MW01625652

MIDNIGHT TO THE BOOM *Painting in India after Independence*

Susan S. Bean

With Homi K. Bhabha, Rebecca M. Brown,
Beth Citron, Ajay Sinha, and Karin Zitzewitz

MIDNIGHT TO THE BOOM

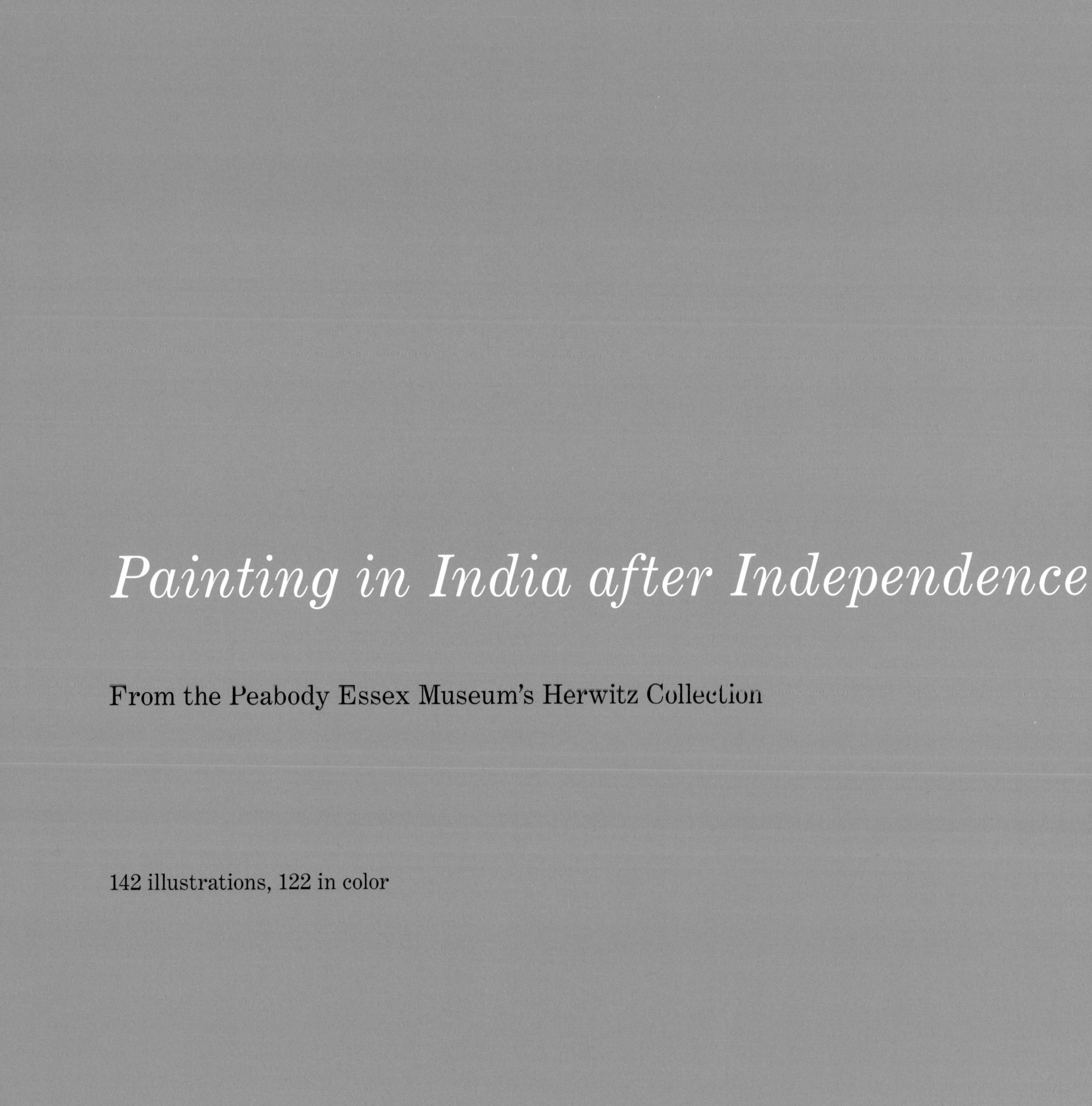

Painting in India after Independence

From the Peabody Essex Museum's Herwitz Collection

142 illustrations, 122 in color

PEABODY ESSEX MUSEUM in association with Thames & Hudson

Midnight to the Boom: Painting in India after Independence from the Peabody Essex Museum's Herwitz Collection accompanies the exhibition of the same name organized by the Peabody Essex Museum, Salem, Massachusetts, on view from February 2, 2013 through April 21, 2013.

First published in 2013 in hardcover in the United States of America by Thames & Hudson Inc., 500 Fifth Avenue, New York, New York 10110

thamesandhudsonusa.com

Published in association with the Peabody Essex Museum, East India Square Salem, Massachusetts 01970

www.pem.org

Library of Congress Catalogue Card Number: 2011946034

ISBN: 978-0-500-23893-6

Coordinated and edited by
Terry Ann R. Neff
t. a. neff associates, inc., Tucson, Arizona

Designed by Fraser Muggeridge studio

Printed and bound in China by Toppan Leefung Printing Limited

This publication and associated exhibition at the Peabody Essex Museum, Massachusetts, were made possible in part by the Chester and Davida Herwitz Charitable Trust and the E. Rhodes and Leona B. Carpenter Foundation.

Support for the exhibition was provided by
Marguerite and Kent Srikanth Charugundla
Dr. Mahesh and Smita Patel

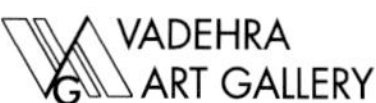

East India Marine Associates (EIMA) of the Peabody Essex Museum

CONTENTS

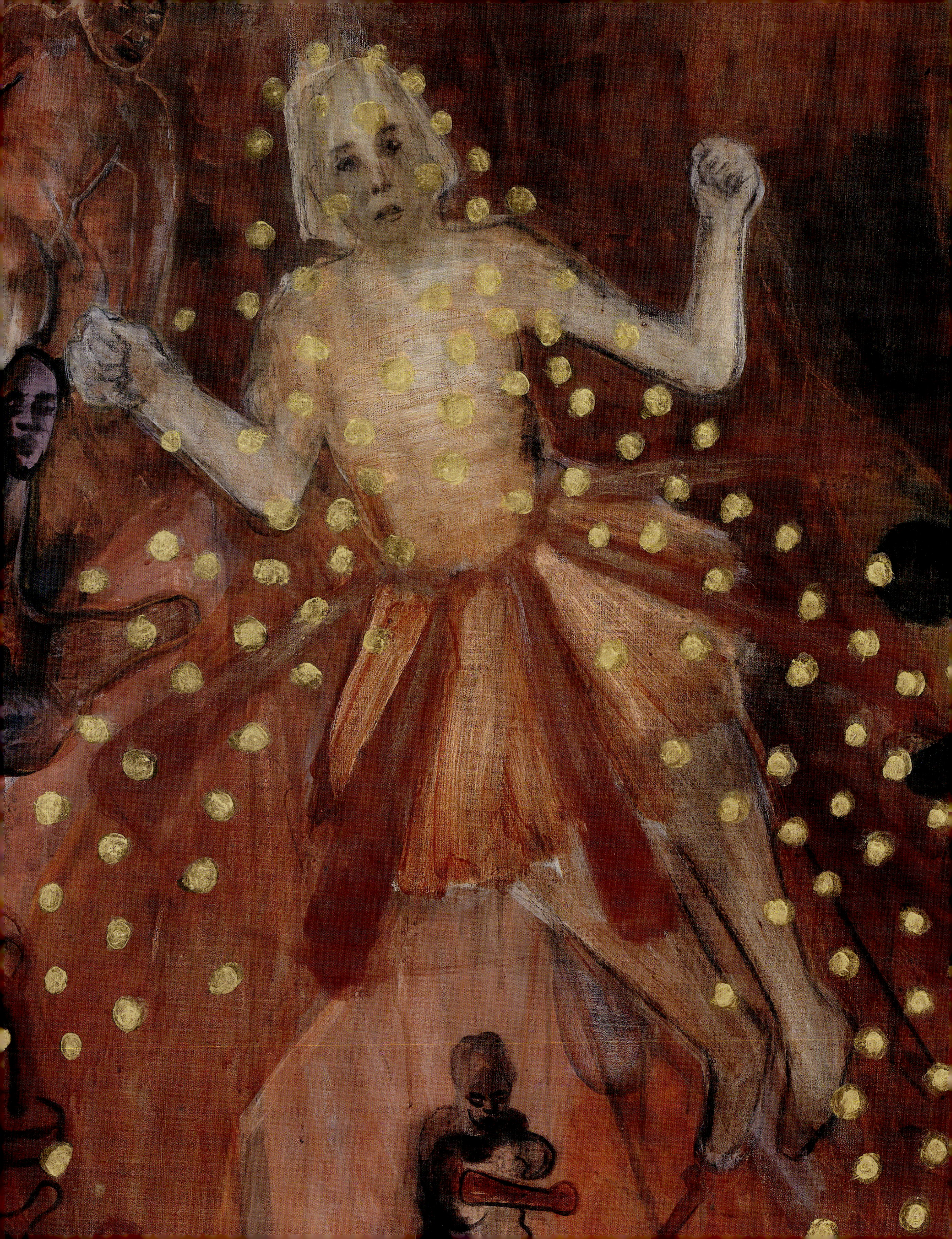

FOREWORD

Today...East and West, yesterday and tomorrow, exist as a confused jumble in each one of us. Different times and different spaces are combined in a here and now that is everywhere at once.

OCTAVIO PAZ

What do India, China, and Europe have in common? On the occasion of *Midnight to the Boom: Painting in India after Independence*, the most fitting answer is their longstanding stature as wellsprings of great painting. Beginning with twelfth-century illuminated manuscripts, India's painting traditions have asserted dynamic relationships with the courtly, colonial, modern, contemporary, and global. Whether religious or secular in origin, painting in India exhibits some fascinatingly persistent characteristics, among them the preference for figuration, a deliberate tension between surface and depth, the prevalence of line as a metaphor for threading and interweaving, and the co-existence of seemingly warring elements, such as raw vigor with delicate patterning and flat color blocking with carefully orchestrated naturalism.

Looming larger than any of these elements, however, is the constancy of percolation not just in India's painting but in India itself, created by integrating, breaking apart, adapting, and rejecting. One of the world's oldest civilizations, India reflects an extraordinary and complicated array of resources, experiences, and inspirations, in large measure set in motion by the spice and silk routes that connected Asia and Europe more than two thousand years ago. The subsequent commercial, artistic, and cultural exchanges across tremendous distances engendered languages, inventions, belief systems, artistic styles, and social customs that still resonate today.

For South Asia in the twentieth century, the year 1947 brought two fundamentally transformative moments: independence from British colonial rule and partition into India and Pakistan. The ensuing political, social, and economic events were of such import for India as a new sovereign state that many of its artists aspired to create a complementary visual language that would be progressive and revolutionary precisely because it expresses both India and the modern. Not surprisingly, painting emerged as the primary arena for these artists, attuned to this medium as an integral part of their cultural heritage, but also determined to proceed with absolute freedom of content, style, and technique. What had been slowly building since early in the twentieth century as resistance to the academic realism promoted by India's colonialist art schools quickly accelerated as a manifestation of independence.

Today, post-independence painting has undergone a tremendous transformation. Cultivating a market is an important step in the maturity of any cultural scene, and a vibrant, increasingly international infrastructure of collectors, dealers, and artists now exists on behalf of India's modern and contemporary art. Since 2005, individual works

Detail of Plate 68.
Nalini Malani,
After Pina Bausch—Mutant B, 1994

by India's key modern painters have regularly exceeded the one-million-dollar mark, generating press coverage that tends to overemphasize market activity rather than address the quality or significance of the works themselves. Countering that trend is a sophistication and stronger body of scholarship that have been growing especially since the 1990s among Indian, American, and European curators and writers. There have also been a series of large-scale surveys, among them *Out of India: Contemporary Art of the South Asian Diaspora* (Queens Museum, 1997); *Century City: Mumbai/Bombay 1992–2001* (Tate Modern, 2001); *Edge of Desire: Recent Art in India* (Asia Society and Queens Museum, 2005–2007); and Paris-Delhi-Bombay (Centre Pompidou, 2011). These surveys, coupled with a series of more tightly focused exhibitions at the Peabody Essex Museum and elsewhere, have addressed the relationship between the traditional and contemporary, the city as muse, and the impact of India's diaspora and globalization on a changed nation.

Today's discourse on art reflects the influence of cultural studies, visual culture, anthropology, and archaeology on art history as well as the impact of the world's rapidly changing demographics. The subsequent focus on diversity has yielded a fascinating duality of desire: to assert the inclusiveness of the global and to articulate the specificity and value of the local, so much so that the word "glocal" has been coined to cope with this duality. Unquestionably, examining how different cultures, whether in Latin America, India, China, and other parts of the world, have interfaced with Euro-American art and culture as a means of reflecting and continuously redefining their identity is relevant to this "glocal" discourse. In the midst of this, however, the concept of modernism as a monolithic, now concluded idiom—although this interpretation has been changing—continues to raise the risk of considering recent chapters in India and elsewhere as more derivative than inventive.

India's artists did not import or copy modernism wholesale, but adapted it and many other resources to the country's specific and often extreme and competing cultural, political, religious, and social circumstances after independence. It was, as the pioneering painter S.H. Raza has asserted, "a vigorous synthesis." Yet, the artistic vitality that arose was not just about identity-driven national cultural politics, but also about the interior and exterior realities and issues of being an artist. So, the more valid question concerns how the modern and modernism have played out in India. At their heart, artists everywhere who have engaged with the modern have wanted to open a window onto a new world, and therefore have frequently asserted individualism, absolute freedom, and rejection of tradition and the norm as necessary to this end. It is a lovely coincidence that the emphasis India's post-independence artists placed on painting, narrative, and figuration between the 1950s and 1980s aligns with similar debates and strategies in the Euro-American art world of the time. Far more than matters of individualism, styles, or processes, however, being modern and being a modern artist is about an attitude that fundamentally positions the individual as an engine of significant change that can radically expand possibilities. It is this attitude that India's post-independence artists have embraced as visual and visualizing citizens who create new and modern meaning.

This project has been long in the making in the best possible sense. Over more than three decades beginning in the 1960s, Chester and Davida Herwitz built a pioneering collection of modern art from India. In addition to fulfilling their personal passion, they aspired to stimulate international attention and appreciation for this new and vibrant chapter in India's art and culture. The penultimate expression of their goal was placing the core of the collection at the Peabody Essex Museum in 2001. The first American museum to collect art from India, PEM counts among its earliest acquisitions historic works from India as a manifestation of the global purview that its seafaring, entrepreneurial founders asserted from the outset in 1799. In keeping with its ongoing efforts to build a collection that reaches beyond the western canon, PEM's acquisition of the Herwitz collection has distinguished it as the first museum outside of India to focus on the achievements of its modern artists. Now, just as at the moment of their largesse in 2001, we are deeply honored that the Herwitzes entrusted the museum not just with ownership and care of their collection, but also with the study, interpretation, and presentation of these works as publicly held ambassadors of India's specific and rich contributions to the world of modern art. The Peabody Essex Museum is pleased to honor the vision and generosity of the late Chester and Davida Herwitz on the occasion of this exhibition and its companion publication.

Midnight to the Boom is the culmination of the critical role that Susan S. Bean, PEM's former curator of South Asian and Korean art, played in the collection's acquisition and the museum's ascension as a primary center for building international appreciation of these artists. We thank her for both her advocacy and scholarship, and join her in thanking Carla, David, and Tom Herwitz and PEM President Robert Shapiro for their wise and supportive counsel from the outset, as well as the many members of the museum's staff, advisors, and authors who have contributed to bringing this project to fruition.

We are especially grateful to the Chester and Davida Herwitz Charitable Trust, the E. Rhodes and Leona B. Carpenter Foundation, Marguerite and Kent Srikanth Charugundla, Dr. Mahesh and Smita Patel, Vadehra Art Gallery, New Delhi, and PEM's East India Marine Associates (EIMA) for their generous support of the exhibition and publication. We are delighted to co-publish this book with Thames & Hudson, and especially thank Susan Dwyer for creating this fruitful partnership. Although the exhibition draws primarily from the museum's Herwitz collection, we deeply appreciate the willingness of several private collectors, galleries, and artists to lend key works to this endeavor.

Beauty, emotion, observation, inquiry, experience, history, humanity, and culture shine forth from the works celebrated in *Midnight to the Boom*, and we salute and thank all of the artists for their individual and collective achievements. Their willingness to engage with life outside of their art and to bring that life into their work has engendered a pluralism that signals their understanding of art and culture as forms of action.

Dan L. Monroe
The Rose-Marie and Eijk van Otterloo Director and CEO

Lynda Roscoe Hartigan
The James B. and Mary Lou Hawkes Chief Curator

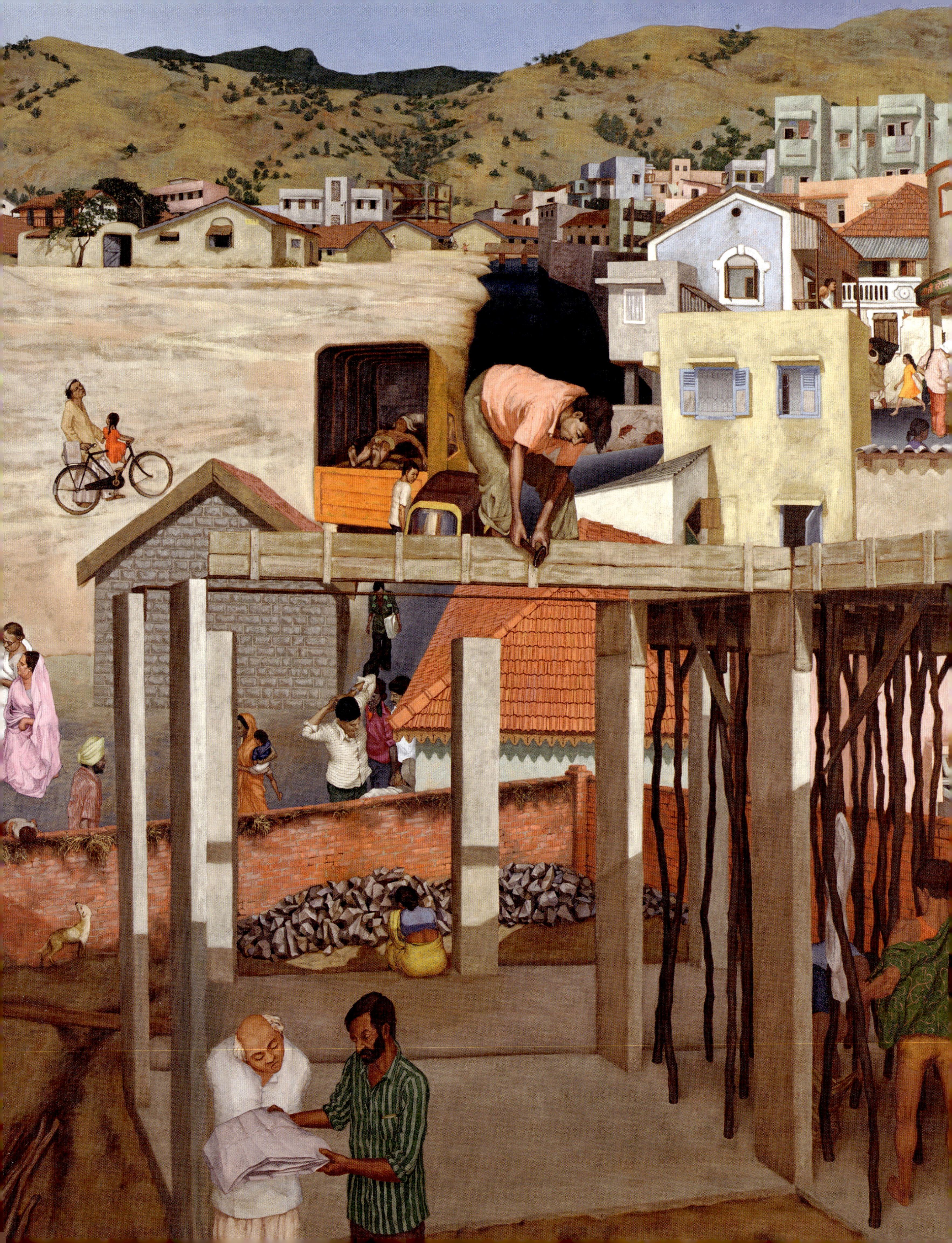

ACKNOWLEDGMENTS

Chester and Davida Herwitz were not just passionate collectors. They believed deeply in India's postindependence art—the subject of this book—and its important place among the modernist art movements across an interconnected world. They also wanted their collection to reside in a public institution for art lovers and scholars far into the future. This exhibition and publication project is part of their legacy. In 2001, the core of the Herwitz Collection was endowed and transferred to the Peabody Essex Museum, which opened the Chester and Davida Herwitz Gallery in 2003. This was in large measure thanks to the efforts of their son Thomas Herwitz; Chester's brother David Herwitz and his wife Carla Herwitz, a PEM trustee; PEM President Robert N. Shapiro; and the visionary leadership of PEM Executive Director and CEO Dan L. Monroe and the museum's board of trustees.

Over the ensuing years of my research on modern Indian art, I have been the beneficiary of the extraordinary, warm generosity of artists, scholars, collectors, and gallerists, who have shared their experience, knowledge, and wisdom. Many artists whose work is part of the Herwitz Collection, and a few the Herwitzes did not collect, spent time with me discussing their work and the art world as they have known it. Especially valuable were in-depth discussions with Bikash Bhattacharjee's family, Rameshwar Broota, Jayashree Chakravarty, Bal Chhabda, Jogen Chowdhury, Vinod Dave, Biren De, Atul Dodiya, K. Laxma Goud, M.F. Husain, Ranbir S. Kaleka, Bhupen Khakhar, Krishen Khanna, Ram Kumar, Nalini Malani, Tyeb Mehta, Akbar Padamsee, Gieve Patel, Sudhir Patwardhan, Ram Rahman, S.H. Raza, Krishna Reddy, Ravinder Reddy, Rekha Rodwittiya, Jamini Roy's grandson Debabrata Roy, G.R. Santosh's son Shabir Hussain Santosh, Gulammohamed Sheikh, Ketaki Sheth, Arpita Singh, K.G. Subramanyan, Anupam Sud, Vivan Sundaram, and Abanindranath Tagore's grandson Amitendranath Tagore.

Many colleagues, curators and art historians, shared their insights into the emergence of India's modern art, its significance at home, its presence in other parts of the world, and current issues in the ongoing discourse on modernism: Nancy Adajania, Monisha Ahmed, Ebrahim Alkazi, Savita Apte, Yashodhara Dalmia, Ella Datta, Saryu Doshi, Tapati Guha-Thakurta, Daniel Herwitz, Mary Jane Jacob, Jyotindra Jain, Marta Jakimowicz, Geeta Kapur, Saloni Mathur, Michael Meister, Partha Mitter, Pratapaditya Pal, Ruby Palchoudhuri, Rashmi Poddar, Ina Puri, Tasneem Mehta, Geeti Sen, Kavita Singh, Gayatri Sinha, and Ashok Vajpeyi. I was privileged to be shown several important collections by their deeply knowledgeable owners, including Tina Ambani, PEM trustee, and Preeti Ambani of the Harmony Art Foundation; Kent and Marguerite Charugundla; Rajiv and Payal Chaudhri; Masanori Fukuoka; Umesh and Sunanda Gaur; Amrita Jhaveri; Jehangir Nicholson; Abishek Poddar; Lekha Poddar and Anupam Poddar of the Devi Art Foundation;

Detail of Plate 70.
Sudhir Patwardhan, *Town*, 1984

Sri and Harsha Reddy; Shilpa and Praful Shah; and Mahinder Tak. Gallerists helped me understand the development of that art market and the evolution of the Indian art world, including Sarah Abraham, Shumita and Arani Bose, Prajit Dutta, Projjal Dutta, Pheroza Godrej, Geetha Mehra, Shireen Gandhy, Peter Nagy, Dadiba and Khorshed Pundole, Rakhi Sarkar and Pratiti Sarkar, Deepak Talwar, Neville Tuli, and Arun Vadhera.

At the Peabody Essex Museum, I am deeply grateful to Lynda Roscoe Hartigan, The James B. and Mary Lou Hawkes Chief Curator, for championing the overall project and piloting the publication to completion in close collaboration with expert editor Terry Ann R. Neff and Director of Exhibition Research and Publishing Kathy Fredrickson. Curator of Contemporary Art Trevor Smith offered wise counsel. Exhibition Assistant Debleena Mitra and Associate Curator for Exhibitions and Research Sarah Chasse did much of the hard work of bringing the exhibition and publication together. Priscilla Danforth, Director of Exhibition Planning, smoothly managed the project, coordinating the masterful work of exhibition designers Dave Seibert and Karen Moreau Ceballos. Chief of Education and Interpretation Juliette Fritsch, educator Gavin Andrews, and Jim Olson, Director of Integrated Media, provided invaluable contributions as part of the project's interpretive team. Will Phippen, Director of Museum Collection Services, and conservators Kathryn Carey, Theresa Carmichael, and Elizabeth Mehlin performed wonders, with the support of Eric Wolin and the museum's collections management staff. Their work enabled museum photographer Walter Silver to produce the splendid images featured here.

The lenders to the exhibition made it possible to mount telling comparisons with works from our own collection. I thank the Baltimore Museum of Art, Brooklyn Museum of Art, Michael Gallis, The Metropolitan Museum of Art, National Gallery of Art, a private collection, and Sri and Harsha Reddy.

I am deeply appreciative of the important contributions of my valued colleagues Homi K. Bhabha, Rebecca M. Brown, Beth Citron, Ajay Sinha, and Karin Zitzewitz, whose writing has illuminated India's art scene in the decades after independence, adding new perspectives on the artists and their work, and broadening the dialogue on late twentieth-century modernist art.

Susan S. Bean
Former Curator of South Asian and Korean Art

NOTE TO THE READER

All plates are of works in the Peabody Essex Museum Herwitz Collection.

The contributing authors are Susan S. Bean (SSB), Homi K. Bhabha (HKB), Rebecca M. Brown (RMB), Beth Citron (BC), Ajay Sinha (AS), and Karin Zitzewitz (KZ).

Personal Names

Although regional usages vary across India, naming systems commonly feature a personal name, which is sometimes preceded or followed by birth place, parent's name, religious sect, profession, caste or clan title, or family name. These secondary names commonly occur as initials. In this publication, the full name of each artist is given in his or her feature essay. Elsewhere, the artist is referred to by his or her most common appellation.

Cities

In recent decades, many cities in India have been renamed in order to replace a Europeanized, colonial form with an earlier name or a name from the regional language. Because most of these changes occurred after the period of *Midnight to the Boom*, the older names are used throughout the book. The most widely cited renamed cities are the following:

Baroda to Vadodara, capital of Gujarat state, in 1974. Both names are in common use. Vadodara is appropriate in official contexts and is the form in Gujarati, the state language. Baroda is customarily used in the transnational and translinguistic art world.

Bombay to Mumbai in 1995. Within the art community, Bombay, considered more cosmopolitan than Marathi-based Mumbai, is more commonly used.

Calcutta to Kolkata, capital of West Bengal state, in 2001.

Madras to Chennai, capital of Tamil Nadu state, in 1996.

Art Schools

Faculty of Fine Arts, Maharaja Sayajirao (M.S.) University of Baroda, commonly referred to as the Baroda art college, founded in 1950.

Kala Bhavana, at Visva-Bharati University, usually referred to as Santiniketan for the village in West Bengal where it is located. The university was founded in 1901 by Rabindranath Tagore, who established Kala Bhavana, the art school, in 1919.

Jamsetjee Jeejeebhoy School of Art, University of Mumbai, commonly referred to as the J.J. School of Art, founded in 1857 and named for the philanthropist who endowed it.

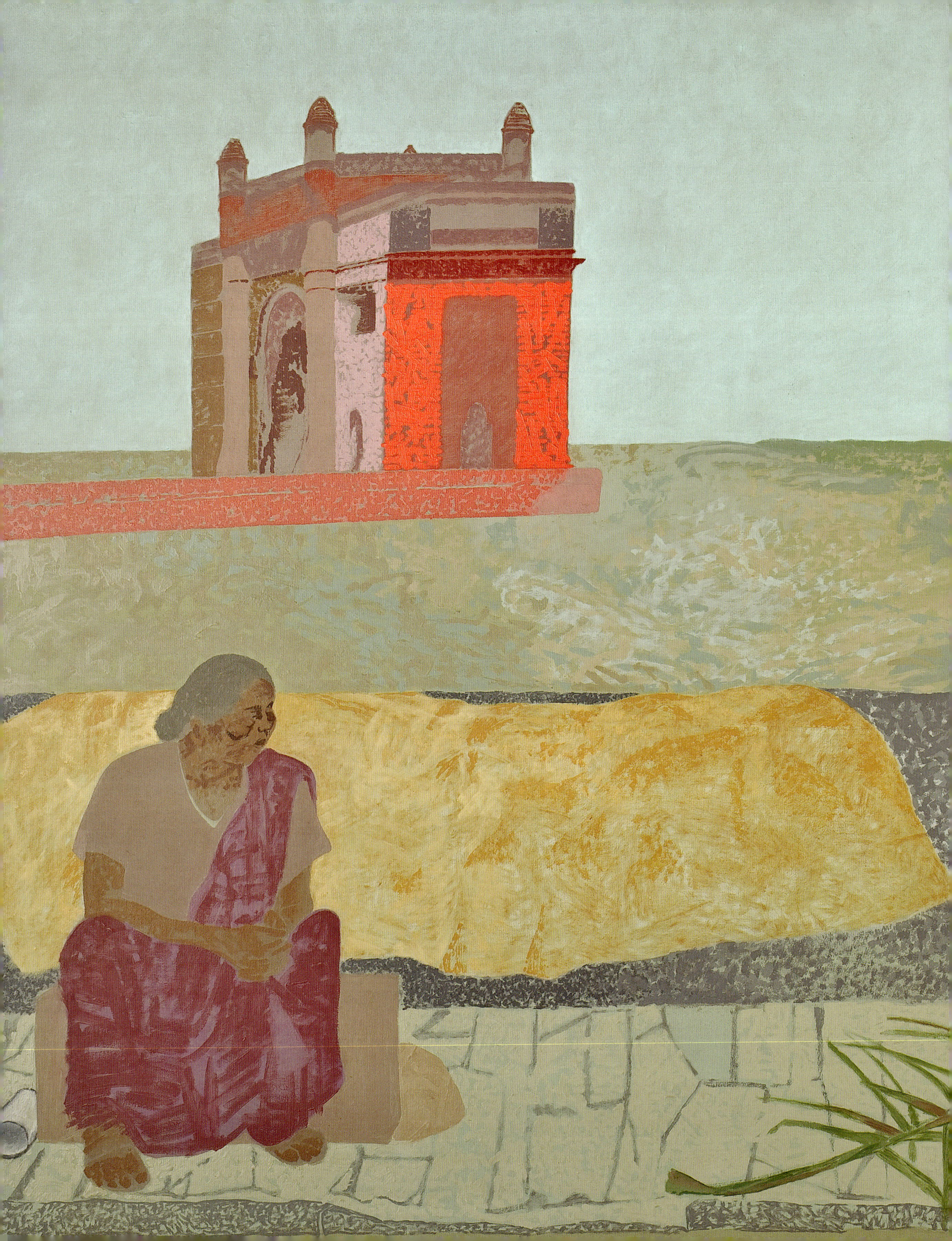

AN AGE OF PAINTING: ART AFTER INDEPENDENCE

Susan S. Bean

A revolutionary art movement asserted itself in India between the declaration of independence at midnight on August 15, 1947 and the economic boom of the 1990s. *Midnight to the Boom* focuses on the three generations of artists responsible for critical shifts in the development of India's modernist art during this period. Subsequently, their achievements and the country's unprecedented boom ushered India's modern and contemporary art into a new era of globalism, a soaring international market, and an explosion in the media and technologies of art.

In the discourse of international modernism that has originated almost entirely in the West, scant attention has been paid to artists working in India or any other place beyond the Paris–New York–London axis. Only relatively recently are modernist movements that arose in centers such as Tokyo, Seoul, Buenos Aires, and Bombay gradually being incorporated into what is becoming a global history. At the same time, most writing on Indian modern art has concentrated on the development of art practice within the context of national cultural politics with barely a nod to the early and ongoing transnational connections of the art movement. *Midnight to the Boom* invites recognition of the significance of India's art for the development of modernist practices globally and is intended to contribute to a broader, more inclusive art history and a fuller awareness of the complex dialogue occurring across the interconnected twentieth century.

Being an artist in these decades in India was not an easy choice. Living in a country where millions lacked adequate food and housing and where sectarian and religious violence erupted regularly, led artists to doubt their right to paint. In the 1960s, Tyeb Mehta commented: "To pick up a brush, to make a stroke on the canvas—I consider these acts of courage, in this country."[1] Yet, in the last half of the twentieth century, these artist-intellectuals played an important role in shaping Indian modernity. By making the leap from small town, local language, caste, and religion to the metropolis, and by expressing their own aesthetic visions, they asserted the importance of individual determination and contributed toward the reconfiguration of Indian culture for a new age, modeling a position at once cosmopolitan, secular, and individualistic.

Most artists who rose to prominence hailed from modest backgrounds. They were neither members of traditional artistic lineages nor part of the Anglicized elite. They had diverse regional, linguistic, religious, and caste origins. Typically, they discovered

Detail of Plate 50.
Gieve Patel, *Gateway*, 1981

their passion for drawing and painting as young students, eventually enrolling in art school and relocating to one of India's major urban centers, where they put aside their cultural and linguistic distinctions for a nationalist, secular, and egalitarian outlook. They quickly learned English, the lingua franca of the intelligentsia. This cultural transformation grounded them firmly in a profoundly cosmopolitan outlook, poised to reach beyond India when opportunities arose.

Painting, long a prestigious practice in India as in the West, became the predominant artistic mode. In part, this preference was pragmatic. In a period with a centrally controlled economy and severe import restrictions, the means for painting and drawing were more readily available than for the complex techniques of printmaking, photography, and sculpture. Moreover, given most artists' limited finances, painting was a practical choice in terms of the cost of materials and the requirements for studio space. Not until the 1990s, after both the economy and the art market had begun to expand, were artists able to readily acquire materials and equipment available internationally.

Two other conditions, best described as absences or voids, ironically served to benefit the artists' individual quests: there was no established canon that restricted freedom to experiment nor was there a market that likewise dictated production. India's own early twentieth-century modernist heritage provided few models to emulate or resist, and Indian artists observed Western modernism's complex narrative of schools and styles from a distance. As a consequence, they were at liberty to pursue their own creative trajectories independent of stylistic trends.

Midnight to the Boom mines the Peabody Essex Museum's Herwitz Collection, the foremost public collection of modernist Indian art outside that country. Davida and Chester Herwitz began thirty years of deepening acquaintance with India in the 1960s on a trip around the world. They discovered India's contemporary art, began to collect, and were soon caught up in the creative excitement of the art world. The Herwitzes responded not only to the dynamism of the Indian art scene, but to its distinctive circumstances and the aspirations of its practitioners. Like most viewers, especially Westerners, they were immediately struck by the clear affinities with European and American modernism, but perhaps because of their growing acquaintance with India and its artists, they perceived its innovative energy. They were also impressed by the global reach of Indian artists who studied and exhibited in Paris, New York, and London, as well as Delhi, Bombay, and Baroda, and while abroad fed their intense interests in world art, whether of the Italian Renaissance, the School of Paris, or the Mexican muralists. For the Herwitzes, contemporary Indian art exuded a vitality that reflected this hybridity, as artists freely drew on the world's art as well as India's rich artistic heritage and translated these varied expressions into distinctive forms.

Chester and Davida Herwitz were also drawn to figurative painting, the predominant mode during these decades. As India's leading art critic, Geeta Kapur, recently commented: "if one were to name a single contribution that Indian artists make to the resources of the 'universal' imaginary, it is the corporeal, passionately enduring 'human image.'"[2] The artist Gieve Patel, making a similar observation in the 1980s, noted that at a time when figurative art was making a comeback in the

West, "there is no such thing here as 'the return of figuration'; figuration never left... today, for many Indian painters the human figure is unquestioned subject matter."[3] Nonetheless, the Herwitzes also admired and collected work by artists with strong affinities for abstraction.

Just as the Herwitz Collection, built by Americans, attests to the transnational location of twentieth-century Indian art, *Midnight to the Boom* reinforces this internationalism with commentary by six United States-based scholars, each deeply engaged with modern India's visual art and culture and actively developing the discourse on modernity to encompass its diverse origins and expressions. Homi K. Bhabha in a conversation with this author reflects on distinctive qualities of art in India after independence, when ad hoc, informal networks and barely commoditized practices energized artists to pursue their own paths with a sophisticated openness to engaging, responding, and translating art from elsewhere. This dialogical, creative hybridity infused their work with a distinctive vigor. Bhabha's interpretation resonates with Patel's observation of the art world in the 1980s: "in the work of painter after painter, a conscious and utterly pertinent borrowing from the whole world of art, irrespective of period or country, ranging from the Italian primitives to the ink-and-brush Sung masters...in each case it is directed towards consolidating a thought or a vision."[4] Karin Zitzewitz maps the emerging formal infrastructure of art schools, a government-sponsored museum, and national and state art academies. An expanding network of international connections greatly increased opportunities for travel, study, and exhibition abroad. Private initiatives to build an art-gallery culture emerged in tandem with the growth of private and corporate collecting. Zitzewitz, from a different perspective, reiterates Bhabha's view of the pivotal importance of informal associations in shaping the character of the movement. Ajay Sinha views "art" as a matter of framing, involving what is around as well as inside the image—context as well as subject and style. From this perspective, he explores how a category of "art" became distinctive within a visual culture dominated by popular prints and cinema. Sinha considers the importance of the emergent realm of the artist's studio as a locus for individual creative production, a place where artists pursued innovative and highly personal practices. Apart from their formal pedagogy, Sinha reveals how art schools shaped painting by creating a secular yet spiritual sense of the contribution of art to vernacular culture—a liberation from demands of the material world and an emotional and intellectual plentitude.

Bhabha, Zitzewitz, and Sinha illuminate cultural and conceptual foundations of India's modern age of painting and set the stage for considering the development of India's art movement through the Herwitz Collection. This author's essay on Davida and Chester Herwitz as collectors explores two shaping forces: their own taste and predilections and the impact the art movement had on them as they became increasingly involved in India's art world. The essay positions the collection as the creation of well-informed yet decidedly individualist tastes. In a field where an established narrative remains emergent, any body of work selected for study necessarily reflects the particular point of view—whether of collector, curator, critic, or historian—that guided the choices made.

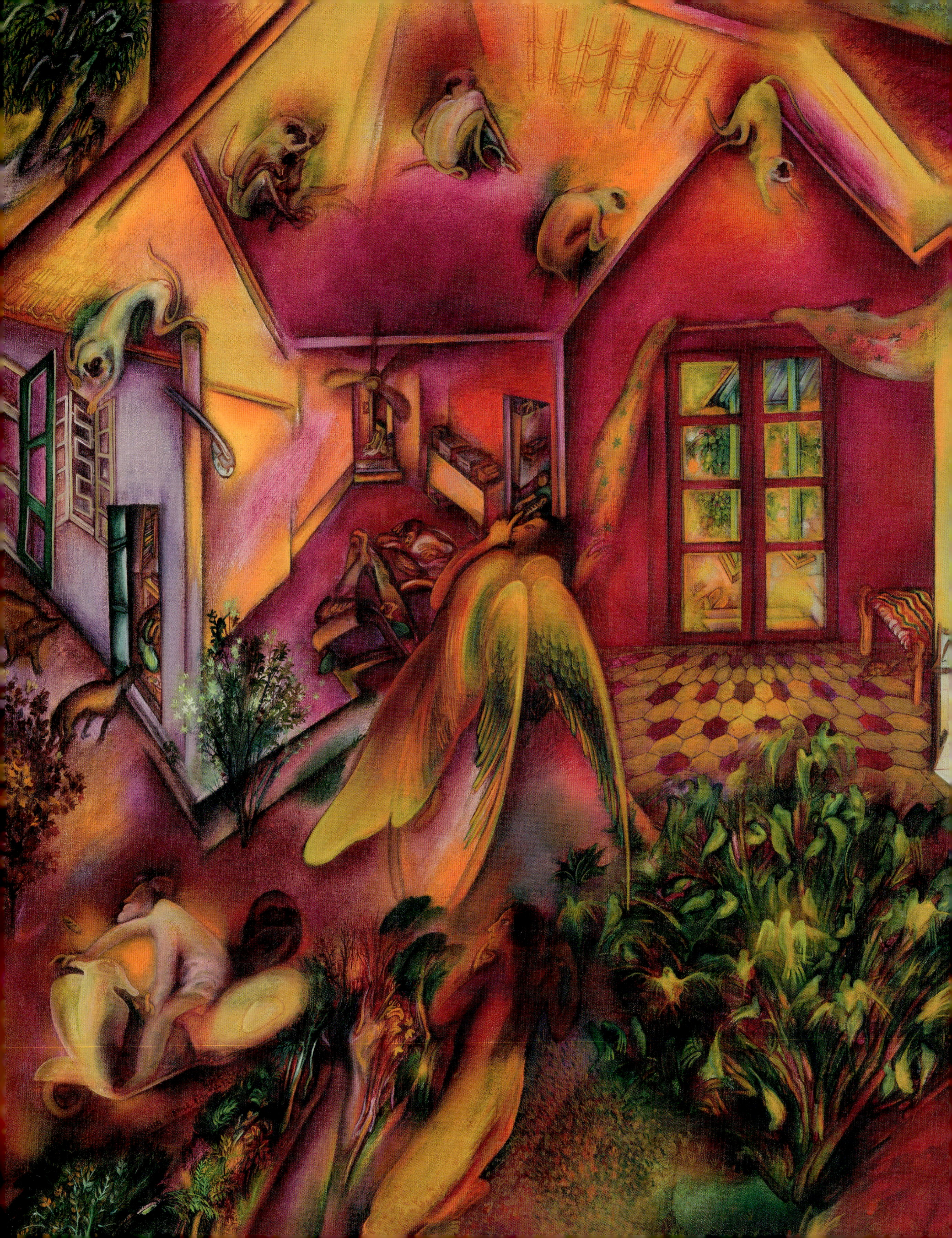

Additional essays frame each of the three generations of artists and the related commentaries on each artist focus on their relationship to their generation and on key works. Rebecca M. Brown presents the first generation, "Pathbreakers," who were young artists in the 1940s, the decade when India won the long struggle for freedom from British rule. These pioneers harbored correspondingly great ambitions for painting in India. They were invigorated by the achievement of independence and deeply scarred by the violence of the partition of India and the assassination of Mahatma Gandhi. They fully embraced the new stature of individuals as citizens and their own role as intellectuals in a new nation, the world's largest democracy. They were eager to reshape India's art world, intent on formulating new aesthetic idioms, deliberate in their deployment of painting basics of color and form they understood as universal. They sought to be at once modern and attuned to the new circumstances of free India. Their artistic arrival coincided with monumental political and social transformation, and their works tend toward the humanistic, transcendent, epic, universal, and cosmological.

The second generation, "Midnight's Children,"[5] introduced by this author, were born in the decade leading up to independence. They established their reputations during the ascendancy of the centralized socialist republic under the leadership of India's founding prime minister, Jawaharlal Nehru. As the daunting challenges of poverty and inequality became increasingly apparent and intractable, the idealism of the immediate postindependence years receded. "Midnight's Children," responding to the conditions of life for the vast majority of India's people, turned away from formal and transcendent concerns toward local realities and textures of personal experience. They focused on particular, individualistic experiments in figural form, explorations of subjectivity, and personal and local narrative.

Looking at the 1980s, amid a resurgence of divisive forces of religion, region, and class that were altering India's social and political landscape, Beth Citron tracks the emergence of a third generation of artists, the "New Mediators." The upsurge of communal and regional loyalties had begun to undermine national unity founded on secularism and equal rights. At the same time, a rise of capitalist enterprise threatened to bring in its wake new inequalities of wealth and privilege. Artists shaping their practices in these years tended toward political engagement, producing works that projected a position and endeavored to engage the viewer. They confronted and reflected on the limitations of the picture space. Trained as painters, many moved away from the canvas as a discrete contemplative universe. Some devised their pictures to project a feminist or Marxist point of view; others pushed beyond the frame, integrating video and installation to dissolve the barrier between art and viewers and enter their space, and to complicate and intensify viewers' experience.

In the 1990s, India's age of modernist painting came to a close. The rapid rise of wealth at home following the opening of the Indian economy and the financial success of Indians living abroad created a boom in the art market. At the same time, the proliferation of art fairs and biennials abroad spawned an unprecedentedly global

Detail of Plate 55.
Gulammohammed Sheikh, *Passing Angel, A Life, Summer Diary*, 1985–87

art scene. As a result, opportunities for artists to show and sell their work increased dramatically. While painting has remained important in India, the directions pioneered by the "New Mediators" generation have pushed painting from the center of the art movement to being one medium among many. *Midnight to the Boom* captures the ethos, culture, and character of India's twentieth-century modernism, when artists appropriated the picture space, building highly individualistic practices, transforming and translating resources from across the world and across time, to become players in the shaping of modernity.

1. Gieve Patel, "To Pick Up a Brush," in *Contemporary Indian Art from the Chester and Davida Herwitz Family Collection* (New York: Grey Art Gallery and Study Center, New York University, 1985), pp. 8–16.

2. Geeta Kapur, "subTerrain: artists dig the contemporary," in Chandrasekhar, Indira, and Peter C. Seel, eds., *body.city: siting contemporary culture in India* (Berlin: Haus der Kulteren der Welt, 2003), p. 67.

3. Patel, p. 9.

4. Ibid., pp. 9–10.

5. The term "Midnight's Children" is taken from the title of Salman Rushdie's prize-winning novel *Midnight's Children* (1981), a tale of two children born at the moment of Indian independence—midnight, August 15, 1947– and switched at birth.

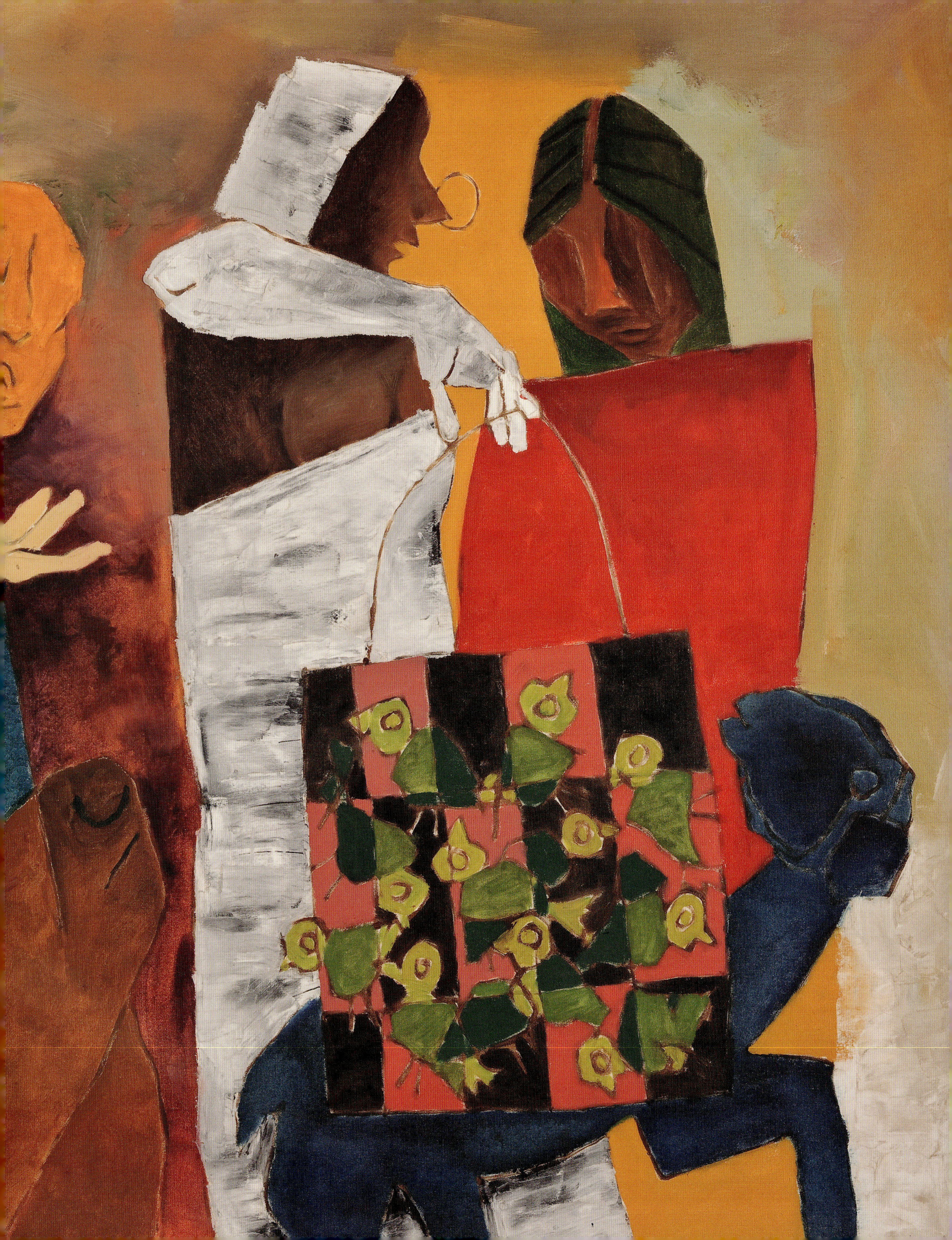

INDIA'S DIALOGICAL MODERNISM

Homi K. Bhabha in conversation with Susan S. Bean

Susan S. Bean: After independence in 1947, India's art movement took off with new energy in new directions. You had the good fortune of being there, as a student in Bombay in the 1960s and early 1970s. What was it like?

Homi K. Bhabha: I was a bit of a fly on the wall, far too young to participate in any meaningful way. I was, however, a very keen-eyed observer, and appreciated the cultural intensity that surrounded my South Bombay world. At that time, South Bombay was the natural meeting-place. In some ways, it still is, because most of the new art galleries are clustered in and around Colaba Causeway. In those days, Bombay's "art mile" was rather sparse in terms of numbers, but the few galleries we had were rich centers of conversation and creativity. Access was easy; artists were open to engagement. I used to go for coffee at the Samovar café and bump into many leading artists, poets, critics, and theater directors. It was lively and buzzing. The demotic "openness" of the art world was what I most clearly remember. It was, to my eyes at least, relatively free of the negative aspects of professionalization that restrict access to the arts. Of course, there is another side to this, too: the absence of bureaucratization also means that there was hardly any state support for art or for artists; and arts education was in poor shape.

SSB: The art world all across India—not just in Bombay—was really quite small at this time, wasn't it? But, instead of being diffuse, dispersed, and isolating, it was vigorously interactive.

HKB: Yes. I think one of the really formative things, at this stage, was the fact that there were relatively few members of this community. Because of that, there was a kind of intensity of interaction. There were internecine wars, but there was enormous energy—good energy and bad energy—and intimacy, and I think this sense of focused creativity, to which I was only partly privy, impressed me greatly. Years later, in my conversations with Akbar Padamsee [in *Akbar Padamsee: Work in Language*, 2010], I came to realize how, among the Progressive Group, there was an enchanted and demonic energy that kept them closely knit in the exchange of ideas and art practice, even when there were personal animosities among them. It was not a big world, in Bombay at least, and you could really touch everything. It was a coterie culture, but not snobbish or exclusive in the way of art cliques. Even a kid like me could participate.

Detail of Plate 6.
M.F. Husain, *Cage V*, 1974

For example, when I was about fifteen, my aunt moved to a new apartment with a very big white wall. I took her to Chemould Gallery and advised her to buy a Ram Kumar (see, for example, Kumar, figure 1). I told her that he was one of the subtlest of these new artists and had a great sense of how to build a structure purely with paint.

I have a pet theory that one reason for such intellectual freedom and energy was that there was no art market worth speaking of. Artists didn't have to keep on claiming their authenticity, originality, or marketability; they could explore what they wanted to explore. You see, if there isn't a market, then all the competitive pressures of wanting to be original or wanting to maintain your market share don't operate to impose a restrictive, signature-centered focus on the art market. This also has the added benefit of avoiding the cult of celebrity that so often obscures the true perception of quality.

SSB: What do you think were the sources of this energy and intensity of interaction in the art community?

HKB: India's urban centers at the time had a richness of cultural exchange, a cosmopolitan culture. You never had to choose Western art over Indian art, or African art over Chinese. Although the art world was not at all sure of itself in an international sense and many of the artists had very little money, there was a certain confidence about being able to cite from wherever you wanted, talk about anything you chose, borrow from here, take from there, make it your own. This tremendous translational vitality would not have been the case if you were brought up to revere certain canons, schools, or great masters.

Vivan Sundaram's iconic painting *People Come and Go* (figure 1) catches the mood of translational cultural exchange rather well. The painting depicts a gathering of artists—Howard Hodgkin and Bhupen Khakhar with a friend. The painting cites several styles—Khakhar's ironic primitivism; the strongly colored, bold forms of Hodgkin's semi-abstracts; Sundaram's own mythic realism. Cultural differences flow in and out of the room brushing up against various signatures of style, mode, and mood. There is no apparent sense of the anxiety of influence, because there is a prevailing mood of translation and conversation.

Years later, when I was made aware that there was a well-established critical perspective, quite popular in foreign climes, suggesting that artists from postcolonial countries were anxiously "imitative" of Western models, I was surprised by the cultural and historical naïveté of what was supposed to be a sophisticated criterion of judgment. Sure, there were good artists and poor artists in the developing world, but to suggest that their "citationality" was a sign of their second-ratedness was to misunderstand the conditions under which they lived and worked. I bet there are more wannabe Warhols or Koons in the art schools of great Western art capitals than in India or Brazil.

SSB: The sophisticated cosmopolitanism you describe was closely connected to India's postcolonial situation—establishing new arenas of action, national and international.

HKB: India's art world, as I recall it, was experimental and left-leaning. Its progressive politics were not nationalistic, but they were inspired by a project of national

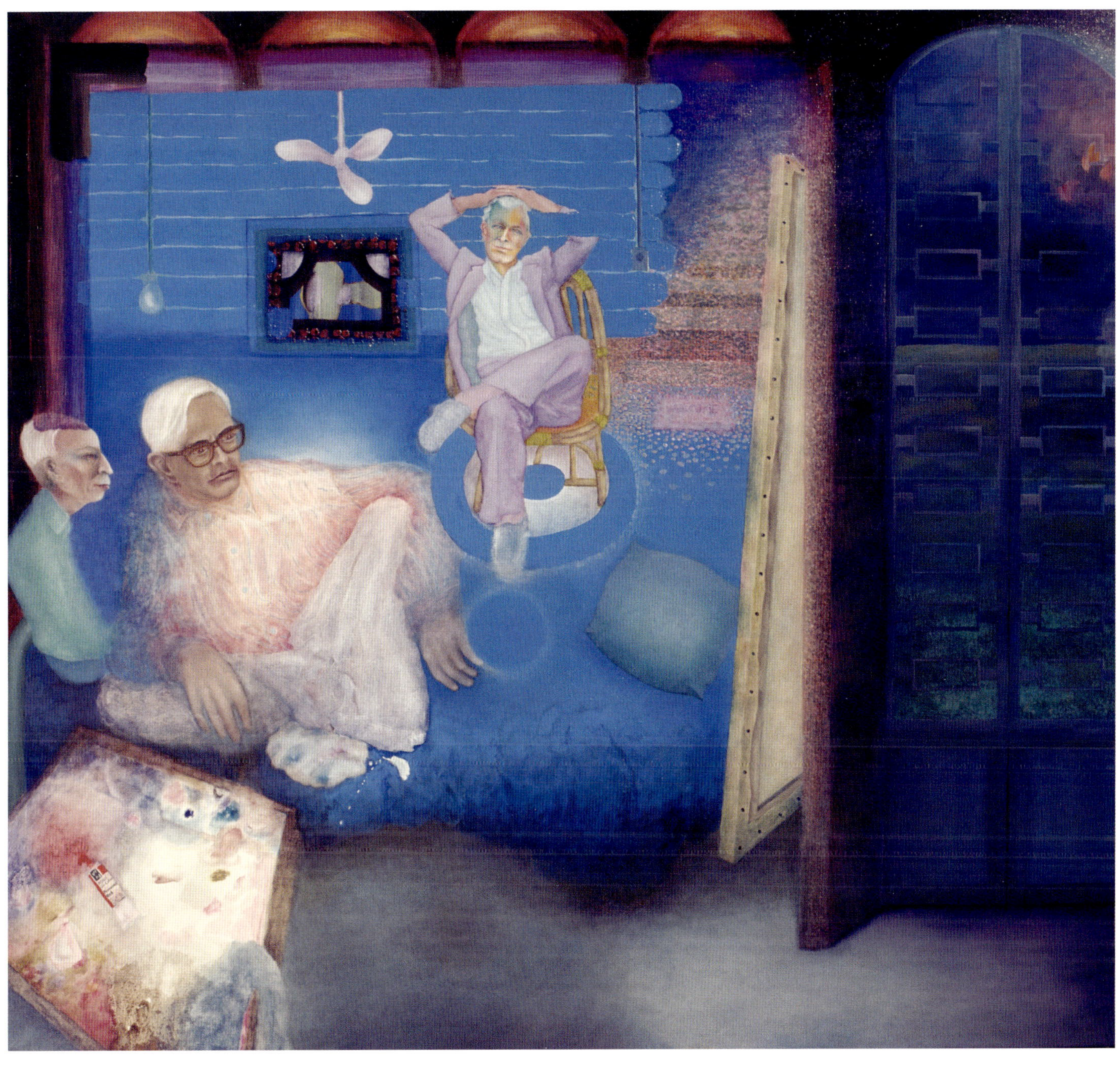

Figure 1.
Vivan Sundaram, *People Come and Go*, 1981
Oil on canvas
48 × 60 inches (123 × 154 cm)
Collection of Rahul and Tejal Amin, Vadodara

recognition and representation. There was a desire to establish a zone of translation in which the language of contemporary art could be used to signify historical forms and contemporary figures that had a local and regional resonance. This translational sense of the many dimensions of "nationness"—rural, urban, symbolic, archival, figurative—did not constitute a nationalist agenda or aesthetic. The early postcolonial ideology of nationness shaped by the Bandung Conference in Indonesia in 1955 had transnational aspirations toward regional development. Frantz Fanon, a pioneering thinker on colonization and its effects, spoke eloquently for this cause when he suggested that to be a nationalist you had first to be an internationalist.

The emphasis on nationness made possible an open field of intercultural experimentation; and effectively resisted cultural or territorial closure. This sense of the nation as a force and a form of cultural mediation reaching out toward larger international or cosmopolitan perspectives has been largely ignored, both historically and theoretically.

SSB: Almost counter-intuitively, you see an energetic, innovative spirit as arising from the aftermath of colonial rule, with its imposition of values and norms that were never swallowed whole, never simply accepted as normal or natural or real.

HKB: The postcolonial condition is more varied than you would think and more ex-centric, although for the longest time the approach was to regard the whole experience of colonization as a straitjacket. Of course, it was a situation of unfreedom, lack of rights, demoralization and dehumanization of people. That must never be denied. But, it also made certain kinds of opportunities for creativity. Often, because there was so much political and cultural pressure against your self-expression as a colonial subject, you sought out ways of being a creative agent of change or intervention by working within the cracks or tensions of the dominant system. Such forms of unrecognized agency often deviate from more conventional traditions of political or cultural resistance. From this point of view, the hegemonic political situation doesn't look much prettier; but the pressure placed upon its tensions, anomalies, and contradictions by emergent, ex-centric, or marginal modes of agency creates a dynamic of ambivalence that both undermines and overlays the dominating power structure. The balance of power shifts, to some degree, because although the status quo remains unchanged, the façade of authority shows up the cracks effected by emergent agents of change. I propose that the creativity or "originality" of modern and contemporary Indian art—its agency—should be viewed from the double perspective I have just outlined.

Somehow, this postcolonial condition, despite many disadvantages politically and otherwise, implants in you a sense that cultural reality, social reality, is always contingent, demanding an act of interpretation. You realize that the conditions of your political marginalization are part of a hegemonic structure dominating you and telling you that the reality you see around you, the reality of exploitation inflicted on your people, is the way things are meant to be. But, you know this is not the way it's meant to be; you understand that this is an interpretation of reality that normalizes inequity and injustice. This insight leads to an approach to culture as interpretation, rather than culture as designation of identities. There is a huge inquisitiveness, not so much about acts of description, but about acts of interpretation; a huge inquisitiveness about what it is to interpret, to know what we see as reality is actually something we understand through interpretation. There is, I think, a rather naïve view fostered by identity politics that suggests that to achieve recognition for your "identity" is to be free. I would rather suggest that to be free is to have the right to interpret and to have your interpretation of history, normativity, or social reality both recognized and institutionalized. It is not the bestowal of identity—or multiple identities for that matter—that empowers you; you need authority to be an agent of transformation or cultural creativity.

That, I think, is one of the innovative values that Indian contemporary artists and writers have given us. They work with, and within, the vocabulary of dominant, international forms and practices, by using their languages but resisting their normative authority or their formal canonicity. They attempt to hybridize cultural forms and figures; to see how much you can cross-fertilize them; how far you can translate them.

SSB: So, for this reason, the sense of a wide universe of possibilities, Indian artists tend to be much more drawn to engaging with art of other times and places.

HKB: Yes, and beyond that, there has been no profound anxiety of influence among the best of our artists and writers—the anxiety comes if you have a desire to overcome the master from whom you learn, to wrestle the master down, to impose your ego. Now, this is not to say that these artists are without ego. I'm just saying that in the practice of assimilation and translation, you see a much more subtle negotiation of influences. In a very profound way, these artists tend to really reflect on moments of *transition*: what it is like to be caught in the midst of different visual languages, verbal traditions, formal conventions, or cultural symbols. I think the richness of this work, the reason why it has made an impact, is that there wasn't this anxiety of citation or quotation. The relationship to celebrated Western art was not perceived as a threat; individuals might feel that they didn't succeed, or whatever, but it was never, I think, perceived at that time in India as a cultural threat.

SSB: This practice of interpretation, of translation, of artists drawing from diverse sources and transforming what they find through their own vision, seems to be especially important to appreciating the tenor and texture of India's art scene during these decades.

HKB: The Eurocentric habit of mind is frequently structured around a *dialectic* that cites non-European objects or ideas in order to subsume them into a new, syncretic totality—a totality that envelops forms of cultural alterity or "otherness" into representations of "exemplarity" articulated to general norms or principles. These normative generalizations often decontextualize cultural differences, and refigure them as mere embellishments to alien histories and dominating contexts. Briefly, the ahistorical description of African art as "primitivism" allows it to be appropriated by Eurocentric discourses in the cause of universalism and progressivism that are all too often self-referential in establishing the authority of the Western intellectual, aesthetic, or epistemological traditions.

In the realms of Indian art—modernist and contemporary—one sees a much more *dialogical* approach to the representation of cultural differences and the influence of diverse aesthetic traditions. Some artists have explicitly reflected on the genealogies of cultural exchange and their enabling effects. For example, in *Old Arguments on Indigenism* (plate 67), Nalini Malani considered her relationships with an earlier generation of third-world women artists. In *People Come and Go*, Sundaram gathered painters from India and abroad whose work has especially moved him. He skillfully referenced the styles of these painters within his own distinctive style of painting, but there is a further sign of the cosmopolitan cultural dialogue that frames the painting and sets its tone. This sign of hospitality is there in the affective and stylistic gesture of the work: you can see it in the posture of the figures as they enter into a circle of companionable conversation; you can see it in the warmth of the paint; you can see it in the different temporal scales—near and far, past and present—that constitutes the *flow* of the image.

SSB: Two other paintings come to mind as particularly focused on this issue of artists' sense of their place in a transcultural art world: M.F. Husain's *Man* (plate 4) and Atul Dodiya's *The Bombay Buccaneer* (plate 63).

HKB: Yes, it's interesting that Husain took Auguste Rodin's *The Thinker* as the central artistic figure for *Man*. And, he gave this figure a kind of open green eye, which may be about the terror of contemplating the creativity of art when one is let loose from traditional moorings and open to infinite possibilities (figure 2). Some details, such as the two plaques with human figures next to the "thinker"—the bull and the goddesslike figure with raised hand—are citations of traditional cultural figures. But, I think that this painting is so much more about figuration and color, about Western modernist art, and how these two elements of art work together in concert. And, if we read it primarily through the figures, we read a much more narrative painting; and if we read it primarily through the juxtaposition of colors, then what comes out is not so much characters or themes, but shapes; even the human figures are made of color blocks that enable other kinds of colors to show. It's almost as if it's a contest of different colors to see what's coming out and what's not coming through. And the intriguing thing about it is the way in which these limited colors create a flow through the painting. You don't feel the limited range of colors is hemming you in, but that they really do represent a large, rich world. It's as if each color spins a different notion of human beingness—the thinker, the artist, the goddess, the grim reaper, or whatever.

Malani's *Old Arguments on Indigenism* has a much greater self-consciousness: about women's issues, about the career of the artist, about the career of the artist as a third-world woman. And, then, the intent to bring together women artists: the work by Amrita Sher-Gil (at right), the Frida Kahlo (center). There is a different feel altogether—self-reflexivity; and in that self-reflexivity there's also a global network of influence, inspiration—but, above all else, a shared painterly and political project.

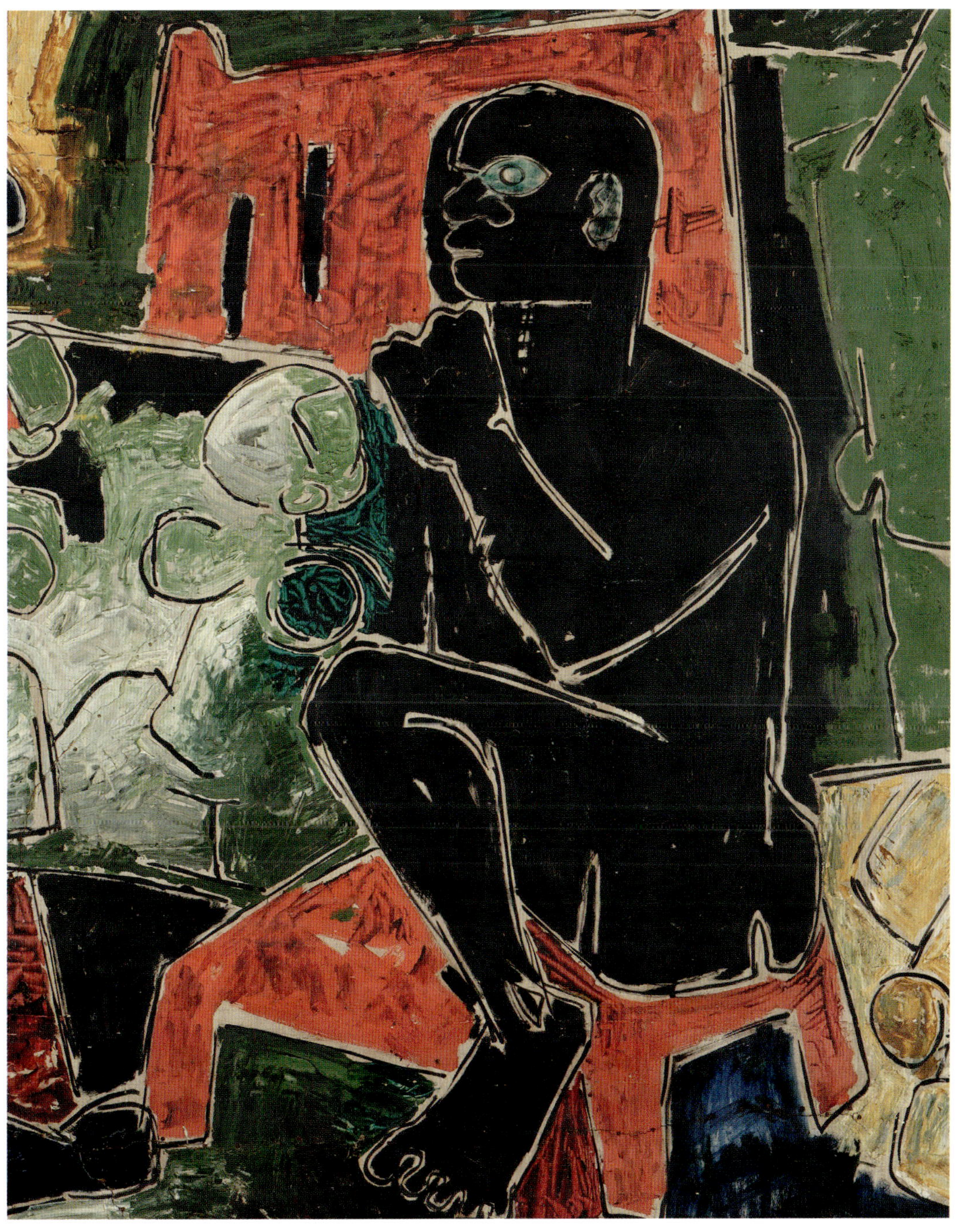

Figure 2.
M.F. Husain, *Man*, 1951
(Plate 4, detail)

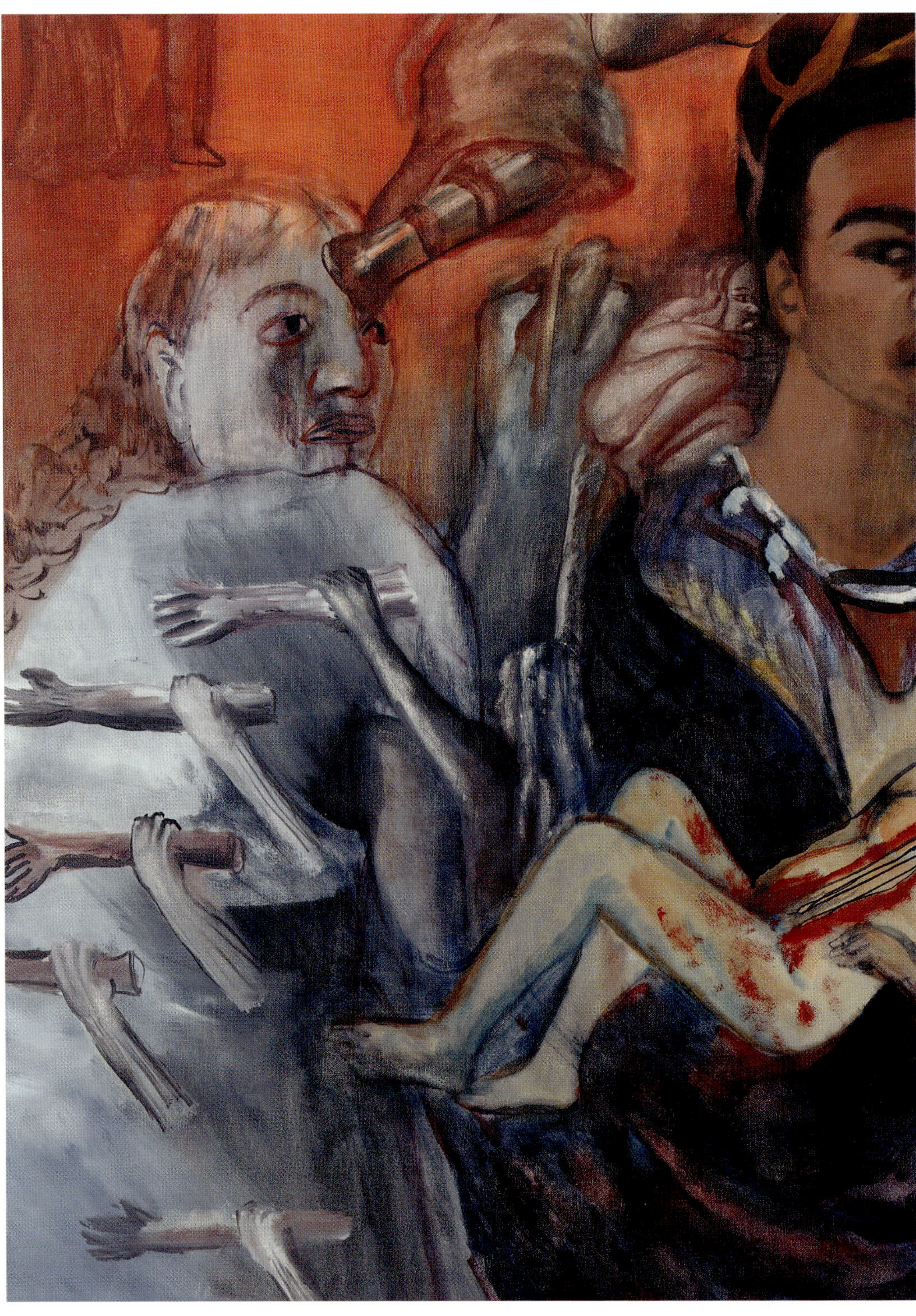

Figure 3.
Nalini Malani,
Old Arguments on Indigenism, 1989
(Plate 67, detail)

There's also a real sense of the psychodrama of the Indian domestic scene of middle-class women, mothers and daughters, about these relationships, about sorrow, the instinct to survive, hysteria, madness; sometimes it's frightening. In the figure to the left of Kahlo, there's a move to escape, to get out of the frame, and, on the other hand, surrounded by the citations of these artists' work, it's almost as if it is their suffering that has made these women into the artists they are. At least as I read it—there's a way in which you can take the suffering and make it art. Malani used something that very often feels like a domestic sphere of women to talk about the political pressures and strictures that play on the domestic sphere from the "outside"—issues to do with the patriarchal power-structure, the law, the distribution of authority, etc.—while creating indentations in the intimate spheres of everyday life. Malani wonderfully portrayed the *presence* of these external pressures as visual *absences* in the picture; they exert a kind of invisible pressure that has to be resisted, and in that tension in between the private and the public she found the shaping force of her work. The quasi-artist figure (at Kahlo's left, probably Malani) holding a paintbrush is both observing and part of the scene; across her body you get these sketches of hands (figure 3). She's there, but she's a ghostly presence. In the awkwardness of her posture is the ambivalence, half looking there and half turning away. Maybe the burden of being a woman artist only ever makes you *half* want it.

SSB: In *The Bombay Buccaneer*, Dodiya also probed his relationship to other artists and to a broad cultural terrain, but his take is teasing and ironic.

HKB: This is painting *after* cinema, *after* Bollywood. Coming out of the traditional form of self-portraiture, you get the popular icon of the Bollywood star. Is there a hint here of a shared celebrity culture between art and the movies? Reflected in the spectacles of the film star you have David Hockney at left and Bhupen Khakhar at right (figure 4). The world has changed; the portrait of the artist has also changed dramatically. By 1994, when this self-portrait was made, the Indian art world had acquired a celebrity gloss boosted by a bullish art market. The mythological musical romances associated with the Bollywood *style* were losing ground to spare, racy Neo-Realist films (with a touch of film noir) that deal with Bombay's Mafioso and the glamour of gangland. It was also around the time of this new kind of popular cinema, which talks so much about crime and the Mafia. Dodiya was actually winking at us and seems to be saying: "One of my eyes reflects Khakhar; the other reflects Hockney. I know; I know this stuff, too, but I want to have a different conversation. I want to have it on the basis of a certain icon of popular culture, and I want to have it on the basis of poster art and the film world." This is about cinema, glamour, consumerism—the painting is branded with the familiar Ralph Lauren logo of a polo player, making a bold, ironic statement about a "brave new India" and the confidence of its rising middle classes. But, it is also about the precarious nature of urban India and its frequent forays into the wild side of corruption, criminality, and exploitation. There's something quite canny about taking a little bit of Braque, or a little bit of Picasso, or a little bit of Hockney, and putting it in a different context—

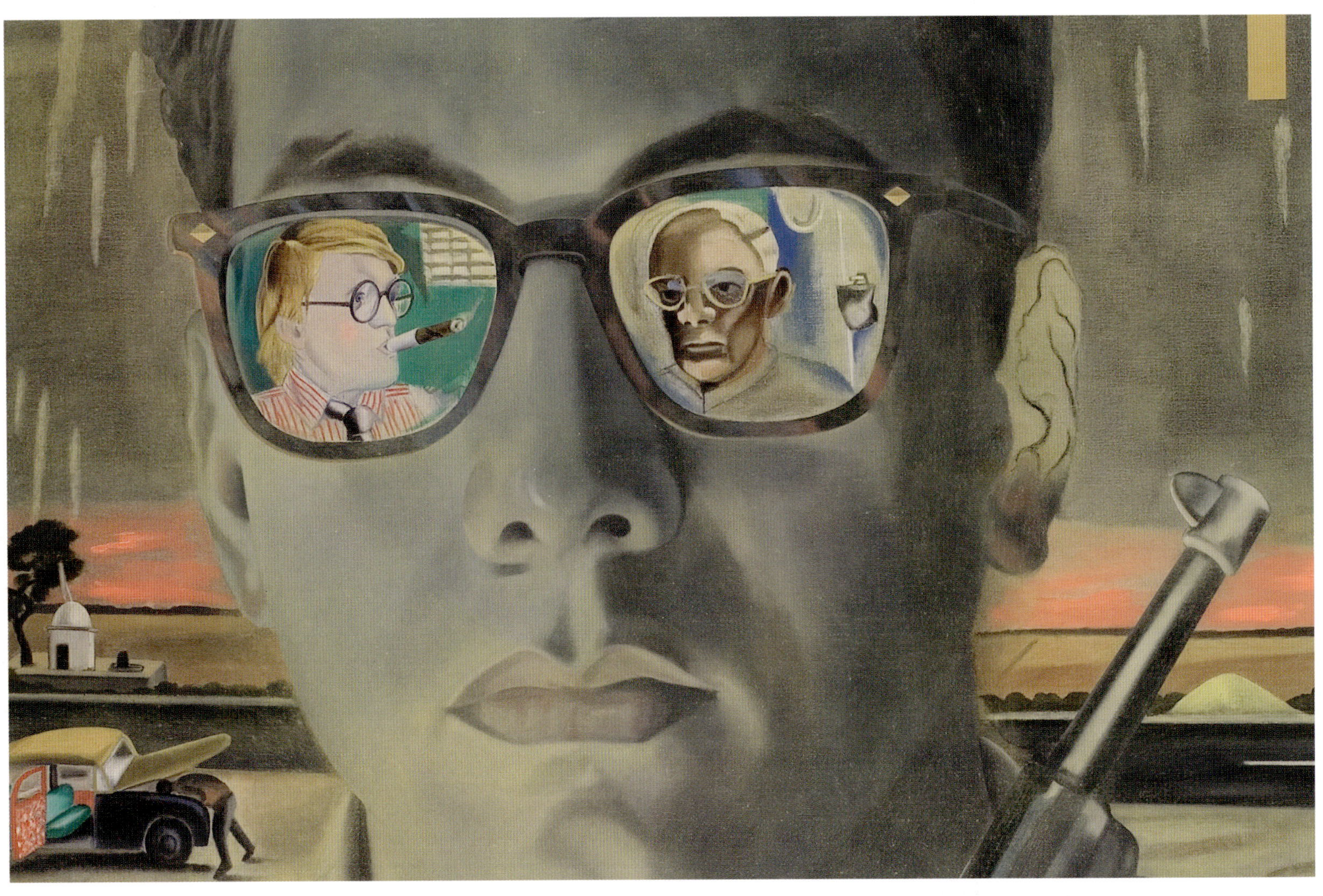

Figure 4.
Atul Dodiya,
The Bombay Buccaneer, 1994
(Plate 63, detail)

the Bollywood context—and saying: "I'm hearing what you're saying, and now I'm giving you something else to think about."

SSB: These works by Husain, Malani, and Dodiya address so reflectively what an artist does, especially an artist coming out of a postcolonial context. Each of them seems to be enacting a kind of rebellion.

HKB: So, the first work, *Man*, is, in a sense, a rather traditional painterly work focused on the artist's traditional labor of mimetic form, and the rather heroic concept of the artist as a shadowed hero. Malani's work immediately opens up a more psychic landscape, which is also to do with painting, but the relationship to it is mediated through the politics of form. It's a much more self-reflective essay, if you like, on the woman as artist, among the transnational lineage of women artists. Her invocation of a gendered tradition of women artists resists the romantic notion of the artist as a sovereign and singular consciousness. And Dodiya's painting has a certain ironic, postmodern self-reflexivity about it. If Malani had her posse of women precursors, Dodiya had his confrères of male masters cited in the painting. But, Dodiya used the media of public culture and poster art to displace "high art" in the direction of a more demotic cultural language and vice versa. A remarkable collection, these three paintings.

It is striking how free these artists seem to have been in their ability to generate a hybridity in their choices and intentions. This comes, I think, from the fact that in India we didn't have cultural institutions that established modernity as an aesthetic and cultural norm. We didn't have dominant, powerful art schools. For example, Bombay's J.J. School was moribund. And, in India, we didn't have a tradition of art criticism, which was desperate to name a particular style of painting: "Mannerism," or "Late Realism," or "Neo-Realism." The absence of a strong institutional presence fostered a certain self-granted permission for the modern Indian artist to experiment, to cite, to quote, and thereby to transform sources for his own work without the guilt of borrowing or being inauthentic.

SSB: To further develop your point, we can take S.H. Raza as an example. He has been quite explicit about his debt to Cézanne for understanding structure in painting. He is also explicit in his admiration for seventeenth- and eighteenth-century Rajput court painting. You are articulating the way he and others approach and work with paintings by other artists.

HKB: Yes, for example, when I saw *Udho, Heart Is Not Ten or Twenty* (plate 14) without knowing anything about about Raza's interest in Cézanne, I said: "My God, why am I so reminded of Cézanne?" In the center, you can really see the presence of Cézanne—in the brushwork, the paint applied in these particular blocks of color, the way they're assembled and constructed (figure 5). You really do see what Raza admired in the way Cézanne constructed a painting with color (see Raza, figure 1). But, one of the beauties is that as he's looking at Cézanne, Rajput court painting is already in his head: harking back to the Rajasthani paintings is the importance of the internal frame (see Raza, figure 2). You can also see the veiled *bindu* (point) looking like a black sun, but

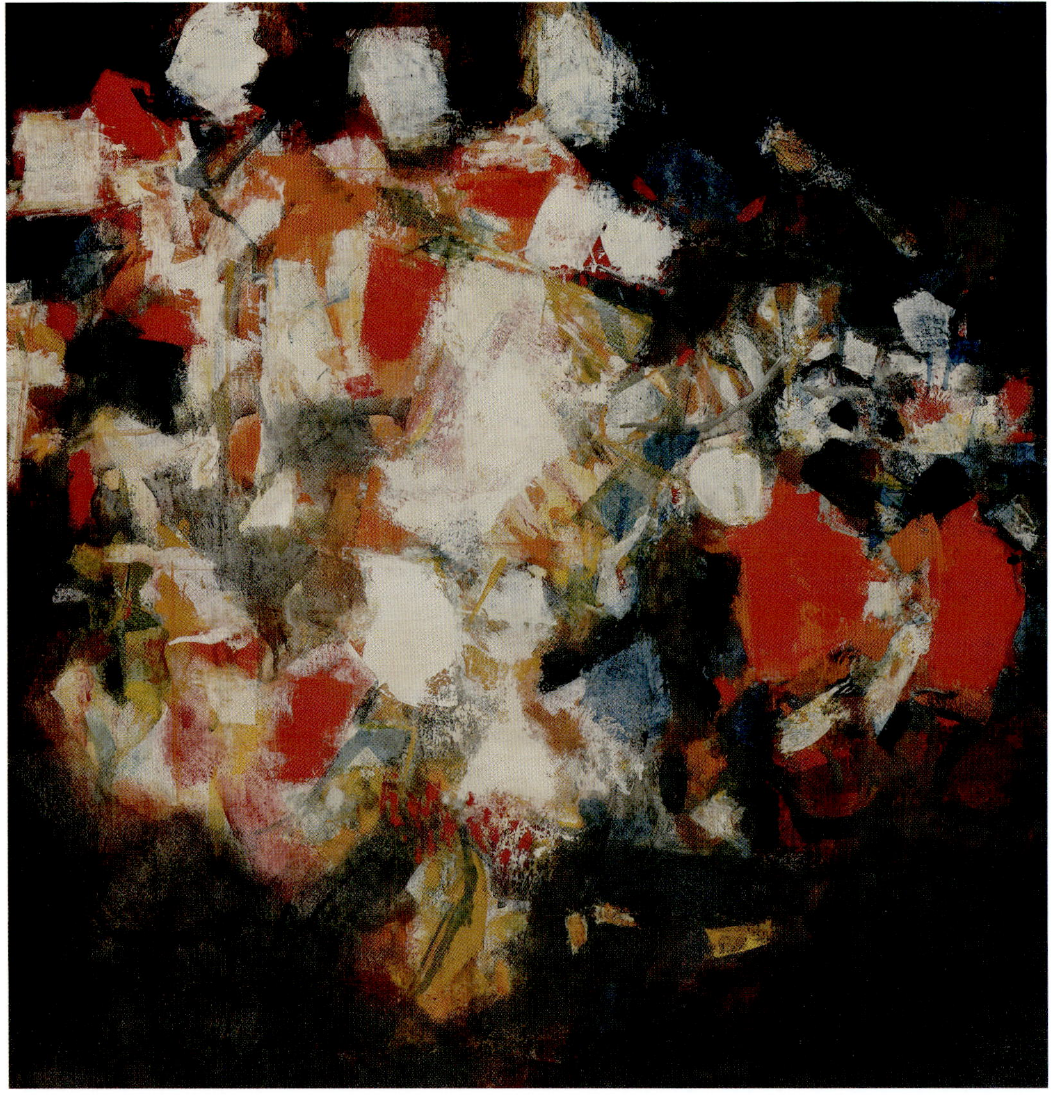

Figure 5.
S.H. Raza, *Udho, Heart Is Not Ten or Twenty*, 1964
(Plate 14, detail)

originating from Raza's childhood practice, instituted by one of his teachers, of meditating on a black circle that somewhere in the future becomes a kind of mystic presence, central to the work itself.

SBB: Our conversation brings out a particular, distinctive quality of much of India's modernist art: the artists' predilection for hybrid, dialogical, transformational practices.

HKB: When you are confronted by the modernity of India, which is so knowing about the cosmopolitanism of its own choosing, then it's a different conversation from one that is fraught with the anxiety of influence, or overwhelmed by a sense of coming belatedly to the drawing board. These artists understood something very profound, which is that if you want a dialogue, you have to take somebody else's words, or, in this case, other approaches to painting, and use them to some degree, in the conversation, as if they were your own.

Editor's Note: This conversation edited by Susan S. Bean synthesizes three sessions in 2011 during which the authors discussed the special character of modernist art in India as they looked at paintings from the Peabody Essex Museum's Herwitz Collection, as well as works and images of works by other artists.

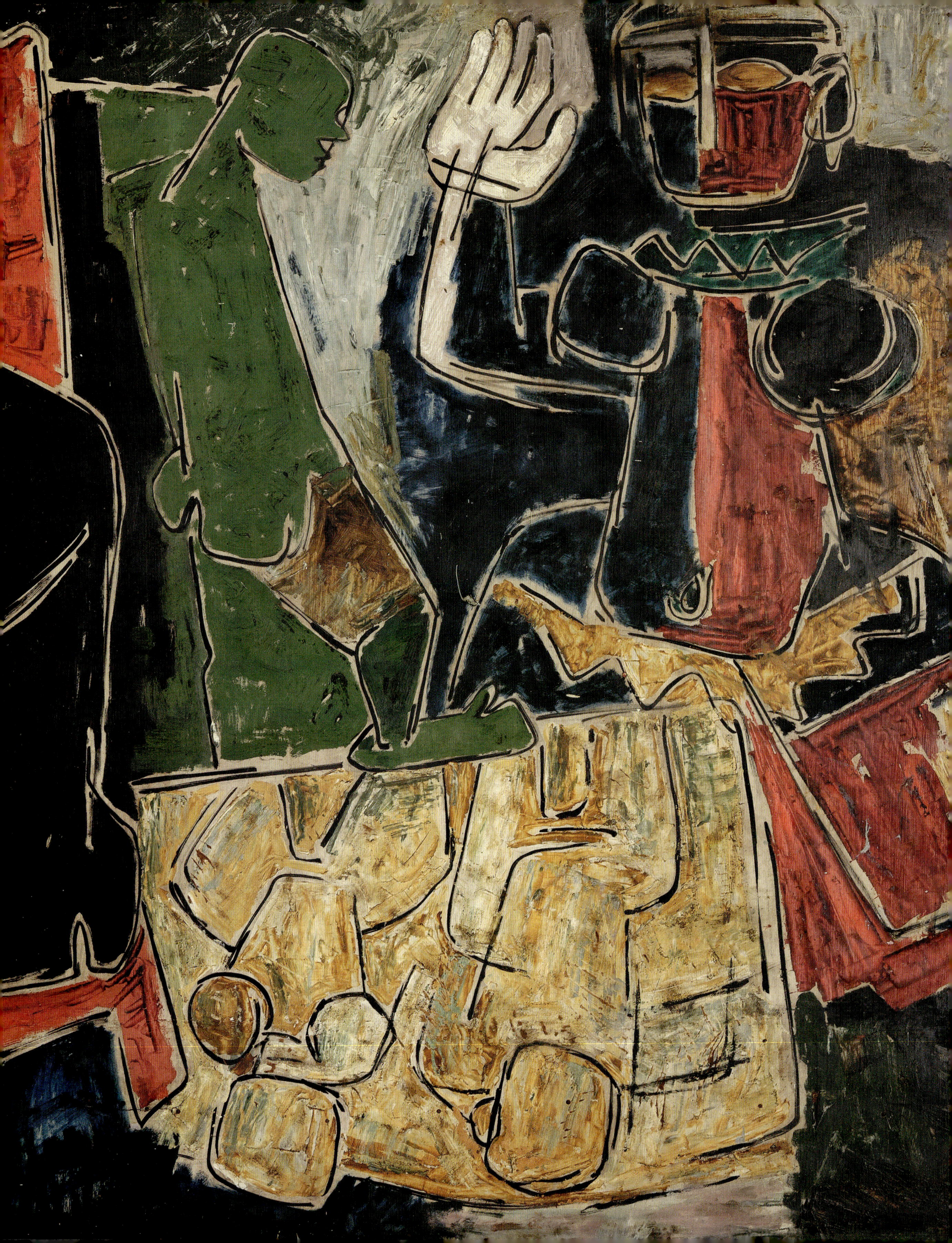

SPACES FOR MODERN ART: THE INDIAN ART WORLD 1940–90

Karin Zitzewitz

A photograph taken in 1951 shows an improbably diverse group of refugees and expatriates from Europe and Indians of various classes, castes, and regional origins (figure 1). They stand together in a small room in South Bombay, jostling for the view of the camera, joined by their shared interest in and commitment to modern art. Behind the group hangs M.F. Husain's *Man* (plate 4), the centerpiece of the event captured by the photo: the artist's first solo exhibition. This snapshot is a significant document of what many in the picture called the "modern art movement."[1] Although it adopted the term "movement" from the struggle for independence from British rule, this group combined the culturally bounded self-assertion of nationalism with the humanist vision associated with a more worldly cosmopolitanism. It saw no contradiction between the two.

Kekoo Gandhy, the gallery owner who also owns this photograph, considered that room, which was called the Artists' Centre, to be a node in an international network of the avant-garde. That network included other sites in India, like the cities of Calcutta, New Delhi, and Madras, and art centers around the world. The artists and patrons who constructed and inhabited these spaces participated in everyday acts of artistic creation and appreciation that ranged from heady sessions in the studio to the mingling described above. They were also conscious of their relationships to other similar spaces and projects across India and abroad. They shared with their patrons the sense of purpose behind the modern art movement, which they thought of as an aesthetic counterpart to other forward-thinking initiatives promoted by the new nation. This community was bound by their belief in the significance of modern art for India and their openness to its pleasures.

Calcutta: The Crucible of Modernism

The story of Indian modernism must begin in Calcutta, the seat of colonial government until 1912 and the country's intellectual hub in the nineteenth and early twentieth centuries. Around the turn of the twentieth century, the Government School of Art, which had been run by the colonial state since the 1850s, rejected its Western-oriented syllabus. It began to encourage students to produce art that was self-consciously Indian *and* modern. Led by its principal, E.B. Havell, a circle of Indian and British

Detail of Plate 4.
M.F. Husain, *Man*, 1951

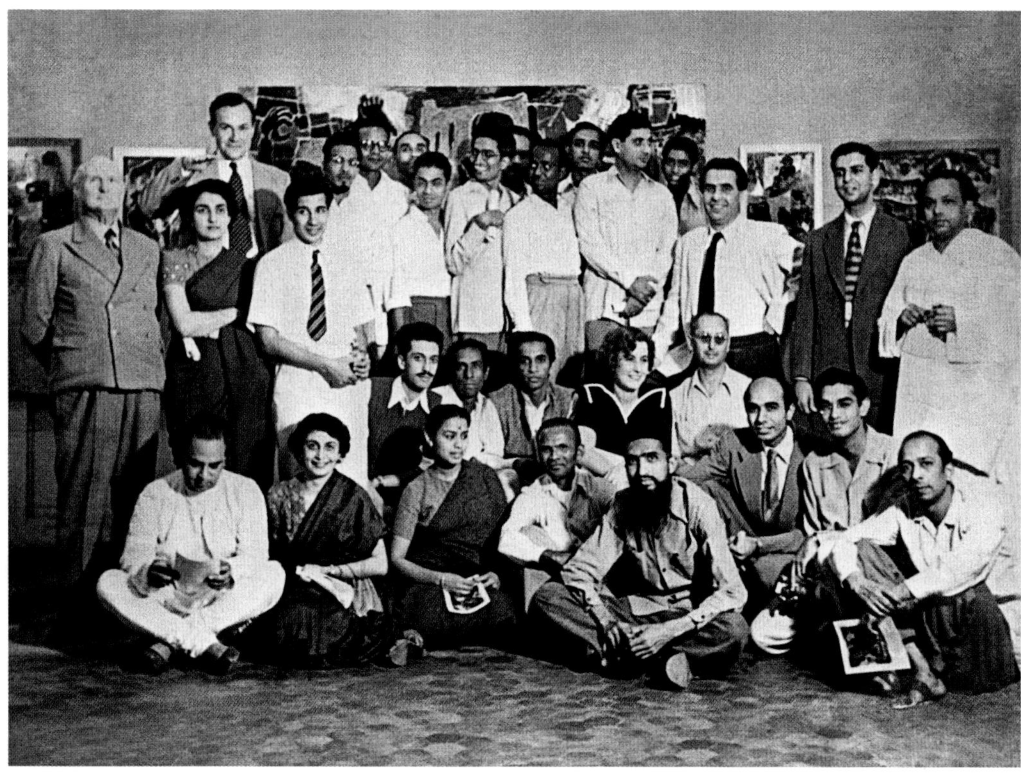

Figure 1.
The Progressive Artists Group and supporters at the Bombay Arts Society Salon, 1951
Left to right: sitting, first row, Dr. Mulk Raj Anand, Siloo Bharucha, Mrs. Renu Khanna, K.H. Ara, M.F. Husain, Bal Chhabda, unidentified, Hazarnis (with folder in hand); sitting, second row, unidentified, unidentified, Laxman Pai, Kathy Langhammer, E. Schlesinger; standing, unidentified, Mrs. Kekoo Gandhy, T.A. Schinzel (behind Mrs. Gandhy), Krishen Khanna (in striped tie), Sadanand Bakre (in glasses, just behind Khanna), D.G. Kulkarni (in glasses, near Bakre), Gaitonde (to Kulkarni's left), A.A. Amelkar, unidentified, Tyeb Mehta, Shiavax Chavda (hands folded in front), Prof. Langhammer (dark tie), Kekoo Gandhy, Manishi Dey.

Collection of Chemould Prescott Road—Contemporary Art Gallery, Mumbai

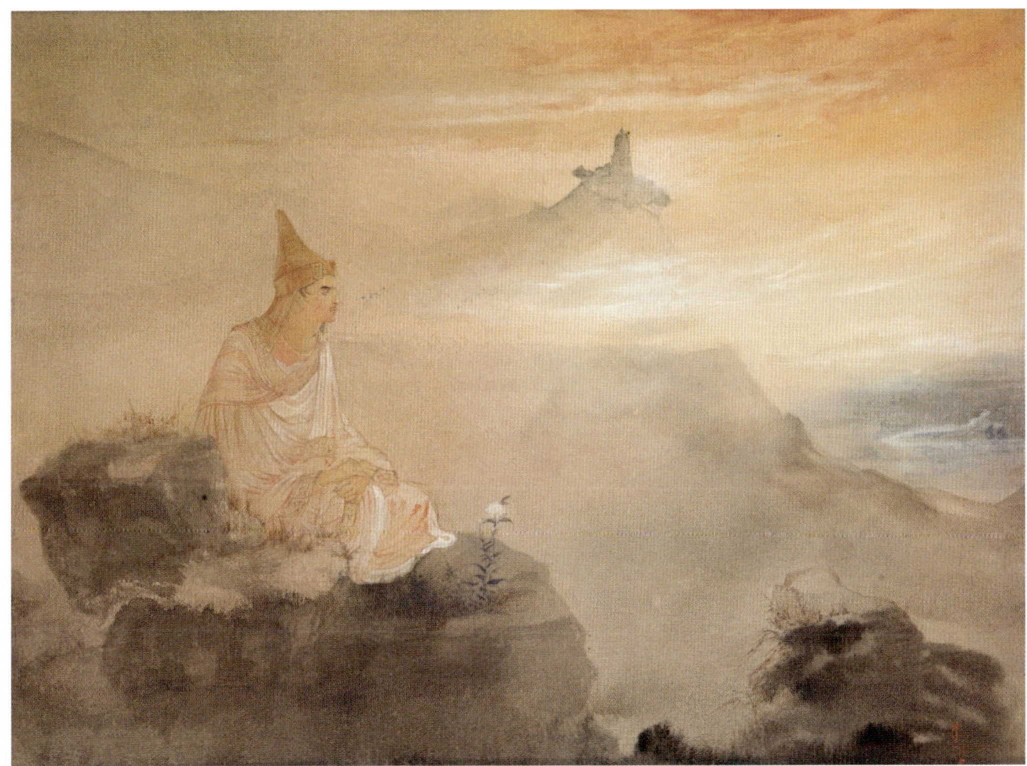

Figure 2.
Abanindranath Tagore,
The Asoka Legend, ca. 1920
Watercolor on paper
9 ¾ × 13 ¾ inches (24.6 × 34.9 cm)
The Chester and Davida Herwitz Collection, Peabody Essex Museum

intellectuals in Calcutta debated what form art in India should take. Directly opposing colonial policy, they declared the post-Renaissance practices of representation and, especially, academic oil painting, to be alien and insufficient.[2] Abanindranath Tagore, whose followers came to be called the Bengal School, developed alternative artistic practices (figure 2). They found indigenous mediums and an alternative sense of scale in the precolonial traditions of India, especially miniature painting, and experimented with contemporary Japanese techniques.

In the 1920s and 1930s, a related group of artists further developed these ideas at Visva-Bharati University in Santiniketan, a village outside Calcutta. This private university founded by Nobel laureate Rabindranath Tagore was an extraordinary hybrid: a cosmopolitan village. Its art department encouraged students to learn from craftsmen as well as the "fine arts" faculty, especially the sculptor Ramkinkar Baij, and Nandalal Bose and Benodebehari Mukherjee, who revived the indigenous practice of mural painting. K.G. Subramanyan (plates 20–23) was among the postcolonial artists trained at Santiniketan, where he assisted Mukherjee in his landmark 1947 mural *Medieval Saints* (Hindi Bhavan, Visva-Bharati, Santiniketan).

Postcolonial Calcutta remained a crucial intellectual center for India, in which art was integrated within a vibrant political, literary, and theater scene. Artists Bikash Bhattacharjee (plates 27–29), Jogen Chowdhury (plates 33–36), and Ganesh Pyne (plates 51–54) all emerged from that milieu. Despite continuing as a center of artistic production, however, it never regained the position it held before independence. That mantle shifted to Bombay.

Bombay: The Cosmopolitan Spaces of a Colonial City

The Artists' Centre, where Husain held his 1950 exhibition, was sponsored by the Bombay Art Society, which had been established in 1888 by and for the colonial elite. According to colonial hierarchy, British artists and patrons dominated at first, but Indians began to submit artwork for consideration shortly after the society was formed. Among the first Indians to compete for the annual gold medal was the largely self-taught, celebrated portraitist and interpreter of Hindu mythology Ravi Varma. The first to win it was M.V. Dhurandhar, who trained at and later became a teacher in Bombay's J.J. School of Art. Of the colonial art schools, the J.J. School was the most committed to the academic style of art, which remained an important part of the curriculum well into the twentieth century.[3]

While the wash-painting technique favored by the Bengal School gained little traction in Bombay, the idea that a modern art could provide a more relevant aesthetic than academic art certainly did. Bombay artists of the 1930s opposed the realism and emphasis on portraiture associated with academism by looking to a variety of modernist models. But, as an anti-academic modernism flourished in the city, even gaining a toehold in the J.J. School, there was enduring opposition to these efforts in the Bombay Art Society. Working in the late 1940s and 1950s, Husain and his fellow members of the short-lived but highly influential Progressive Artists Group continued to frame themselves against the academic tradition. However, they also rejected the romantic and ethereal style they associated with the Bengal School, finding very different answers to the question of what relationship Indian modernism was to have to its artistic history.

These artists favored the creation of a modernism conversant with Postimpressionist styles of painting developed in France and Germany that subordinated naturalism to the exploration of formal elements of color, line, and form, which they viewed as free from direct associations with the colonial state.[4] Their patrons, particularly a small group of Central European Jewish refugees who came to Bombay during the Second World War, found in the Progressive Artists an alternative Indian modernism that was a sharp rebuke to the Indian academic tradition and the colonial culture it had come to represent. Looking to reform the Bombay Art Society to their tastes, these artists and patrons embraced this form of modernism as the only one suited to the moment. With the colonial associations of the art school and exclusivism of the art world as a foil, this group positioned itself as a socially engaged avant-garde appropriate to both Bombay's cosmopolitanism and India's nationalism.

These artists gathered in informal spaces like the Artists' Centre, which was rented on their behalf by a relatively wealthy refugee, the Austrian pharmaceutical manufacturer and collector Emmanuel Schlesinger. They found an alternative source of artistic training in an informal salon held in the home of Walter Langhammer, a painting teacher and artist from Vienna who fled to India with his Jewish wife and her mother. German refugee Rudolph von Leyden, a cartoonist and graphic artist for the *Times of India*, took on the crucial role of critic, championing his favored modernists in the pages of his newspaper. Remaining active in the art scene throughout the 1940s and 1950s, these three men gathered a wide array of supporters, from diplomats to businessmen to intellectuals, often also making use of the talents of foreigners passing through. This community was the basis of the modern art world of Bombay.

Bombay's modern artists and art patrons shared two apparently divergent points of view: one looking outside the country and one looking within. To some, the city and its European patronage made it a gateway to training in the West. This attitude fostered the migration of a number of Bombay modernists to Paris and London, including Progressive Artists F.N. Souza and S.H. Raza (plates 14–17), as well as Akbar Padamsee and Tyeb Mehta (plates 9–13). Raza went to France in 1950 on a scholarship from the Alliance Française after attracting the support of Langhammer and von Leyden (figure 3). The latter produced a handsome book about the artist in 1959. Raza's experience in Paris changed his work significantly, as he turned from watercolor to oils and experimented with abstraction (figure 4). In 1956, he won a major prize in Paris, which led to sponsorship by a gallery, and he remained in France for much of his adult life.

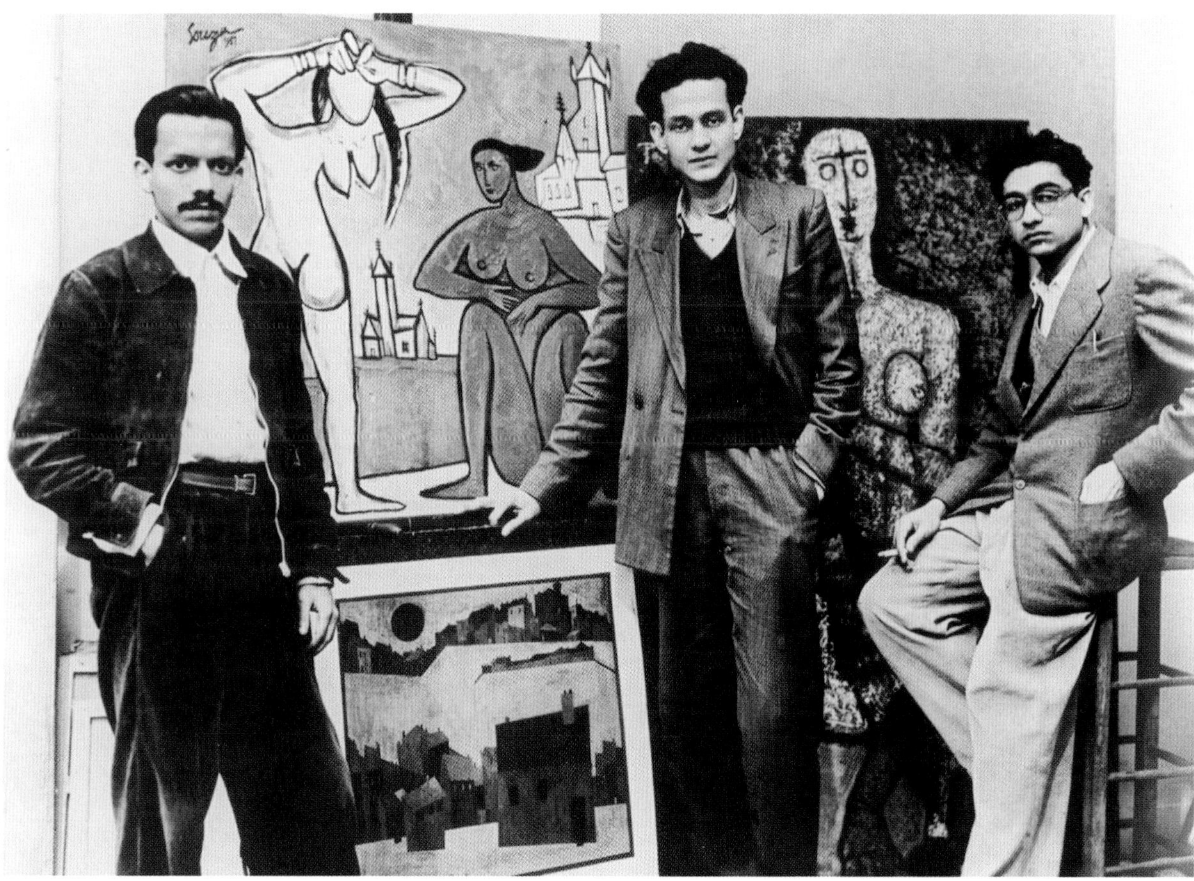

Figure 3.
Left to right: F.N. Souza, S.H. Raza, and Akbar Padamsee in Montparnasse, Paris, 1952
Collection of S.H. Raza

However much Bombay looked outward toward the West, it also remained a key center for national institutions committed to the promotion of modern art. Among the first important contributions to come from Bombay was *Marg*, a magazine founded in 1946 by the socialist writer Mulk Raj Anand with sponsorship from the Tata industrial group. Casting a wide net over India's aesthetic terrain, *Marg* was a forum for modernist design and urban planning as well as essays on art and art history.[5] In its earliest days, it carried a crucial section of reviews from around India. Unlike other art criticism, which was printed only in the city editions of newspapers, *Marg* made it possible for people to be informed about the direction that modern art was taking around the country.

The core group of artists and refugees also pressed for the establishment of institutions for the exhibition of modern art. Most enduring has been the Jehangir Art Gallery, a space carved out of the grounds of Bombay's Prince of Wales Museum (now Chhatrapati Shivaji Maharaj Vastu Sangrahalaya) in 1952. For some years in the 1950s, the Bhulabhai Desai Institute thrived in the posh neighborhood of Warden Road, supporting theater, music, and dance as well as art, and fostering the careers of many who went on to lead arts organizations around India. Tyeb Mehta described the institute as something like a clubhouse, where artists would discuss their work over cups of tea. It also housed the short-lived Gallery 59, which sold modern Indian art.

The first two enduring commercial galleries were founded in the city in 1963. Kali Pundole converted his Fort business district space, originally a watch shop, into the Pundole Art Gallery, through which he also amassed an important collection. Gallery Chemould grew out of a framing business founded during the war and was housed inside the Jehangir Art Gallery (see Sinha, page 54). Its directors, Kekoo and Khorshed Gandhy, became active in the Bombay Art Society in the early 1940s and were a major force in the modern art movement in Bombay and nationally. Into the 1970s, these two galleries remained the only ongoing commercial spaces in Bombay, where they worked to cultivate a consistent audience for modern art. Among the most prominent collectors was nuclear physicist Homi Jehangir Bhabha, who not only bought works for his own collection, but also for the halls of the Tata Institute of Fundamental Research at the southern tip of the city.[6] Corporate collecting was also important: the Times of India, Air India, the Taj Mahal Hotel, and Proctor and Gamble all amassed sizable collections.

Nevertheless, Indian patronage was limited and prices remained quite low. Artists were open to foreign collectors and many felt that modern art was more appreciated outside of India than within. Accustomed to much higher prices in Europe and the United States, foreigners especially in Bombay and New Delhi were able to assemble relatively large collections. Prominent among these collectors were Davida and Chester Herwitz, who began to collect Indian art in the late 1960s.

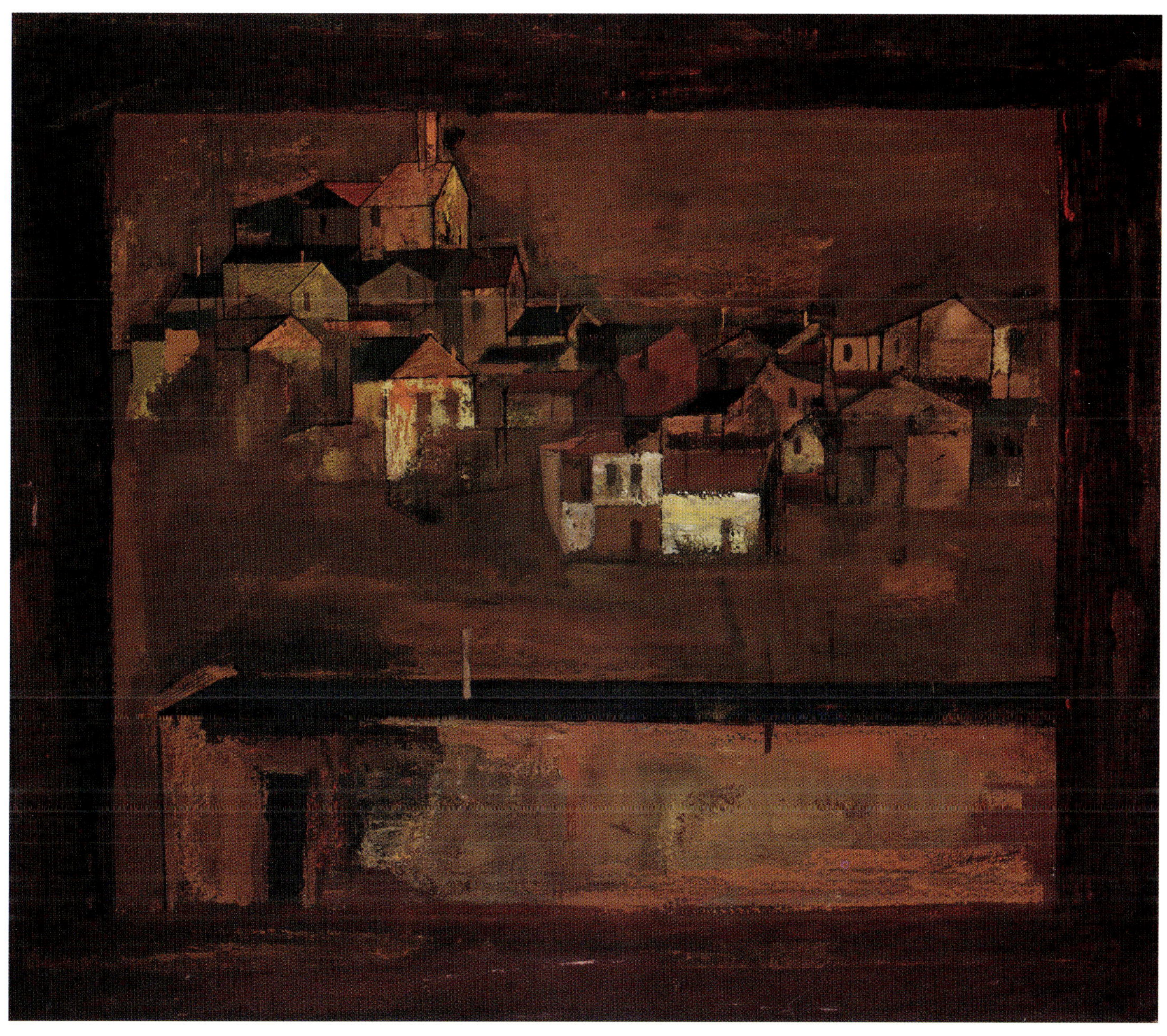

Figure 4.
S.H. Raza, *Untitled*, 1953
Oil on paper
22 ½ × 26 ½ inches (57.2 × 67.3 cm)
The Chester and Davida Herwitz Collection,
Peabody Essex Museum

New Delhi: Art Institutions for a New Nation

As India's struggle for independence drew to a close, debates over who would determine the character of national art institutions accelerated. Conferences held in 1947 and 1948 helped to solidify a network of modern artists groups scattered across India—an important way in which artists organized themselves at this time.[7] Many groups resembled the Progressive Artists: they worked with but also exposed the shortcomings of urban societies encouraging art patronage. In New Delhi, the most important was the All India Fine Arts and Crafts Society, founded in 1928. At independence, this society assumed it would merely extend its reach to the nation as a whole, but in 1954 it was instead succeeded by three national academies: one for literature, one for performing arts, and one for fine art, the Lalit Kala Akademi. The National Gallery for Modern Art was founded in the same year.

Popular magazines such as *Illustrated Weekly of India* joined *Marg* and, later, the academy-sponsored *Lalit Kala Contemporary*, to discuss what sort of art should be encouraged. While some argued for the revitalization of indigenous modes of painting, others debated between modernism and socialist realism. The Lalit Kala Akademi's annual exhibition became a lightning rod for these debates well into the 1960s. Overall, the academy has had a catholic sense of taste, which, it argued, has demonstrated its properly democratic support of a variety of current artistic practices. Its activities have accompanied other state efforts to encourage a wide array of art, including the establishment of the All India Handloom and Handicrafts boards, which attempted to salvage and create markets for indigenous crafts.

In terms of the conditions of exhibition and collecting, Delhi differed considerably from Bombay. Each scene piggybacked the dominant force of social organization for the elite: in Calcutta, that was the larger intellectual milieu; in Bombay, it was big business; in Delhi, it was the central government and the international diplomatic and aid institutions that attempted to influence the new nation. At times, art world activities took on the character of cultural diplomacy.

Jawaharlal Nehru, the first prime minister, thought modernist design and architecture had enormous potential for shaping the country's development. He invited internationally renowned figures to India, most famously the international-style architect Le Corbusier, who designed a new capital, Chandigarh, for the partitioned state of Punjab. Nehru's administration also gave a voice to two passionate advocates for the preservation and development of India's craft traditions, however. Folk art advocates Pupul Jayakar and Kamaladevi Chattopadhyay led the Handicrafts and Handloom boards, respectively, establishing strong state-run networks of patronage for these "traditional" arts.[8] While these two projects might seem mutually exclusive, they were often supported by the same people. Groups committed to India's modernization and international exchange often supported both modern design and craft.[9]

A crucial example is the Rockefeller Foundation, which funded the Handicrafts Board while also supervising a rural credit scheme through the Indian Cooperative Union. Governor Nelson A. Rockefeller was a significant force in the New York art world, sitting on the board of The Museum of Modern Art while amassing one of the most important private collections of African, Oceanic, and pre-Columbian art in the world. Modern art was on the foundation's agenda from the time it entered India. Tom Keehn, the foundation's representative in India in 1953–61, was instructed by Rockefeller to survey modern art and culture because, as he noted, little attention had been paid to those areas.[10] Keehn and his wife, Martha, befriended painters in Delhi, including Husain and Ram Kumar (plates 7 and 8), and collected their works.

In 1955, MoMA, which had by then established itself as a legitimizing force in the art world, mounted a show highlighting Indian textiles and jewelry.[11] It was explicitly described in Cold War terms, as a gesture of American support for Indian culture that might counter Russian influence. When exhibitions director Monroe Wheeler toured India, Keehn introduced him to artists and proposed that MoMA do an exhibition of modern Indian art. Wheeler declined. As Keehn reported: "Monroe said, 'You are doing good work. Keep at it. But these artists are not ready for the New York Museum of Modern Art.'"[12]

The Rockefeller Foundation helped establish the Kunika Gallery inside the government-run Handicrafts Emporium—then and now the center of tourist shopping in the city. It followed the taste of its founding director, Richard Bartholomew, and exclusively showed modern artists. Bartholomew was an accomplished artist, curator, and critic; he later became head of Lalit Kala Akademi. He championed the work of Kumar, whose early paintings expressed urban anomie, but who had turned by the late 1950s to increasingly abstract land- and cityscapes (figure 5). Bartholomew co-authored a book on Husain that was published by Harry N. Abrams in 1971.[13] Despite his critical acumen, the gallery struggled financially, so Kekoo and Khorshed Gandhy were invited from Bombay to put the gallery back into the black.[14]

The Gandhys hired Roshan Alkazi to manage the gallery, which they renamed Kunika-Chemould Art Centre, and gave her complete control over the exhibition schedule. Roshan Alkazi was married to Ebrahim Alkazi, who had been associated with the Bhulabhai Desai Institute in Bombay before he moved to Delhi to direct the new National School of Drama. In Bombay, the Alkazis had been closely associated with the same group of artists supported by the Gandhys, and these artists and their Delhi associates became the core of the Kunika-Chemould roster. Important collectors themselves, the Alkazis went on to found their own gallery, Art Heritage, in 1977. Other significant commercial galleries included the Kumar Gallery, led by a former employee of Kunika-Chemould, and the Dhoomimal Art Gallery at Connaught Place, which had been founded in 1936.

The Rockefeller Foundation additionally influenced Indian modern art through its artist residency program in New York, which was briefly aligned with MoMA. The six-to-nine-month residencies were often formative experiences. Mehta's time in New York led him to discover the paintings of Barnett Newman, which prompted Mehta to introduce the formal device of the diagonal into his paintings—a celebrated moment in the development of his work (plate 10).

It is easy to overstate the impact of the Rockefeller Foundation's activities, and therein falsely characterize the internationalism of Indian art as an alliance with the West. In fact, Indian artists also built productive relationships with countries of the global South, as artists looked to similar artistic movements in Africa and Latin America, as well as Japan. One concrete exchange occurred in 1963 with the exhibition

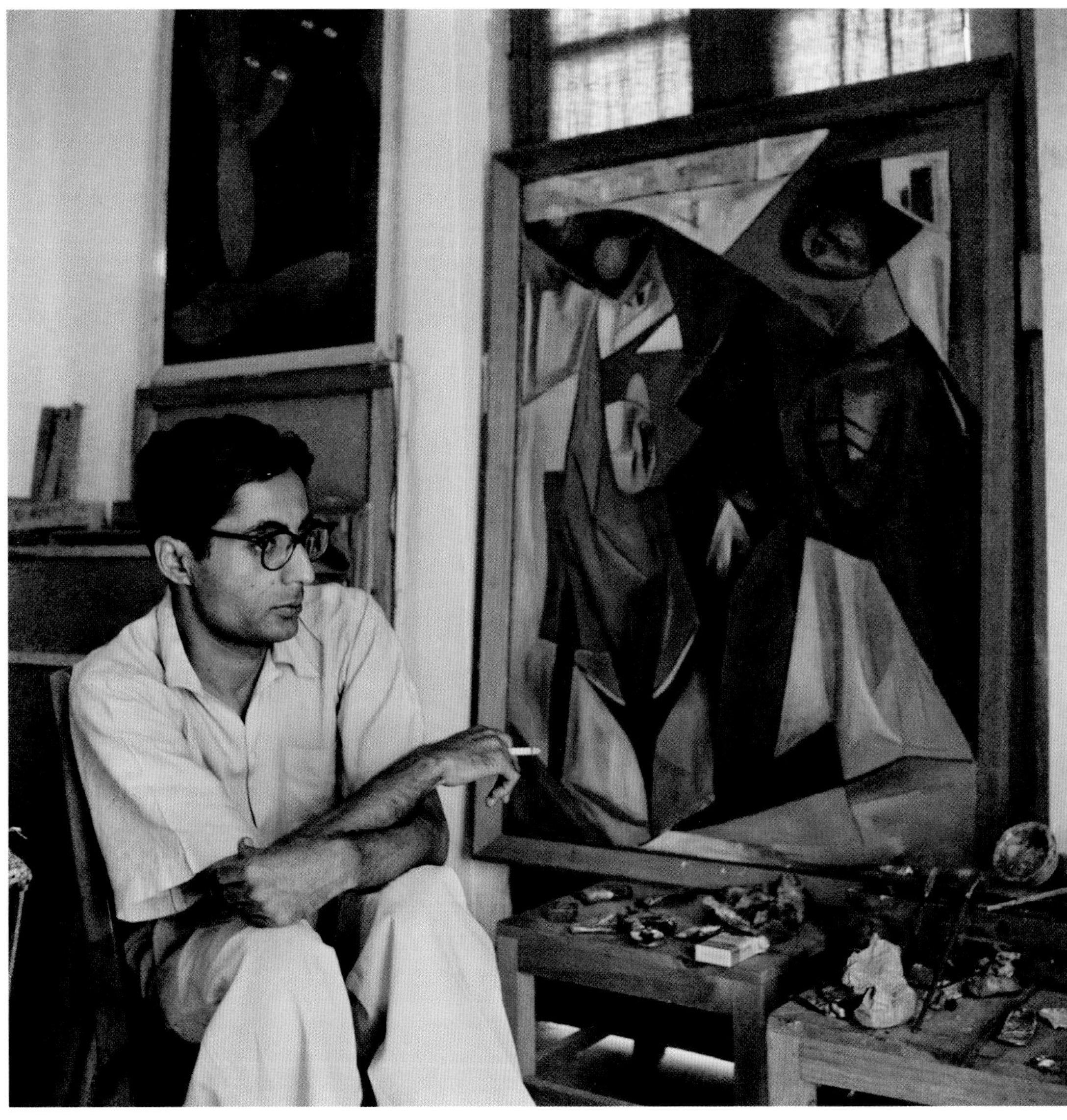

Figure 5.
Richard Bartholomew,
Ram Kumar in His Gole Market Studio, New Delhi, 1956
Collection of Pablo Bartholomew

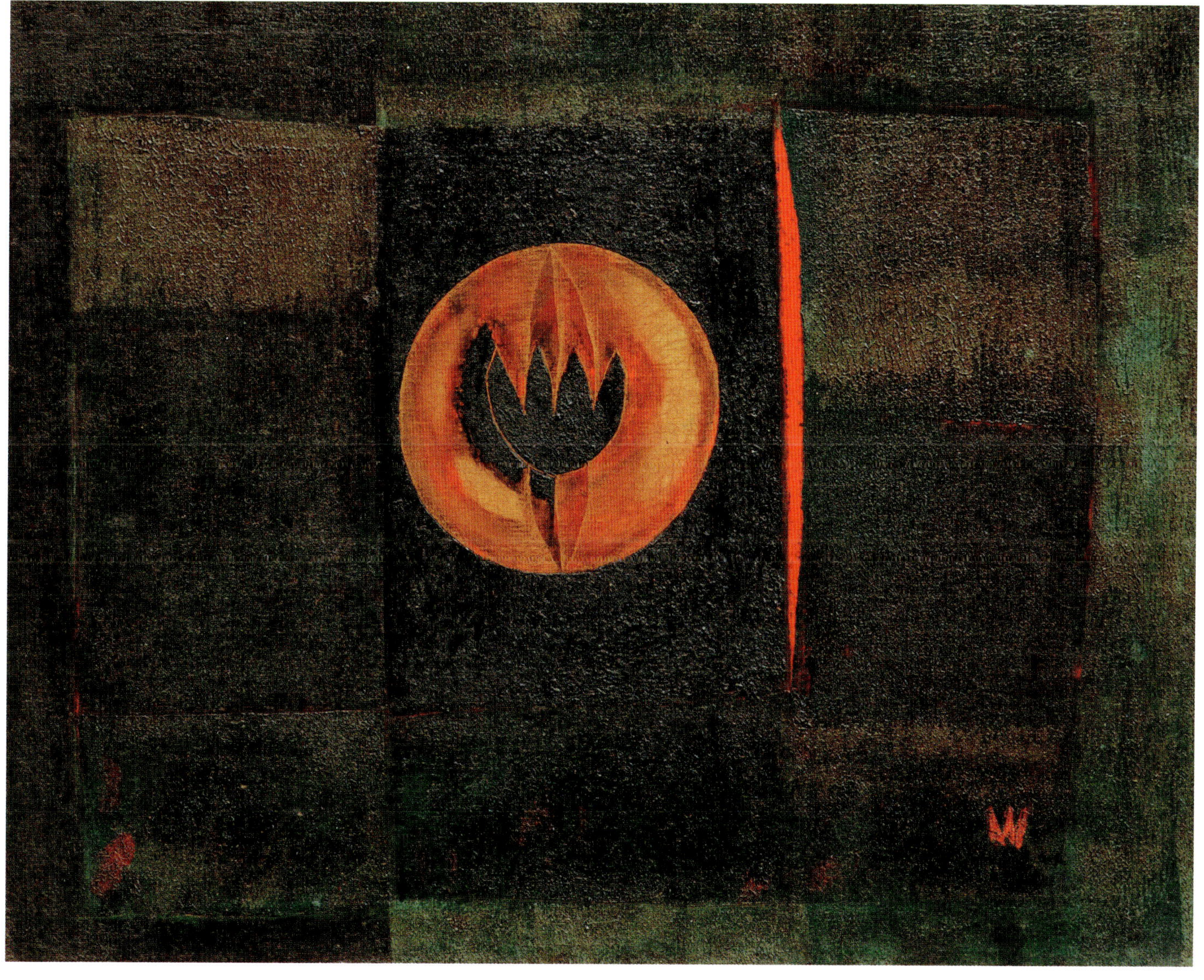

Figure 6.
J. Swaminathan, *Untitled*, 1964–65
Oil, sand, and pigment on canvas
24 × 30 inches (61 × 76.2 cm)
J. Swaminathan Foundation

of Group 1890. The group was led by Delhi artist J. Swaminathan (figure 6), a close friend of Surrealist poet Octavio Paz, the Mexican ambassador to India. Paz encouraged the group to draw upon the insights of structural anthropology to reconnect art to an intuitive and elemental source. While some artists found that source in the body, others looked toward a spiritual realm. That impulse found fruition in the style of painting associated with G.R. Santosh (plates 18 and 19) and Biren De (plates 1 and 2), Neo-Tantrism, which drew on the mandala form to create images that converged in interesting ways with color-field painting.

But, modern art in New Delhi remained tied to larger projects aiming at India's rapid development throughout the first decades of independence. An important source of employment for many prominent artists was the Weavers' Service Centre at the All India Handloom Board. The center employed artists as designers charged with reworking traditional textile patterns for national and international markets.[15] K.G. Subramanyan (plates 20–23), a polymath artist and writer who has advocated the alignment of modern art with craft, worked there from 1958 to 1961. He developed "bleeding madras" plaid, which was a crucial contribution to the preppy style of the American Northeast.[16] Before and after his work with textiles, Subramanyan was a professor of painting in Baroda's influential art institution.

Baroda: A Postcolonial Avant-Garde

Founded in 1950, Maharaja Sayajirao University in Baroda, Gujarat, sought to distinguish itself from universities with roots in the colonial era. The faculty of fine arts was integrated with the university, and became the first art school in India to include a department of art history and to award bachelors and, later, masters degrees. Its curriculum was assembled from a number of sources, combining British academic training with post-Bauhaus ideas of art education popular in the United States. Key faculty, like Subramanyan and sculptor Sankho Chaudhuri, were trained in the Indian- and Asian-derived techniques developed in Santiniketan, and a large number of early students and faculty were educated at Dakshinamurti, a school in Bhavnagar, Gujarat, noted for its social commitment. Situated in the milieu of Gandhian nationalism, Baroda's faculty was personally and politically progressive and believed that art must be engaged in society. This dynamic institution became the petri dish of India's avant-garde.

Baroda faculty and students had their hand in many of the most important radical art movements, including Group 1890. The school fostered a number of different aesthetic agendas. For example, the painting department contained both Subramanyan (figure 7), whose work combines modernist playfulness with attention to craft tradition, and Nasreen Mohamedi (plates 44–47), whose spare drawings evince an extraordinary discipline and economy of expression. But, in the 1970s, Baroda became associated with figurative narrative painting, which was embraced by artists wishing to reject Neo-Tantrism and other trends as insufficiently grounded in social life. These artists spread their opinions through the magazine *Vrishchik* (Scorpion). Geeta Kapur's early essays appeared in its pages; by the end of the decade, she had emerged as the most inventive and insightful critic and curator of modern Indian art.

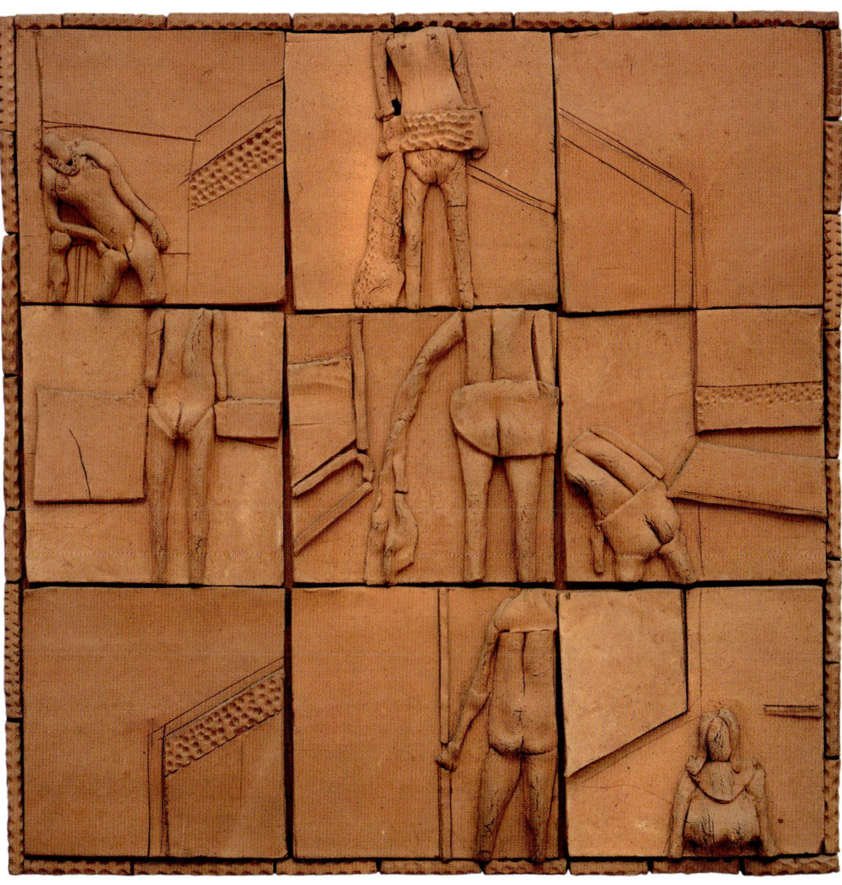

Figure 7.
K.G. Subramanyan, *Bathers*, 1971
Terracotta
25 × 25 inches (63.5 × 63.5 cm)
National Gallery of Modern Art, New Delhi

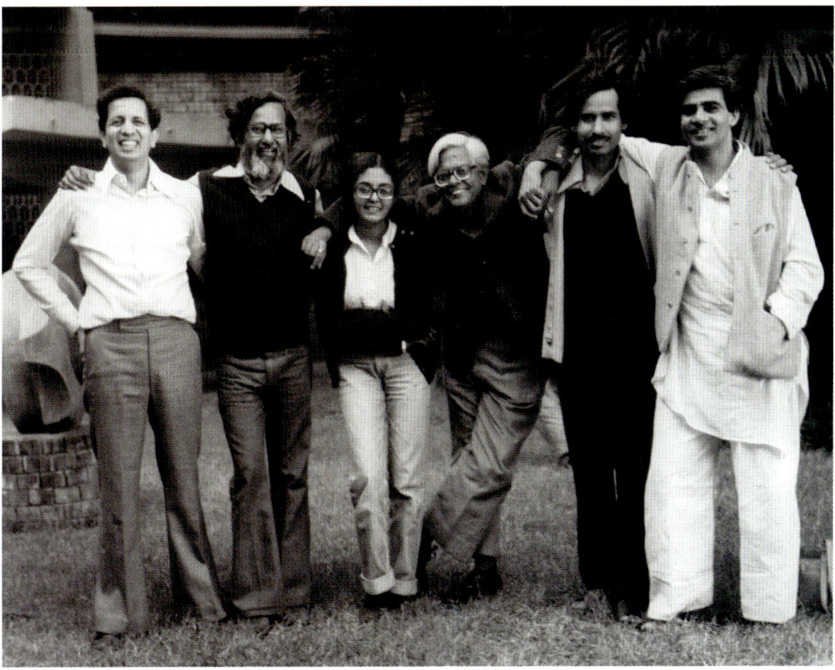

Figure 8.
Artists who participated in the *Place for People* exhibition, 1981. Left to right: Sudhir Patwardhan, Gulammohammed Sheikh, Nalini Malani, Bhupen Khakhar, Jogen Chowdhury, Vivan Sundaram, 1981
Collection of Vivan Sundaram

These artists honed their commitment to figuration in a series of group shows leading up to their most eloquent expression, the 1981 *Place for People* exhibition at the Jehangir Art Gallery. The show brought together work by Jogen Chowdhury, Bhupen Khakhar (plates 41–43), Nalini Malani (plates 66–68), Sudhir Patwardhan (plates 69–71), Gulammohammed Sheikh (plates 55–57), and Vivan Sundaram (figure 8). Geeta Kapur's extensive catalogue essay discussed the role of the figure in Indian and Western art.[17] Although commonly associated with Baroda, this exhibition identified a question vital to many artists around India: what space might the figure occupy in modern Indian art?

This group initially positioned themselves as radicals reacting against the dominant artists of their time. But, as their ideas proved convincing, they soon became the new establishment. They advanced their point of view through a series of new institutional forms. An annual art camp held in the hill station of Kasauli fostered the careers of younger artists. Kapur and Sundaram created a new critical forum in the *Journal of Arts and Ideas*, which greatly expanded the study of Indian art and popular visual culture.[18] As the Bombay modernists had done, this group worked to provide new venues for artists to develop and show their work.

Just as the previous generation balanced nationalism with cosmopolitanism, these artists looked to engage with the world outside of India. Perhaps the most important opportunities abroad were provided by the government-sponsored Festivals of India, which were held in major world cities between 1982 and 1987.[19] Among the events were two exhibitions of the Herwitz Collection, one in New York University's Grey Art Gallery and the other in the Phillips Collection in Washington, DC. The crowning recapitulation of the ambitions of artists in the 1950s—those denied their show at MoMA—came when Patwardhan, Khakhar, Sheikh, and Arpita Singh (plates 58–61) were all given solo exhibitions at the Centre Georges Pompidou in Paris.

The boom in modern Indian art that followed this period has had many positive effects, but it changed the ad hoc nature of the Indian art world, professionalizing what had been an extraordinarily informal creative process. The gallerist Kekoo Gandhy, whose stories have influenced many historians of modern Indian art, has emphasized the informal creative energies that dominated the most productive art institutions in India. He has given the impression that the art world is at its best when small groups of people advance big ideas, or when enduring visions are realized on shoestring budgets. What the present world of Indian art shares with this period is its divided point of view. The dual responsibilities to build a national art community and to participate in a global artistic process remain the driving forces behind Indian art.

1. The pioneering gallerist Kekoo Gandhy is particularly fond of this term. See Karin Zitzewitz, *The Perfect Frame: Presenting Indian Art* (Mumbai: Gallery Chemould, 2003); and Yashodhara Dalmia, *The Making of Modern Indian Art: The Progressives* (New Delhi: Oxford University Press, 2001).

2. See Tapati Guha-Thakurta, *The Making of a New 'Indian' Art: Artists, Aesthetics and Nationalism in Bengal, c. 1850–1920* (Cambridge: Cambridge University Press, 1992); and Partha Mitter, *Art and Nationalism in Colonial India, 1850–1922: Occidental Orientations* (Cambridge: Cambridge University Press, 1994).

3. See Mitter.

4. See Dalmia and also Geeta Kapur, *Contemporary Indian Artists* (New Delhi: Vikas Publishing House, 1978).

5. Gyan Prakash, *Mumbai Fables* (Princeton, New Jersey: Princeton University Press, 2010).

6. Mortimer Chatterjee and Tara Lal, *The TIFR Art Collection* (Mumbai: Tata Institute of Fundamental Research, 2010).

7. See Zitzewitz.

8. See Pupul Jayakar, *The Earthen Drum: An Introduction to the Ritual Arts of Rural India* (New Delhi: National Museum, 1980); and Kamaladevi Chattopadhyay, *The Glory of Indian Handicrafts* (New Delhi: Clarion Books, 1985). 9. The reasons for this are complex, having to do both with the development of art education in India, as discussed in Guha-Thakurta and in Mitter, and the role of craft in the nationalist movement, as discussed in Emma Tarlo, *Clothing Matters: Dress and Identity in India* (Chicago: University of Chicago Press, 1996); and Rebecca M. Brown, *Gandhi's Spinning Wheel and the Making of India* (London: Routledge, 2010).

10. Thomas Keehn, ed., *India Ink: Letters from India by Martha McKee Keehn, 1953–61* (New Delhi: Vadehra Art Gallery, 2000).

11. Saloni Mathur, "Charles and Ray Eames in India," *Art Journal* 70, 1 (Spring 2011), pp. 34–53.

12. Keehn, p. 87.

13. Richard Bartholomew, "Paintings of Ramkumar," *Hindustan Times*, October 1955, p. 6; Richard Bartholomew and Shiv S. Kapur, *Maqbool Fida Husain* (New York: Harry N. Abrams, ca. 1971).

14. Kekoo Gandhy, conversation with the author, 2003.

15. Nilima Sheikh, "A Post-Independence Initiative in Art," in Gulammohammed Sheikh, ed., *Contemporary Art in Baroda* (New Delhi: Tulika Press, 1997), pp. 53–143.

16. K.G. Subramanyan, *The Magic of Making: Essays on Art and Culture* (Calcutta: Seagull Books, 2007), pp. 189–202.

17. Geeta Kapur, "Partisan Views about the Human Figure," in *Place for People* (Bombay: Jehangir Art Gallery, and New Dehli: Rabindra Bhavan, 1981), n.p.

18. Most issues of the *Journal of Arts and Ideas* are available online at The Digital South Asia Library, http://dsal.uchicago.edu/.

19. *India: Myth & Reality—Aspects of Modern Indian Art* (Oxford: Museum of Modern Art, 1982); Carla M. Borden, ed., *Contemporary Indian Tradition: Voices on Culture, Nature, and the Challenge of Change* (Washington, DC: Smithsonian Institution Press, 1989).

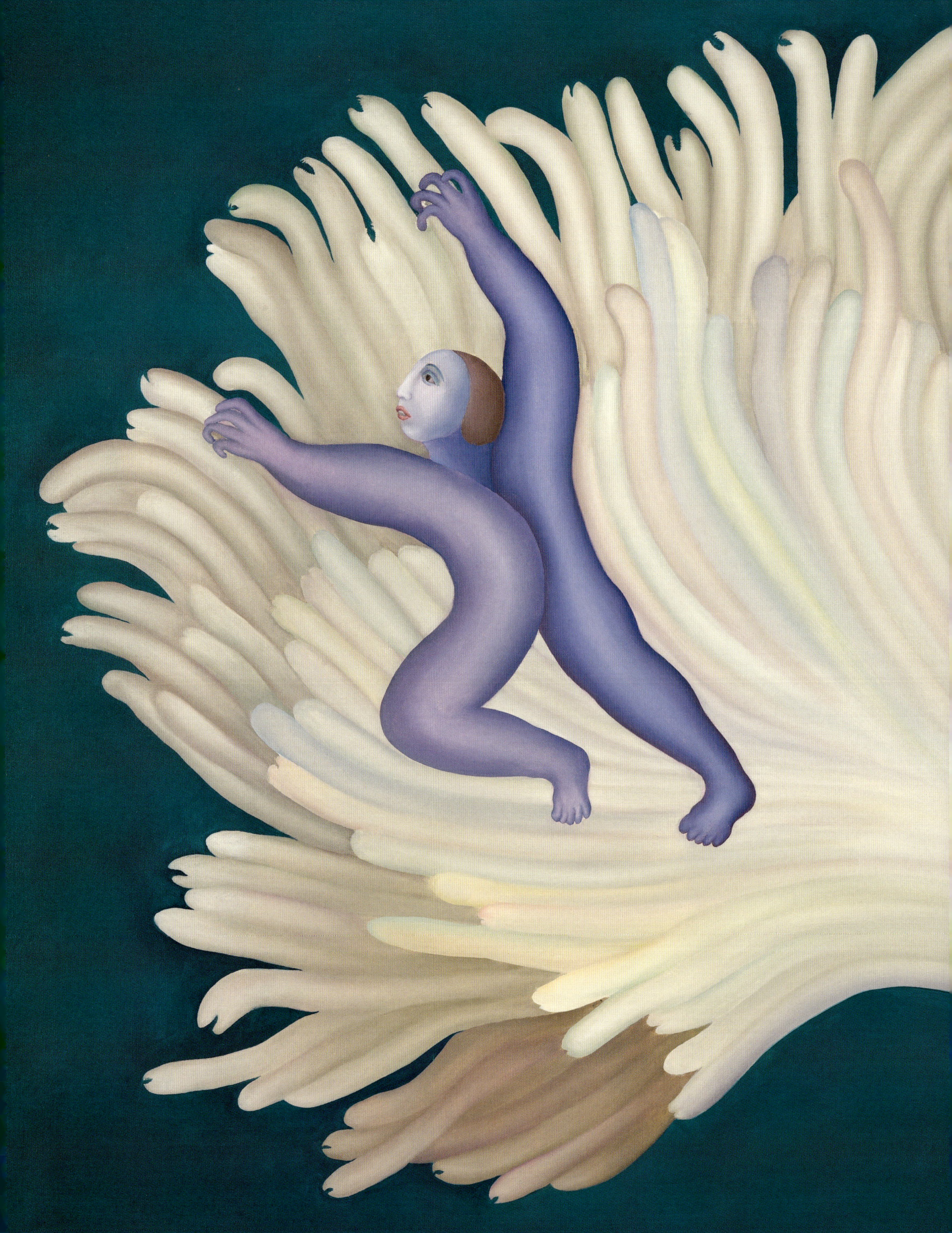

FRAME/WORKS AND THE EMERGENCE OF "ART" IN INDIA AFTER INDEPENDENCE

Ajay Sinha

How do images become something called art? In principle, Manjit Bawa's untitled painting from 1987 (plate 26) could be seen as a religious icon of Lord Krishna slaying the snake demon Kaliya, from the ancient text the Bhagavata Purana. The painting's display in a gallery rather than a shrine does not disallow this interpretation, since museums—including the Peabody Essex Museum—sometimes show images dressed as if for worship in the original religious context.[1] During the second half of the twentieth century in India, a particular conception of aesthetic value was produced through ways of what could be called *cultural framing*. This framing process made "art" a term of value for image-making and the term came to be taken for granted as an integral part of the imagery produced by artists such as Bawa and others.

Framing Art: Painting as "Art"

In the decades before independence, art was literally a matter of framing. This is exemplified by the early ventures of Kekoo Gandhy, a Parsi entrepreneur who founded one of India's first independent commercial art galleries.[2] In the 1940s, with the assistance of a Belgian acquaintance who saw a market potential in making frames for mass-produced prints of gods and goddesses, Gandhy set up a frame factory at his house in a Bombay suburb. He soon gained a British government contract for framing paintings made by Italian prisoners of war who had been captured during British expeditions in North Africa, and employed to make paintings for army establishments under a government project called MURART. Gandhy entertained the prisoners at his home (making use of their culinary skills) along with young Indian artists such as M.F. Husain (plates 3–6), K.H. Ara, F.N. Souza, and Mohan Samant. He had come to form these connections through friendships with other European refugees, principally the Austrian painting teacher and commercial artist Walter Langhammer (see Zitzewitz, page 40).

Thus, through social networks, Gandhy developed his vision. He helped artists frame paintings, employed them in his factory, and initiated sales of their work at his house and at other similar gatherings during a time when the Bombay Art Society

Detail of Plate 26.
Manjit Bawa, *Untitled*, 1987

was the only major exhibition venue. The society had been established in 1888 as a civic institution for the British elite; artists competed for medals and the public could purchase tickets to view their works. Gandhy's interest and investment in paintings may have been piqued at least in part by a paradoxical demographic shift within the institutionalized art world. Government-sponsored societies, established in all colonial cities in the nineteenth century, saw over time a spike in ticket sales despite dwindling of membership, with one unexpected effect. As Shukla Sawant noted, they "succeeded in turning 'Art' into a commodity that could be consumed if not possessed by more than just the elite."[3] Gandhy astutely sought commercial possibilities for this new civic commodity.

Framing and selling "art" as opposed to the inexpensive, popular images of deities and saints known as "god prints" involved particular challenges (figure 1). Unlike the existing vast network of artists, publishers, and distributors that brought mass-produced images to markets in cities, towns, and villages, the circulation of unique paintings—art—required specific sites for display and sale, as well as cultivation of affluent buyers and patrons.[4] Gandhy claimed a wall on the lobby level of the newly built Metro Cinema and called it the Metro Art Corner. He later moved his exhibition project to a window at the Taj Mahal Hotel, and then to a storage facility on bustling Princess Street amid textbook and stationery shops, wholesale warehouses, and commercial photo studios that connected the British administrative enclaves to the native, mostly Parsi, business district. Eventually, in 1963, he established the Chemould Art Gallery and Frame Shop on the second floor of the Jehangir Art Gallery, next to the Prince of Wales Museum.

Gandhy's story offers a good example of a new, entrepreneurial framing of art—both literally and symbolically—within what Kajri Jain has called a "vernacular culture industry."[5] At the Metro Art Corner, in the 1940s, Gandhy pitched art as a new kind of commodity in an Anglicized cultural and bureaucratic context. The Art Deco movie hall was owned and operated by the American studio Metro-Goldwyn-Mayer as an outlet for Hollywood films. Decorated with murals by students at the J.J. School of Art under the British modernist Charles Gerard, it attracted a clientele of educated, English-speaking urbanites who distinguished themselves from the rural and slum-dwellers who purchased bazaar god prints and watched Hindi- and Marathi-language films in the cheaper theaters. Gandhy offered the cosmopolitan sensibilities of this professional and industrialist class one more mark of distinction.

The vernacular culture industry also shaped the identity of artists who migrated to the city from small towns and villages. Seeking the opportunities available in Bombay, most enrolled in the J.J. School of Art, exhibited in the annual shows of the Bombay Art Society, painted banners and posters of commercial films, and produced illustrations for English- and regional-language magazines as well as paperback books and product advertisements. Boundaries between commercial image-making and the emerging category of high art were fluid. Husain, for example, came from the small town of Pandharpur in South Maharashtra in the 1930s and earned a living by painting movie billboards. Tyeb Mehta (plates 9–13), from Kapadvanj in Gujarat, dabbled in the film industry before turning to painting. S.H. Raza (plates 14–17) arrived from the small town of Damoh in the Central Province and worked as a designer and block

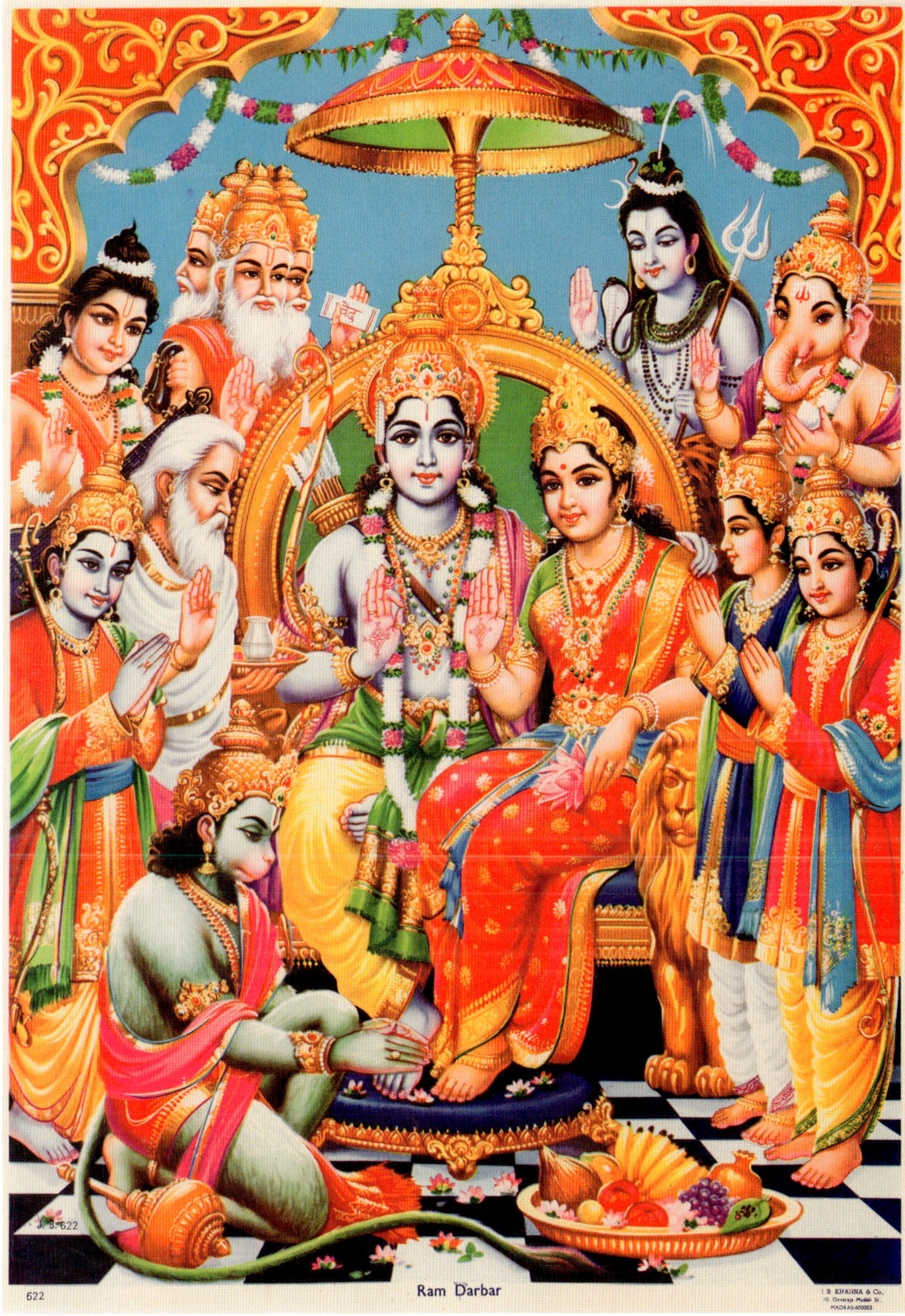

Figure 1.
Ram Darbar (Rama and Sita enthroned, surrounded by Hanuman, Shiva, Ganesha, Brahma, and other Hindu gods), 1980s
Chromolithograph by J.B. Khanna
18 × 13 inches (45.7 × 33 cm)

Peabody Essex Museum, Gift of the Davida Herwitz Fine Arts Trust

maker before joining the school of art faculty. Just as Gandhy was exhibiting Indian artwork at the Metro Art Corner, a graduate of the J.J. School, S.M. Pandit, was painting posterboard advertisements for window display at the same Metro Cinema. While Husain gravitated to the art circle of Gandhy and his cohort of Parsi collectors and European immigrants, Pandit set up an independent company, the Young Artists Commercial Studio, and specialized in "Hollywood-style" gods and mythological figures, making Shiva look like Tarzan for the popular market that had originally inspired Gandhy's frame shop.[6]

Institutional Frames: The Art School

Bombay's art scene was part of a wartime cosmopolitanism developing in some measure away from colonial institutions. But, the prestige of art as an exclusive aesthetic and social practice was also being shaped, possibly more fundamentally, within the art schools themselves. Important role models included Nandalal Bose at Santiniketan's Visva-Bharati University, K.C.S. Paniker in Madras at the Government College of Fine Arts and later at Cholamandal, and K.G. Subramanyan (plates 20–23) at the art school in Baroda. At Bombay's J.J. School, teachers and students mingled under the institutional mission to craft the new, civic commodity away from the marketplace.

The example of Shankar B. Palsikar is especially instructive. Unlike those mentioned above, who shaped an experimental curriculum for relatively new and progressive art schools, Palsikar worked within the framework of the painting department of a well-established colonial institution. Born in the industrial town of Bhandara in northeastern Maharashtra, he trained at the J.J. School in 1942–47, taught painting there until 1968, and served as dean until his retirement in 1975. Probably because he was immersed in the institution's bureaucracy, he seems known to only a small group of students. Critics stopped mentioning him by the 1950s, despite a gold medal from the Bombay Art Society in 1950.[7]

Mehta affectionately described Palsikar's inspiring presence at the art school:

> Palsikar had a lot of students whom he influenced. If you see the early Gaitondes [Vasudeo S. Gaitonde]—not his abstracts but even earlier, they were inspired by the technique Palsikar used. Mohan Samant, myself, even Akbar [Padamsee] to some extent, were very close to Palsikar.... Palsikar chose the kind of conventions that were true to his expression. His reference to European sensibility was far less. He was deeply buried in Indian aesthetics and he was a *bhakta* [devotee] of Shiva. At the same time he was aware of what was happening elsewhere. When I was in my third year at the J.J. School of Art he gave me a book by Kandinsky which concerned the spiritual in art and told me to read it.[8]

This statement describes a great teacher whose charisma lay not in his mastery of any particular style of painting—Indian or Western—by which the school's curriculum was divided, but rather in what Mehta called the "expression" of a versatile mind and a mode of being. Palsikar brought paintings to life in his legendary classroom demonstrations. Dazzled by "unbelievable color effects,"[9] students like Mehta not only surrounded the master in awe, but also became enchanted by the act of painting as some sort of mystical, magical process. Within the school's somewhat bohemian atmosphere, the aura of art palpably became a framework for self-representation.

Framing Visions: The "Spiritual"

The "spiritual," a frequent term in student testimonials regarding Palsikar, was an operative concept. Nebulous as it might be, it springs from a few sources, Indian and European, with interconnected connotations. In the 1940s, Bombay's German and Austrian refugees introduced the spiritual in the image of an enlightened, urban model from just twenty years earlier, beleaguered and threatened in wartime Europe. Imbued with the Weimar Republic's utopian vision of liberal democracy and emancipation from imperial rule, they imagined a public life based on cultural revival and an integration of urban media and design aesthetics, inspired by the Bauhaus and possibly tinged with bohemian, Kabalistic mysticism. The Bauhaus ideal of an all-encompassing, socially transformative, aesthetic system had already inspired the culture of Rabindranath Tagore's Visva-Bharati University at Santiniketan, when Tagore returned from Germany and arranged for the first exhibition of artists such as Wassily Kandinsky and Paul Klee in Calcutta in 1922. Indeed, this event may have been the reference point for Palsikar's pedagogy at the J.J. School of Art.[10]

On the whole, the spiritual was considered counter-cultural, a retreat from and critique of current politics, the art market, and one's own social and economic situation—in short, a liberation into intellectual and emotional plenitude. The genealogy of this vision can be traced back to nineteenth century Calcutta where the priest and urban saint Ramakrishna Paramahansa gathered middle-class youth within the Dakshineswar temple and modeled a mode of detachment from the entrapments of the city.[11] Ramakrishna embodied spirituality in an idiosyncratic set of behaviors, but he preached what Jeffrey Kripal described as universal mysticism based on "*vyakulta* (anxious desire)," a yearning for the divine whose intensity could release one from worldly bonds and kindle higher knowledge in the form of ecstasy.[12] In the early twentieth century, the Calcutta artist Abanindranath Tagore referred to the spiritual as an organizing principle for art-making, equating art with "the cult of the mind and spirit" rooted in yogic practice and Indian aesthetics.[13] If Paramahansa embodied intellectual restlessness as a mode of being in a religious context, Tagore imagined a more nationalistic form of art practice. His nephew, Rabindranath Tagore, made the spiritual operative at his university as a humanistic value that transcended both, religion and national politics.[14]

Over time, such "spiritual" figures come to inhabit the self-image of an artist. According to Atul Dodiya (plates 62 and 63), three pictures hang on the wall across from his bed: that of Paramahansa (figure 2), that of another modern saint, Ramana Maharshi (figure 3), and a drawing by Akbar Padamsee (figure 4). The first two images are mass-produced framed photographs sold in the bazaars, but Padamsee's work belongs to another class, the visual representation of the artist's creative energy. Dodiya wrote that Padamsee was fascinated by the mystic Paramahansa, but the "prophet," as he calls the drawing, is not intended to be specifically recognizable. Rather, it represents an epiphany similar to the saint's own. The implication is that the saint's intellectual and emotional yearning might have also informed that artist's own wide-ranging artistic experiments, and this is what fascinated Dodiya. For him, Padamsee's power lay in the material effects produced in his images so that they seemed to bristle with imagined, visionary adventures. Padamsee's heads seemed "moulded out of lumps of pockmarked earth." Like smoldering geological entities, they "pulse and glow repeatedly at different moments in Padamsee's oeuvre." When Dodiya tried to copy one, he discovered how his "mimic's vanity was scattered, blown apart, like the very charcoal dots in his [Padamsee's] work."[15] In other words, an imitation of the "spiritual" lineage adorning his bedroom led to an eruption of uncanny epiphanies in his own artwork.

Framing Places: The Artist's Studio

The primary site for such visionary adventures is the artist's studio. In 1969, Padamsee received the prestigious Nehru Fellowship and founded the Vision Exchange Workshop (VIEW), a project to bring artists together to experiment across various media, including photography and film. Meenakshi Shedde described the workshop as a "thriving beehive in 1969–72, encouraging cross-pollination of artistic disciplines and practices, with experiments in painting, etching, and filmmaking."[16] Padamsee called the workshop an "anti-institution," according to the poet Arvind Krishna Mehrotra, who, having no experience with cameras or enlargers, made photograms inspired by Dadaism and Surrealism. What struck Mehrotra most was that the Dadaist "anti-institution" was the artist's own ancestral home, the Taher Mansion, where the distinction between image-making and life blurred.[17]

The performative aspect of the studio was brought closer to the public and commercial domain at the Bhulabhai Desai Institute in Bombay. Named for a Gujarati lawyer and nationalist leader during the 1940s, the institute was established in 1951 by his daughter-in-law, Madhuriben Desai, with the assistance of the left-leaning writer Soli Batliwala, at Bhulabhai Desai's sprawling old mansion on Warden Road. Here, a variety of cultural practitioners—painters, musicians, filmmakers, and dancers—were given work spaces, display venues, and lecture halls. Husain, Gaitonde, Nasreen Mohamedi, and others had studios. The filmmaker and painter Bal Chhabda opened his Gallery 59 for displaying art, naming it for the founding year. Ebrahim Alkazi staged plays on the lawn. Ravi Shankar played sitar. Visitors who came for performances and the art gallery could also see an artist at work:

> In the evenings after a hard day's work, Husain, Gaitonde and Tyeb Mehta would relax in the verandah and one could wander from one studio to another watching the Progressive painters and sculptors to the sound of a sitar, a tabla, a voice practicing the scales or the foot-beats of a dancer. Or else one could sit on the terrace in the

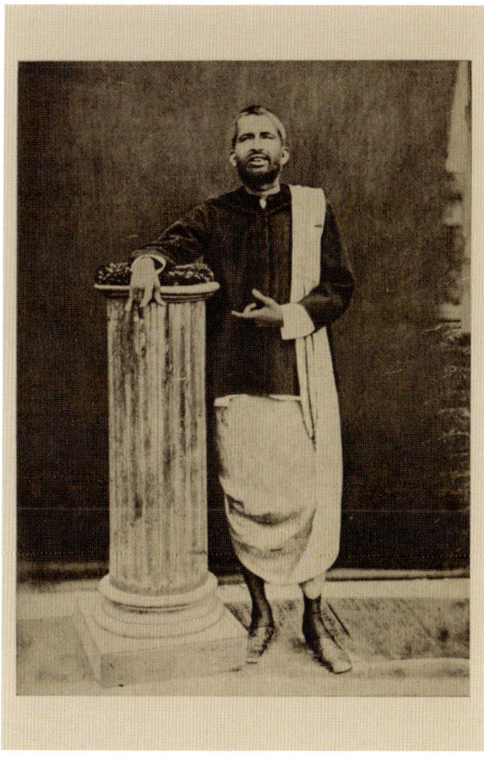

Figure 2.
Ramakrishna Paramahansa
Commercial print from nineteenth-century photograph
Collection of Atul Dodiya

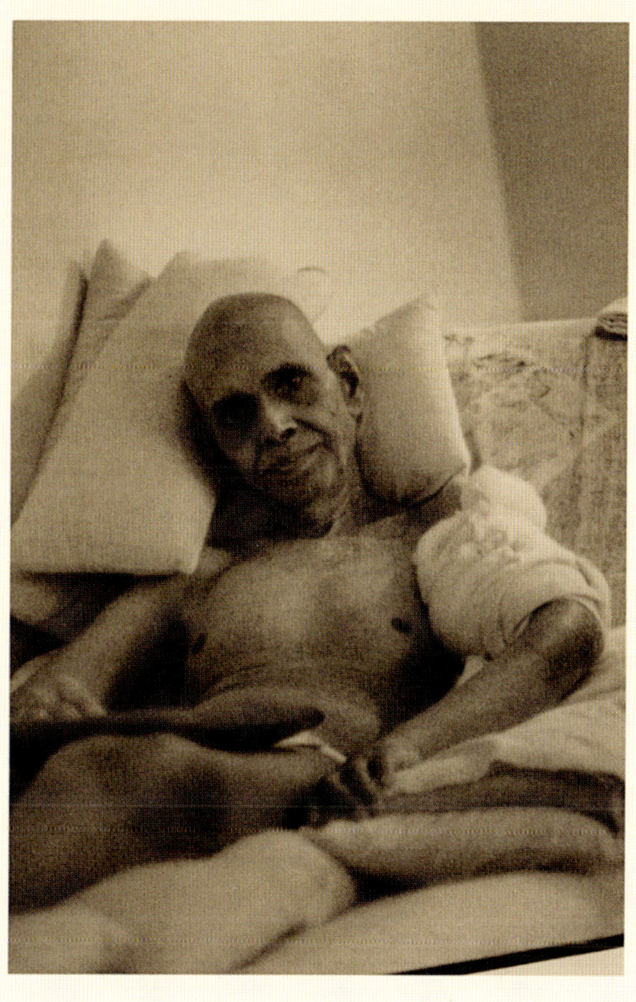

Figure 3.
Ramana Maharishi
Commercial print from mid-twentieth-century photograph
Collection of Atul Dodiya

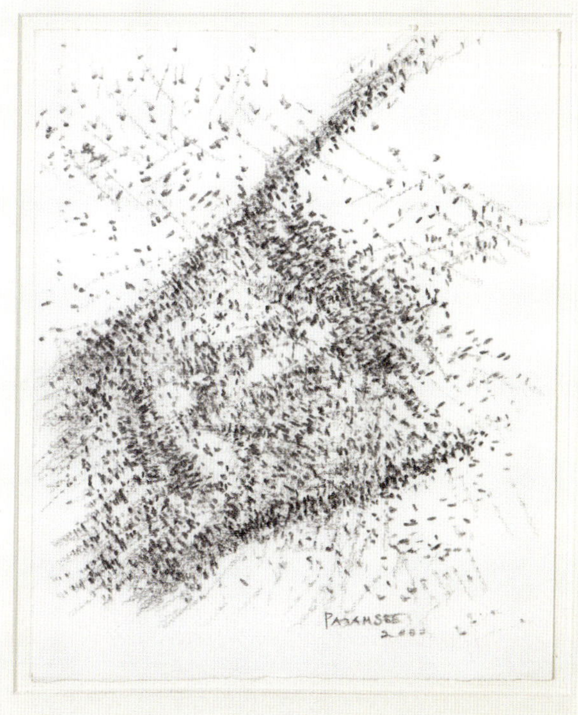

Figure 4.
Akbar Padamsee, *Head*, 2000
Graphite on paper
11 × 9 inches (27.9 × 22.9 cm)
Collection of Atul Dodiya

> cool sea breeze watching Alkazi putting the Theatre Unit through the paces for *Arms and the Man* or *Murder in the Cathedral*.[18]

The visibility of the studio was quite the opposite of image practices of popular art such as calendar prints or movie posters, where the studio is hidden and the artist's identity is limited at best to an overlooked corner signature.[19] By contrast, the artist was the governing fantasy and organizing principle of a new art system, to which the urban public gravitated. Moreover, artistic arenas were by definition self-referential, assuming and defending the possibility of something called "art."

The public visibility of the studio as a site for artistic experimentation was new in mid-century India. The only precedents were the Tagore ancestral home of Jorasankho in Calcutta, where, however, only the elite gathered, and the art program at Visva-Bharati University in Santiniketan, which functioned as a remote forest retreat. Moreover, when art was first differentiated from crafts as a new, self-conscious cultural practice in the early twentieth century, the nature of studio practice was expressed only in personal sketchbooks while the art itself emphasized nationalistic themes.[20] The decades after independence seem to register a shift from concerns about styles—Indian or Western—to a new referent, namely, the artist him- or herself, and artistic process became a consistent preoccupation.

Framing Practice: The Artist and Artistic Process

The new practice of art-making was, thus, marked by the overarching presence of the artist and myriad references to the image-making process. Therefore, the initial exemplar, Bawa's *Untitled* (Krishna fighting Kaliya), should be located within this new self-referential art practice, conveying an artist's unique vision. Layers of translucent paint evoke the deep, luminous blue-green of the ocean without actually depicting it. Blue, amoebic Krishna cradled delicately by serpent-hoods swaying like tentacles of an underwater creature turns the painting into an epiphany.

Looking at artworks as a record of inspired invention might shed light on the difference between Rameshwar Broota's *Man through the Ages* (plate 31) and a calendar image of the visionary Swami Vivekananda, shown standing against skyscrapers of Chicago during the Parliament of World Religions in 1893, where he swayed a Western audience toward Indian spirituality (figure 5). Visual anthropologist Christopher Pinney read the calendar image as a representation of "moral collision," whereby the high-rises, representing the "materialistic aspirations" of the West, provide a scale for the figure, whose "spiritual heights" nevertheless exceed it.[21] In Broota, we witness a similar drama unfolding at a cosmic scale when sharp architectural details penetrate and dissolve into the body. But, unlike the popular print, Broota's image creates a sense of ambiguity and indeterminacy. It reflects the unfamiliar rather than the familiar, showing simply a naked man against a dark landscape. The tension arises between the cosmic scale of the imagery and the human flesh and bone on which it is based. The human form morphs under the viewer's eyes, turning steely despite its wrinkled skin.[22] The eerie

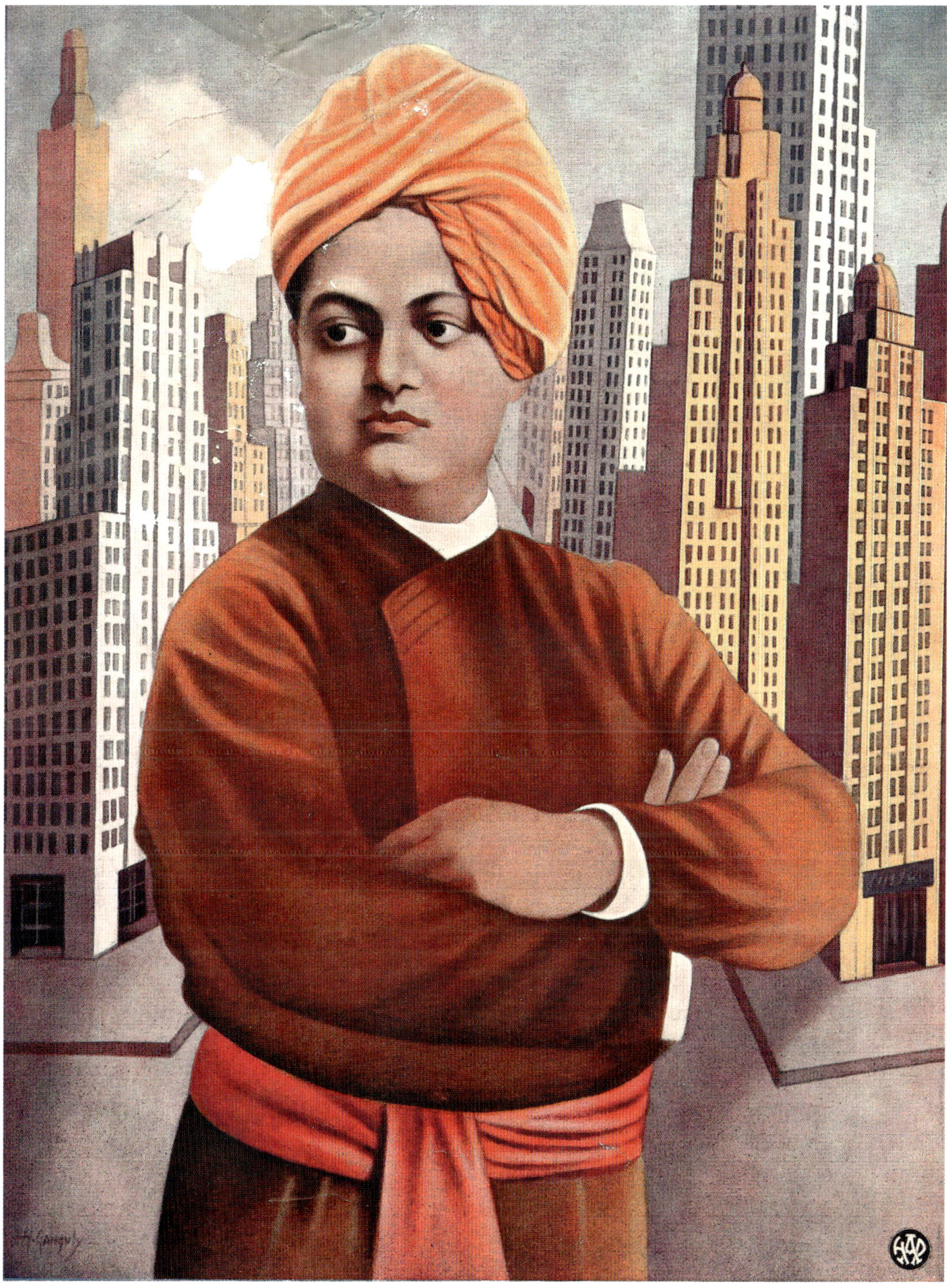

Figure 5.
Swami Vivekananda in Chicago, ca. 1942
H. Ganguly, artist; unknown publisher
Chromolithograph
11 × 8 inches (27.9 × 20.3 cm)
Collection of Christopher Pinney

specter looks like a humanoid machine, thanks to the black and silver paint and crosshatchings made by a stylus, whose scratches can almost be heard as it devours what paint had produced.

Seeing the artwork as a record of artistic process, whether explicitly or implicitly present, can illuminate many paintings from this time. Gieve Patel picked his subjects from everyday life in the city, then laid them out on canvas as a forensic puzzle. The random, banal imagery—a woman arriving early at a ceremony (*Early Guest*, plate 49), another drying her acid-yellow sari while a stray onlooker stares (*Gateway*, plate 50), two men resting near a cart (*Two Men with Handcart*, plate 48)—has the quality of an accidental encounter. It is as if the viewer experiences the city not through the clarity of a guidebook or stories told by a resident bard, but mimetically, like a snapshot: fragmented and saturated with a sensory excess that requires—yet ultimately defies—analysis. In *Gateway*, incidental details, such as the palm frond or the flip-flop dangling at the edge of the pothole, gain unusual sharpness against a ground that seems to wither and vaporize around them. As in a color negative, chromatic relations are altered, suffused with mid-afternoon glare. The result is a sense of puzzlement and wonder at what seems like a retinal afterimage.

In postindependence India, what distinguished art from other kinds of images was its performative, self-referential, pointedly personal form. This reminds us that "art" is a matter of framing, involving what is around as well as inside the image—the context as well as the subject and style. The art value of a Bawa, a Broota, or a Patel can be understood only by looking on both sides of the frame.

1. *Faces of Devotion: Indian Sculpture from the Figiel Collection*, an exhibition at the Peabody Essex Museum, 2010–12.

2. Kekoo Gandhy, "The Beginnings of the Art Movement," in "City of Dreams: A Symposium on the Many Facets of Bombay," *Seminar* 528 (August 2003).

3. Shukla Savant, "Artist Collectives in the Age of Anxiety, 1940–50," in *Art and Visual Culture in India, 1857–2007*, ed. Gayatri Sinha (Mumbai: Marg Publications, 2009), p. 138.

4. Kajri Jain, *Gods in the Bazaar: the Economies of Indian Calendar Art* (Durham, North Carolina: Duke University Press, 2007), especially chapter 2: "When the Gods Go to Market."

5. Ibid., pp. 13–16, for a definition of the phrase.

6. Rajesh Devraj, "Making Showcards," in Deepali Dewan, ed., *Bollywood Cinema Showcards: Indian Film Art from the 1950s to the 1980s* (Toronto: Royal Ontario Museum Press, 2011), p. 32. See also Kajri Jain, "The Showcard: Traveling Still," in ibid., pp. 44–48.

7. Review of the Bombay Art Society exhibition at the newly built Jehangir Art Gallery, *The Times of India*, February 3, 1952, reprinted in Yashodhara Dalmia, *The Making of Modern Indian Art: The Progressives* (New Delhi: Oxford University Press, 2001), pp. 291–92.

8. Dalmia, p. 68.

9. Ibid.

10. Partha Mitter, *The Triumph of Modernism: India's Artists and the Avant Garde, 1922–1947* (London: Reaktion Books, 2007).

11. Sumit Sarkar, "'Kaliyuga,' 'Chakri,' and 'Bhakti': Ramakrishna and His Times," *Economic and Political Weekly* 27, 29 (July 18, 1992), pp. 1543–59, 1561–66.

12. Jeffrey Kripal, *Kali's Child: The Mystical and Erotic Life of Ramakrishna Paramahansa* (Chicago: The University of Chicago Press, 1998), p. 25.

13. Quoted in Tapati Guha-Thakurta, *Monuments, Objects, Histories: Institutions of Art in Colonial and Postcolonial India* (New York: Columbia University Press, 2004), pp. 162–63.

14. Ramachandra Guha, "Travelling with Tagore," in *Theorizing the Present: Essays for Partha Chatterjee*, eds. Anjan Ghosh, Tapati Guha-Thakurta, and Jakani Nair (New Delhi: Oxford University Press, 2011), pp. 152–87.

15. Atul Dodiya, "Untitled," trans. from Gujarati by Gieve Patel, in *Akbar Padamsee: Work in Language*, eds. Bhanumati Padamsee and Annapurna Garimella (Mumbai: Marg Publications in association with Pundole Art Gallery, 2010), p. 283.

16. Meenakshi Shedde, "Art in the River of Life," in ibid., pp. 310–11.

17. Arvind Krishna Mehrotra, "Koffee Korner," in ibid., p. 279.

18. Minakshi Raja, "Going My Way," *Afternoon Dispatch and Courier*, September 30, 1995, quoted in Dalmia, p. 72.

19. Jain, pp. 171–215. Christopher Pinney, *Photos of the Gods: The Printed Image and Political Struggle in India* (London: Reaktion Books, 2004), p. 190.

20. Tapati Guha-Thakurta, *The Making of a New 'Indian' Art: Artists, Aesthetics, and Nationalism in Bengal, c. 1850–1920* (Cambridge: Cambridge University Press, 1992).

21. Christopher Pinney, "Some Indian 'Views of India': The Ethics of Representation," in *Traces of India: Photography, Architecture, and the Politics of Representation, 1850–1900*, ed. Maria Antonella Pelizzari (Montreal: Canadian Centre for Architecture; and New Haven, Connecticut: Yale Center for British Art, 2003), pp. 262–75.

22. Dario Gamboni, "Composing the Body Politic: Composite Images and Political Representation, 1651–2004," in *Making Things Public: Atmospheres of Democracy*, eds. Bruno Latour and Peter Weibel (Karlsruhe: ZKM Center for Art and Media, and Cambridge, Massachusetts: MIT Press, 2005), pp. 162–95.

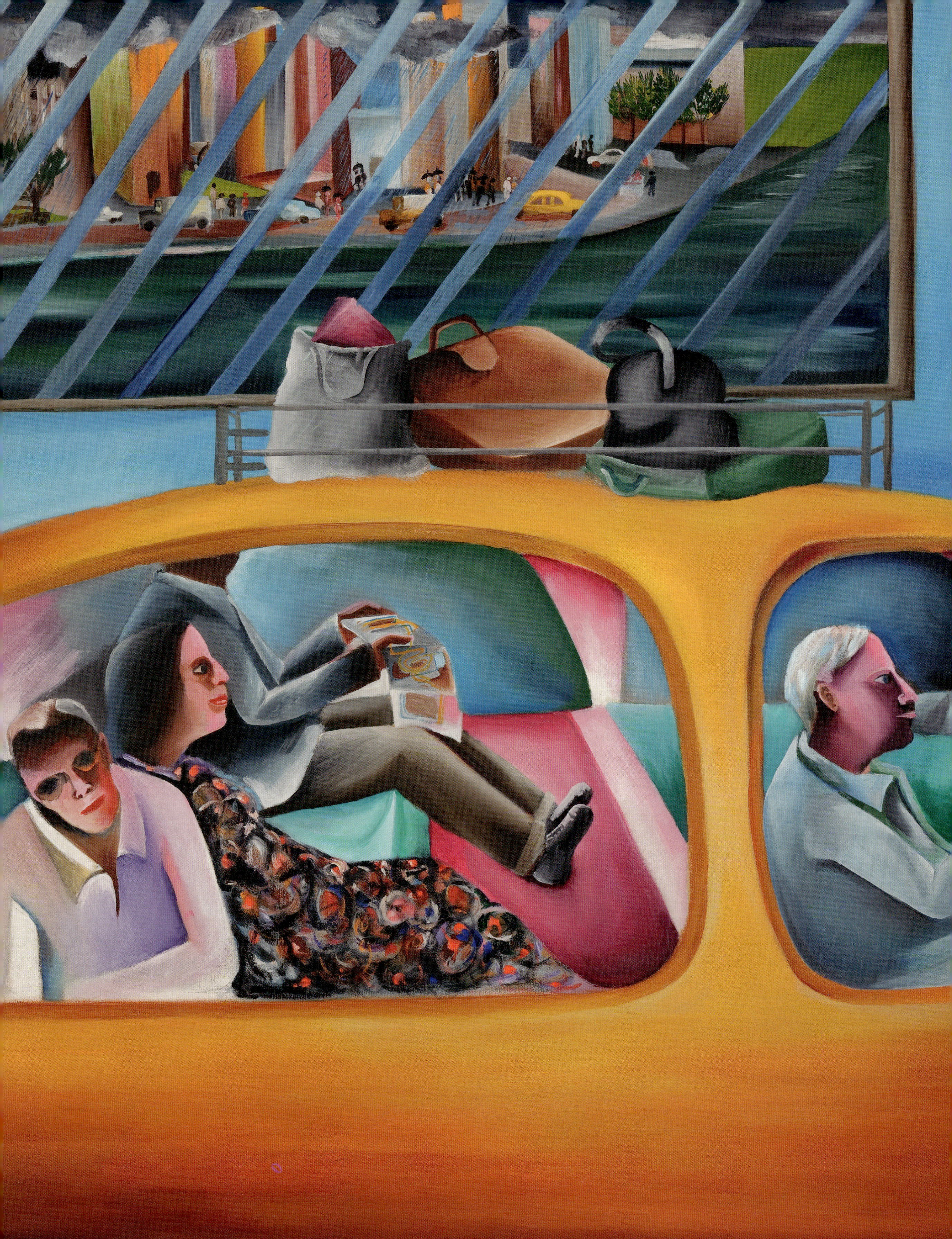

AMERICAN COLLECTORS OF INDIAN ART CHESTER AND DAVIDA HERWITZ

Susan S. Bean

I think Chester Herwitz played a major role in building up contemporary art, for twenty-five, thirty years, very religiously going there, meeting artists. No one [else] has done that, not even any person from my country. This is dedication. We were lucky to meet him and to spend time with him. He had a brilliant mind and the passion, you know, that fire. He was not buying painting just to collect, to make a statement, or for status. No. He was crazy about painting. – M.F. Husain[1]

In 1974, the Worcester Art Museum in Massachusetts mounted *Paintings by Husain*, the first solo exhibition in an American museum for M.F. Husain (plates 3–6). Chester (1927–1999) and Davida ("Davey," 1930–2002) Herwitz, who had recently begun collecting Husain's paintings in earnest, were the exhibition's instigators and masterminds (figure 1). They lent their own paintings and arranged to borrow works from the American collectors Thomas and Martha Keehn, Harold Leventhal, and Harry N. Abrams. The exhibition, the first of many forays by the Herwitzes into the art world as international impresarios of Indian art, carried all the hallmarks of what distinguished them as collectors: ebullient, articulate enthusiasm for the art and dogged determination to collect and present twentieth-century art from India. They not only built what would quickly become the most important private collection of this work outside India, they got to know the artists, encouraged them, and sought ways to get their work seen. In less than twenty-five years, by the time of Chester's death in 1999, the Herwitzes had acquired well over four thousand paintings, works on paper, sculptures, and photographs by artists from India. In addition to contemporary art, they formed significant collections of embroidered quilts from Bengal (*kantha*), nineteenth-century Kalighat paintings from Calcutta, and silver jewelry and ornaments from across the subcontinent.

For the Worcester exhibition, Chester Herwitz enlisted former ambassador to India John Kenneth Galbraith, whose wife's portrait by Husain hung in their Cambridge, Massachusetts, home, to write for the small exhibition catalogue. He also arranged for T.N. Kaul, Indian ambassador to the United States, to serve as the official patron of the exhibition. In addition, Chester wrote letters to museum directors and prominent art critics inviting them to view the works and consider hosting the

Detail of Plate 41.
Bhupen Khakhar, *First Day in New York*, 1983

exhibition or reviewing the art. He brought Husain from India to be the guest of honor for the event and sought to connect him with important American commercial art galleries. Efforts such as these multiplied over the years and ultimately earned him recognition by the Indo-American Society, which in its annual awards in 1996 honored Chester Herwitz, alongside Dr. Manmohan Singh, then India's finance minister, and Mother Teresa.

The Herwitzes first visited India in 1962 on an around-the-world tour to celebrate Chester's success in building a one-man operation making leather belts and accessories into a prosperous fashion and accessory design and manufacturing company. The couple's shared enthusiasm for travel, art, and collecting became an increasingly important aspect of their relationship. In India, they were captivated by the cacophony, bustle, and energy. Rich and poor, sacred and secular, private and public—categories so carefully separated in America—jostled for space and attention. On a second visit, they went to the National Gallery of Modern Art in New Delhi where they saw Husain's murallike painting *Zameen* (1955), which they felt embodied the colors of India's streets, its vitality and excitement.[2] They returned to India in the summer of 1969 on a second world tour, this time with their three young sons. Their favorite sites were ancient places, like Varanasi and south Indian temple towns, still teeming with people going about their business. Years later, Chester Herwitz characterized these early visits to India as opportunities to experience an authentic, visual drama of life on the streets: people praying, consulting, being shaved, selling nails, boxes, lathes, pipes, garlands. Roads filled with horses, bullocks, camels, bicycles, motor bikes, Mercedes, elephants, cows, children—a drama of color with pink turbans and tie-dyes against white. And the contradictions—riches and poverty, floods and drought, cold and heat, high caste and untouchable, slipshod building and painstaking craftsmanship.[3]

The Herwitzes, already collectors of contemporary art as well as antique furniture and decorative arts, began to buy an eclectic mix of silver ornaments and textiles related to Chester's profession in the fashion industry and also contemporary and traditional court-style paintings. They made their first major purchase of Indian contemporary art in 1972 at Espace Cardin in Paris, where Husain's "Mahabharata" series, painted for the previous year's São Paulo Biennial, was on view. According to Husain, Chester knew his work from the 1971 Harry N. Abrams publication *Husain*. The Herwitzes bought eleven canvases. On their next trip to India, they arranged to meet Husain.[4]

The trips to India were becoming annual affairs lasting a month or two, with an evolving elaborate routine. In the fall, Davida sent their itinerary to everyone they hoped to see. They booked the same room at the Taj Mahal Hotel in Bombay and became members of the Indian International Centre in New Delhi, where they stayed each year (figure 2). They made regular visits to Madras, Calcutta, Hyderabad, and Baroda. They became avid collectors of Husain's work and extended their interests to other artists, some introduced by Husain and others whose work they saw in galleries. During their visits, they called on artists, attended openings, lectures, concerts, dinner parties, and eventually weddings of art-world friends they made over the years. These trips and their relationships in India became the center of their lives. In a 1980 lecture at the Delhi College of Art, Chester described himself as a successful fashion designer

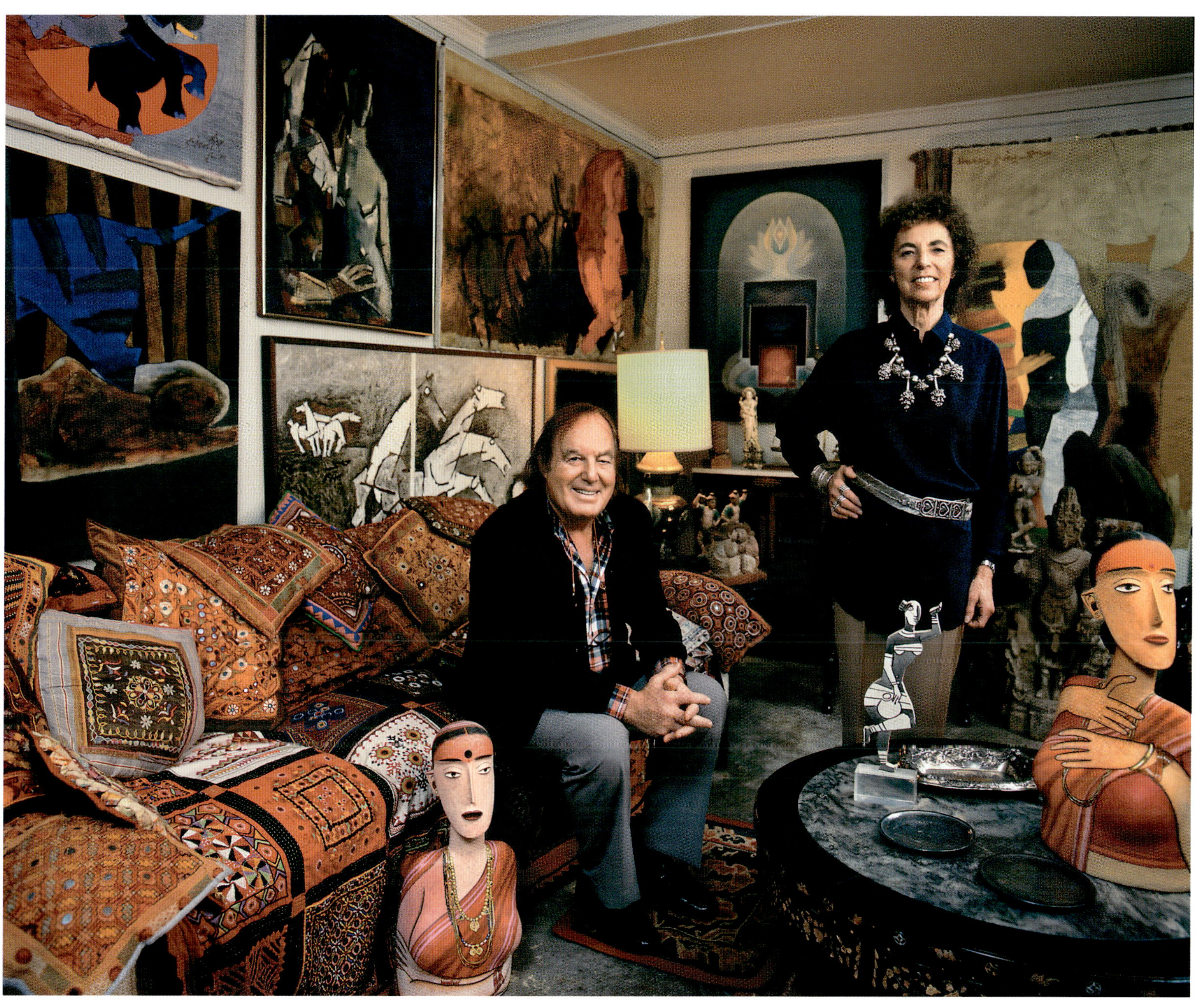

Figure 1.
Chester and Davida Herwitz at home, Worcester, Massachusetts, 1995
Herwitz Archive, Peabody Essex Museum

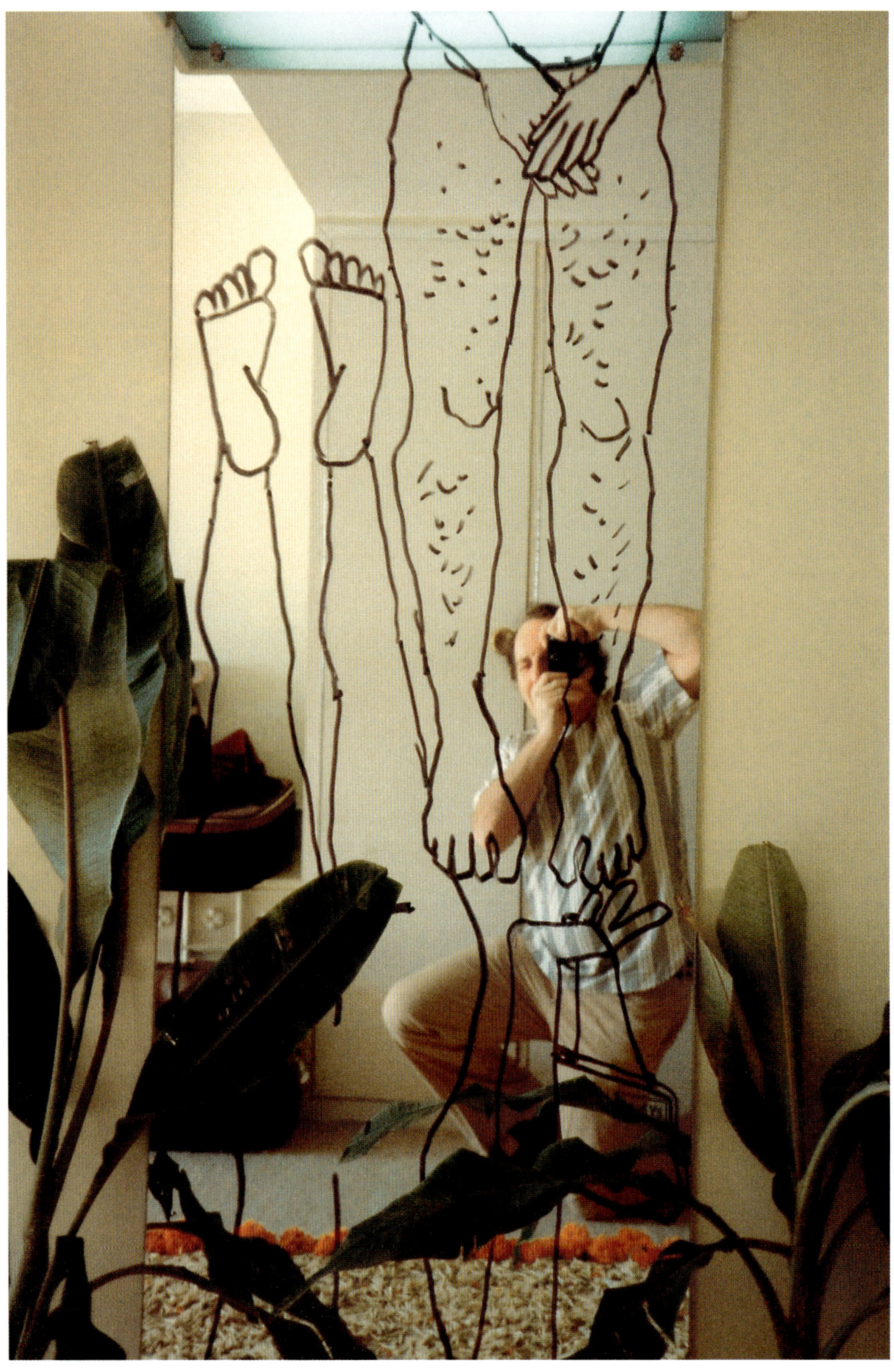

Figure 2.
Chester Herwitz, photograph of the Herwitzes' hotel room mirror painted by M.F. Husain, Bombay, 1983
Herwitz Archive, Peabody Essex Museum

and manufacturer who had sold all but one of his companies in order to devote himself more fully to Indian art.[5] In India, the Herwitzes were active participants in the Indian art world and important collectors; at home in Worcester, their position as a prominent, civic-minded couple was far less stimulating and exciting.

Chester and Davida engaged Indian painting at every level—visually, sensually, intellectually. In a 1983 letter to his son Thomas, Chester wrote: "This morning I made what I think is a real discovery about Contemporary Indian Art and as you might well imagine I am very excited. In thinking about Indian paintings, particularly those in my collection, what I think is common to most of the paintings has something to do with contradiction, conflict, duality, opposites, polarization, etc." As examples, he cited Husain's "splits," the "diagonals" of Tyeb Mehta (plates 9–13), the black-and-white geometric drawings of Nasreen Mohamedi (plates 44–47); the "Tantric work" of Biren De (plates 1 and 2) and G.R. Santosh (plates 18 and 19); Somnath Hore's wounds; the *bindus* of S.H. Raza (plates 14–17). Acknowledging a tendency for over enthusiasm, he concluded with self-deprecating humor: "I could go on, Tom, but I just wanted you to have a record that on this date, July 13, 1983, I made this intellectual discovery."[6] Two Herwitz sons, Thomas, now a lawyer, and Daniel, now a university professor, were drawn in. In 1978, while a student at Williams College, Thomas conducted a research project interviewing artists including Husain, Raza, Bal Chhabda, Badri Narayan, and Santosh, critic Richard Bartholomew, and gallerist Kali Pundole. Daniel, a 1984 PhD from the University of Chicago in the philosophy of aesthetics, returned to India in 1987 to complete a book on Husain based on the Herwitz Collection.[7]

In his notes for the 1980 lecture at the Delhi College of Art, Chester pinpointed his motivations for collecting: "Why I collect. Love of art. Excitement and fascination with living art." He wrote that collectors "experience something difficult to describe…and want to continue that experience…even to refine and enhance the feeling." Of his own experience, he remarked:

> My commitment is to the artist. Usually [I] look for several years either at the work or at reproductions of the work—student work and of course current work… sketches…sometimes acquire work not at the highest level but important in development or point of departure in work. For me there is more to a work of art than a picture…there is the person, the living flesh and blood of an artist…the vision of the person…it all sort of comes together amounting to an extraordinary experience…that is the artist as a person intertwines with the artistic creation of the viewer-collector. I believe fine art is twice created…once by the artist and again in the relationship of art to viewer…. [The collector] brings passion and encouragement; preserves art; loans for exhibiting; studies and loves the art.[8]

Chester Herwitz loomed large in physique and personality. A star football player in college, he tackled collecting in a similar spirit. Expressive and articulate, he conveyed affection and disdain, opinions and appreciation. Davida, elegant, warm, and gracious, shared the passion for Indian art and guided the building of the collection, teaming with Chester to make selections. Davey was also the mediator who softened Chester's rough edges and smoothed over his gaffs. In India, the couple and their collection acquired a mythic aura. Chester, more vocal and assertive, became known as a voracious collector, snapping up dozens of works before they ever left the artists' studios. Pioneering Bombay gallerist Pheroza Godrej recalled first meeting Chester when she found him sitting impatiently on the stairs outside her Cymroza Gallery waiting for the doors to open so he could have first choice from an exhibition of Arpita Singh (plates 58–61).[9] He was competitive, always ready to outmaneuver potential buyers by arriving first (or even early) for an opening or a studio visit. Chester bargained for lower prices with gallerists and artists alike; he convinced artists to save their best work for his annual visits. Some in the art world saw his tactics as emanating from the power of foreign wealth and objected that he took work away from India to be housed in a private American collection. For them, he represented the face of American neo-imperialism. Others welcomed the Herwitzes' collecting as an indication of the transnational significance of art being produced in India.

The Herwitzes actively supported the careers of artists whose work they acquired. Chester recommended Gieve Patel (plates 48–50) for a fellowship at the Smithsonian Institution's Wilson Center: "In my view Gieve is the most original, creative 'younger' artist in India, laden with talent which transcends the boundaries of traditional art disciplines in such a way that his painting is sublimely poetic, his poetry conjures sharp unforgettable images...."[10] He wrote to the curator of the Department of Graphic Arts at the National Gallery of Art offering to show her work by K. Laxma Goud (plates 37–40 and figure 3).[11]

The Herwitzes were keenly aware of the difficulty in finding a platform for contemporary Indian art in the West. In the run-up to the U.S. Festival of India in 1985–86, Chester wrote to Richard Bartholomew, then secretary of the Lalit Kala Akademi:

> I wish I could give you some solid news with regard to exhibitions of contemporary Indian Art during the festival period. It appears that many exhibitions of antiquities, craft and the like are firmly in place all across the U.S.A. Such is not the case with contemporary art. You know that I am very willing indeed to loan to any museum, but nothing is really nailed down, although there are some reasonably good prospects. These words seem so shallow when one is aware of the intense interest I have that the power and beauty of the works of many Indian artists be seen by the American public.[12]

The Herwitzes did whatever they could, advocating for and lending to exhibitions, lecturing, and supporting publications. In 1987, the couple made a list of the exhibitions they had lent to in the 1980s (figure 4). There were four in the United Kingdom in 1982.[13] During the 1985–86 U.S. Festival of India, four exhibitions were mounted from the Herwitz Collection.[14] During the French Festival of India in 1986, they lent to three solo shows at the Centre Georges Pompidou: Sudhir Patwardhan (plates 69–71), Bhupen Khakhar (plates 41–43), and Arpita Singh.

The Herwitzes understood that an international market was a critical component in bringing art from India into the mainstream of the twentieth century. In 1995–96, the Herwitzes in partnership with Sotheby's took a bold step: the very first

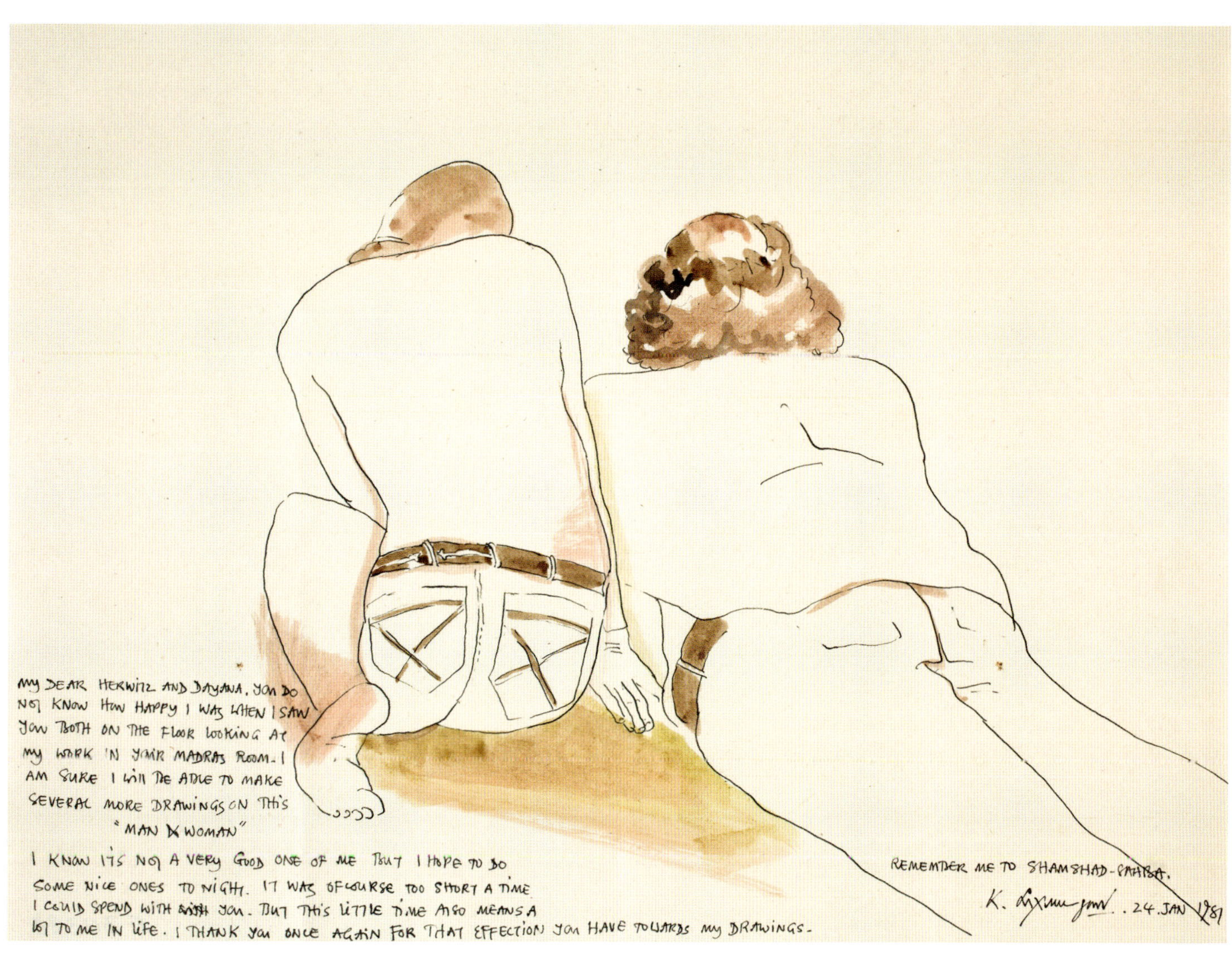

MY DEAR HERWITZ AND DAYANA. YOU DO NOT KNOW HOW HAPPY I WAS WHEN I SAW YOU BOTH ON THE FLOOR LOOKING AT MY WORK IN YOUR MADRAS ROOM. I AM SURE I WILL BE ABLE TO MAKE SEVERAL MORE DRAWINGS ON THIS "MAN & WOMAN"

I KNOW IT'S NOT A VERY GOOD ONE OF ME BUT I HOPE TO DO SOME NICE ONES TONIGHT. IT WAS OF COURSE TOO SHORT A TIME I COULD SPEND WITH ~~WITH~~ YOU. BUT THIS LITTLE TIME ALSO MEANS A LOT TO ME IN LIFE. I THANK YOU ONCE AGAIN FOR THAT EFFECTION YOU HAVE TOWARDS MY DRAWINGS.

REMEMBER ME TO SHAMSHAD-SAHBA.

K. Laxma goud. 24. JAN 1981

Figure 3.
K. Laxma Goud, letter to the Herwitzes with a drawing of them looking at his work, Madras, 1981
Ink and watercolor on paper
10 × 13 ½ inches (25.4 × 34.3 cm)

The Chester and Davida Herwitz Collection, Peabody Essex Museum

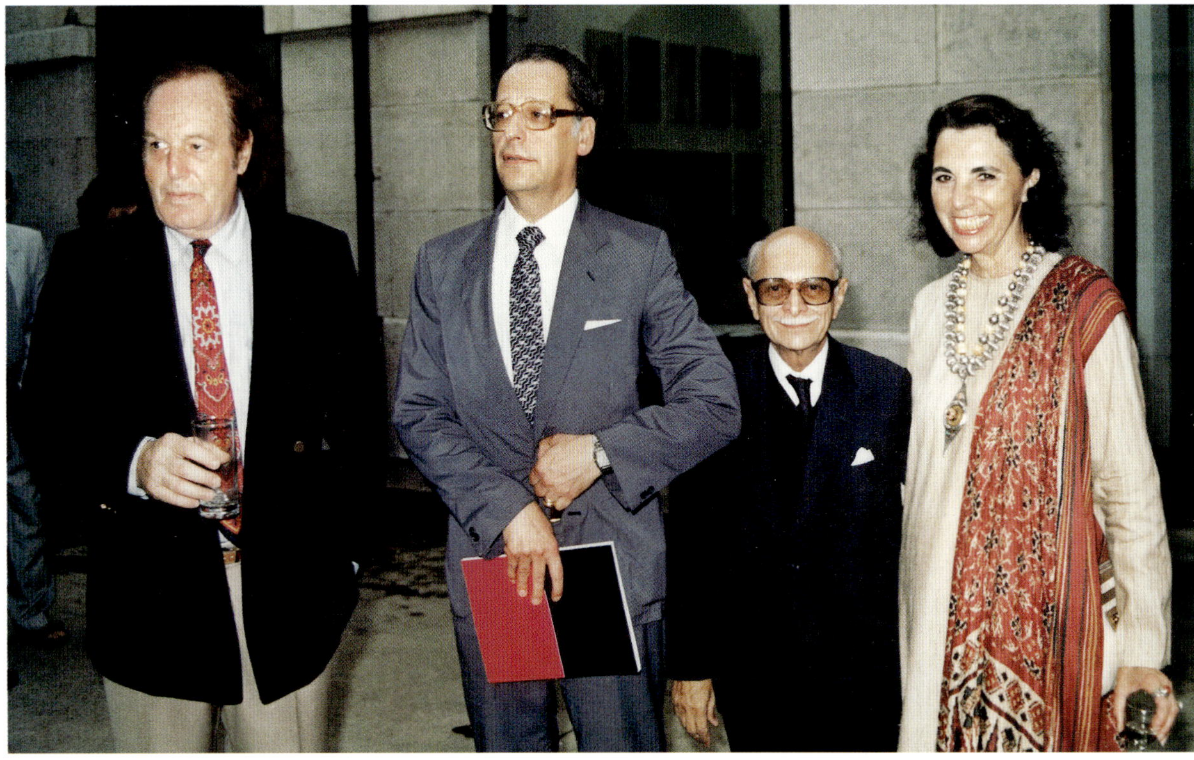

Figure 4.
Left to right: Chester Herwitz, Geneva city government official, Jehangir Nicholson, and Davida Herwitz at the *Coups de Coeur* exhibition, Geneva, 1987
Herwitz Archive, Peabody Essex Museum

international, high profile sale of contemporary Indian art. They selected works from their collection to be sold at two auctions in New York to fund a private trust that would support Indian art. This strategic move is widely credited with launching international demand: the auctions marked the beginning of the rapid rise of the contemporary Indian art market. The Herwitzes had, over the years of building their collection, also recognized the importance of museum exhibitions and collections to the public appreciation of art. Their many efforts to organize and lend to exhibitions culminated in their decision to place the heart of their collection in a public museum where it could stimulate American and international awareness and interest in modern and contemporary Indian art. In 2001, when the Peabody Essex Museum acquired the Herwitz Collection, it created the first ongoing program dedicated to modern and contemporary Indian art outside India.

Chester and Davida Herwitz had discovered in postindependence Indian painting an art movement firmly anchored to its Indian locale, yet dynamically in dialogue with art of other times and places. They made it their purpose not only to build a collection, but to bring this art from India to the West, positioning it to expand established views of twentieth-century art toward a global vista that would encompass multiple lineages of modernism.

1. M.F. Husain, telephone interview with the author, June 10, 2006, Herwitz Archive, Peabody Essex Museum, Salem, Massachusetts (hereafter Herwitz Archive).

2. Chester Herwitz, notes for a lecture in Worcester, Massachusetts, 1985, Herwitz Archive.

3. Chester Herwitz, notes for a lecture, 1980s, Herwitz Archive.

4. M.F. Husain, conversation with the author, October 8, 2003, Herwitz Archive. See Shashi Tharoor and Susan S. Bean, *Epic India: M.F. Husain's Mahabharata Project* (Salem, Massachusetts: Peabody Essex Museum, 2006).

5. Chester Herwitz, notes for a lecture at the Delhi College of Art, 1980, Herwitz Archive.

6. Chester Herwitz, letter to Thomas Herwitz, July 13, 1983, Davey's Handbag Collection, Worcester Historical Museum, Worcester, Massachusetts (hereafter Worcester Historical Museum).

7. Daniel Herwitz, *Husain* (Bombay: Tata Steel, 1988).

8. Chester Herwitz, notes for a lecture at the Delhi College of Art, Herwitz Archive.

9. Pheroza Godrej, conversation with the author, December 2007, Herwitz Archive.

10. Chester Herwitz, letter to James H. Billington (Director, Fellowship Office, Wilson Center, Smithsonian Institution), September 29, 1982, Worcester Historical Museum.

11. Chester Herwitz, letter to Ruth Fine, October 5, 1982, Worcester Historical Museum.

12. Chester Herwitz, letter to Richard Bartholomew, July 3, 1984, Herwitz Archive.

13. Loans from the Herwitzes to exhibitions in the United Kingdom, 1982: Tate Gallery, London: *Six Indian Painters*; Museum of Modern Art, Oxford: *India: Myth & Reality—Aspects of Modern Indian Art*; Royal Academy, London: *Contemporary Indian Art: The Gesture, and Motif,* and *Stories, Situations.*

14. Loans from the Herwitzes to exhibitions for the Festival of India in the United States, 1985–86: Grey Art Gallery and Study Center, New York University, New York: *Contemporary Indian Art from the Chester and Davida Herwitz Family Collection*; Hood Museum, Dartmouth College: *Indian Painting of the 80s from the Herwitz Family Collection*; The Phillips Collection, Washington, DC: *Indian Art Today—Four Artists from the Chester and Davida Herwitz Family Collection*; Worcester Art Museum, Worcester, Massachusetts: *Flowers of the Vine—Contemporary Indian Painting from the Chester and Davida Herwitz Collection* and *Flame of Many Colors—Contemporary Indian Painting from the Chester and Davida Herwitz Collection.* In addition, the Herwitzes loaned works by De and Santosh to the Frederick S. Wight Art Gallery at UCLA for *Neo-Tantra* (catalogue edited by Edith Tonelli).

PATHBREAKERS

The First Generation

Biren De

M.F. Husain

Ram Kumar

Tyeb Mehta

S.H. Raza

G.R. Santosh

K.G. Subramanyan

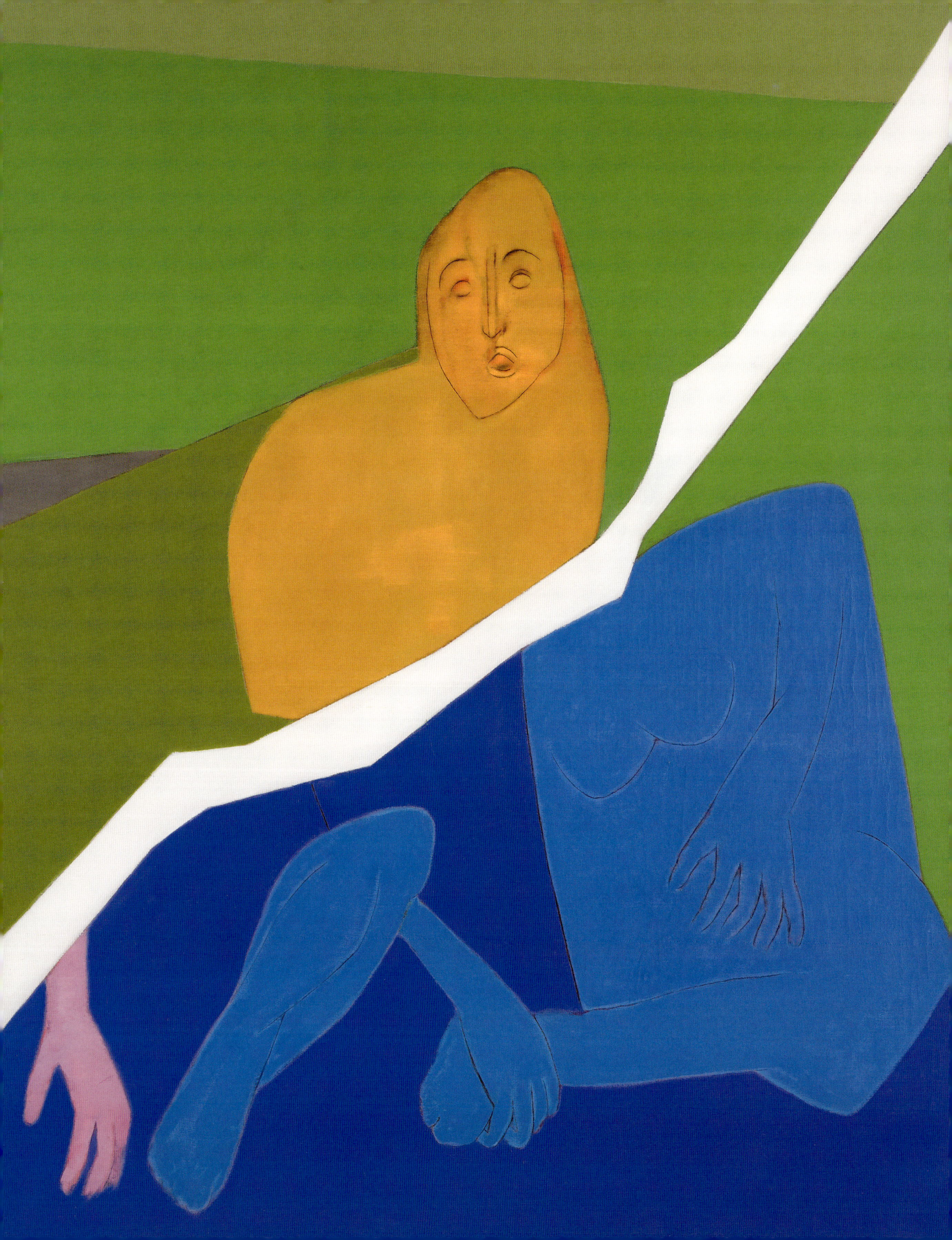

PATHBREAKERS: THE FIRST GENERATION

Rebecca M. Brown

In the decades prior to India's independence in 1947, artists across the subcontinent, including Jamini Roy (figure 1), Nandalal Bose, and Amrita Sher-Gil, had begun to define subjects and painting styles suitable for a modern Indian art. Through productive dialogue and contentious debate, they forged a variety of paths toward establishing India as a cultural and political entity.[1] With India's independence, these contested directions continued to develop, breaking new ground and engaging with the challenges facing the new nation. Independence paired hope with despair: the partition of the subcontinent into India and Pakistan claimed as many as five hundred thousand lives and displaced millions of people, producing considerable poverty and ongoing religious conflict.[2]

While a need to "catch up" hovered over this first pathbreaking generation, so did an energetic buzz of possibility, fed by the idea that India, a longstanding center for global culture, had more than a peripheral contribution to offer modern art. But, how could art be simultaneously modern and Indian? If modern art involves the pursuit of abstraction and the purity of paint, if it seeks out universal truths and human commonalities, and if it emerges in metropolitan centers such as Paris, London, and New York, then how can India's artists be both universal and responsive to concerns specific to South Asia?[3] Navigation of the paradox of how to be modern and Indian followed several interlinked pathways: transforming existing subject matters in new stylistic directions, turning to the cosmology and spiritual traditions of the subcontinent to explore innovative modes of abstraction, exploring the centrality of the figural for South Asian image traditions, and engaging with the politics and history of the new secular nation. All of these paths involved struggle and negotiation, and from that dynamism emerged the energy embodied in the "Pathbreakers" generation.

Some artists, convinced of the primacy of color and form, moved toward abstraction as a mark of the modern. Ram Kumar (plates 7 and 8) and S.H. Raza (plates 14–17), both members of the Progressive Artists Group of Bombay (1947–52), pursued this path, but neither abandoned a crucial link to the visual language of South Asia, retaining links to local subjects and seeking inspiration in historical painting traditions. Kumar shifted from painting figural groups to exploring abstracted angular forms of the holy city of Varanasi, at first populated with a figure or two, but eventually devoid of inhabitants. Raza turned from watercolor sketches of

Detail of Plate 10.
Tyeb Mehta, *Untitled*, 1973

picturesque Indian landscapes to compartmentalized expressionist compositions and geometric linearity.

Other artists pursued abstraction in concert with an investigation of Tantra, a Buddhist and Hindu spiritual tradition that emerged in the fifth century CE and focused on the union between the microcosm and the macrocosm, through sexual metaphor or by linking celestial forms (sun, moon) with bodily ones (seed, womb). In the 1960s, Tantra became part of a larger global pursuit of Asian spirituality. Biren De (plates 1 and 2) associated celestial forms with blossoms and seed shapes; G.R. Santosh (plates 18 and 19) painted ethereal images focused on generative symbolisms related to plant, human, and cosmological forms. While never a formal or unified movement, the artists loosely grouped under the label "Neo-Tantra" developed a modern, abstract art that had its roots in Indic visual culture.

The "Pathbreakers" generation did not focus solely on the abstract or the spiritual; indeed, complete abstraction was rare, and a concern with representation—of the figure, the landscape, or the urban—constituted the foundation of most work of this period. Alongside poets, novelists, musicians, and playwrights, artists sought an Indian modern art in the context of a nation struggling to anchor itself in secular humanism. The period from 1947 to 1964 is often called the Nehruvian era, after India's first prime minister, Jawaharlal Nehru, who encouraged rapid industrialization with a series of five-year economic plans inspired by the Soviet model. During this time of growth and optimism, many artists produced critical contributions to political and social issues such as poverty, the representation of women, religious communal tensions, and India's position in the Cold War (figure 2).

The Progressive Artists Group in Bombay took its activist name from the longstanding commitment to leftist politics found within the visual, performing, and literary art communities in South Asia. While "progressive" came to describe the formal experimentations and appropriations of these Bombay artists, an undercurrent of Marxism, support of workers and farmers, and a focus on the plight of the common people infused many works from this period.

Some artists merged contemporary political subject matter with vernacular styles and mediums. In his reverse paintings on acrylic and his watercolors, K.G. Subramanyan (plates 20–23) drew from local and historical Indian arts to create a fresh vision of everyday objects and intimate portraits; his reconfigured iconic images of deities bring the transcendent into the everyday. In *The Great Show with Beasts and Goddess* (plate 22), Subramanyan critically examined the powerful goddess Durga in the context of the increasing political power of the Hindu right at the end of the 1980s.[4] Political-religious tensions played a central role for many of these artists. Tyeb Mehta (plates 9–13) explored the fracturing of the subcontinent at partition through the diagonal, partial dismembering of anonymous human bodies. An increasingly fraught relationship with Pakistan, culminating in the 1965 war, encouraged artists to engage critically with religious difference, often combining multiple religious symbols in one work to underscore the human elements that bring us together, or exploring the legacies of communal religious violence.

Despite the regular appearance of women and goddesses in the work of this generation, women artists were few. Issues of gender emerged through a critical

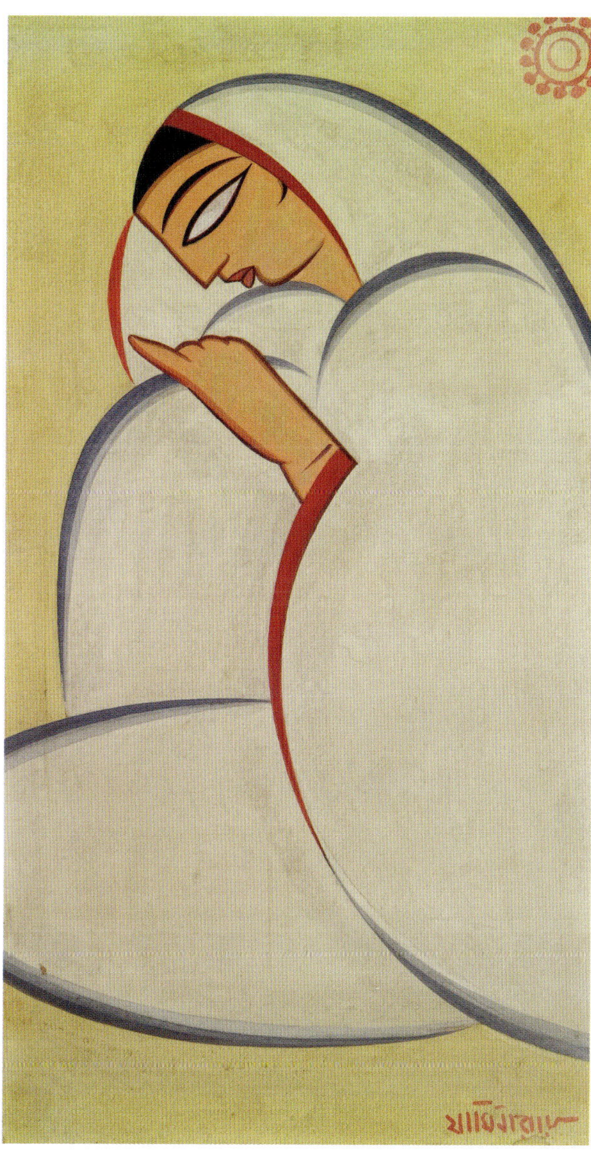

Figure 1.
Jamini Roy, *Untitled*, ca. 1945
Watercolor on paper
27 ¼ × 15 inches (69.2 × 38.1 cm)
The Chester and Davida Herwitz Collection,
Peabody Essex Museum

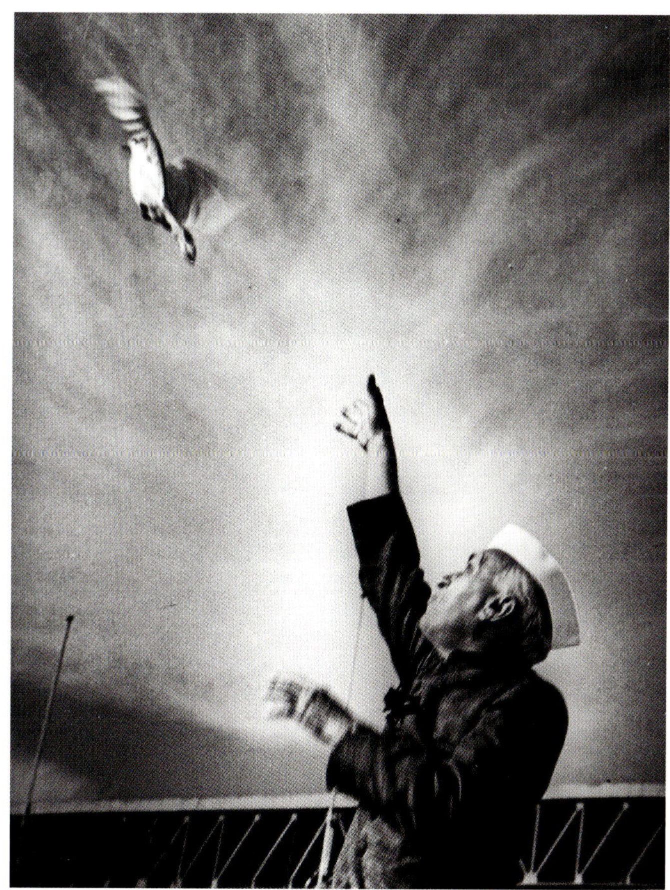

Figure 2.
Homai Vyarawalla, *Pandit Nehru Releasing a Dove at a Function at the National Stadium, New Delhi*, 1950
Homai Vyarawalla Archive in the Alkazi Collection of Photography, New Delhi

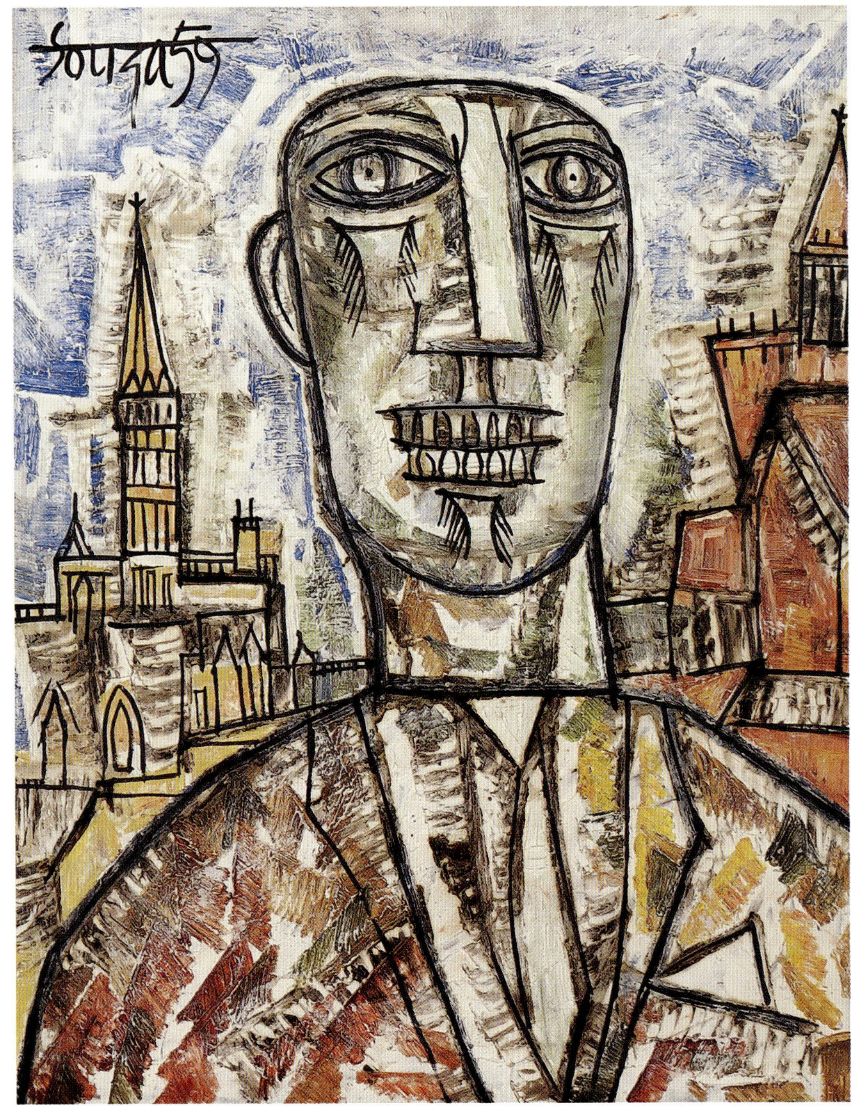

Figure 3.
F.N. Souza, *Man in Townscape*, 1959
Oil on board
30 × 24 inches (76.2 × 61 cm)
Collection of Umesh and Sunanda Gaur

engagement with the feminization of India—a re-evaluation of the village against the masculine, industrialized urban, and an exploration of feminine spirituality, particularly the connection between power (*shakti*) and the goddess, as in *The Great Show*. The "Pathbreakers" generation carved out a counter-argument to the masculinity of European modernism by focusing on the everyday, the spiritual, and village craft, which was often practiced by women. *Cage V* (plate 6), for example, is from a series by M.F. Husain (plates 3–6) that explores the limitations and boundaries of women's lives in India: the formal language of the flattened, limited geometric forms the women inhabit echoes the confinement symbolized by the birdseller's cage. Husain also explored the universal feminine, specifically bodily and spiritual sacrifice, in *Mahabali* (plate 5). Many in this generation also depicted the mundane lives and struggles of ordinary people, but made of them iconic examples of humanity, whether Subramanyan's *Parsi Couple* (plate 23) in their living room, F.N. Souza's haunting head paintings (figure 3), or the burdened figures of Husain's *Peasant Couple* (plate 3). Husain, along with other artists of this generation, invested these themes with a modernist, universal language, weaving global visual idioms into local narratives and lives, a maneuver seen most clearly in *Man* (plate 4). Unlike later generations who challenged the very idea of a universal human experience, this first generation after independence used that modernist tenet to speak directly to global concerns.

These artists were "Pathbreakers" not just for Indian art, but also for modernism around the world. The Cold War and global decolonizations in the 1950s and 1960s encouraged conversations and exchanges outside the orbit of Euro-America and the USSR. Artists traveled and exhibited from São Paulo to Fukuoka, Mexico City to Sydney, and often lived and studied in New York, Paris, or London. Their works provide rich examples of a modernism that bridges local and universal and a number of paths that join together spirituality and secular humanism. And, while these artists blazed new trails, they also relied on South Asian precedents. Whether addressing Indian epics, historical violence, rural and popular techniques, or appropriating an ancient spiritual tradition, the "Pathbreakers" created new idioms that are remarkably and forcefully both Indian and modern.

1. Partha Mitter, *The Triumph of Modernism: India's Artists and the Avant-Garde, 1922-1947* (London: Reaktion Books, 2007); Sonya Rhie Quintanilla, ed., *Rhythms of India: The Art of Nandalal Bose* (San Diego: San Diego Museum of Art, 2008); Yashodhara Dalmia, *Amrita Sher-Gil: A Life* (New Delhi: Penguin Viking, 2006); Sona Datta, *Urban Patua: The Art of Jamini Roy* (Mumbai: Marg Publications, 2010).

2. The death toll from partition ranges from two hundred thousand to five million, with most estimates hovering around five hundred thousand. See Gyanendra Pandey, *Remembering Partition: Violence, Nationalism and History in India* (Cambridge: Cambridge University Press, 2001). In addition, as many as twelve million South Asians migrated to the other side of the new border, splitting up families and contributing to widespread poverty. See Urvashi Butalia, *The Other Side of Silence: Voices from the Partition of India* (Durham, North Carolina: Duke University Press, 2000).

3. For further discussion, see Rebecca M. Brown, *Art for a Modern India, 1947–1980* (Durham, North Carolina: Duke University Press, 2009).

4. Karin Zitzewitz, "The Secular Icon: Secularist Practice and Indian Visual Culture," *Visual Anthropology Review* 24, 1 (2008), pp. 12–28.

BIREN DE

Born in Faridpur, Bengal (now in Bangladesh), 1926–2011 died in Delhi
Lived and worked in Delhi

Biren De's paintings radiate and glow. Rich color fills his canvases, anchoring his compositions on a nodal point that serves as the generative source for energy that flows outward, across the space of the painting but also three-dimensionally, toward the viewer and across time. His early work, as for many of his generation, focused on the figural, but during the 1960s he turned toward abstraction, developing his mature vocabulary from a range of sources, especially imagery associated with Tantra.

De was born in Faridpur, Bengal (now in Bangladesh) and from 1944 to 1949—spanning the year of independence in 1947—he studied at the Government College of Art and Craft in Calcutta. He then taught in the Delhi Polytechnic's Art Department, traveling to the United States in 1958–60 as a Fulbright scholar, and he exhibited around the world, starting with the Salon de Mai in Paris (1951) and including biennials in Tokyo (1959), São Paulo (1961), Venice (1962), and Sydney (1973). In the 1950s, he was an accomplished portraitist, painting the young Indira Gandhi (figure 1), two Indian presidents and the archbishop of Delhi, as well as his colleagues, including, in 1951, the writer and photographer Richard Bartholomew.[1]

De's life in Delhi and his teaching position at the College of Art situated his work in the dynamic context of the capital during this first decade after independence. Alongside Ram Kumar (plates 7 and 8) and others, he developed his figural idiom by examining historical Indian mural painting at Ajanta in Maharashtra as well as the vernacular painting of tribal groups like the Santhals of Bihar and Bengal. When he went to New York in 1958, he was already experimenting with an ethereal figural form and the North American art scene, especially the dominance of Abstract Expressionism, furthered his detachment from representational imagery. Returning to Delhi, De spent the 1960s developing a style that bridged the figural and the abstract. De's social circle in Delhi included Ajit Mookerjee, an art collector and intellectual interested in the philosophy and visual culture of Tantra, an aspect of both Buddhism and Hinduism that emerged in the fifth century CE. Tantra centers on an understanding of the universe as "the concrete manifestation of the divine energy of the godhead," which Tantric practitioners or *tantrikas* channel through the microcosm of the human body and its energies, often in the context of phallic and vaginal imagery.[2] European scholarship from the nineteenth and early twentieth centuries, shaped by conservative views on sexuality, considered Tantra a taboo and esoteric element of these two religions and counter to the primary flow of religious practice in India. However, as Indian and Euro-American intellectuals of the 1960s valorized India's religious traditions as a resource for self-transformation, Tantra became a popular focal point for the era's experimentations with both the sexual and the spiritual. Alongside European and North American artists exploring Asia's religious traditions, several Indian artists began to appropriate imagery from Tantric material into their work.[3]

De's personal familiarity with Mookerjee's collection of Tantric art contributed a great deal to the development of his new abstraction in the 1960s. Even before the publication of Mookerjee's *Tantra Art* in 1966, De exhibited his new iconography in a solo show at the Kumar Gallery, Delhi, in 1964.[4] De expressed ambivalence about his connection to Tantrism and his participation in what some started to call a "movement" of Neo-Tantrism. In statements from the 1970s and 1980s, he often explicitly linked his work to Tantra, while he later distanced himself, indicating that his concern lay primarily in a generative energy, more universal than the particularities of Tantric practice and visual culture.[5] At a conference in Delhi in 1986, De articulated his relation to Tantra:

> To me, the essential meaning of Tantra is expansion: expansion of Consciousness.... Tantra lures us along a numinous path, giving us from time to time visions of effulgent Light and Wholeness (Mandala); at the very end of this path is the promise of our deliverance—through surrender of self to the Supreme Energy that governs the universe.[6]

Unlike his contemporary G.R. Santosh (plates 18 and 19), who delved more directly into imagery of union and cosmic diagrams, De focused on the universal elements of Tantra that tapped into the "surrender of self," producing a language of celestial forms and rich pulsating canvases balanced between historical Indic visual culture and contemporary experimentations with abstraction. De's compositions emanate from a central single point or *bindu* (seed). In some of his works, phallic and vaginal elements overlap one another, but in *You—July '70* (plate 1) and *August '78* (plate 2) the focus is on the circular and the forms perhaps even transcend the gendered division within Tantra. The abstractions invite a range of readings: as a celestial form (sun, star, moon, eclipse, black hole), as a lotus or flower blossom, or simply as radiating or pulsating energy. The deceptively simple titles often record only the month and year of the painting, but they also signal an embedded concern with time. Seeds, generation, unfolding energy, and growth all embody processes that develop in time, and the circular format of his compositions evokes the cycle of birth, death, and rebirth found in multiple Indic belief systems. – RMB

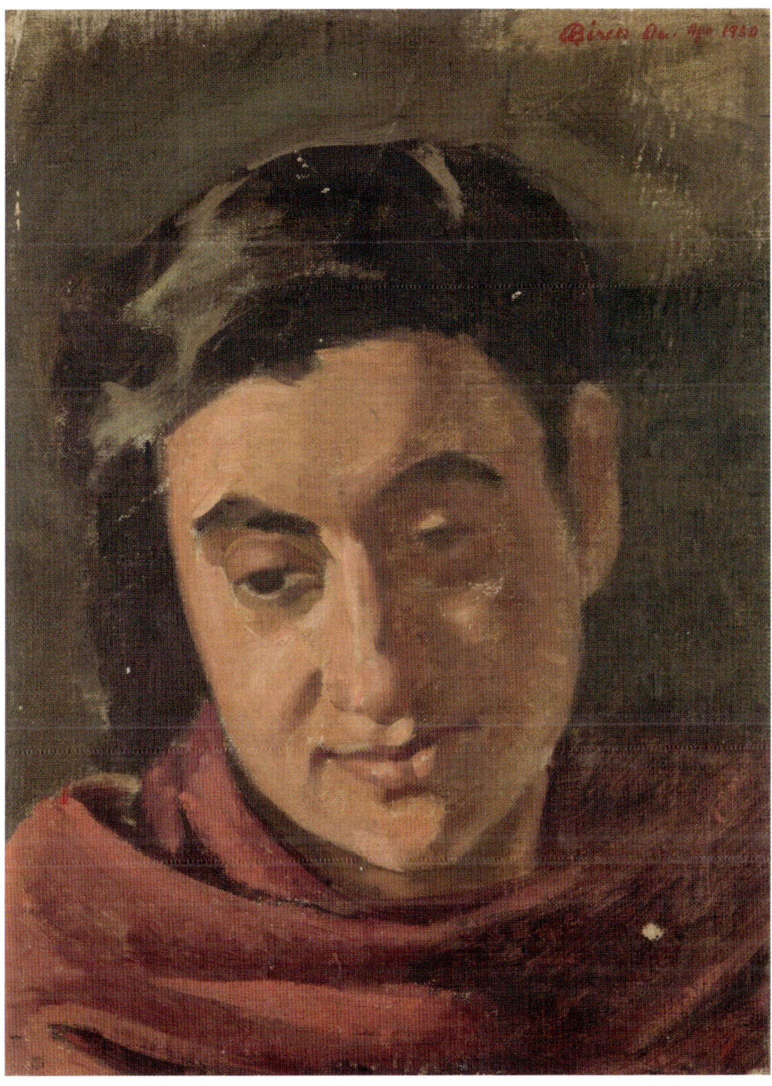

Figure 1.
Biren De, *Portrait of Indira Gandhi*, 1950
Oil on canvas
14 × 11 inches (35.6 × 27.9 cm)
The Chester and Davida Herwitz Collection, Peabody Essex Museum

1. The painting was entitled *Portrait of a Writer*. See Aveek Sen, "Vanishing Point," in *Richard Bartholomew: A Critic's Eye* (Mumbai: Chatterjee & Lal, New Delhi: PhotoInk, and New York: Sepia International, 2009), pp. 84–95.

2. David Gordon White, "Tantra in Practice: Mapping a Tradition," in David Gordon White, ed., *Tantra in Practice* (Princeton: Princeton University Press, 2000), p. 9.

3. For more on Tantra and twentieth-century Indian art, see Edith Tonelli, ed., *Neo-Tantra: Contemporary Indian Painting Inspired by Tradition* (Los Angeles: Frederick S. Wight Art Gallery, University of California, Los Angeles, 1985); Achinto Sen-Gupta, "Neo-Tantric 20th-Century Indian Painting," *Arts of Asia* 31, 3 (May/June 2001), pp. 104–15. See also Rebecca M. Brown, "P.T. Reddy, Neo-Tantrism, and Modern Indian Art," *Art Journal* 64, 4 (Winter 2005), pp. 26–49.

4. Ajit Mookerjee, *Tantra Art* (New Delhi, New York, and Paris: Ravi Kumar Gallery, 1966). Mookerjee collaborated with Philip Rawson to exhibit his collection at the Hayward Gallery in London in 1971, with a catalogue by Rawson: *Tantra* (London: Arts Council of Great Britain, 1972). An expanded version appeared as Philip Rawson, *The Art of Tantra* (Greenwich, Connecticut: New York Graphic Society, 1973); in 1978, it was made part of the Thames and Hudson World of Art series. See Sen-Gupta, pp. 107–12. Sen-Gupta dates the Kumar Gallery show to 1965; the gallery's website includes it in its listings of shows for 1964.

5. Frank Thompson, "The Splintered Glass: Painting and Religion in Modern India," *Studies in Religion/Sciences Religieuses* 10, 2 (June 1981), pp. 175–86. Several obituaries for De mention this ambivalence as well.

6. Biren De, "Pictorial Space—A Journey Within," in *Concepts of Space, Ancient and Modern*, ed. Kapila Vatsyayan (New Delhi: Indira Gandhi National Centre for the Arts, 1991), p. 572.

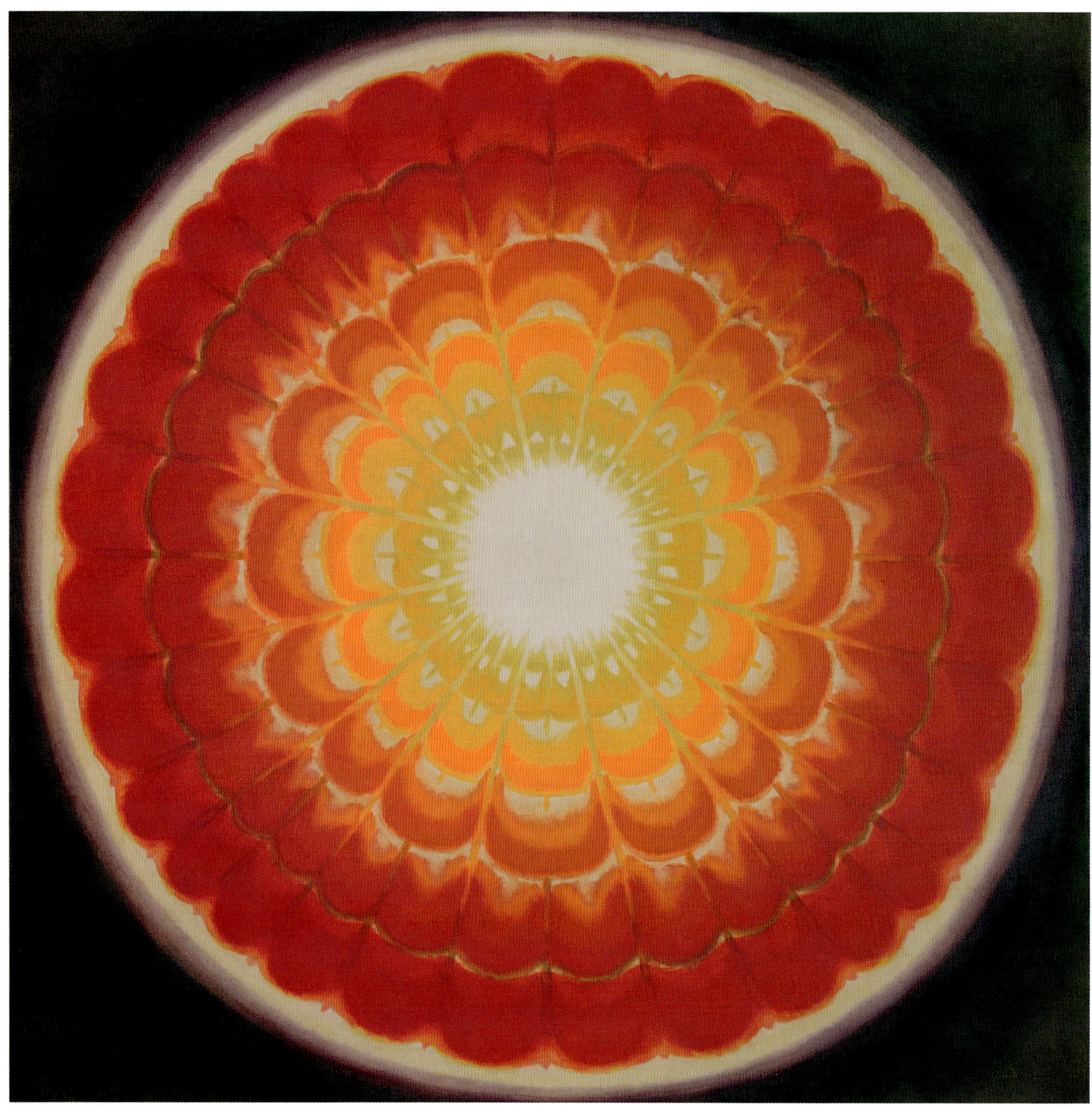

Plate 1.
You—July '70, 1970
Oil on canvas
51 × 52 inches (129.5 × 132.1 cm)

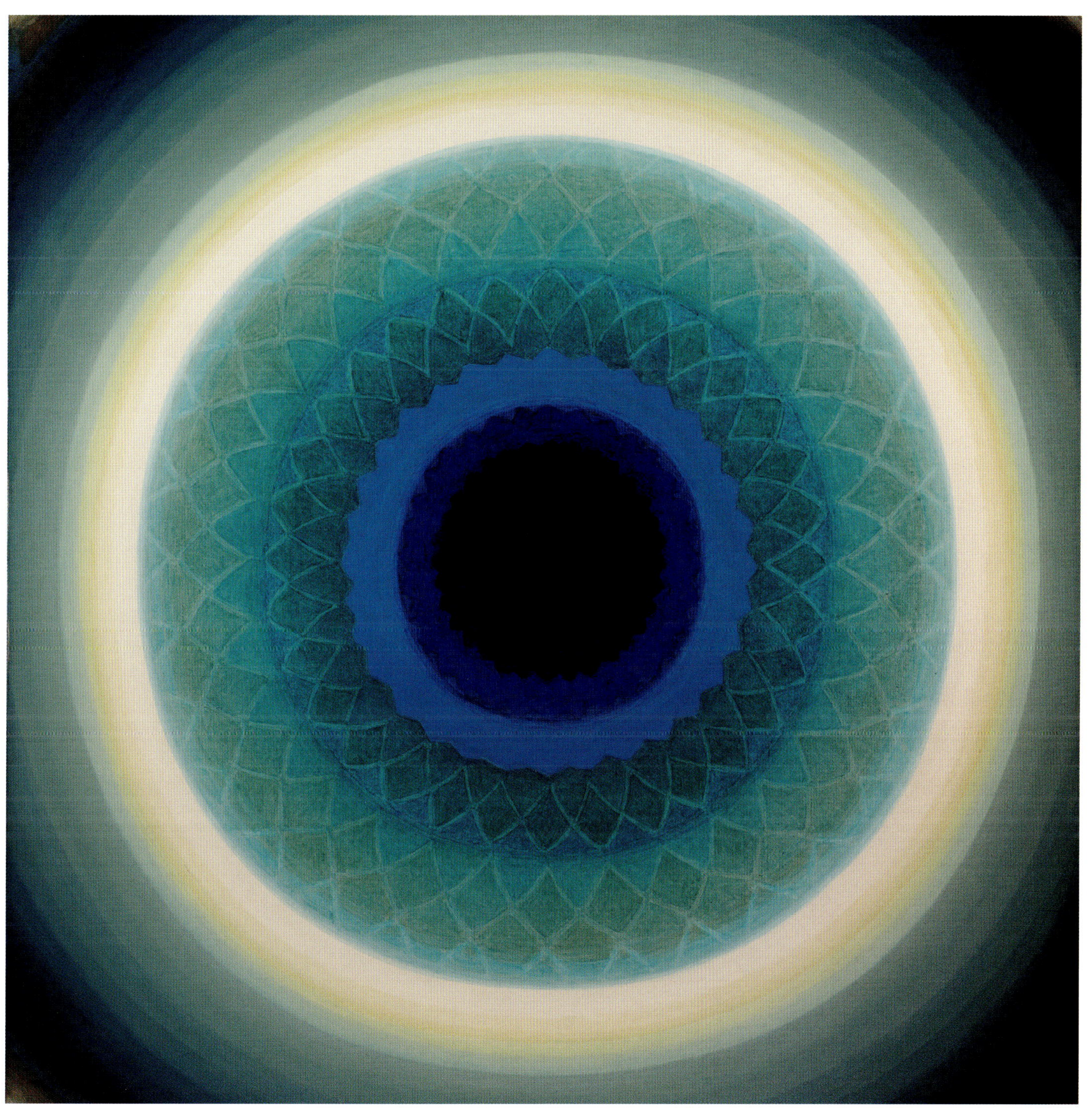

Plate 2.
August '78, 1978
Oil on canvas
49 ¾ × 49 ½ inches (126.4 × 125.7 cm)

M.F. HUSAIN

Born in Pandharpur, Maharashtra,
1915–2011 died in London
Lived and worked in Bombay

Maqbool Fida Husain achieved a celebrity in India reserved for film stars and politicians. His murals in airports, hotels, and public buildings have been seen by millions. He hobnobbed with the Nehru-Gandhi family, Bollywood stars, and Mother Theresa. His paintings likewise are larger than life, projecting the epic of India's people and civilization in a thoroughly modernist language. The most nationalist of the "Pathbreakers" generation, Husain, a Muslim, died in self-imposed exile, hounded out of the country by Hindu extremists offended by his depictions of Hindu deities. His personal tragedy testifies to art's centrality in contemporary culture wars.

Husain made his debut on the art scene in 1947, the year of India's independence, winning an award at the Bombay Art Society's exhibition. He had left provincial Indore for Bombay ten years earlier with no money and great ambition. He eked out a living as a cinema billboard painter and children's furniture designer, painting when he could, often late into the night. In the late 1940s, things began to move quickly for him. The artist F.N. Souza, impressed by his work, brought Husain into the newly organized Progressive Artists Group, a loose association of like-minded young artists eager for public and private forums for the new directions they were taking in their work. They collaborated with pathbreakers in other arts—poets, writers, and theater people. They also found supporters among émigrés from Hitler's Europe, who had settled in Bombay and joined its art world. One of them, Emmanuel Schlesinger, was among the first to collect Husain's work, helping to enable the artist to paint full time. Through these Europeans, Husain discovered German Expressionism. He especially admired the work of Emile Nolde and Max Beckman, but it was their expression of individual freedom that most deeply resonated with Husain's experience of liberation as British power gave way to Indian sovereignty. The Expressionists' emphasis on conveying inner feelings in paint, color, and brushstroke encouraged him to move away from representations of the observed world to projections of deeper realities.

In 1948, Husain traveled with Souza to Delhi to see the exhibition *Masterpieces of Indian Art* at Government House (now Rashtrapati Bhavan). In this intense, unprecedented experience of Indian art, Husain found resources for his own developing practice: figural form in Gupta sculpture (fourth-sixth centuries), and the bold colors of seventeenth- and eighteenth-century Pahari painting. In subsequent sketching trips to the temples of Khajuraho and the Chola bronzes in the Government Museum, Madras, he worked out his distinctive approach to line. *Peasant Couple* (plate 3)[1] embodies Husain's evolving approach. Dark, intense, earthy colors energize the composition by contrasting the verticality of the figures with a strongly diagonal background of black and yellow shapes. The sturdy farmer and his wife who fill the canvas seem excavated from color, defined by white line with contours emphasized in sharply laid down black. Husain's take on a new India follows that of Gandhi, in which the rural masses are the backbone of the nation.

Man (plate 4), one of Husain's most published works, is an enigmatic, chaotic assemblage of figures, a simultaneously mystifying and eloquent expression of postcolonial modern life.[2] A clear reference to Auguste Rodin's iconic *The Thinker*, a black figure seated on a thronelike red chair dominates the canvas. He holds a rectangle enclosing human figures; a similar "Gupta period" friezelike form lies beside him, upside down.[3] This "thinker" is a creator, an artist, like Husain. At the upper right, a goddesslike figure makes a reassuring gesture, but beside her is a vaguely menacing, slouching green man, perhaps alluding to the ignorant, brutal aspect of human nature. On the left side of the canvas, an upside-down man rests on a bull, ubiquitous in rural India and associated with the god Shiva. These perplexing, tantalizing juxtapositions demand decipherment from both the viewer and the Man. His large green eye observes the bewildering swirl of opposing and contradictory forces—ancient and modern, Eastern and Western, hopeful and anxious, powerful and vulnerable, chaotic and creative—that surround the artist-intellectual in postindependence India.

Husain's career thrived during the 1950s and 1960s. He traveled to China, Russia,

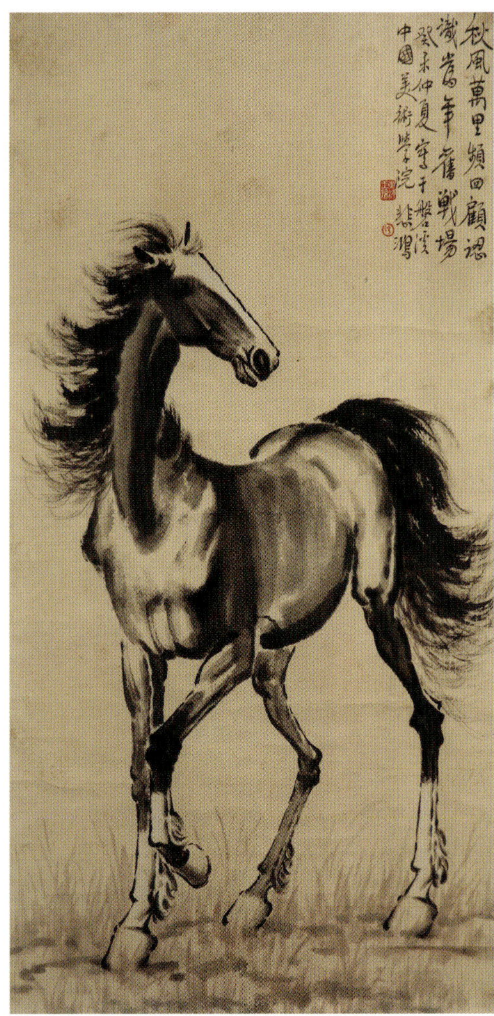

Figure 1.
Xu Beihong, *Horse*, 1943
Hanging scroll
Ink on paper
41 ¼ × 20 ½ inches (104.8 × 52.1 cm)
Collection of Michael Gallis

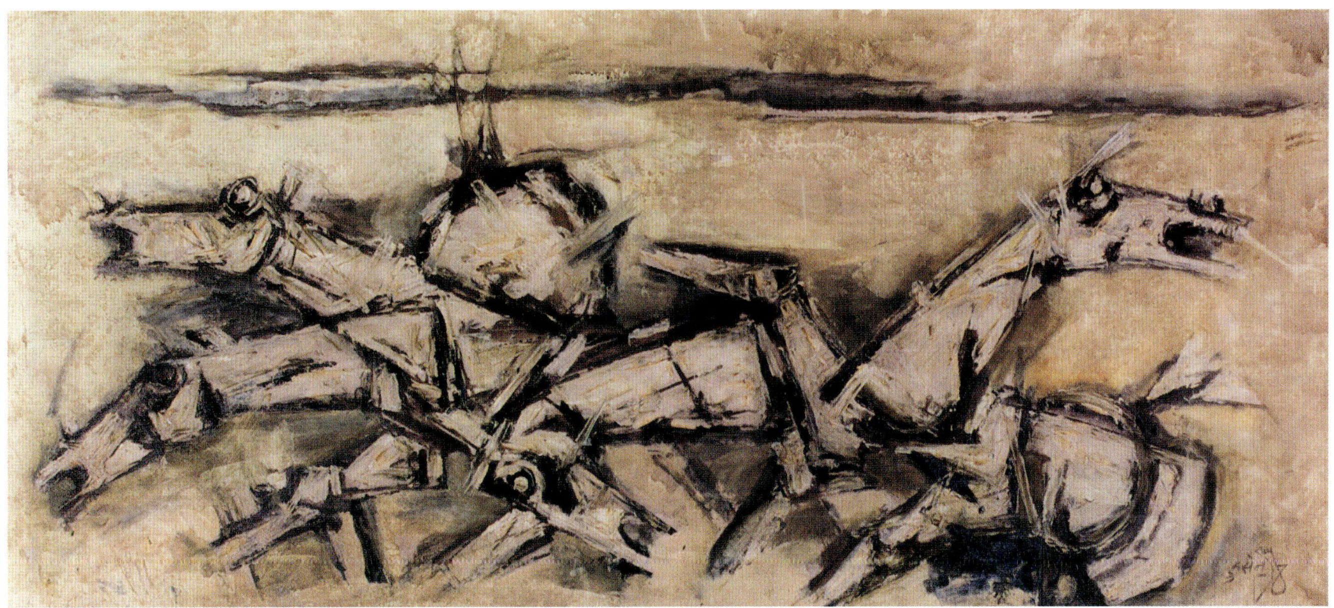

Figure 2.
M.F. Husain, *Lightning Horses*, ca. 1979
Oil on canvas
43 × 100 inches (109.2 × 254 cm)
Collection of Sri and Harsha Reddy

Europe, and Great Britain; he had solo gallery exhibitions in Zurich, Prague, Frankfurt, Tokyo, Rome, Baghdad, and Kabul. His work was shown at the Salon De Mai in Paris and biennials in Venice and São Paulo. In Beijing in 1951, Husain met renowned painter Xu Beihong, and saw his famous paintings of horses (figure 1). Husain was amazed by the vitality and grace of the animals. He infused his own horses, already a favorite subject, with a new vigor based in the brush-and ink-lines of the Chinese master (figure 2).

By the early 1970s, Husain had achieved international recognition that would not be matched by an artist from India until the emergence of the more global contemporary art world. The 1971 São Paulo Biennale honored Husain and Picasso as the two special invitees. That same year, Harry N. Abrams released a monograph on Husain, the first by an international art publisher on an Indian artist. Husain painted unceasingly and continued to explore new platforms for his art. He became increasingly populist and connected to Indian public culture. In 1968, he loaded a cart with paintings from his "Ramayana" series, hitched up oxen, and went to share the works with village people in Andhra Pradesh. At the same time, he unabashedly manipulated the art-world elite, demanding unprecedented prices because he understood the relationship between cost and an artist's standing. His forays into marketing are widely acknowledged for the public attention brought to the Indian art world.

Mahabali (plate 5) and *Cage V* (plate 6), enigmatic allegories of woman's plight, are epic works of these mature, confident, increasingly public years, and exemplify a stylistic shift toward having the figure reign supreme and relegating color to a strong supporting role. In *Mahabali*, a female torso emerges from an earth-tone background. The source of life, uniquely powerful yet essentially self-sacrificing, she towers over a red, womblike shape containing a group of line-drawn figures. In *Cage V*, a girl in virginal, bridal red with eyes downcast listens to a woman in white holding out a cage with green parrots ensnared in its decorative grid. Two other women accompany them; the four figures poignantly evoke the confinement of women in all the stages of life.

Husain often asserted that his paintings should be pure visual experiences—felt, not read. In a letter to Davida Herwitz in 1974 in response to a plea for explanations of paintings selected for exhibition, he wrote: "After completion of these paintings a year later the painter himself re-enters into some of these works through the backdoor as a stranger [and] the same works may reflect another prism of thought."[5] Husain's modernist mythologies with outsized mortals and re-envisioned deities are intended as allusions, gatherings of cultural and personal icons within which contemporary viewers might experience their own profound and perplexing place in the scheme of things. – SSB

1. *Peasant Couple* has been referred to by different titles, including *Balram Street*, *Kisan (Rhythm of Life) (Paris)*, and *Midday Meal*.

2. *Man* has attracted multiple interpretations as an allegory of modernity, including Ebrahim Alkazi, *M.F. Husain: The Modern Artist and Tradition* (New Delhi: Art Heritage, 1978), p. 9; Yashodhara Dalmia, *The Making of Modern Indian Art: The Progressives* (New Delhi: Oxford University Press, 2001), pp. 102–103; Daniel Herwitz, *Husain* (Chattanooga, Tennessee: Hunter Museum of Art, 1988), p. 8; Geeta Kapur, "Modernist Myths and the Exile of Maqbool Fida Husain," in *Barefoot Across the Nation: Maqbool Fida Husain and the Idea of India*, ed. Sumathi Ramaswamy (New York: Routledge, 2011), pp. 22–24.

3. M.F. Husain, conversation with the author, December 3, 2009, Herwitz Archive, Peabody Essex Museum, Salem, Massachusetts.

4. Susan S. Bean, "East Meets East in Husain's Horses," in *Lightning: From Private Collection of Marguerite and Kent Charugundla* (New York: Tamarind Gallery, 2007), pp. 11–16.

5. M.F. Husain, letter to Davida Herwitz, September 12, 1974, Herwitz Archive, Peabody Essex Museum, Salem, Massachusetts.

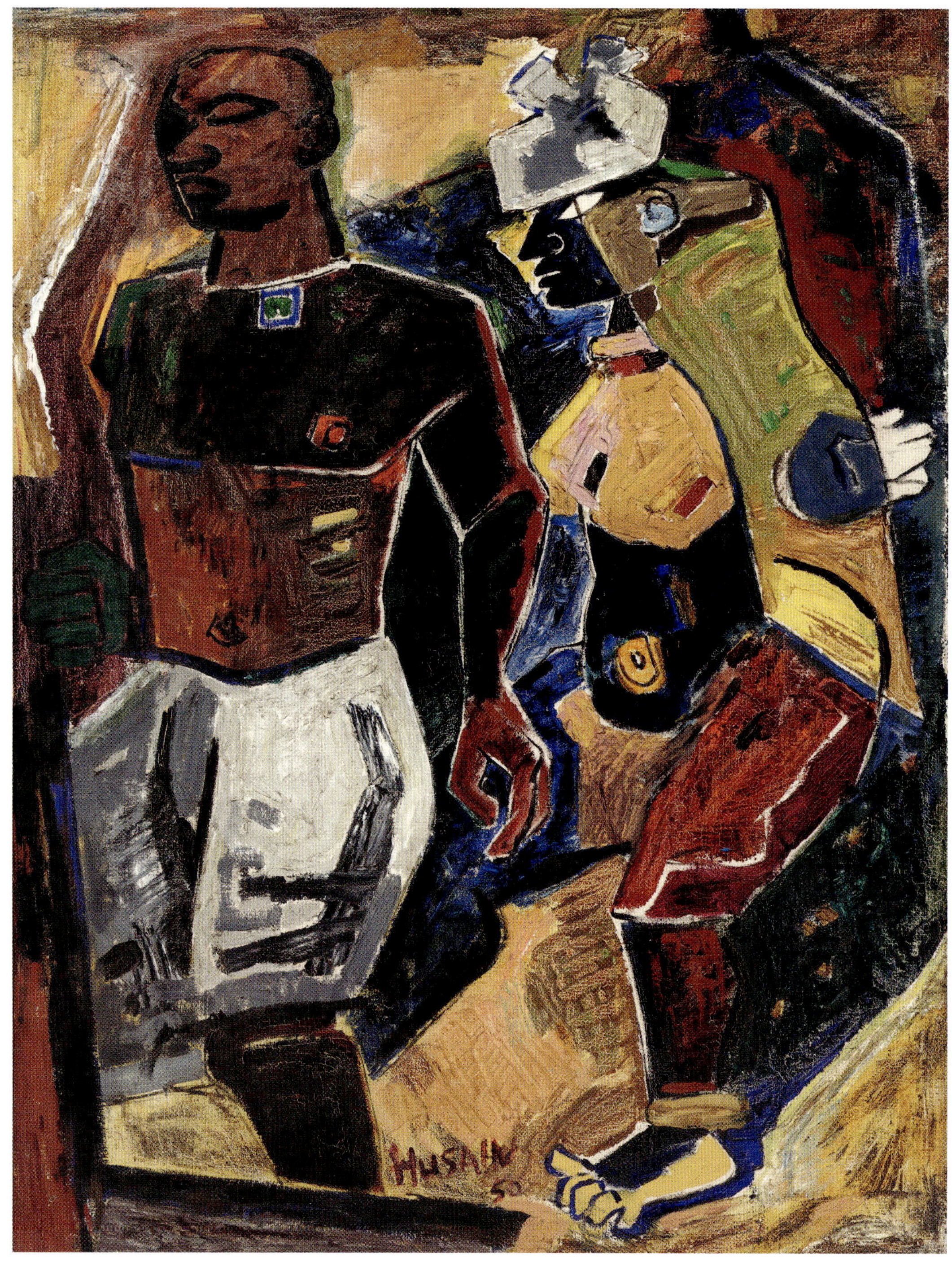

Plate 3.
Peasant Couple, 1950
Oil on canvas
47 ½ × 36 ½ inches (120.7 × 92.7 cm)

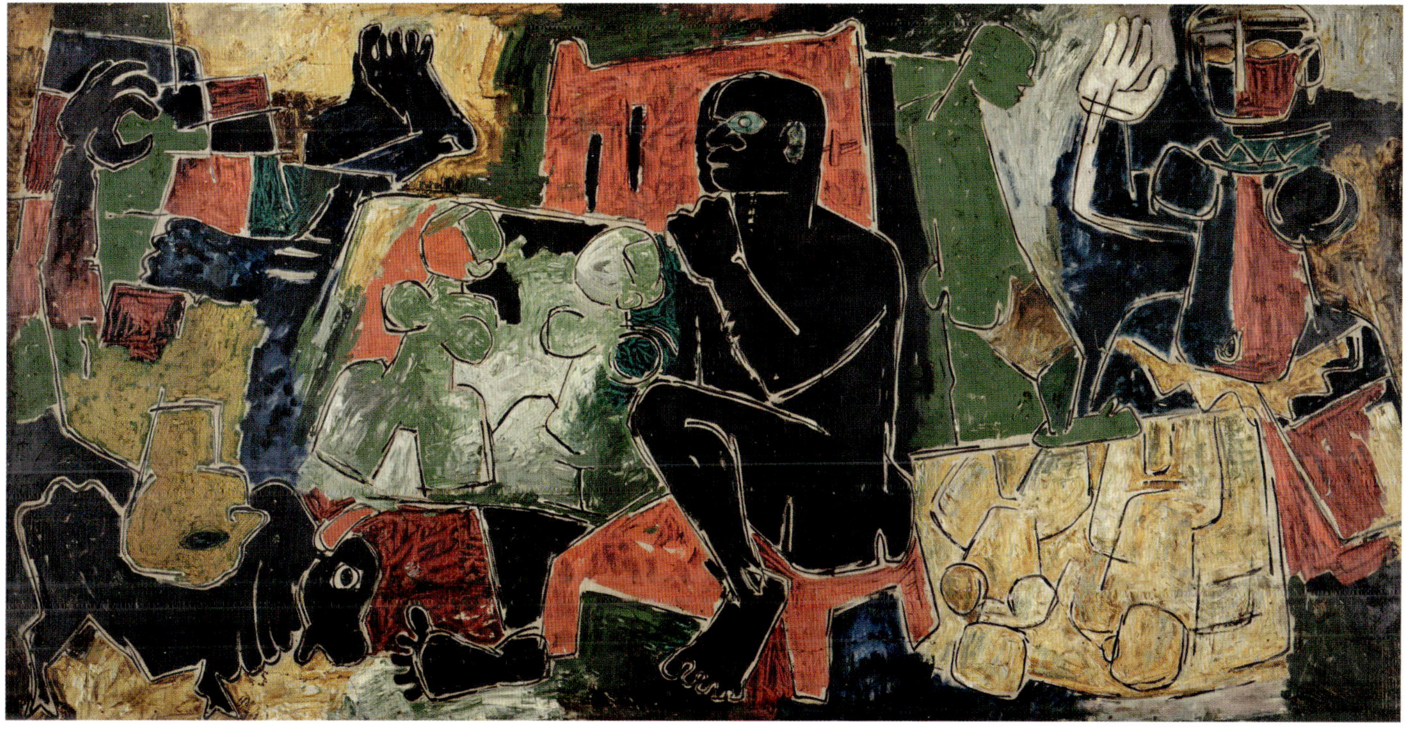

Plate 4.
Man, 1951
Oil on fiberboard
48 × 96 inches (121.9 × 243.8 cm)

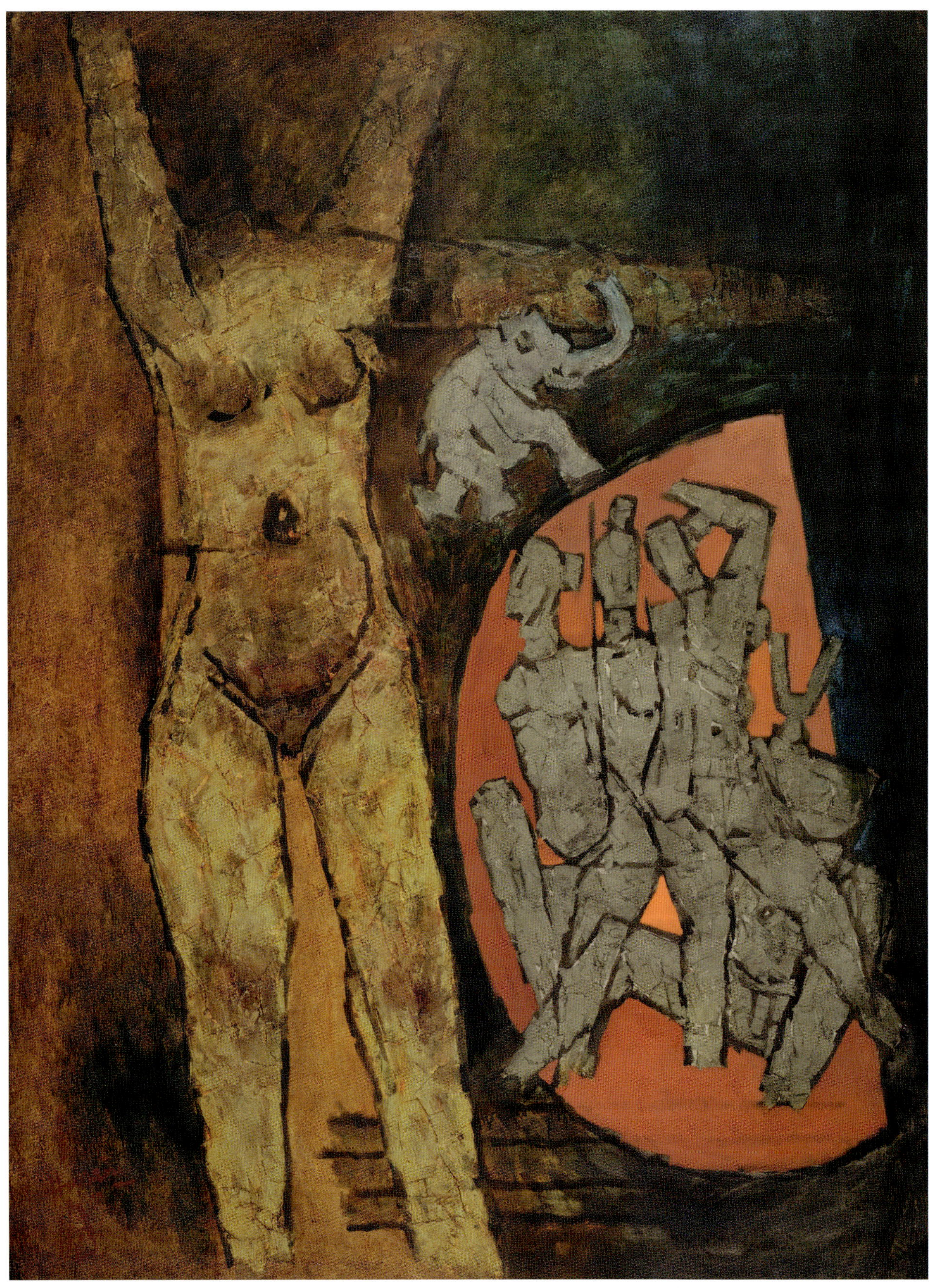

Plate 5.
Mahabali, 1972
Oil on canvas
93 ¾ × 69 ½ inches (238.1 × 176.5 cm)

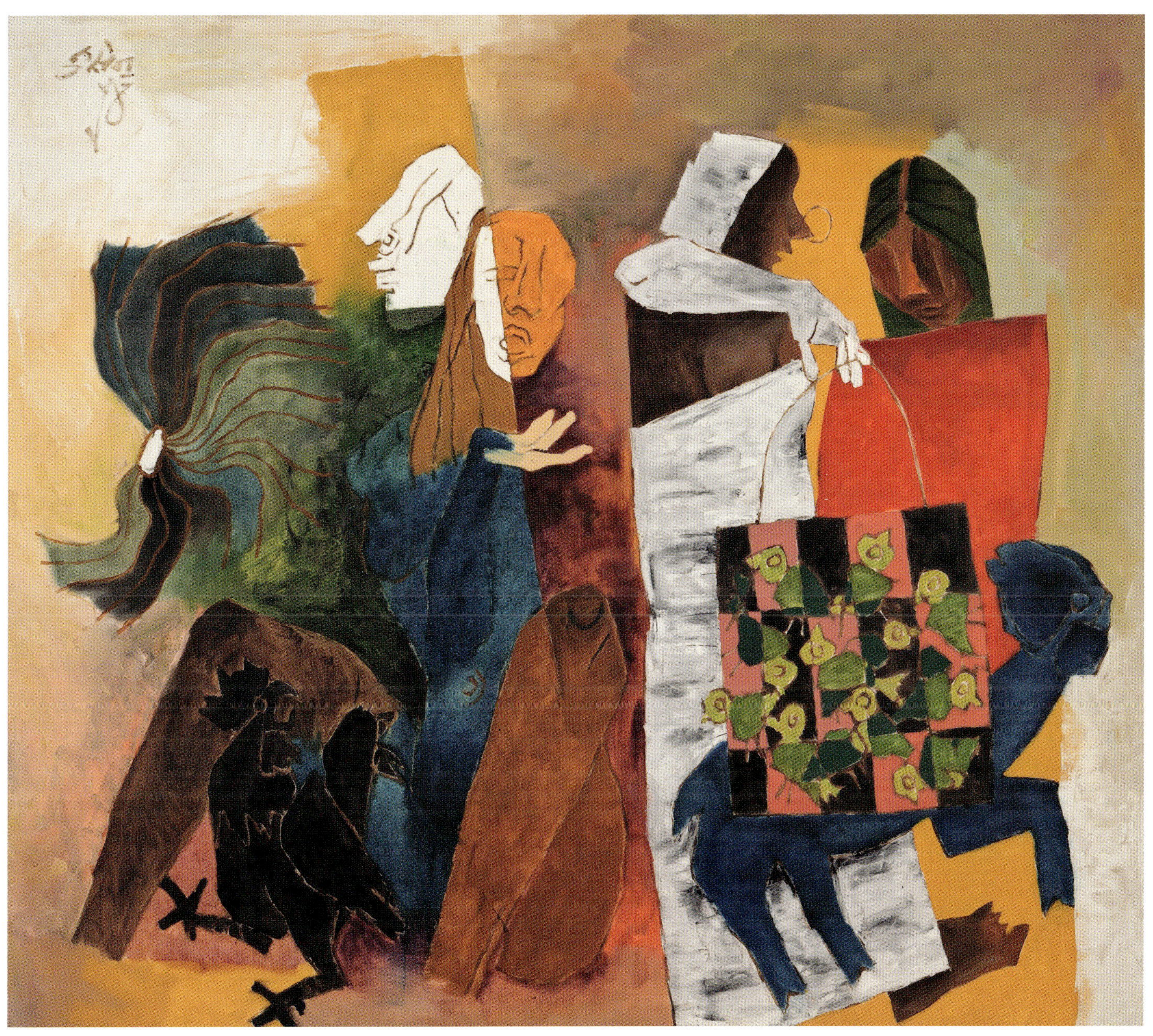

Plate 6.
Cage V, 1974
Oil on canvas
68 ¼ × 78 ¾ inches (173.4 × 200 cm)

RAM KUMAR

Born in Simla, Himachal Pradesh, 1924
Lives and works in Delhi

My figures were taken from the streets I saw around me, and I did reflect their sense of confusion, their search for identity, their alienation.
Ram Kumar, 1986[1]

In 1956, thirty-one-year-old Ram Kumar had already experienced a great deal. He had witnessed the upheavals of partition and India's independence, and in 1950–52 had lived in Europe, where he painted with Fernand Léger and André Lhote in Paris and joined the French Communist Party.[2] His book in Hindi on his European experiences was to be published in 1957.[3] Kumar already held a master's degree in economics and had studied in Delhi with Sailoz Mukherjea, a modernist painter who combined India's folk art traditions with vibrant brushwork, executing local subjects in an international style. Mukherjea's paintings built on the earlier generation of the Bengal School—which painters of Kumar's generation challenged.

A young painter and writer in the decade after independence, Kumar navigated a dynamic terrain of competing pathways for modern Indian art. Like many artists in this decade, he joined several groups, including the Delhi Silpi Chakra and the Progressive Artists Group, to assert a new idiom for modern Indian art.[4] The previous generation had gained legitimacy by embracing the bucolic (and sometimes sentimental) Indian countryside; Kumar looked toward the urban and the plight of the rising middle class.

The figures in *Unemployed Graduates* (plate 8), painted in 1956, boldly face front and assert their qualifications through their European business attire while their shoulders droop and their wide eyes stare questioningly out of the canvas. Likewise, In *Burden* (plate 7), of the same year, there is little sentimentality. Unlike rural depictions of Indian women wearing picturesque saris and carrying water jugs on their head, Kumar's Indian womanhood is a figure crowded by the three small children who hover behind her. Her arms push against the picture plane, highlighting the confined urban spaces and emphasizing the weight of her familial burden. Kumar did not evade the realities of urban life in 1950s India. He addressed the pressures on the "modern woman" and the lack of opportunities for the upwardly mobile, educated lower middle classes. He painted urban decay and struggle rather than large-scale violent upheavals.

In these early paintings, Kumar took his stylistic cues from Amrita Sher-Gil, Léger, Amedeo Modigliani, and broadly from expressionism and Cubism. Several commentators have compared his work to that of Ben Shahn in its graphic qualities and its nod to social realism. That realism also appears in his Hindi fiction, in which, as in his painting, he explored the alienation of the urban individual and viewed city dwellers as continually experiencing a feeling of exile.[5]

Kumar is best known, however, for his later cityscapes and abstract landscapes. In the late 1950s, he began focusing on the urban form instead of its inhabitants, painting abstracted architectonic cities and landscapes (figure 1). He told filmmaker Satyajit Ray that he found the human figure to be a distraction that drew the eye away from elements of the painting that constitute its life.[6] Kumar began a series of studies of Varanasi, the holy city on the Ganges river, overlaying the sacredness of the site with the alienation of modern urban life. He turned from overtly political themes to explore the quality of exile that he felt formed the basis of Indian experience. These Varanasi paintings and his later experimentations with fully abstracted landscapes pushed the boundaries of Indian painting. In them, Kumar explored the intersection of the sacred and the secular, the fast-paced modern urban life with the ostensible timelessness of religious space, and the traces of the human on the physical world. The elimination of people from his cityscapes did not signal an erasure of humanity from his work; as for Nasreen Mohamedi (plates 44–47), the incidental mark of the human on the sacred riverbank or the rural vista became a way to explore how the modern world included moments of loneliness and alienation alongside moments of wonder and awe.

Kumar's early figural period presages his later work. He has claimed that in his cityscapes, he left behind the political in favor of self-reflection. But, the effort to define a city like Varanasi in paint echoes the struggle he articulated in his unemployed graduates and burdened woman. Kumar may no longer engage in the heated debates of his youth, but his work continues to present a nuanced engagement with socio-political concerns. – RMB

1. Prema Viswanathan, "The Human Figure Is a Distraction," *Free Press Journal* 19 (October 1986). Available online via the Centre for the Study of Culture and Society, http:// http://cscs.res.in/. Accessed June 28, 2011.

2. Gagan Gill, ed., *Ram Kumar: A Journey Within* (New Delhi: Vadehra Art Gallery, 1996), p. 234; biographical information about the artist follows Gill's text.

3. Ram Kumar, *Yuropa ke skaica [Sketch of Europe]* (Noida, India: Remadhava, 2007; originally published 1957).

4. These two groups have manifestos that are somewhat at odds: the Progressives largely eschewed politics and focused on formal concerns while the Silpi Chakra group participated more directly in a political milieu in Delhi. Membership in these groups was often more casual than the term "group" suggests. My thanks to Atreyee Gupta for her insights on Kumar's participation in various groups. For more on the Silpi Chakra, see her "The Promise of the Modern: Silpi Chakra and the Politics of Art in New Delhi," in *Twentieth Century Indian Art*, eds. Partha Mitter and Parul Dave Mukherji (New Delhi: Art Alive Gallery, in press).

5. See Geeta Kapur, *Contemporary Indian Artists* (New Delhi: Vikas Publishing House, 1978), pp. 57–74 for more on these issues in Kumar's early work.

6. Viswanathan.

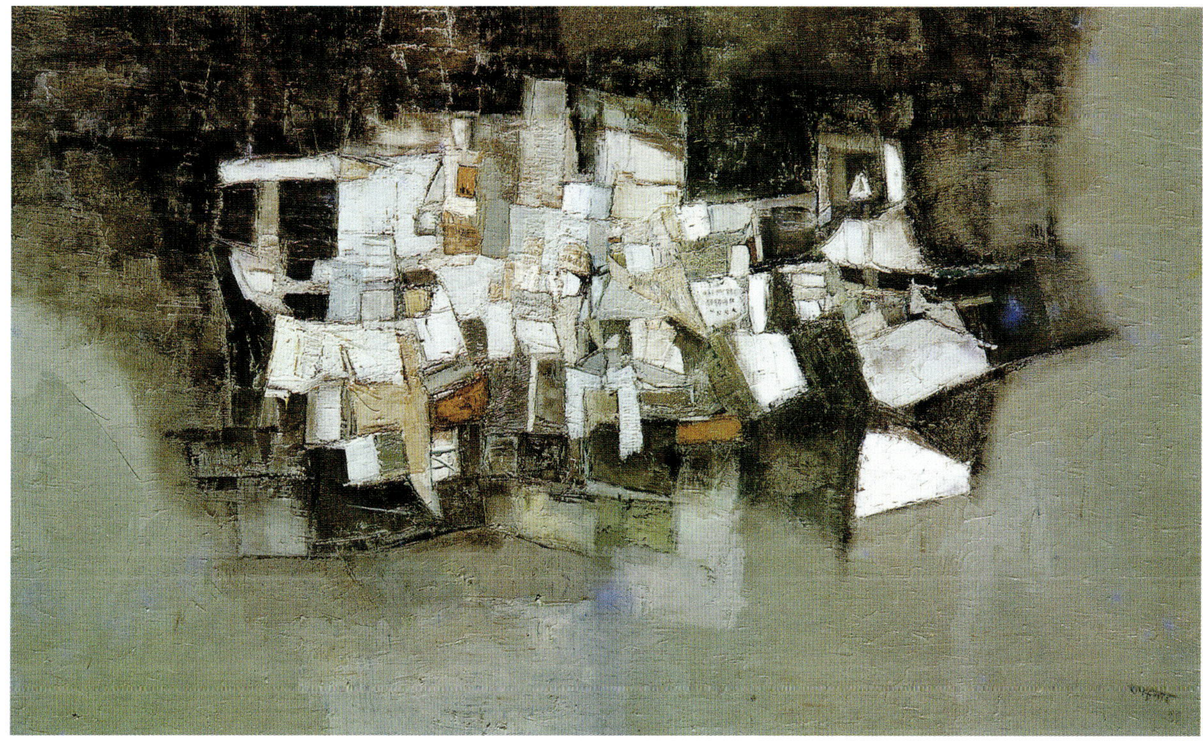

Figure 1.
Ram Kumar, *Varanasi*, 1966
Oil on canvas
50 × 70 inches (127 × 177.8 cm)
Vadehra Art Gallery, New Delhi

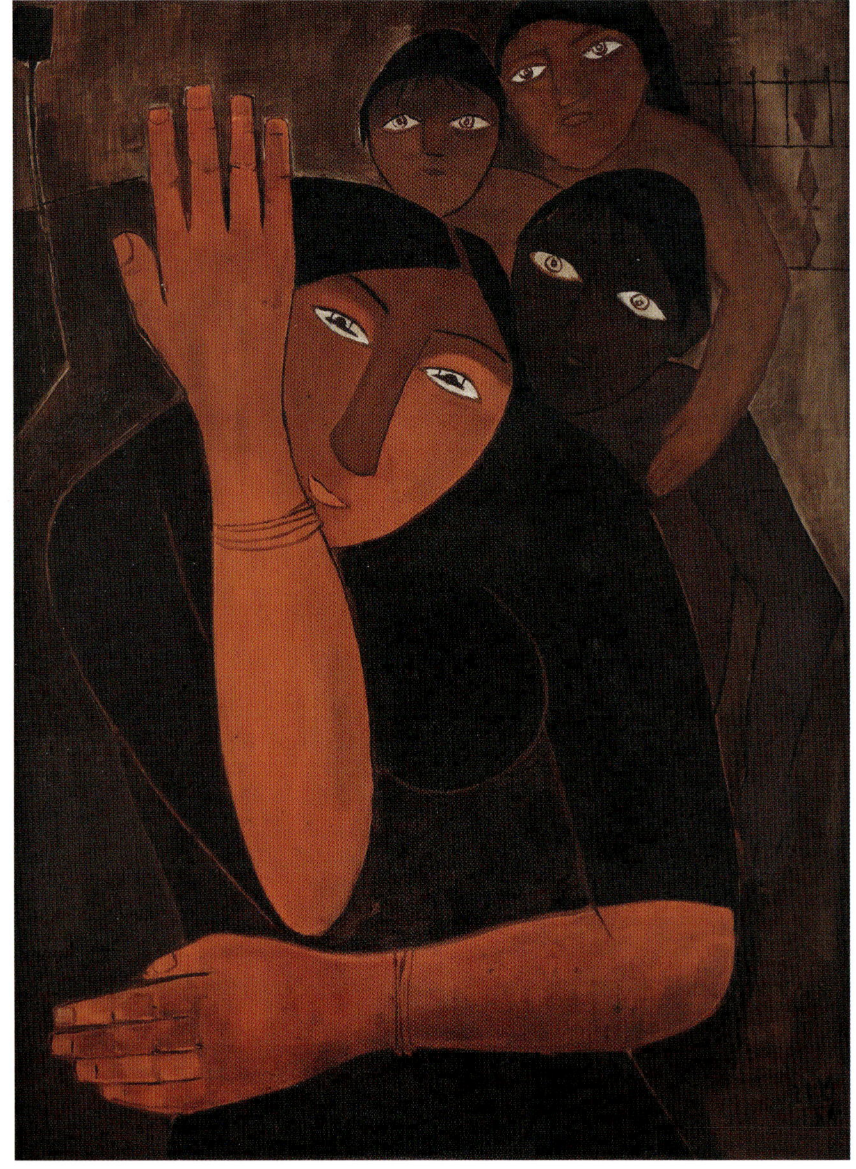

Plate 7.
Burden, 1956
Oil on fiberboard
31 ½ × 23 ½ inches (80 × 59.7 cm)

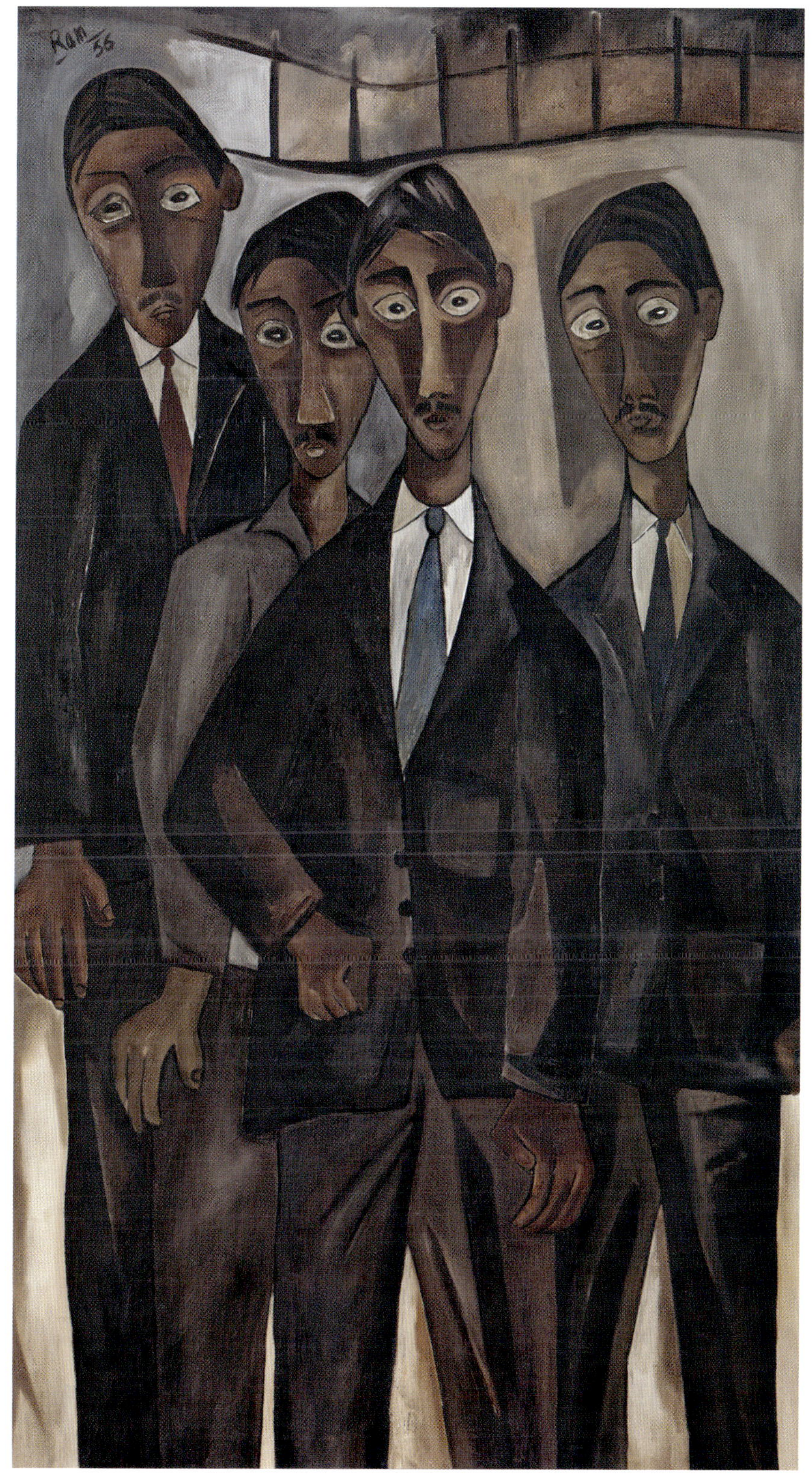

Plate 8.
Unemployed Graduates, 1956
Oil on canvas
46 × 26 inches (116.8 × 66 cm)

TYEB MEHTA

Born in Kapadvanj, Gujarat, 1925–2009 died in Bombay
Lived and worked in Bombay

When sectarian violence anticipating Indian partition in 1947 rendered it impossible for Tyeb Mehta to travel from his home on Mohammed Ali Road, Bombay's predominantly Muslim area, to a job as a film editor's assistant in distant Tardeo, a friend suggested that he instead enroll as a painting student in the nearby J.J. School of Art. From his graduation in 1952 until his death in 2009, Mehta's traumatic experience of partition remained the structuring element of his artistic career, focusing his stylistic sensibility and defining the deliberately restricted repertoire of the themes he painted. These included solitary and grouped human figures, trussed bulls, falling birds, and the Hindu goddesses Kali and Durga, all interpreted in response to partition violence or the artist's consciousness of his position as a Muslim in contemporary India.

In 1969, back in India after a long stay abroad in London and New York, Mehta developed the diagonal as a seminal device and subject. Though it has long been thought that the diagonal entered Mehta's work as a hasty and haphazard solution to a formalist problem,[1] it refers closely to the artist's ongoing concerns with the relationship between figuration and abstraction, as well as international artistic currents. It became his primary compositional element for the next decade, as in an untitled canvas from 1973 (plate 10). Within India, the diagonal referred symbolically and psychically to partition and the country's subsequent cultural and religious fragmentation. In relation to international modernist expression, the form reinterpreted the "zips" in the "Onement" series (figure 1) by American Abstract Expressionist Barnett Newman, which Mehta had likely seen in 1967 in New Delhi at the Lalit Kala Akademi or at The Museum of Modern Art (figure 2) while in New York on a Rockefeller Fellowship in 1968–69; he cited the experience as "a revelation."[2] Unlike Newman, however, Mehta consciously adhered to figuration throughout his career. Despite his interest in the formalist principles of abstraction that led Euro-American modernism, Mehta believed that the figure (animal or human, naturalistic or abstracted) distinguished his work—and the aspirations of Indian modernist art—from that of the West. Additionally, while Newman's "zips" cleanly bisect the canvas, Mehta's angular diagonals divide the plane into jagged segments. The form serves as a symbol of cultural and religious scission and as a product of the artist's intellectual engagement with existentialism and international notions of "Universal Man."

As he developed the diagonal in the early 1970s, Mehta's early attraction to expressionism (preponderant among modernist artists in India after independence), seen in works such as *Untold Element* (plate 9), gave way to painting a flattened and clean planar surface. In the untitled 1973 painting, Mehta positioned overlapping faces, torsos, and errant limbs on both sides of the diagonal form, and distinguished individual figures and geometric planes through color. By the end of the 1970s, Mehta reintegrated the canvas into a single picture plane and began to "reassemble" figures from fragments, as in the untitled canvas from 1979 (plate 11). His reconfiguration of the human subject roughly as individual quadrants of color blocks echoes Mehta's representation of trussed or otherwise distressed bulls beginning in the 1950s and underscores the parallels he drew between the bull and the human figure. The bound or ripped-apart bull symbolizes the human slaughter that Mehta had witnessed in Bombay during partition. Mehta described the bull as "a statement of great energy...blocked or tied up. The way they tie up the animal's legs and fling it on the floor of the slaughterhouse before butchering it.... The trussed bull also seemed representative of the national condition...the mass of humanity unable to channel or direct its tremendous energies."[3]

Mehta's figures appear predominantly androgynous until around 1972, when he began to articulate some subjects as female, primarily through the suggestion of breasts, though he also began to delineate soft facial features of individual feminine figures around the same time. Subsequently, many of Mehta's unnamed human figures appear female. One example, *Sequence* (plate 12), represents a rare instance when the artist experimented with allusions to narrative compositions (at a moment, perhaps related, when the narrative figuration movement

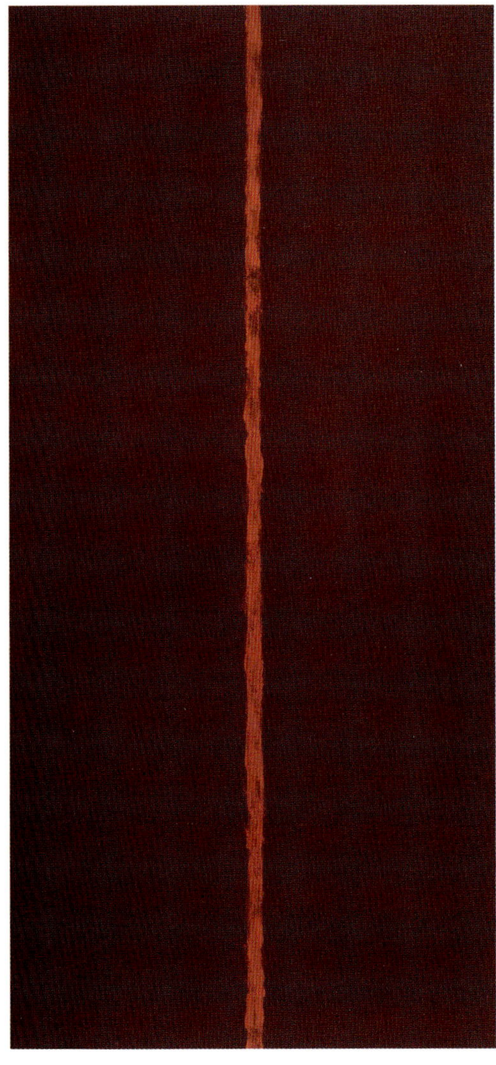

Figure 1.
Barnett Newman, *Onement III*, 1949
Oil on canvas
71 ⅞ × 33 ½ inches (182.6 × 85.1 cm)
The Museum of Modern Art, New York,
Gift of Mr. and Mrs. Joseph Slifka

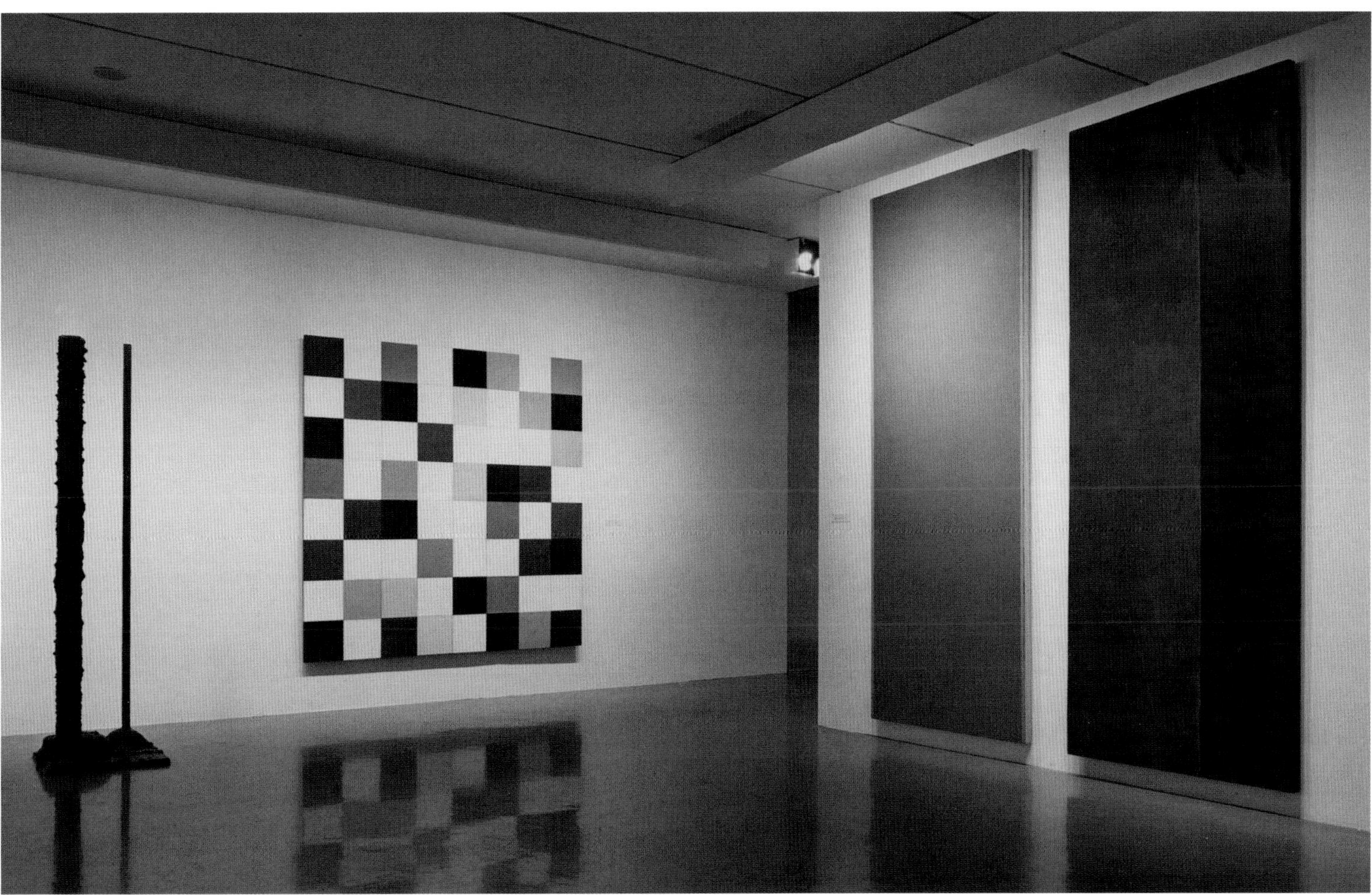

Figure 2.
Art of the Real exhibition, The Museum of Modern Art, New York, July 3, 1968 through September 8, 1968
The Museum of Modern Art Archives, New York

in Indian art was at its height). Here, four female figures are distinguished from the trussed bull at the lower right: one attends to the animal, two hover closely, the fourth approaches the group.[4]

Notable exceptions to Mehta's focus on the female form are designated subjects, such as *Rickshaw Puller* (plate 13), in which the exaggerated musculature indicates the figure's profession and, accordingly, his gender. As in other of Mehta's compositions that emphasize an action rather than a state of being, moving the vehicle (rendered as an abstracted, ambiguous form) structures the figure at its helm.

Works by Mehta from the 1970s and early 1980s highlight the unified vision of the artist's practice and his linear, reductive mature style. Mehta noted that with the absence of a rapid turnover of movements in the development of contemporary art in India,[5] "we accepted something from the West which was universal, and rejected avant-gardism. We wanted to create our own identity."[6] More than for other leading modernists in India, however, Mehta's subjects and point of view were obsessively singular throughout his life; they left an enduring imprint on twentieth-century Indian art and cultural history. – BC

1. Ranjit Hoskote, "Images of Transcendence: Towards a New Reading of Tyeb Mehta's Art," in *Tyeb Mehta: Ideas, Images, Exchanges* (New Delhi: Vadehra Art Gallery, 2005), pp. 17–19; Gieve Patel, "Contemporary Indian Painting," *Daedalus* 118, 4 (Fall 1989), pp. 195–96.

2. Nikki Ty-Tomkins Seth, interview with Tyeb Mehta, "The Human Figure is What I Primarily React To," *The Sunday Observer* (Bombay), February 1984, pp. 14–15.

3. Ibid., p. 14.

4. The placement of the bull seems to echo Mehta's *The Diagonal No. 3* (1969), the first work he painted in the "Diagonal" series after returning from New York.

5. Patel, p. 200.

6. Tyeb Mehta, interview with the author, February 4, 2007.

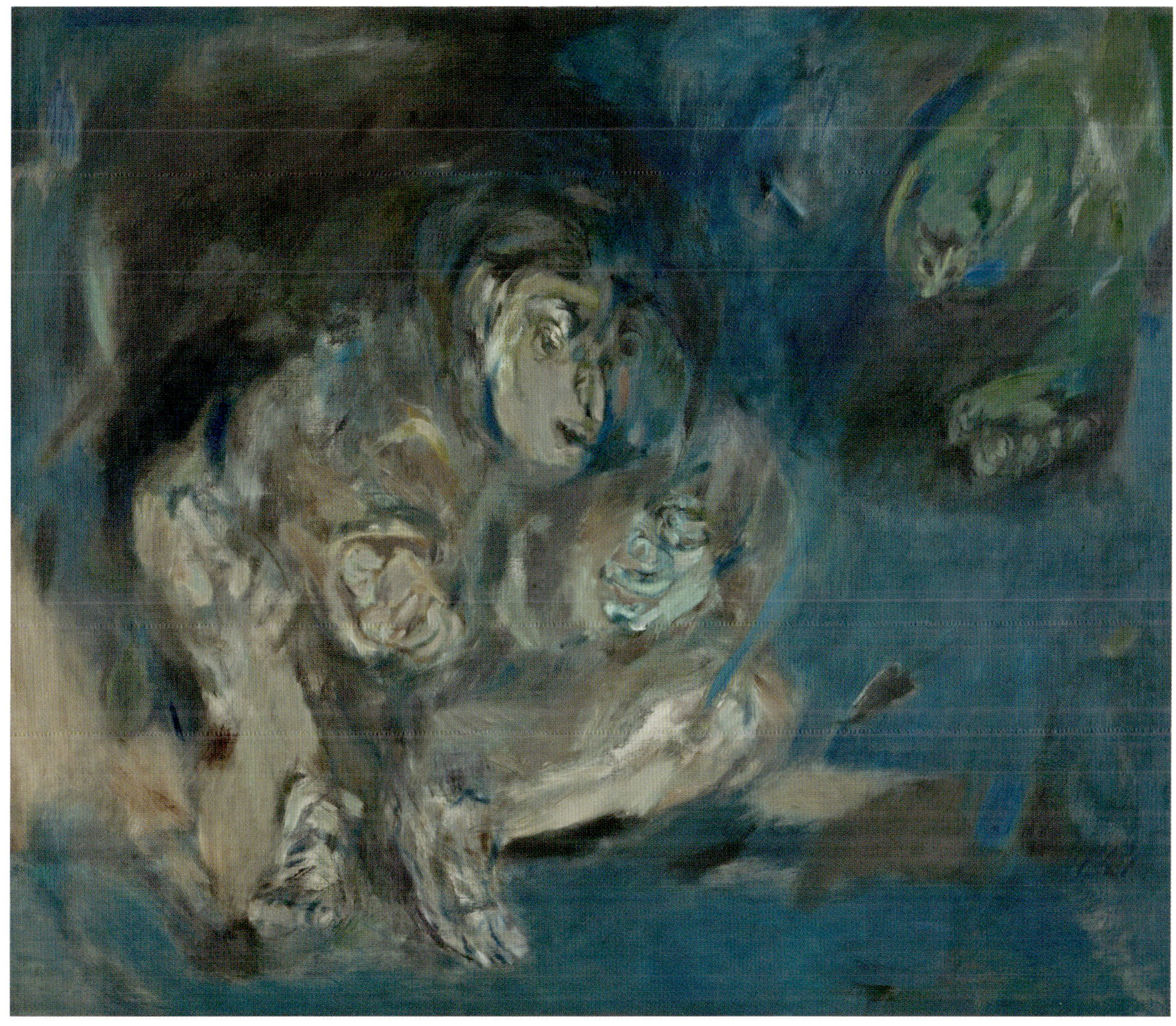

Plate 9.
Untold Element, 1965
Oil on canvas
49 × 58 ½ inches (124.5 × 148.6 cm)

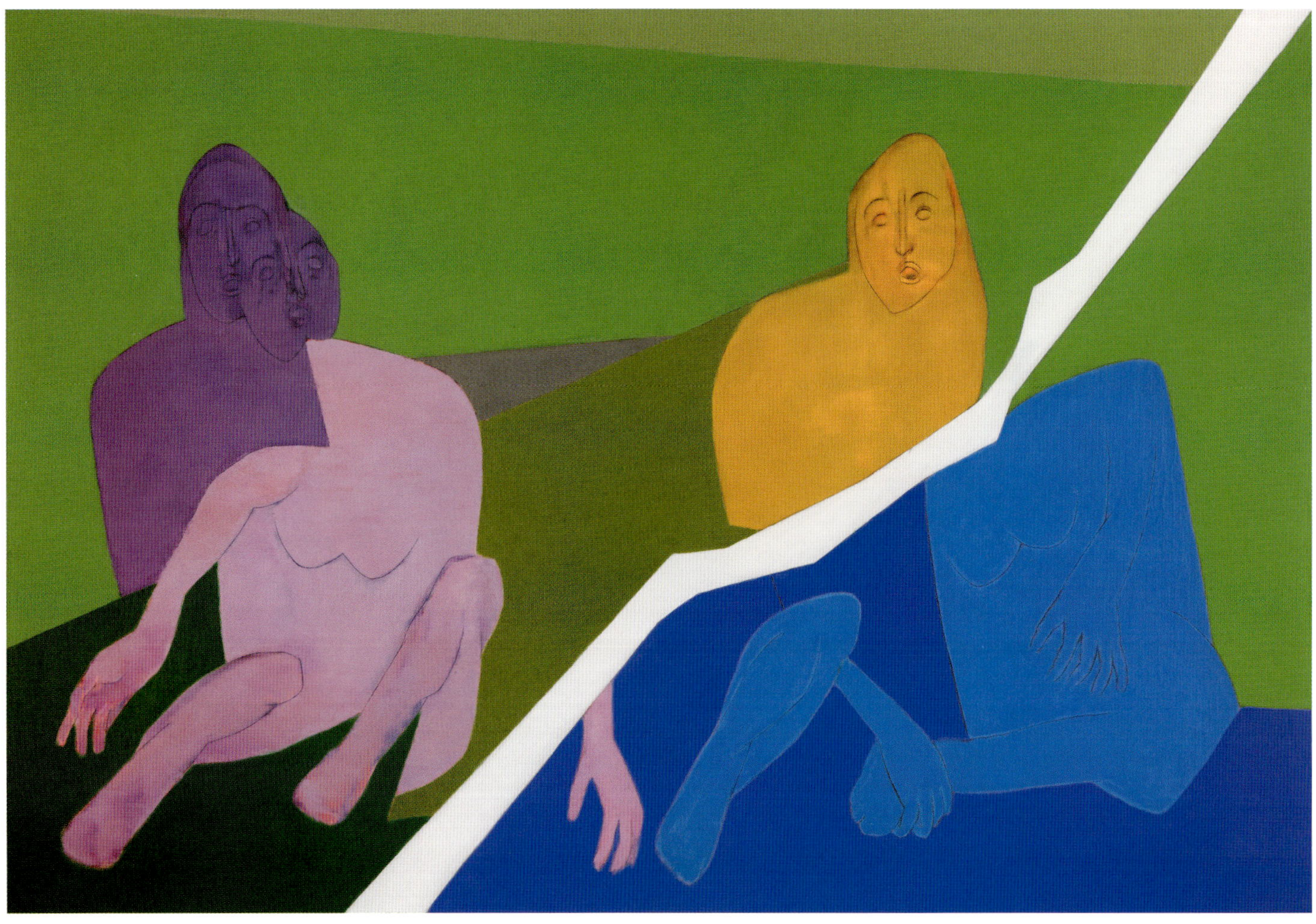

Plate 10.
Untitled, 1973
Oil on canvas
69 ⅛ × 102 inches (175.6 × 259.1 cm)

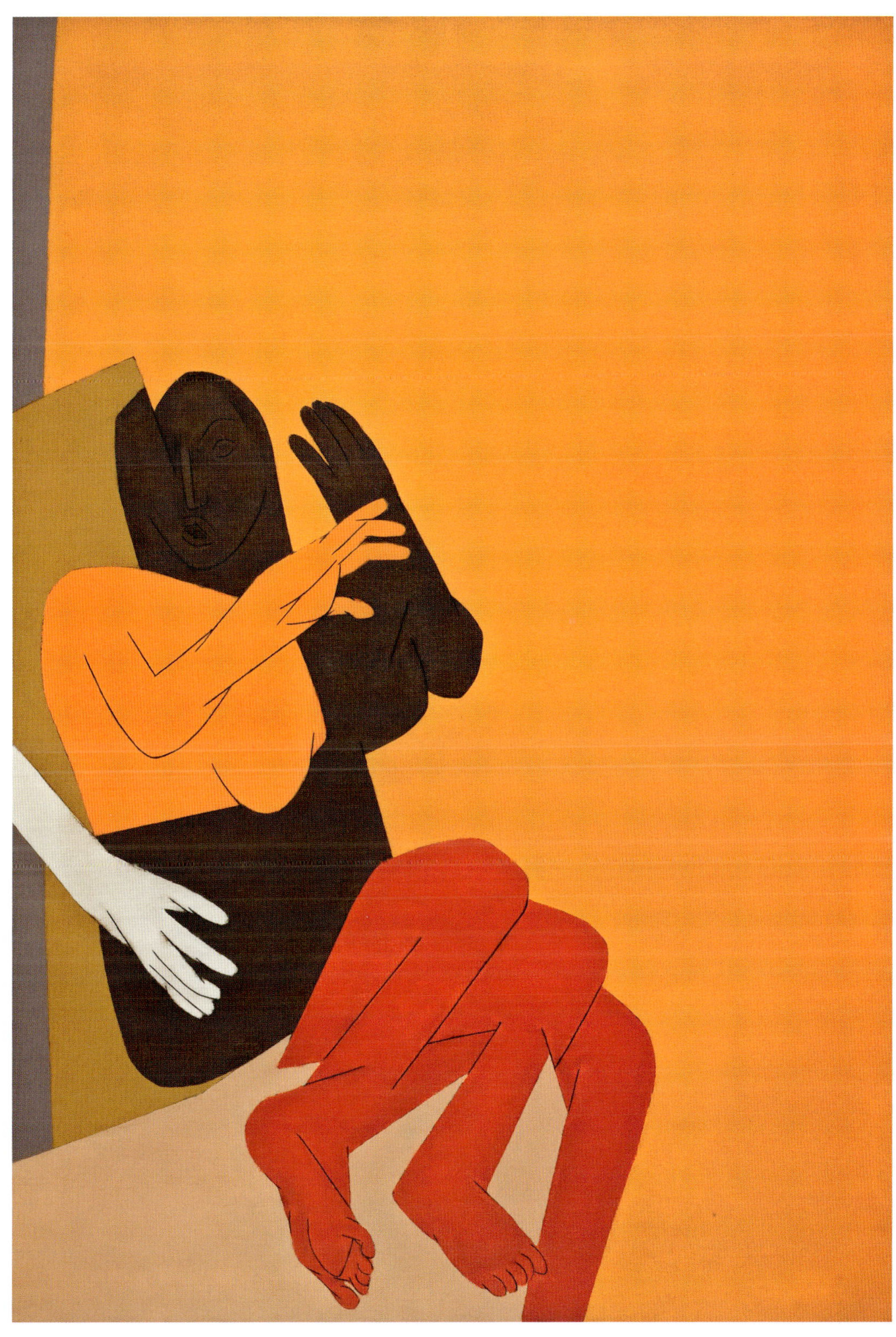

Plate 11.
Untitled, 1979
Oil on canvas
59 ½ × 41 ¾ inches (151.1 × 106 cm)

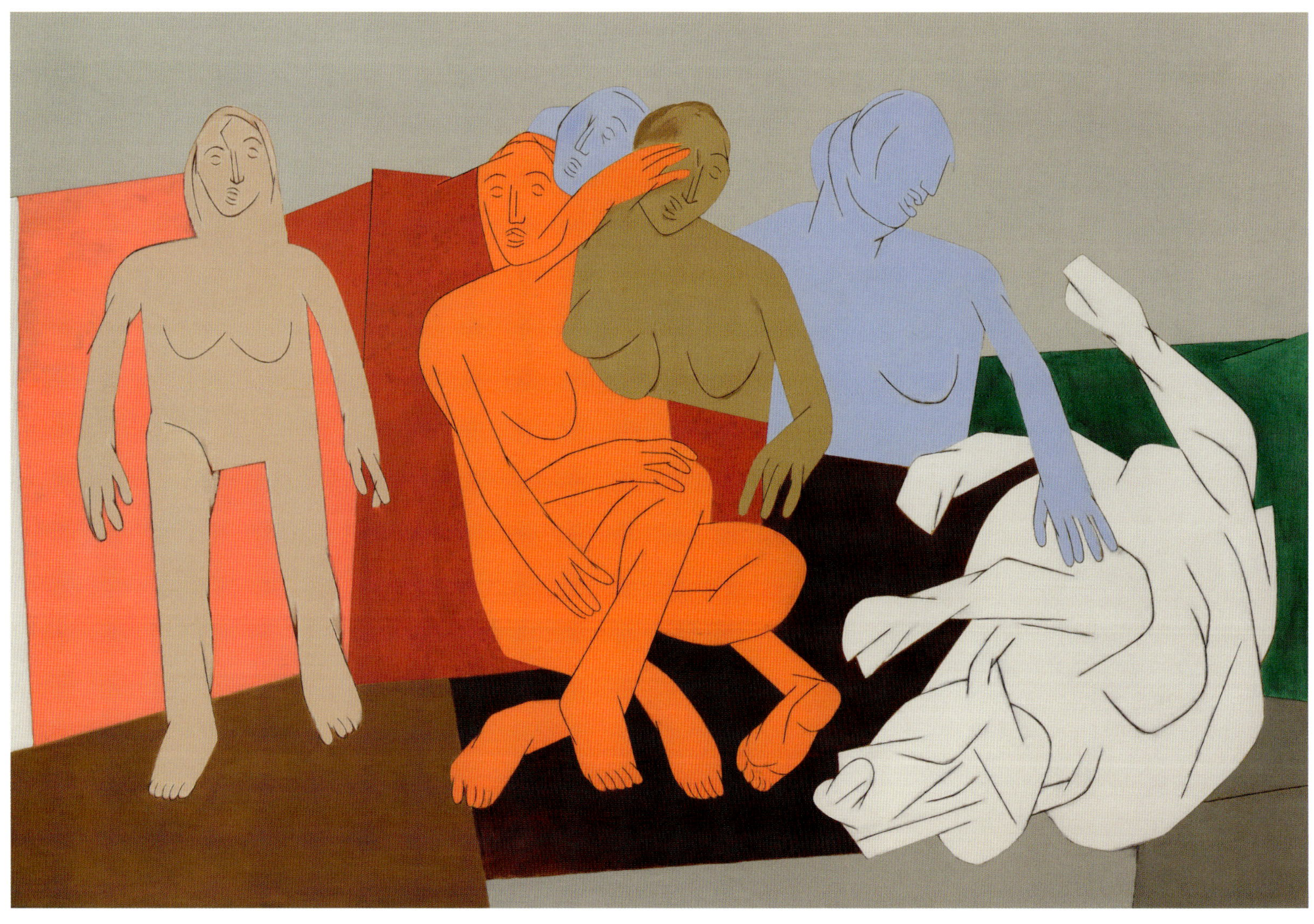

Plate 12.
Sequence, 1981
Oil on canvas
69 × 102 ½ inches (175.3 × 260.4 cm)

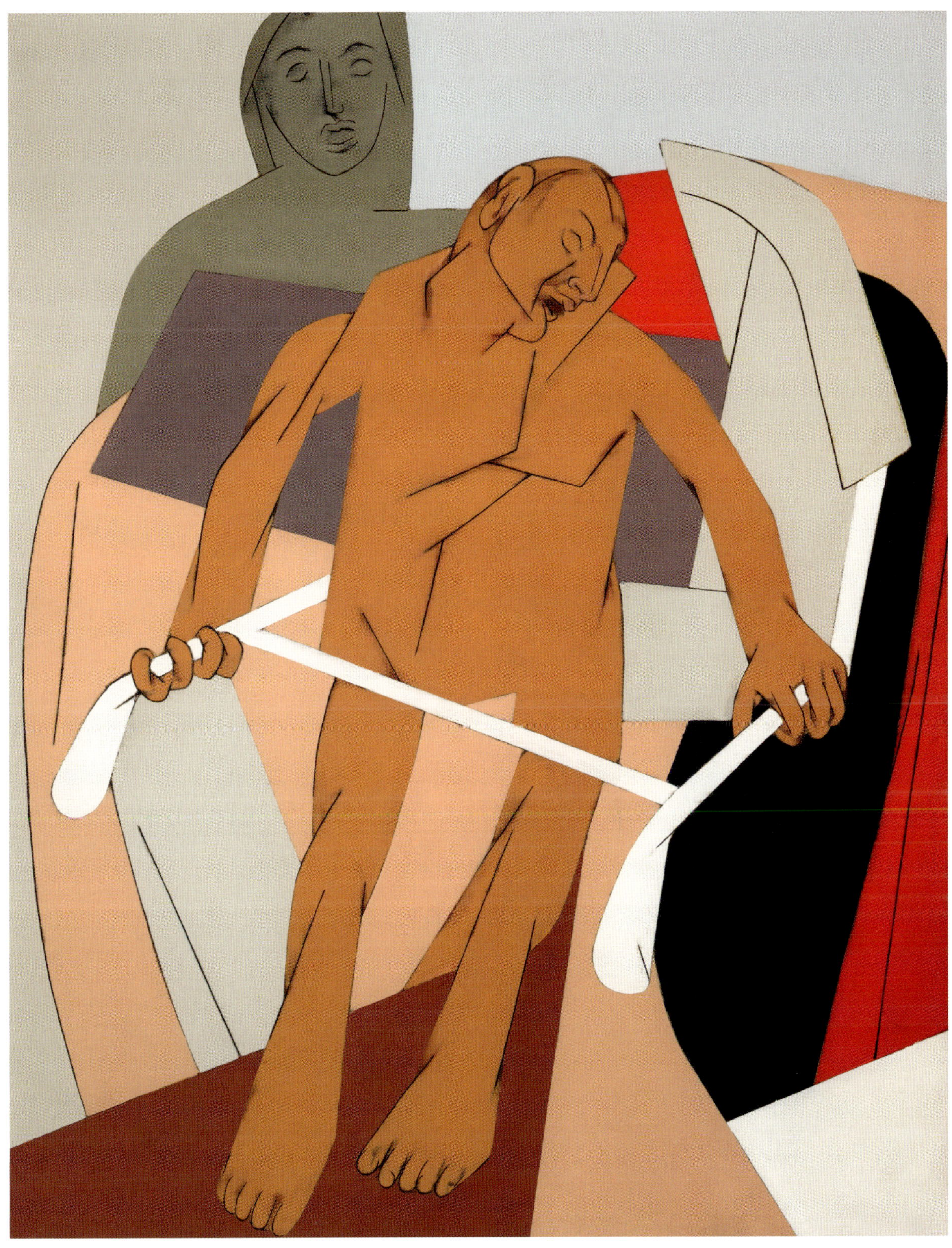

Plate 13.
Rickshaw Puller, 1982
Oil on canvas
60 ½ × 48 ⅛ inches (153.7 × 122.2 cm)

S.H. RAZA

Born in Babaria, Madhya Pradesh, 1922
Lives and works in Delhi after sixty years in Paris

Ever since his student days in Bombay when he painted watercolors of familiar views in the city, Sayed Haider Raza has been absorbed with place. He has moved, it seems inexorably, from representational to abstract landscapes and then cosmic scapes. From the beginning, he has been absorbed with the construction of these terrains: "in Bombay I realized that a painter should know his language as a writer should know the vocabulary, the grammar, the meaning of words...."[1] In 1940s Bombay, Raza found a congenial group of ambitious young artists: "we looked at paintings which were significant because of the colour orchestration, the relationship of the lines, spaces, and the right kind of proportion. All this was vital to painting and in each other's work, we looked for what Clive Bell has called 'significant' form."[2]

In the painting *Udho, Heart Is Not Ten or Twenty* (plate 14),[3] Raza merged two of his key resources in his quest for significant form: Rajput court painting of the seventeenth and eighteenth centuries, and the canvases of Paul Cézanne. Cézanne's place in Raza's self-education is singular. In 1947, Raza met the French photographer Henri Cartier-Bresson in Kashmir. Cartier-Bresson admired the young artist's work and advised him to study Cézanne in order to learn how to construct a painting.[4] Raza, already an admirer of the School of Paris, became determined to go to France. He studied French in Bombay and secured a scholarship through the French consulate. When he arrived in Paris in 1950, Cézanne was his priority: "I went to the museum again and again and tried to understand what was construction according to Cézanne."[5]

Simultaneously, Raza studied Rajput court painting. Like many of his contemporaries, he had seen the exhibition organized by the British in Delhi in 1948 to mark the establishment of India as a sovereign republic. For most of these artists, this exhibition provided their first significant exposure to the richness of Indian art. Raza was deeply moved: "Even at that early age—I must have

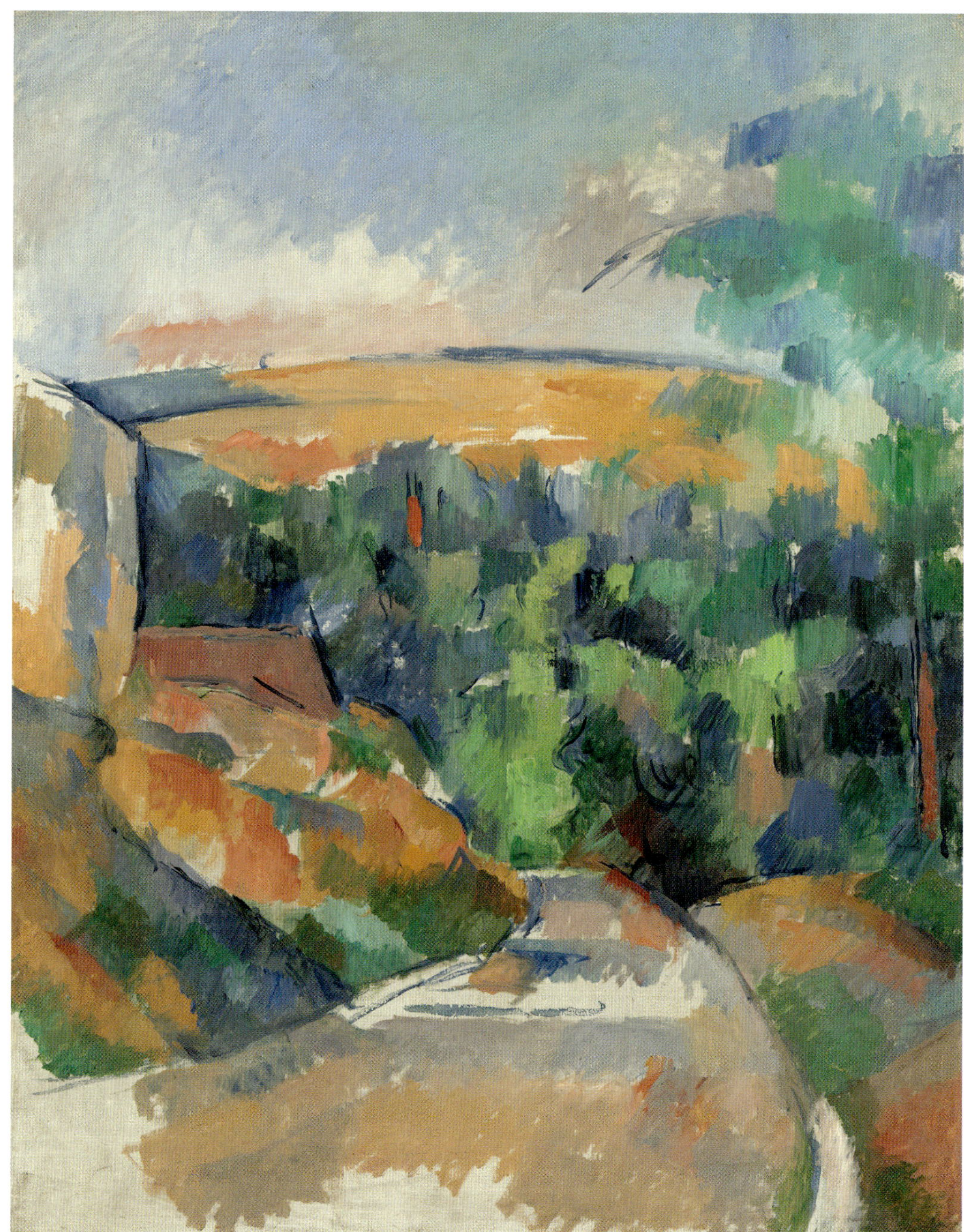

Figure 1.
Paul Cézanne, *The Bend in the Road*, 1900–1906
Oil on canvas
31 ¼ × 26 inches (81.9 × 66 cm)
National Gallery of Art, Washington, DC, Collection of Mr. and Mrs. Paul Mellon, 1985.64.8

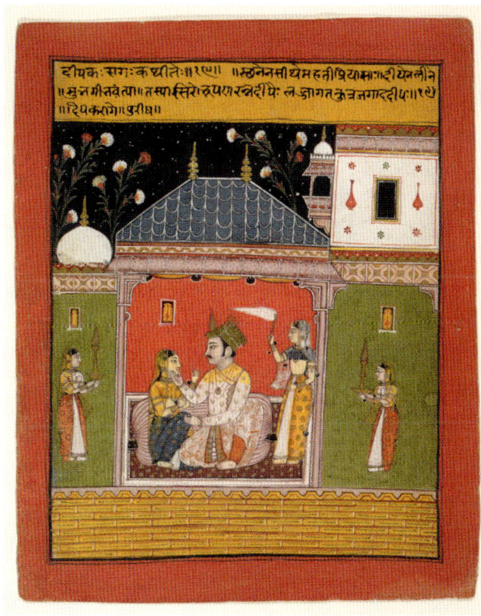

Figure 2.
Dipak Raga, page from a dispersed Ragamala series, 1630–40
Ink and opaque watercolor on paper
9 ½ × 7 ¾ inches (24.1 × 19.7 cm)
The Metropolitan Museum of Art, New York, Gift of the Kronos Collections, 1982.462.4

been about 24 or 25—I thought there was something extremely important in the Mughal miniatures, Rajput paintings, Jain miniatures and, of course, Indian sculpture."[6] He was intrigued by the way Rajput painters used color structurally, not naturalistically, to create vistas of palace compounds, gardens, forests, and hills.[7]

In *Udho, Heart Is Not Ten or Twenty*, Raza seems to have paid double homage, combining his interest in Rajput painting with his lessons from Cézanne. Juxtaposing *Udho* and Cézanne's *The Bend in the Road* (figure 1) highlights his debt to the French artist's way of constructing a coherent landscape through the application of broad strokes of color. Raza's palette, however, with its dominant black, red, and white, makes reference to the Rajput devices for enclosing pictorial space and incorporating inscriptions within the picture to create an explicit link between painting and poetry. A seventeenth-century miniature depicting the musical mode *Dipak Raga* (figure 2) offers an example of what so intrigued Raza. The strong primary color palette structuring the landscape, the red border, and inscription in their own way constitute a geometry of color.

L'Été '67 (plate 15), painted just a few years after *Udho*, shares a similar structure, but indicates new directions Raza took following a brush with American Abstract Expressionism during a summer spent in California and New York. The abstract landscape is enclosed in a red border, as in *Udho*, but the application of paint is looser and freer. The black circle, placed like a sun, is drawn from Raza's childhood: "my teacher Shri Nand Lalji Jharia...put a dot on the white wall of a veranda asking me to sit down and simply look at it forgetting play, study and everything else.... I started meditating on the point in the solitude of my little rooms in Bombay or elsewhere and later in my home in Paris."[8] In the coming years, the circle became increasingly important, signifying the undifferentiated cosmos, origin, and creation.

The 1960s was a transitional period in which Raza fully integrated his French apprenticeship with his Indian roots. His work found recognition, attracting steady gallery representation. In 1956, Raza had become the first non-French artist to win the prestigious Prix de La Critique. Despite these successes, he felt a need "to go back to my sources, to the sources of my country, to my civilization, to my roots, to my childhood and try to study more seriously the fundamental principles that underlie the Indian arts, Indian painting, music, dance, philosophy, literature and poetry."[9]

By the 1980s, Raza felt that he had mastered the handling of color and form. In *Rajasthan II* (plate 17), he mined the Rajput division of picture space into rectangular areas that carry a visual narrative. The strongly structured composition in Raza's elemental Indian colors—red, black, white, green/blue, and yellow—conveys the essence of Rajasthan's searing, stark, majestic landscape. In *Bindu, La Terre* (plate 16), the black sun has evolved into the *bindu*. Raza recalled a night in southern France when "the revelation of the 'Bindu' came to my mind as a point of departure; a unity of tremendous force, power, energy which the Bindu contained both as an idea and as a seed, a drop, a unity, a geometrical form, a point, a circle containing all the different geometrical shapes, triangles and colours."[10] For Raza, the realization of the *bindu* was a second birth, the beginning of his ongoing explorations of the cosmic orchestration of color-form. – SSB

1. Sayed Haider Raza and Ashok Vajpeyi, *Passion: Life and Art of Raza* (New Delhi: Rajkamal Books, 2005), p. 41.

2. Yashodhara Dalmia, *Journeys: Four Generations of Indian Artists in Their Own Words*, 2 vols. (New Delhi: Oxford University Press, 2011), vol. 1, p. 53.

3. The title, inscribed at the top of the painting, is taken from a well-known medieval *bhakti* (devotional) verse by Surdas (ca. 1480–1580). The *Gopis* (milk maids) tell Udho, the sage and friend of Krishna, that because the heart is only one, and it is already devoted to Krishna, there is no room for others—mortal or divine. Ashok Vajpeyi, e-mail to the author, March 9, 2011, Herwitz Archive, Peabody Essex Museum, Salem, Massachusetts.

4. Raza and Vajpeyi , p. 37.

5. Ibid., p. 56.

6. Ibid., p. 42.

7. Dalmia, p. 52.

8. Raza and Vajpeyi, p. 61.

9. Ibid., p. 60.

10. Ibid., p. 61.

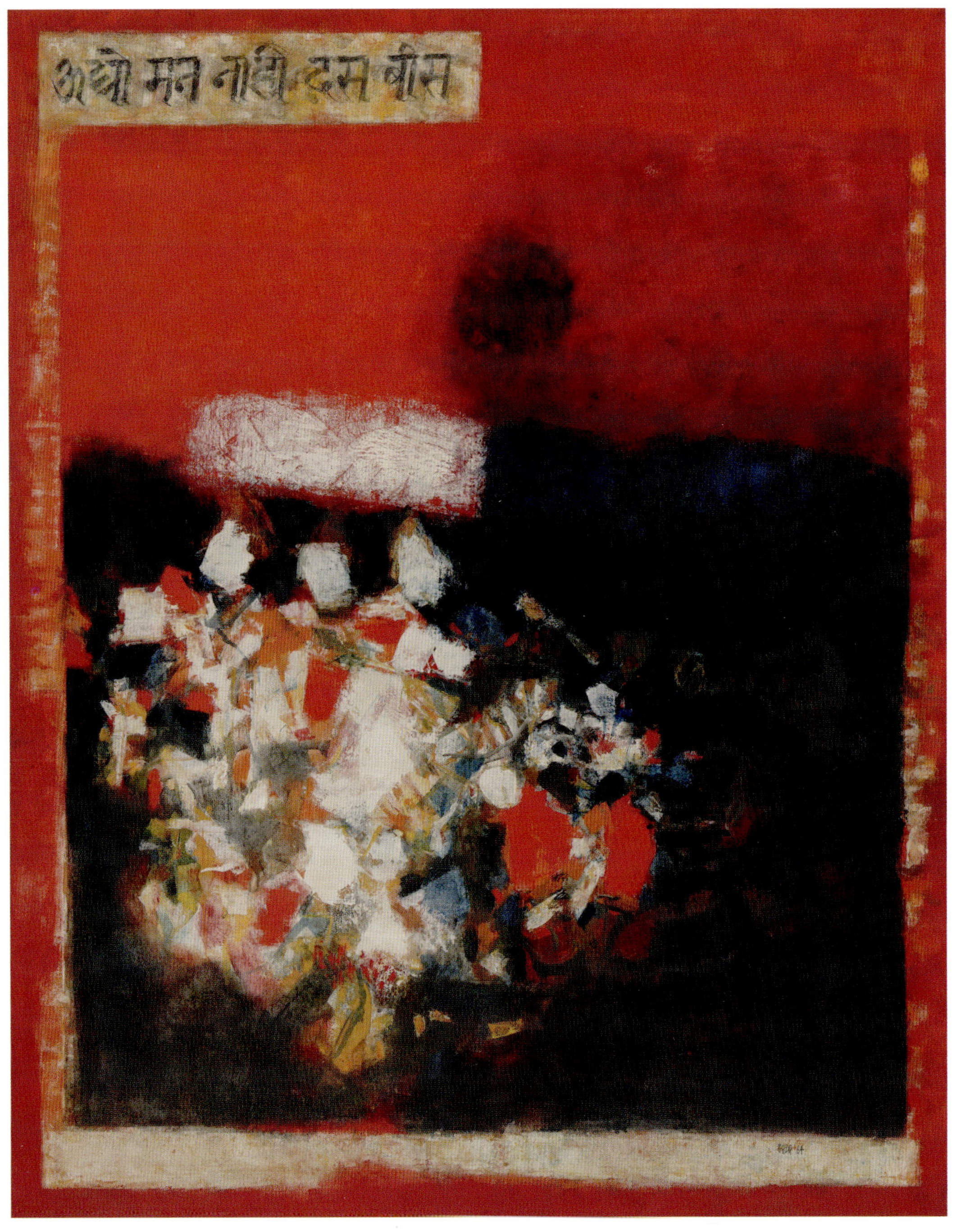

Plate 14.
Udho, Heart Is Not Ten or Twenty, 1964
Oil on canvas
50 × 40 inches (127 × 101.6 cm)

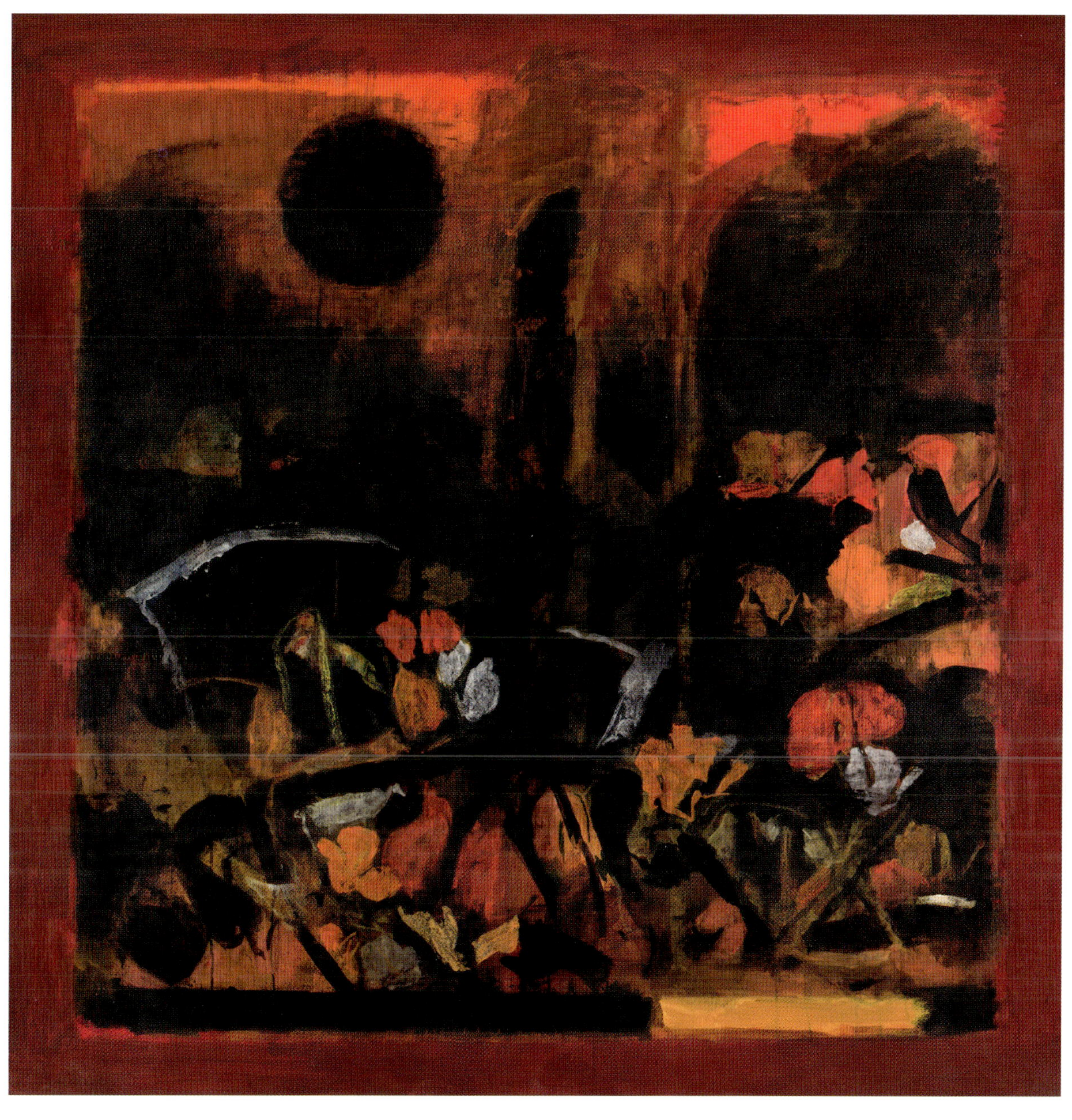

Plate 15.
L'Été '67, 1967
Oil on canvas
59 ¼ × 59 ¼ inches (150.5 × 150.5 cm)

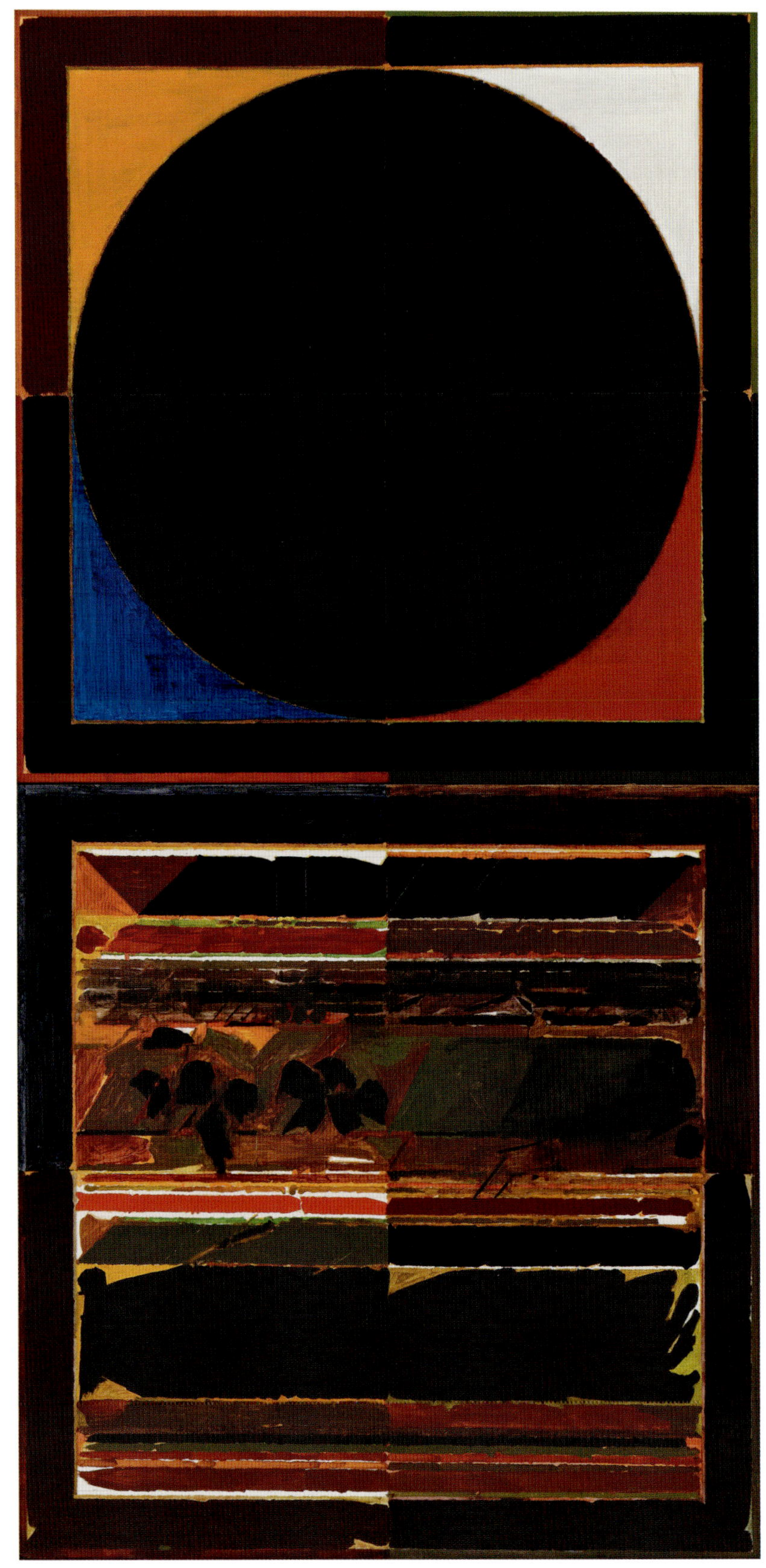

Plate 16.
Bindu La Terre, 1983
Oil on canvas
Two panels, each 63 ¼ × 31 ¼ inches
(160.7 × 79.4 cm)

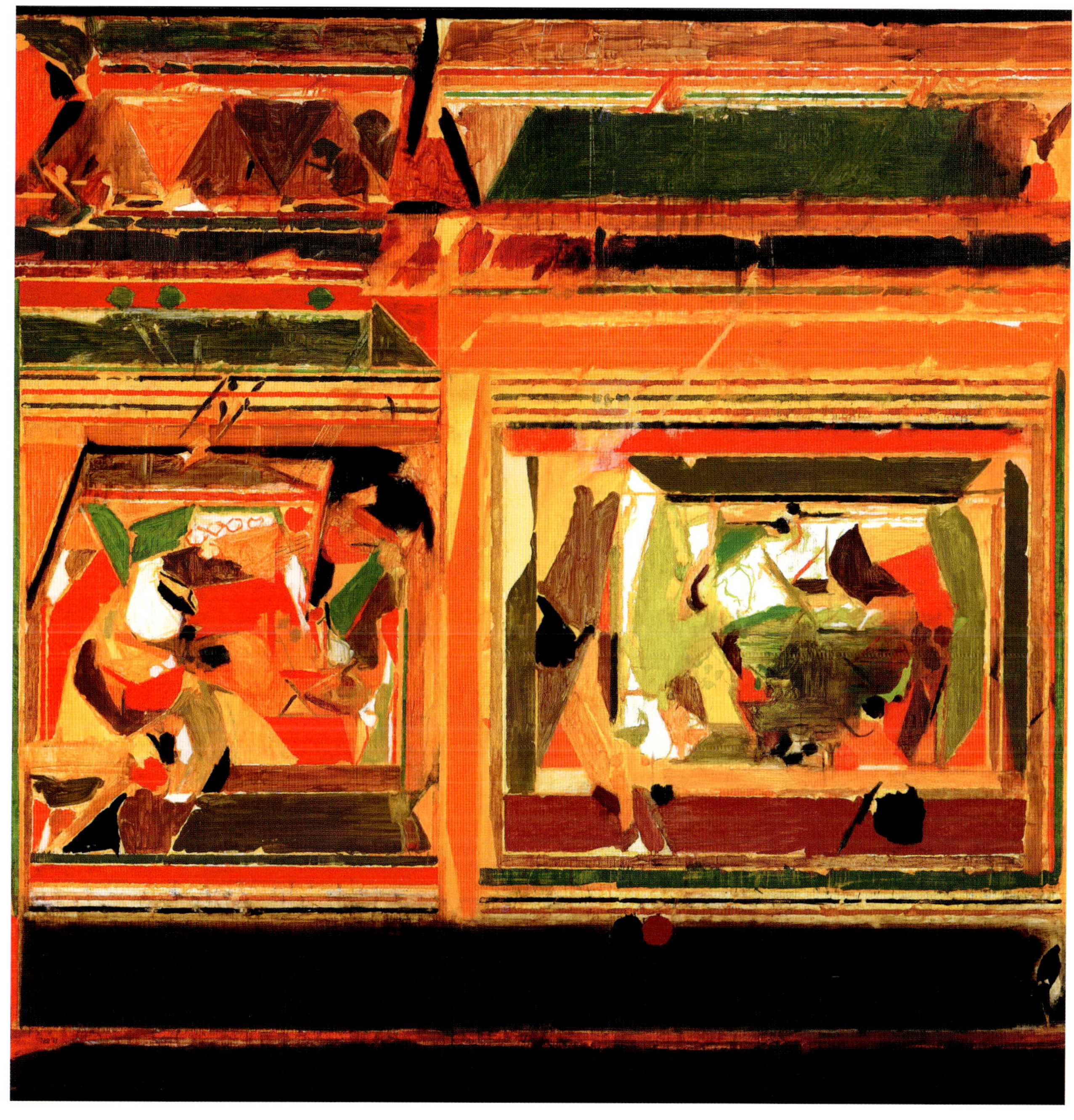

Plate 17.
Rajasthan II, 1983
Oil on canvas
68 ⅞ × 68 ⅞ inches (174.9 × 174.9 cm)

G.R. SANTOSH

Born in Srinagar, Kashmir, 1929–1997
died in Delhi
Lived and worked in Delhi

Gulam Rasool Santosh, like Ram Kumar (plates 7 and 8), Gieve Patel (plates 48–50), and others was a poet and author as well as an accomplished painter. His poetic sensibility can be detected in his paintings through the careful use of color and brushwork to produce forms that hover slightly in front of backgrounds that threaten to envelop them. With Biren De (plates 1 and 2) and others, he turned toward abstraction but did not fully embrace it. Santosh's compositions explore bodily form, growth, and union. Two untitled paintings ten years apart (plates 18 and 19) both convey a stillness within the dynamism of generative, ovoid elements. The Indic religious traditions of Tantra, Kashmiri Shaivism, and Sufism ground all of Santosh's artistic practice.

Santosh was born Gulam Rasool Dar in Srinagar, Kashmir. As a youth, he took up drawing and painting, focusing on landscapes of the mountains and lakes around him. In 1954, a government scholarship enabled him to study in Baroda at Maharaja Sayajirao University, where he worked closely with the figural expressionist painter N.S. Bendre. After a few successful years in Bombay, he settled in Delhi in 1960. He never lost his connection to Kashmiri poetry, landscape, and spiritual traditions.

Santosh's relocation to the capital coincided with an influx of Tibetan exiles, driven out by the Chinese government in 1959 along with the Dalai Lama.[1] Rising interest in the complex geometric mapping found in painted mandalas from the Himalayan region led to the publication of several books, including Ajit Mookerjee's highly influential *Tantra Art: Its Philosophy and Physics* (1966) and *Tantra Asana: A Way to Self-Realization* (1971). Even before these publications, Santosh discovered his own connection to Tantra. After a pilgrimage in 1964 to the ice-formed Shiva lingam (phallic emblem) in the Amarnath cave in southern Kashmir, Santosh began incorporating Kashmiri Shaivism into his work. This eighth-century Tantric philosophy asserts the oneness of all things, and understands the energies of the universe as emanating from Shiva's feminine power of the cosmos, Shakti. The play of Shiva's static consciousness and Shakti's dynamic power establishes and sustains the universe.[2] Santosh's abstracted iconographies began to grow out of his study of this Kashmiri approach to the worship of Shiva. His interest in Tantric imagery emerged from an intellectual and personal commitment: "My paintings are based on the male and female concept of Śiva and Śakti and, therefore, construed as Tantra."[3]

The paintings illustrated here represent one side of Santosh's oeuvre. The dominant ovoid or circular egg form emphasizes the feminine, but the phallic principle is evident in the strong vertical symmetry and vertical elements along the central axis. In other works, Santosh expanded from an abstracted egg or vaginal form to incorporate bodies in union, sometimes with stylized silhouettes of legs, torsos, and heads surrounded by halos or clouds, but more often turning to an upward-pointing triangle for the masculine and a downward-pointing triangle for the feminine (figure 1).

The earlier untitled painting (plate 18) incorporates a central point often called *bindu* (seed) in the Tantric tradition. It forms the center for organic shapes that emerge from it and light—enlightenment—hovers here at its core. Kashmiri Shaivism teaches that each person is already enlightened and needs only to become aware of that enlightenment. This work and the painting of a decade later both explore the idea of oneness with the universe in the subtle shifts between the forms and the background; their potent stillness expresses the combination of Shiva and Shakti in abstracted visual form.

In addition to grounding his work in Indic visual culture, Santosh participated in a wider shift, found in the work of North American artists such as Mark Rothko, Frank Stella, and others who explored geometries and color fields to understand spiritual connections to the universe. Santosh's paintings engage with a larger cultural movement that incorporates the Beat poets, counter-culture filmmakers, and musicians seeking enlightenment through personal explorations of India's spiritual texts and traditions. The resultant works appealed to European and North American collectors similarly participating in a celebration of a timeless, spiritual, and sexually intriguing India.[4]

While Santosh's works can reinforce this stereotyping of the subcontinent, they can also complicate that simplistic view. His oeuvre emerges from a syncretic Kashmiri culture in which Hindu practices developed in dialogue with Islamic Sufi traditions and Mahayana Buddhist practices. Santosh himself came from a Muslim Kashmiri background. He married a Hindu, took her name in place of Dar, and moved comfortably back and forth between poetic Urdu text and modernist oil paint. The choice of a philosophical tradition focused on *oneness* also suggests that Santosh sought solace from the divisive political landscape of post-Nehruvian India. His work seeks out the modern and the universal in a specific religious tradition of the subcontinent. Like many other modernists, Santosh explored art and cultural philosophies outside of his own upbringing. He did not have to look far from home to develop his own modernist idiom, which instead of turning to the secular, grew from religious faith and practice. – RMB

1. Clare Harris, *In the Image of Tibet: Tibetan Painting after 1959* (London: Reaktion Books, 1999).

2. For more on Kashmiri Shaivism, see Peter Heehs, *Indian Religions: A Historical Reader of Spiritual Expression and Experience* (New York: New York University Press, 2002), pp. 243–51; Paul E. Muller-Ortega, *The Triadic Heart of Śiva: Kaula Tantricism of Abhinavagupta in the Non-Dual Shaivism of Kashmir* (Albany: State University of New York Press, 1989).

3. G.R. Santosh, Santosh, *A Decade of Realization* (New Delhi: Chanakya Gallery, 1978), quoted in Frank Thompson, "The Splintered Glass: Painting and Religion in Modern India," *Studies in Religion/ Sciences Religieuses* 10, 2 (Spring 1981), p. 180.

4. Juan Guardiola, "Modern India: An Introduction," in *India Moderna* (Valencia: Institut Valencià d'Art Modern, 2008), p. 349. See also Rick Fields, *How the Swans Came to the Lake: A Narrative History of Buddhism in America* (Boulder, Colorado: Shambala, 1992); Theodore Roszak, *The Making of a Counter Culture: Reflections on the Technocratic Society and Its Youthful Opposition* (Garden City, New York: Doubleday, 1969).

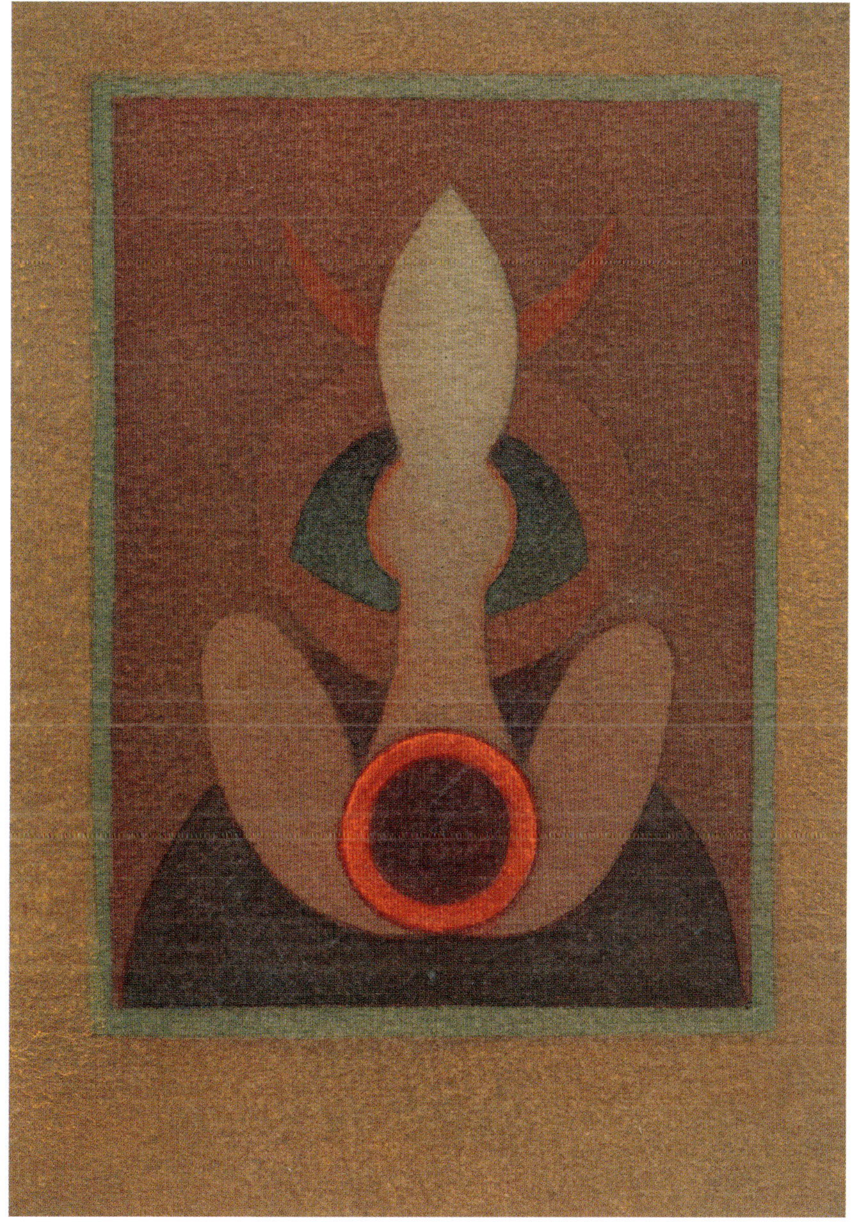

Figure 1.
G.R. Santosh, *Untitled*, 1974
Watercolor on paper
7 ½ × 5 ¼ inches (19.1 × 13.3 cm)

The Chester and Davida Herwitz Collection, Peabody Essex Museum

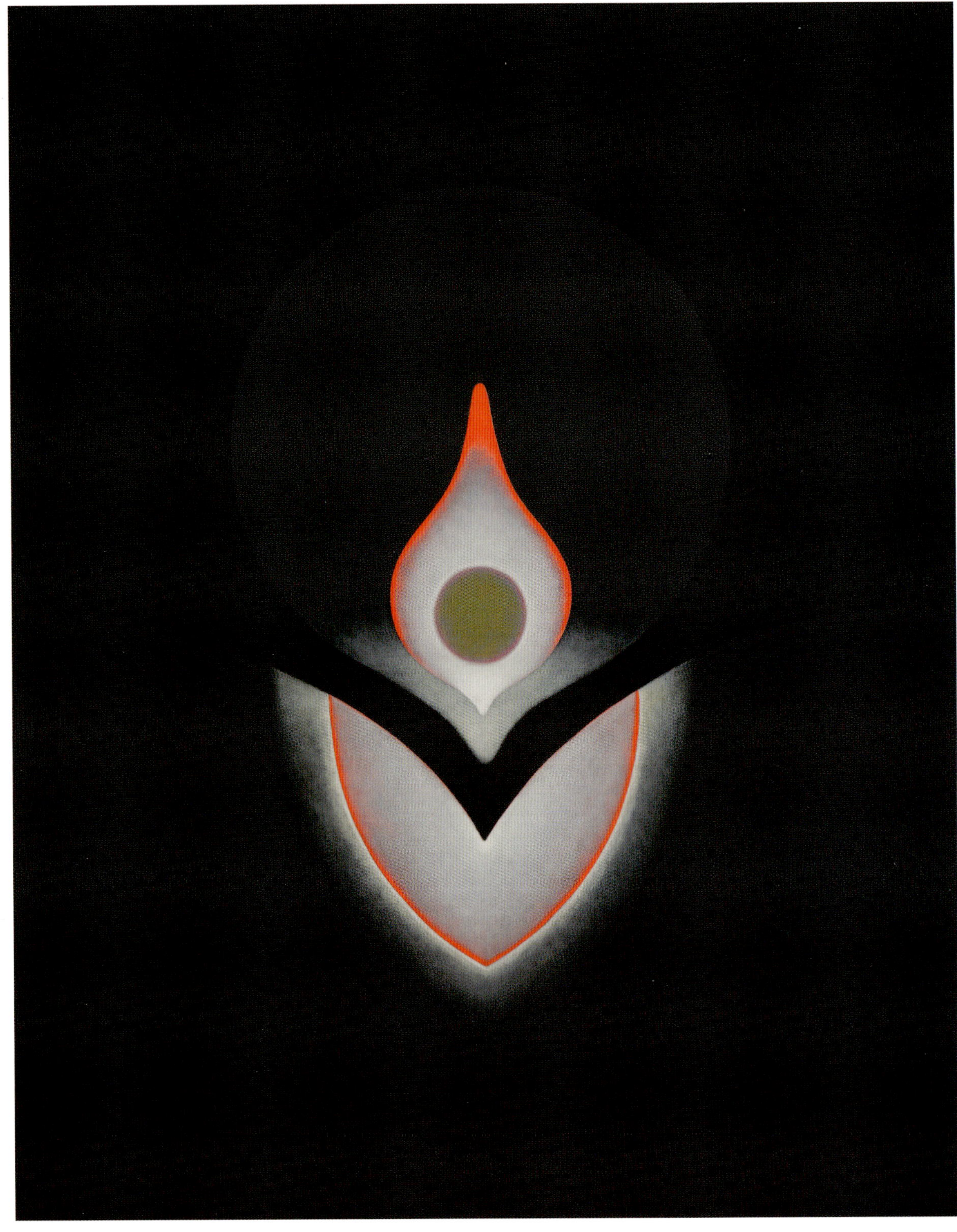

Plate 18.
Untitled, 1973
Oil on canvas
50 × 40 inches (127 × 101.6 cm)

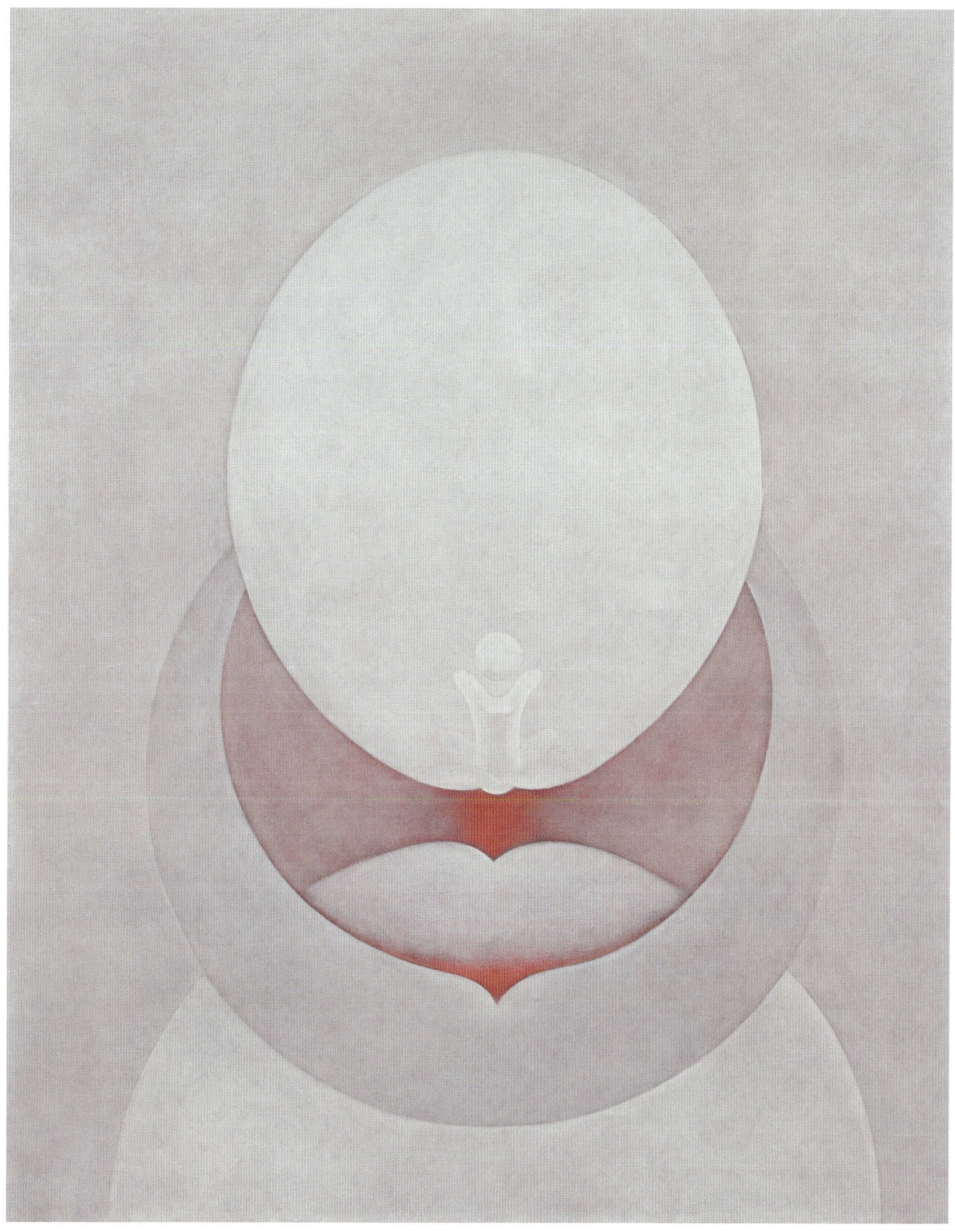

Plate 19.
Untitled, 1983
Oil on canvas
50 × 40 inches (127 × 101.6 cm)

K.G. SUBRAMANYAN

Born in Kuthuparamba, Kerala, 1924
Lives and works in Baroda

Kalpathi Ganapathi Subramanyan's art is playful yet disciplined, grounded in both modernist aesthetics and India's vernacular visual tradition. An emeritus professor of painting in Santiniketan at Visva-Bharati's Kala Bhavan, the art school from which he received his own training from 1944 to 1948, Subramanyan is among the most individual and influential of modern Indian artists. While he was successful from a relatively young age, he is rightly celebrated for his work after 1980—a period that many view as the pinnacle of his career.[1]

Subramanyan was raised in Mahe, a French colonial possession in what is now the state of Kerala.[2] Precocious and surrounded by Indian nationalists fleeing the British colonial state, as a teenager Subramanyan joined a Marxist reading group and the local Rationalist Society before gravitating toward Gandhianism. He became a student leader at Presidency College in Madras during the 1942 Quit India movement. Arrested, he was sentenced to six months in the Alipuram Camp Jail alongside other political prisoners, but their acquaintance served only to disillusion him with politics.

While a student in Madras, he had shown his drawings to the principal of the Art College, who recommended further study. After his conviction barred him from enrollment in state-sponsored universities, Subramanyan sought admission to the art school at Visva-Bharati, a private university that had been set up by the polymath Bengali intellectual Rabindranath Tagore in the village of Santiniketan, West Bengal. Subramanyan enrolled in 1944, and began his training under the uniquely anticolonial art syllabus devised by Nandalal Bose and his colleagues. Bose presided over master classes with craftsmen, encouraged collective work and collaboration among students, and required them to study across media. Subramanyan thrived under this system and became close with some of his teachers, including Ramkinkar Baij and Benodebehari Mukherjee. In his last year of college, Subramanyan assisted Mukherjee in his landmark 1947 mural *Medieval Saints* (Hindi Bhavan, Visva-Bharati, Santiniketan).[3]

Subramanyan took these lessons with him to the new Faculty of Fine Arts at the Maharaja Sayajirao University in Baroda, Gujarat, where he began to teach painting in 1951. Although he left several times—for a year at the Slade School in London, for a period as a designer for the Handlooms Board, and for a Rockefeller fellowship to New York—Subramanyan was a guiding influence in Baroda until 1980, when he moved back to Santiniketan to be a professor. Formally employed in the department of painting, Subramanyan was also an accomplished printmaker, illustrator, muralist, and sculptor, as well as one of the most articulate art theorists in India.[4] In these decades, Subramanyan produced disciplined and formally driven paintings and graphic works, on the one hand, and toys (see Bean, "Midnight's Children," figure 1) and narrative relief sculptures (see Zitzewitz, figure 7) that engaged with craft traditions and collaborative practice, on the other. For all its diversity, his work in this period is characterized by a decisive split between high modernism and vernacular culture.

His most consequential single work from this time is the 1963 mural in Lucknow at the Ravindralaya Theatre, which was named for Rabindranath Tagore.[5] Eighty-one feet long and nine feet high, *The King of the Dark Chamber* is based on Tagore's allegorical morality play denouncing the corruption of excessive pride. Constructed from thirteen thousand ceramic pieces, some standard prefabricated units and others individually designed, the relief is effectively a sculptural collage. This highly ambitious work combines Subramanyan's deployment of the high-modernist grid—seen throughout his subsequent painting—with the enormous respect he held for the cultural legacy of Bengal. The mural is one of his most accessible works from this time; its strong narrative tempers the artist's astringent impulses.

This synthesis of narrative accessibility and formal discipline came to characterize Subramanyan's best work and is especially evident in what is widely lauded as the artist's most inventive turn: the reverse painting on acrylic that he began during a 1977 stint as a visiting artist at Santiniketan (plates 20 and 21). Beginning in 1980, Subramanyan produced works of art that are formally and conceptually complex but also winning, playful, and deeply integrated with the visual culture of his adopted home of West Bengal. His paintings, which draw on various traditions of popular painting, take a satirical look at middle-class life. Typically, as in *Girl Eating Rasagolla* (plate 20), they lampoon and eroticize domestic plenitude, showing voluptuous housewives at tables overloaded with fruit.

The animals that star in Subramanyan's paintings are important subjects across his oeuvre, serving as symbols of play, domesticity, and desire. Here, they are portrayed in frames within the frame—a compositional device that Subramanyan has used frequently to construct interior spaces out of gridded planes. In *Parsi Couple* (plate 23), a hunched and morose man and woman sit with their dog in a room whose walls seem ready to collapse. Floating over their heads, the head of an animal—perhaps a dog, perhaps a bull—lends an ominous allegorical possibility to what might have been (but is surely not) a portrait of friends.

The complex painting *The Great Show with Beasts and Goddess 2* (plate 22) belongs to a series of paintings of the goddess Durga in her most represented terrible form, killing a buffalo demon. Subramanyan was fascinated by the goddess, who is an icon of both the elemental contest between good and evil and its transcendence. The Durga image captures the sense of the mutability of form and identity that Subramanyan claimed was a common principle of Indian visual culture. – KZ

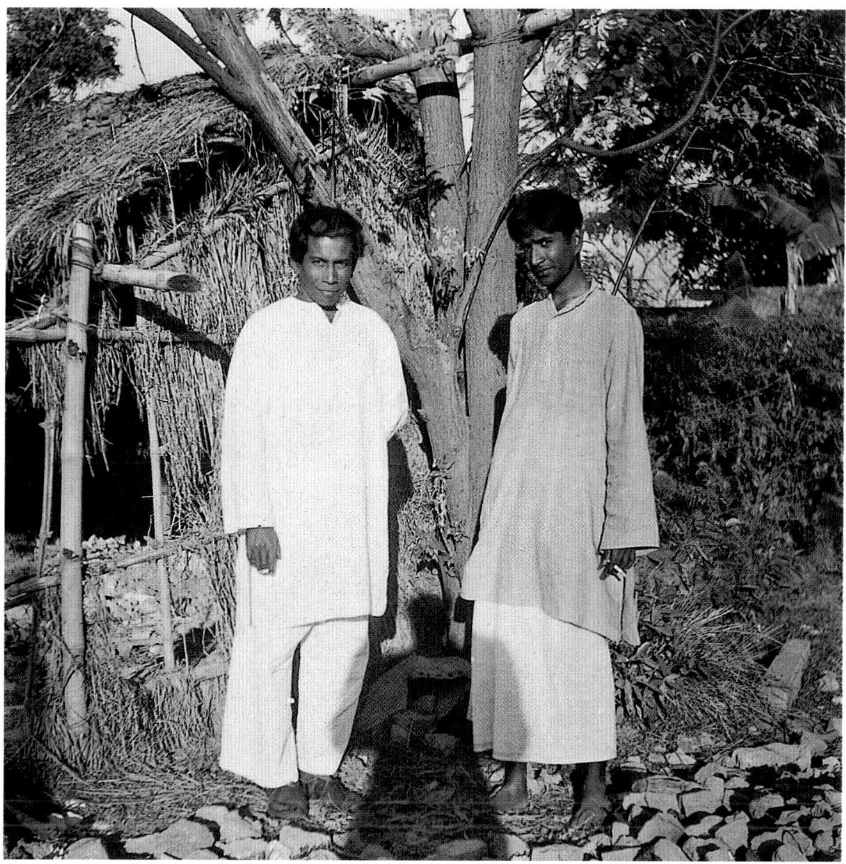

Figure 1.
Ramkinkar Baij and K.G. Subramanyan in Santiniketan, 1947
Collection of K.G. Subramanyan

1. See Geeta Kapur, "Mid-Century Ironies: K.G. Subramanyan," in *When Was Modernism: Essays on Contemporary Cultural Practice* (New Delhi: Tulika Press, 2000), which builds on her *K.G. Subramanyan* (New Delhi: Lalit Kala Akademi, 1987), pp. 87–144.

2. R. Siva Kumar, *K.G. Subramanyan: A Retrospective* (New Delhi: National Gallery of Modern Art, 2003).

3. Jayanta Chakrabarti, R. Siva Kumar, and Arun Kumar Nag, *The Santiniketan Murals* (Calcutta: Seagull Books in association with Visva-Bharati, 1995).

4. See Subramanyan's books of essays, all published by Seagull Books, Calcutta: *Moving Focus* (1978; reprinted 2006), *The Living Tradition: Perspectives on Modern Indian Art* (1987), *The Creative Circuit* (1992), and *The Magic of Making: Essays on Art and Culture* (2007).

5. Discussed in Nilima Sheikh, "A Post-Independence Initiative in Art," in Gulammohammed Sheikh, ed., *Contemporary Art in Baroda* (New Delhi: Tulika Press, 1997), pp. 53–143.

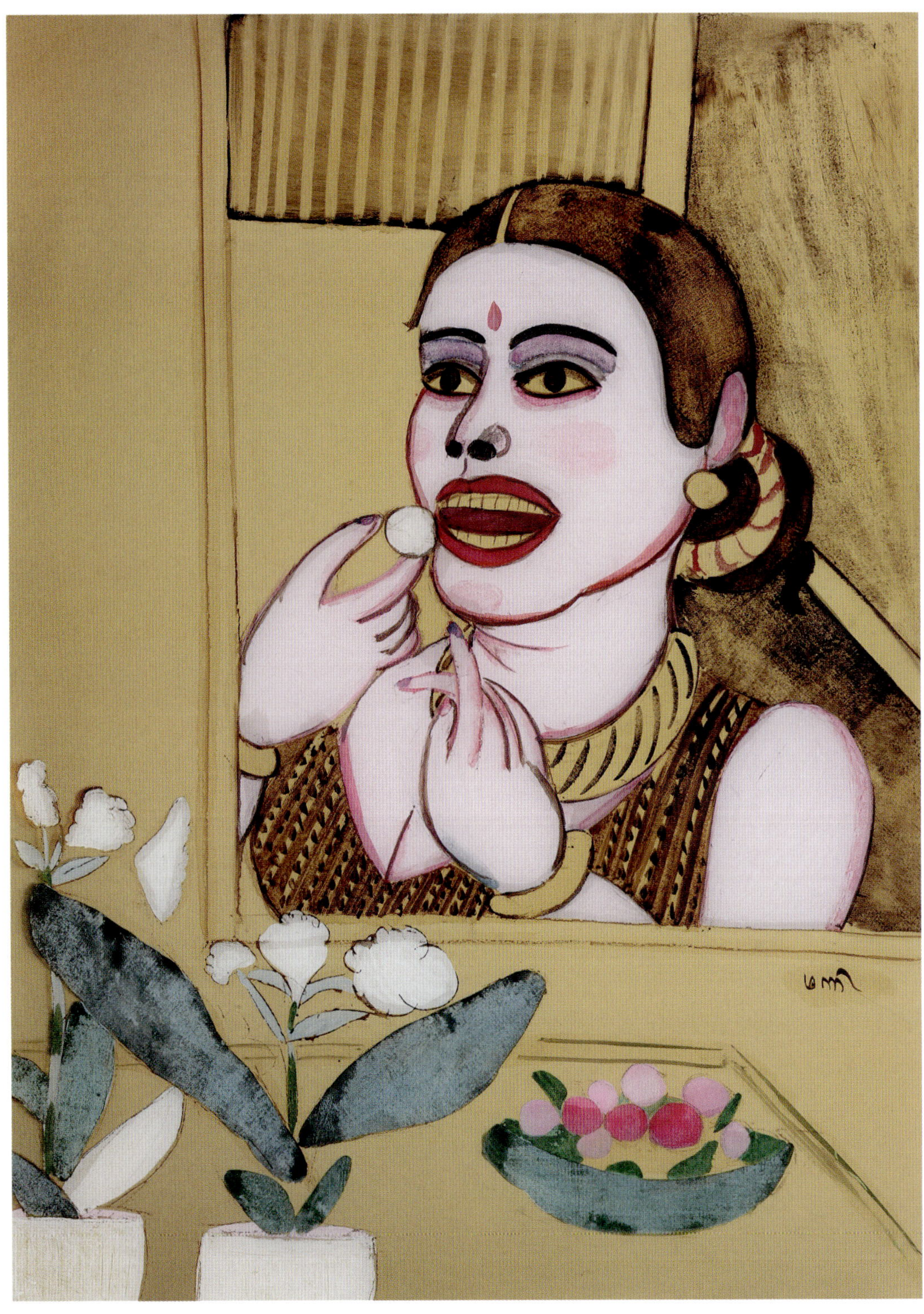

Plate 20.
Girl Eating Rasagolla, 1980
Reverse painting on acrylic
24 × 18 inches (61 × 45.7 cm)

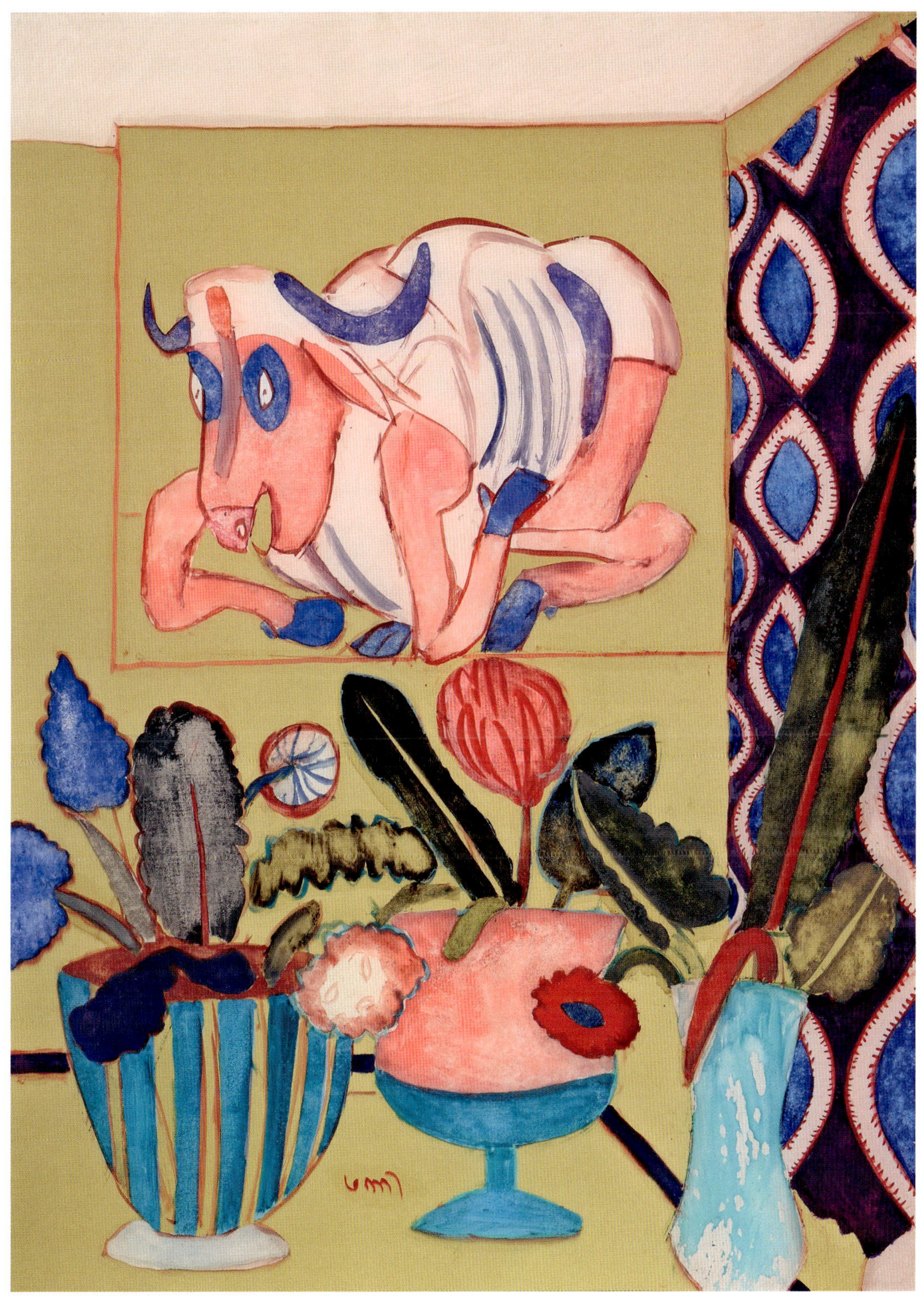

Plate 21.
Pots of Flowers and Pink Cow, 1980
Reverse painting on acrylic
24 × 18 inches (61 × 45.7 cm)

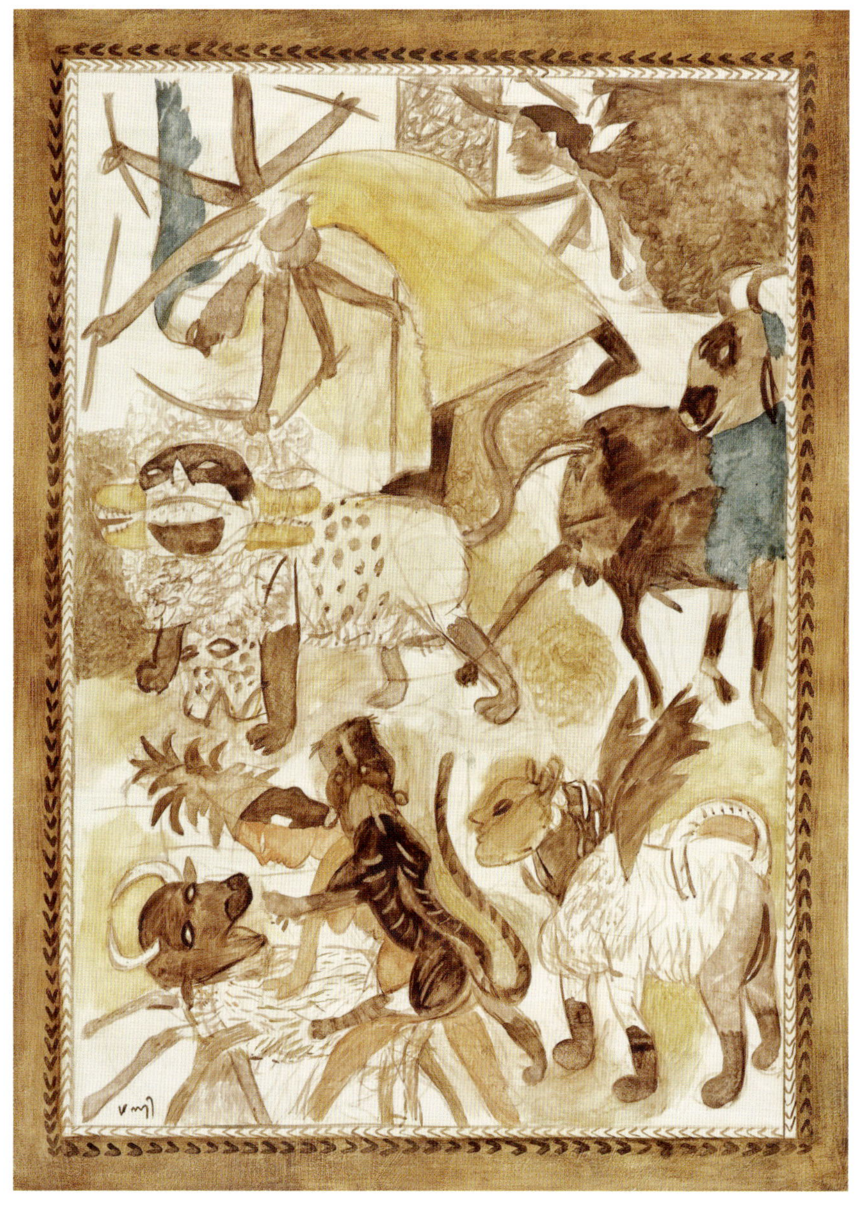

Plate 22.
The Great Show with Beasts and Goddess 2, 1989
Watercolor on paper
29 ¾ × 21 ¾ inches (75.6 × 55.3 cm)

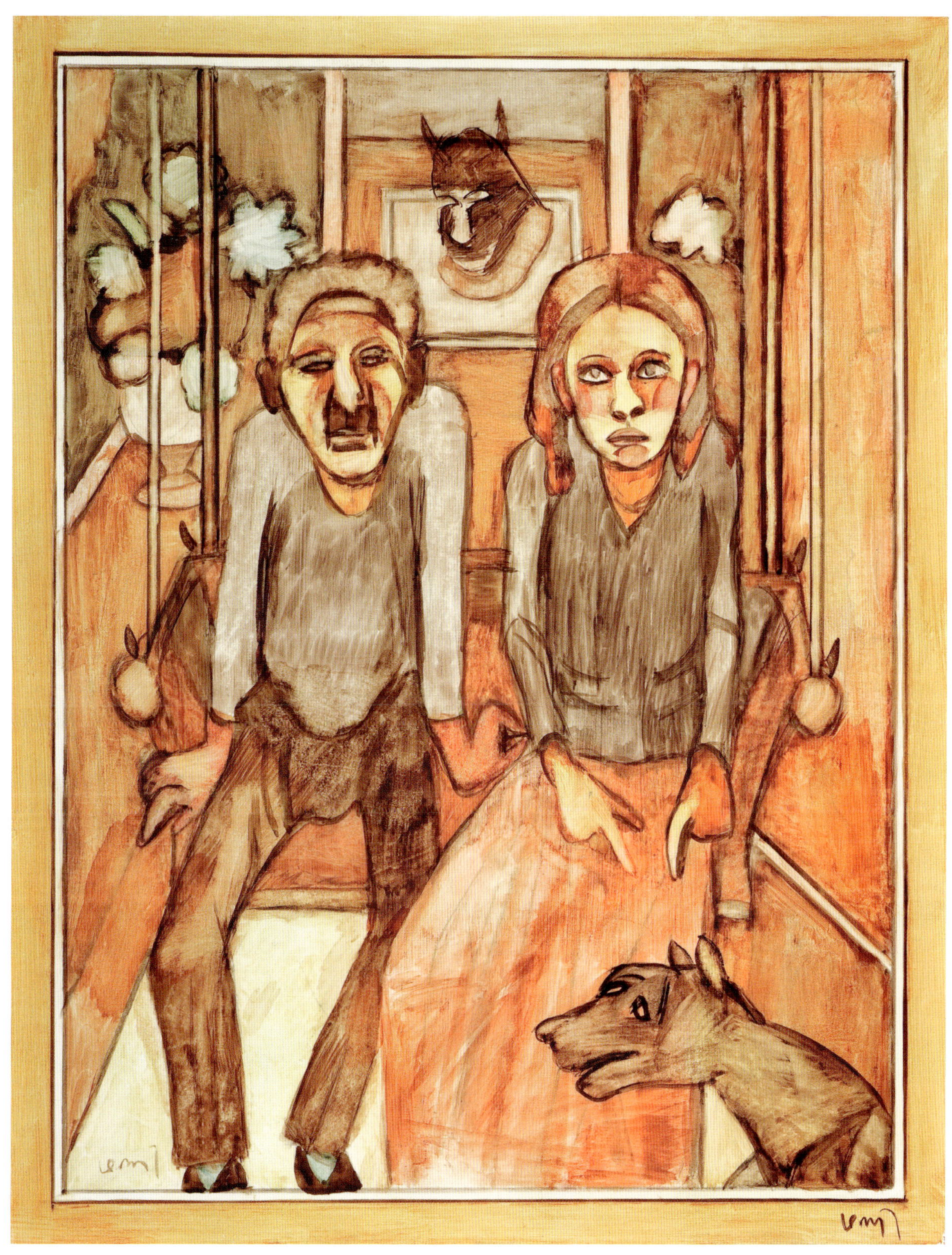

Plate 23.
Parsi Couple, 1990
Watercolor and varnish on paper
28 × 22 inches (71.1 × 55.9 cm)

MIDNIGHT'S CHILDREN

The Second Generation

Manjit Bawa

Bikash Bhattacharjee

Rameshwar Broota

Jogen Chowdhury

K. Laxma Goud

Bhupen Khakhar

Nasreen Mohamedi

Gieve Patel

Ganesh Pyne

Gulammohammed Sheikh

Arpita Singh

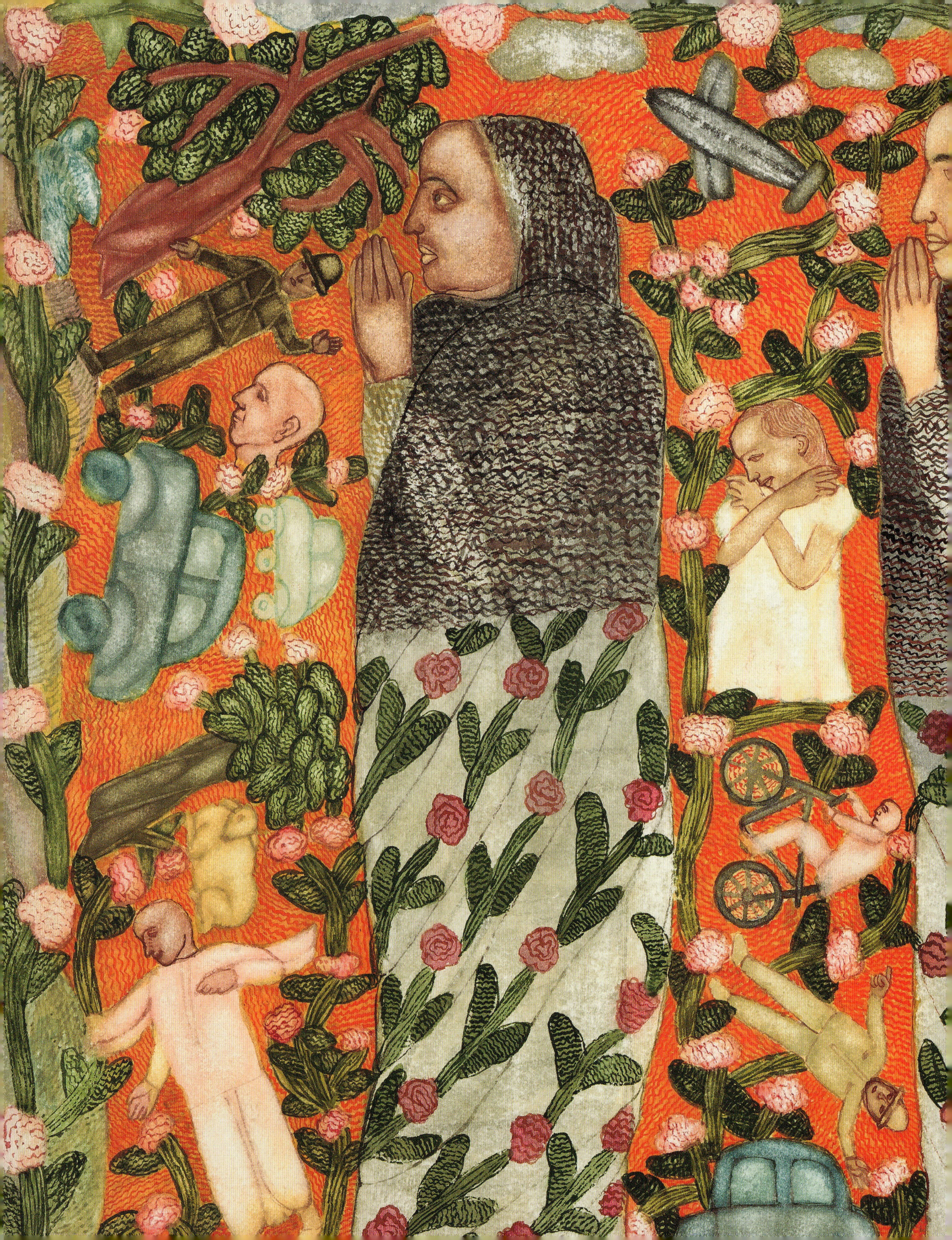

MIDNIGHT'S CHILDREN: THE SECOND GENERATION

Susan S. Bean

In the 1970s, a new generation of artists began to make waves. They had grown up as citizens of a sovereign nation during a time when the euphoria and idealism of independence faded steadily in the face of India's gargantuan challenges. The new nation's democratic constitution and centrally planned economy had given all its citizens a voice in their future, a promise of decreasing poverty, and greater access to education and other social services. Despite the national commitment to social equality, gaps were immense between the interests and needs of the wealthy, powerful elite and the vast majority of the poor; between urban centers and the sweeping rural hinterland; between the rights and advantages of men and the subservient place of women; between the well educated and the illiterate masses; between Hindus and religious minorities; and between privileged high castes and exploited low castes. Existing fissures, often manipulated for political gain, had broadened. Tensions between Hindus and Muslims, unresolved by the partition of British India, erupted with increasing frequency. Local and regional interests marshaled vote blocks to become centers of political power. Civil servants, politicians, industrialists, and farmers all sought to profit by gaming the system.

Artists, mostly urban intellectuals from many different religious, linguistic, and regional backgrounds, shared a commitment to personal creativity and a cosmopolitan outlook. They strongly supported India's founding ideals of social inclusiveness, secular government, equal justice, and economic opportunity. This postindependence generation was acutely aware of being caught between those ideals and stark realities. Gieve Patel (plates 48–50), painter, poet, and critic, described India as a "country almost always on the brink of dismemberment...that seems all the time on the point of falling apart."[1] He and many of his contemporaries turned away from the transcendent themes of the "Pathbreakers" generation—modernist visual cosmologies and universal, epic humanism—toward highly subjective approaches to painting. While working with modernist fundamentals of form and color, these artists made explicit links to classical Indian court painting and popular art as platforms for developing strongly individualistic practices. They were committed to the representation of local and personal experience.

Although there was no organized movement and artists took their own paths, the shift was widespread and discernible across the country—in Delhi and Bombay, to the

Detail of Plate 61.
Arpita Singh, *The Worshippers*, 1989

east in Calcutta and Santiniketan, and in the south where the artists' commune Cholamandal was established in 1965. Also in the 1960s, Baroda's art college, founded at Maharaja Sayajirao University shortly after independence, emerged as a vital center. Without roots in colonial curriculum, its art faculty and students were free to explore new directions. The university hired K.G. Subramanyan (plates 20–23) and the sculptor Sankho Chaudhuri from Santiniketan's art school at Visva-Bharati University, north of Calcutta, a university that was dedicated to educational practice simultaneously cosmopolitan and rooted in its locale. Subramanyan brought to Baroda his deep respect for the local, indigenous, living arts practiced by lineage-based artists all across India—painters, potters, sculptors, weavers, and embroiderers (figure 1). This infusion of aesthetic and cultural ideals from the preindependence early modernism of Santiniketan inspired and supported the new directions that Baroda students would take, making local realities the center of their art (figure 2).

The increasing salience of gender in the art community also served as an impetus for this turn toward the personal. The freedom movement had given women unprecedented roles in public life and the new nation made them full citizens, with voting rights and equal justice. Women's participation in the art community was small, but increased steadily. In the second generation, women artists like Nasreen Mohamedi (plates 44–47) and Arpita Singh (plates 58–61), as well as B. Prabha, Anjolie Ela Menon (figure 3), and Madhvi Parekh, made places for themselves in the art world. The nature of femininity and masculinity, of interest to first-generation artists such as M.F. Husain (see page 87), took on new importance, for example, for Rameshwar Broota (plates 30–32) sourcing masculinity from his own body; Singh, responding to her housewifely fantasies and fears; Bikash Bhattacharjee (plates 27–29) probing the connections between divine and mortal feminine powers; and Bhupen Khakhar (plates 41–43) projecting homosexual desires and anxieties.

A few second-generation artists in Baroda were especially influential in shaping this shift to the local and personal. Gulammohammed Sheikh (plates 55–57), who had studied at Baroda, joined the faculty on his return from three years in Great Britain. Initially hired to teach art history, he brought his deep interest in Western and Indian art to visual narrative. His lectures, articles, and conversations with colleagues had an impact on students and other artists in Baroda and beyond. Khakhar, who completed a master's degree at the art college in 1964 and lived and worked in Baroda, also became a key player in the art scene. A part-time chartered accountant, he felt as connected to the city's working-class culture as to the intellectual life of the art community. From his position straddling these two subcultures, he developed a style centered around deceptively unsophisticated figuration and garish colors adopted from popular art and décor that vividly captured the taste of ordinary people in a way that was not merely about them, but of them. Mohamedi, who joined the art college faculty in 1972, pursued a practice outwardly at odds with her cohort, dedicated as it was to the pursuit of pure spatial geometries in black and white. Yet, she was esteemed by her peers and beloved as a teacher for the personal intensity of her practice, the purity of her modernist aesthetic, and the complete integration of her art practice with her way of life. The critic, historian, and curator Geeta Kapur, a member of this generation, extended Baroda's influence through her writing. She helped forge a new path for

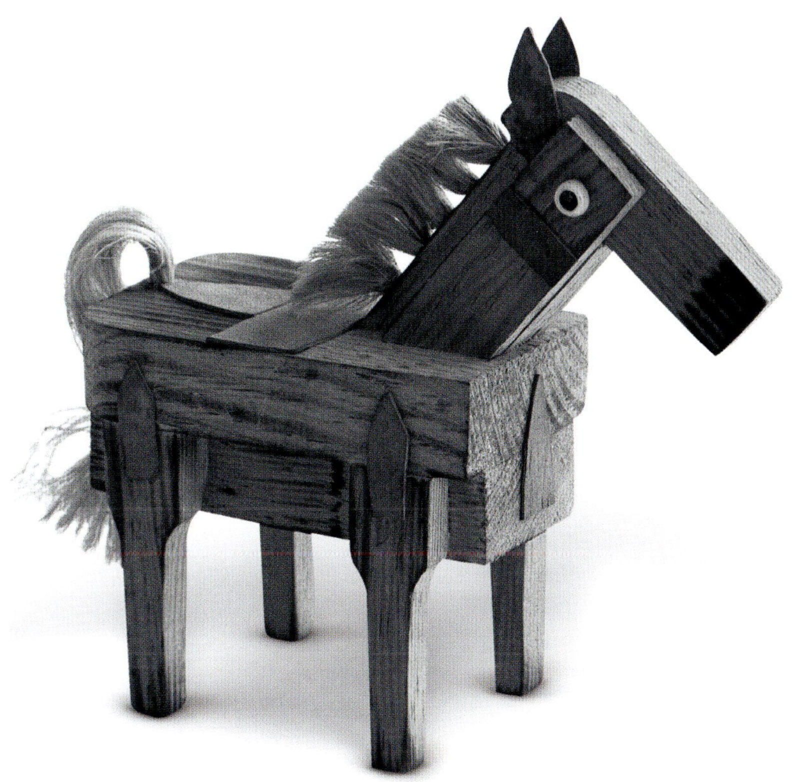

Figure 1.
K.G. Subramanyan,
Toy, ca. 1970
Wood and mixed media
Collection of the Baroda Fine Arts Faculty

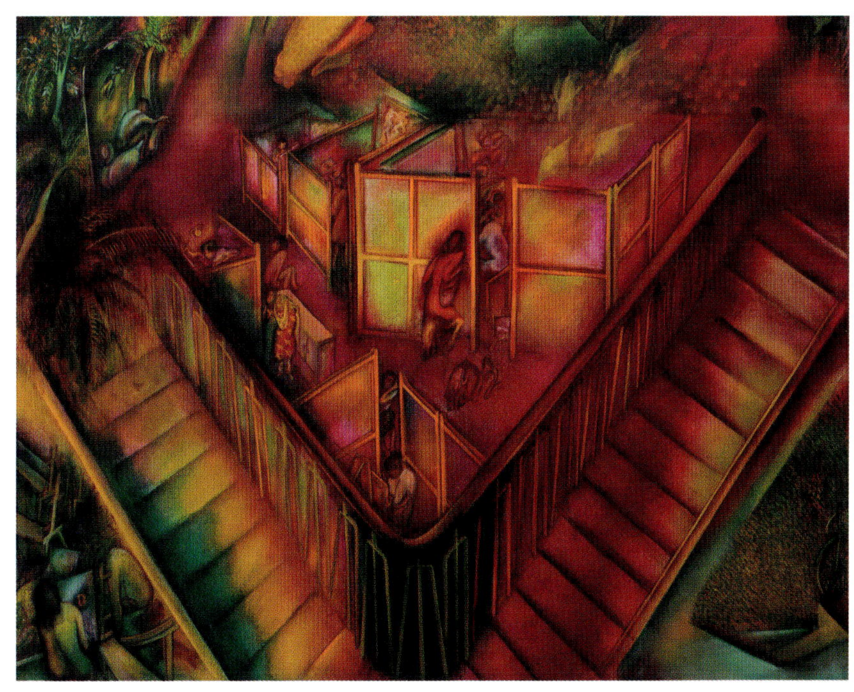

Figure 2.
Gulammohammed Sheikh,
Passing Angel, A Life, Summer Diary,
1985–87
(Plate 56, detail of students' studios at Baroda's art college)

Indian art criticism, linking it to a transnational discourse while probing deeply into the practices of Indian artists, articulating the aesthetic aims of this generation and its forebears, and helping to chart the course for a socially and politically committed art community in India.[2] The increasingly lively debates on art were given new outlets in *Vrishchik* (Scorpion), which Sheikh and Khakhar edited and published in Baroda from 1969 to 1973, and later in the *Journal of Art and Ideas*, edited by Kapur and her colleagues and published in Delhi from 1982 to 1999.

Artists of this generation in Baroda and beyond confronted the human figure with new intensity, determined to explore innovative approaches. Broota, using his body as model, sought to represent the contradictions of modern man—bewildered, yet strong. K. Laxma Goud (plates 37–40) drew the people of his native village, giving them sturdy, if sometimes ravaged, bodies, and lavishing faithful and laborious detail on their clothing and ornaments. His drawings are like ritual offerings, invoking the warmth, eroticism, and authenticity of the people who have been the cornerstones of his life. Khakhar, Singh, Manjit Bawa (plates 24–26), and Jogen Chowdhury (plates 33–36) jettisoned all deference to anatomical correctness, in part to free themselves of its roots in colonial pedagogy. Bawa composed his figures from fluid shapes emanating from brushstrokes and meticulously contoured in his signature neon colors. Chowdhury created sagging, rotund forms as send-ups of the Bengali middle class, skewering their love of money, idleness, and sweets. Khakhar developed a willfully naïve figuration to impart an informal, down-home intimacy and whimsical sincerity to his portrayals of friends, family, and neighbors. These artists and others reinvented figural form in dialogue with the postcolonial conundrums that structured their lives.

Second-generation artists also retooled pictorial space for its potential to tell stories. Painting in India, as elsewhere, had long been a favorite medium for storytelling, especially to present episodes from history and religious lore. In the "Pathbreakers" generation, artists such as Husain and Subramanyan charted new directions in their modernist, idiosyncratic reinterpretations of mythologies. Their younger colleagues made still more radical assaults on pictorial space, revolutionizing visual narrative by adapting traditional forms to express the conditions of their lives. This movement was most powerfully articulated in Baroda by Sheikh and Khakhar, within an art network that extended among others to Patel in Bombay, Vivan Sundaram and Singh in Delhi, and farther afield in Calcutta in the work of Bhattacharjee and Ganesh Pyne (plates 51–54). They privileged personal experience and local realities from intensely subjective positions, combining autobiographical and descriptive imagery. The results are compositions so particularized that viewers often cannot tap into the narrative intentions. Instead, the artists intended to lure viewers into the picture space by intriguing them with juxtapositions of imagery that they might use to make up their own stories, becoming collaborators in the creative process. "Midnight's Children" established pictorial space as a deeply contemplative arena in which to reconsider perceptions of people and their place in the world.

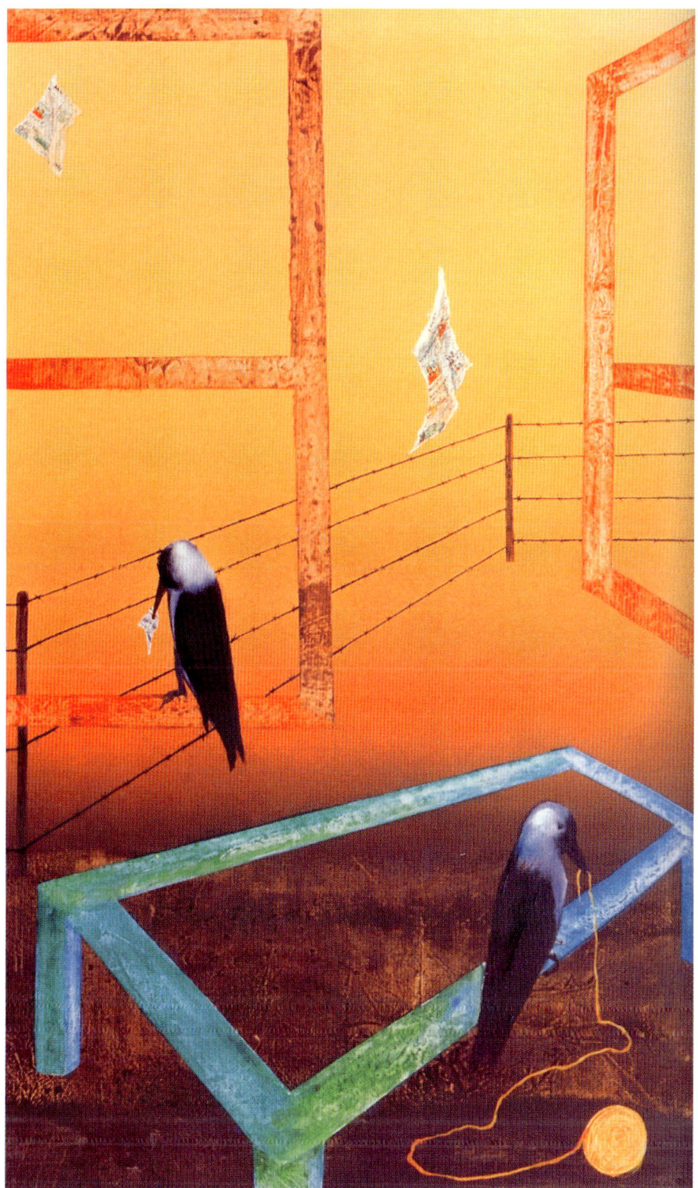

Figure 3.
Anjolie Ela Menon, *November*, 2004
Oil on fiberboard
36 × 24 inches (91.4 × 61 cm)
Peabody Essex Museum, Gift of Aicon Gallery, 2004

1. Gieve Patel, "Contemporary Indian Painting," *Daedalus* 118, 4 (Fall 1989), p. 176.

2. See especially Geeta Kapur, *Contemporary Indian Artists* (New Delhi: Vikas Publishing House, 1978), and *When Was Modernism: Essays on Contemporary Cultural Practice in India* (New Delhi: Tulika Press, 2000).

MANJIT BAWA

Born in Dhuri, Punjab, 1941–2008
died in Delhi
Lived and worked in Delhi

In 1979, at Dhoomimal Gallery in New Delhi, Manjit Bawa showed a group of paintings that were hailed as a stunning synthesis of his earlier figural work and recent experiments with abstract, colorful organic shapes on a flat monochrome ground. The artist J. Swaminathan, who wrote the catalogue essay, called the exhibition a breakthrough and Bawa "a painter of true significance on the Indian scene."[1] In the new work, Bawa composed figures of biotic shapes forming oddly elongated limbs on softly rounded bodies. Creatures in unexpected bold hues emerge from the action of the brush with no nod to anatomical study.

Krishna and the Cows (plate 24) exhibits some refinements of the new style. The shapes, weirdly unnatural and disquieting, have become surprisingly lyrical in their placement and juxtapositions. In the early 1980s, Bawa fulfilled an ambition he set for himself in reaction to art-school exercises exhorting students to emulate the work of Western and Indian masters: he created his own figural form, distinct from the work of other artists. Drawing and plein-air sketching were central to this project, and Bawa's accumulated archive attests to an ongoing evolution. Even after achieving his goal, he continued to hone the forms.[2] *Krishna and the Cows* depicts the deity as a flute player—a subject type that became a recurring favorite. Bawa, himself a flautist, felt an affinity with Krishna the cowherd playing to his flock, as he did with Ranjha, the flute-playing Punjabi folk hero. But, Bawa's musical proficiency created a deeper connection for him between music and painting. He habitually painted while listening to Indian and Sufi classics, and he strove to transfer the rhythms of the music to canvas. He also believed that painting was akin to playing music in that one returned to the same melody or composition over and over, creating a deeper, more fulfilling, awareness.[3] Bawa deployed his repertoire of images, whether deities or animals, like religious icons, formally placed and centered on the canvas for the viewer's contemplation.

Equally vital to the effect of Bawa's work is his brilliant play with color. His childhood memories of color were strong: green paddy fields, blue waters of the Beas River; bold, strong hues of the local embroidered *phulkari* shawls, the riot of color during the spring festival of Holi.[4] While still a young artist, he consciously struggled to harness these experiences in his work. After art school, Bawa went to London where he specialized in serigraphy. For a period, he earned his living in a silkscreening studio and later he taught the technique. But, his attachment was to painting. His mastery of serigraphy instilled an appreciation of the power of luminous pure color and sharply delineated forms. Nonetheless, it was not until 1973 that he began to use flat color in his paintings.[5]

Bawa remembered vividly how the conscious manipulation of color emerged for him as an artist:

> my first encounter with the colour red… [came] at the end of a long day's trek…. Before my eyes I saw a sight I will never forget—brilliantly hued Flame of the Forest blossoms! These glorious *tesu* [flowers] seemed to be spraying red all over the barren rocky landscape. The evening's last red-orange rays lit up the entire stretch of area into a volcano of violent red. Instantly charged, I took out my sketchbook…but…I could not get it right…experimenting for many more years with different shades of red—cadmium, rose madder, scarlet, vermillion, post-box, Indian red, until finally it came to be a part of my oeuvre.[6]

Dharma and the God (plate 25) exemplifies the astonishing potency of color in Bawa's work. The flat, monochromatic ground creates simultaneously a sense of void and a sensation of color as cosmic plentitude. The figures appear to be in colorless white, yet their contours, features, and volume are made up of delicate applications of many hues. The subject of the painting is the story of the weeping bull, the personification of Dharma (universal order, righteousness). Three legs (representing austerity, cleanliness, and mercy) have been cut off by Kaliyuga (the current age of degeneration) and Dharma stands trembling upon the remaining leg, truth.[7] In Bawa's rendering, a deity sits astride the bull facing the viewer, like a religious icon. Here, as in much of his work, the artist has translated the stories he grew up with into an individual vision, aesthetic and numinous.

An untitled painting from 1987 (plate 26) exemplifies the style he sought to achieve. Set against an enveloping deep blue firmament, at once a vast emptiness and a strong presence, Krishna triumphs over the snake demon Kaliya, who succumbs and becomes Krishna's devotee. But, the story is subordinated, sublimated to Bawa's study of color and form. Krishna's body, composed of two blue sinuous forms modeled to impart volume, stretches across a multitude of similarly tubular, delicately shaded, complexly colored serpentine heads. The narrative and figural references are made into a substratum for aesthetic assertion. In conveying his purpose, Bawa liked to cite Rabindranath Tagore's assertion that the visible world is just a vast procession of forms and that the artist's goal is to capture the play of forms, not for any emotional or intellectual purpose, but simply for its own sake.[8] – SSB

1. J. Swaminathan, *Manjit Bawa* (New Delhi: Dhoomimal Gallery, 1979).

2. Aman Nath, "Manjit Bawa," *Swagat*, April 1985, p. 23.

3. Manjit Bawa, *Manjit Bawa* (as told to Ina Puri) (Mumbai: Sakshi Gallery, 2002), pp. 8–12.

4. Manjit Bawa, *Manjit Bawa in His Own Words* (as told to Ina Puri) (New Delhi: Roli Books, 2000), p. 13.

5. Geeti Sen, *Image and Imagination: Five Contemporary Artists in India* (Ahmedabad: Mapin Publishing, 1996), p. 79.

6. Bawa, *Manjit Bawa*, pp. 8, 10.

7. Sen, p. 95.

8. Bawa, *Manjit Bawa*, p. 6.

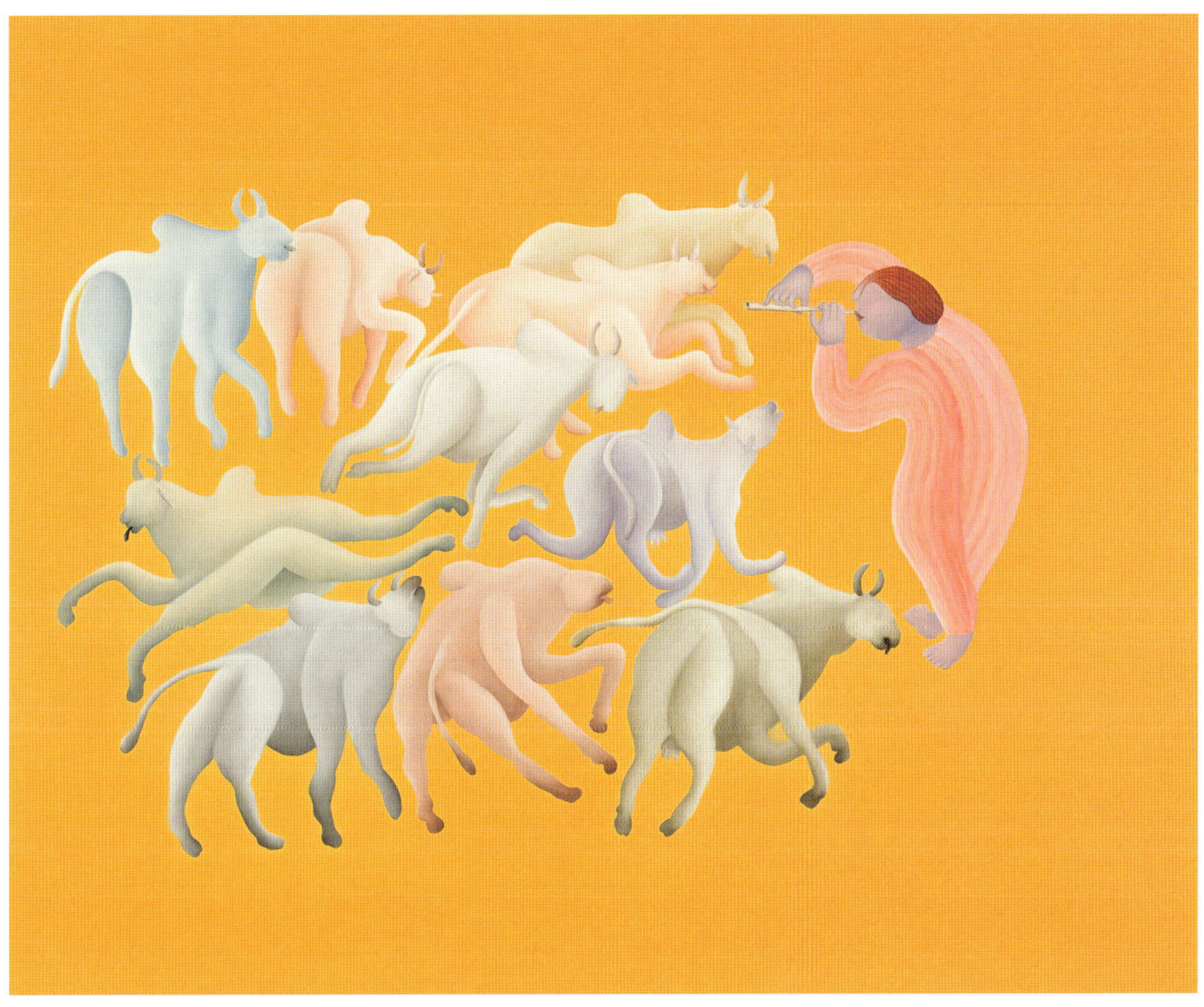

Plate 24.
Krishna and the Cows, 1981
Oil on canvas
48 × 60 inches (121.9 × 152.4 cm)

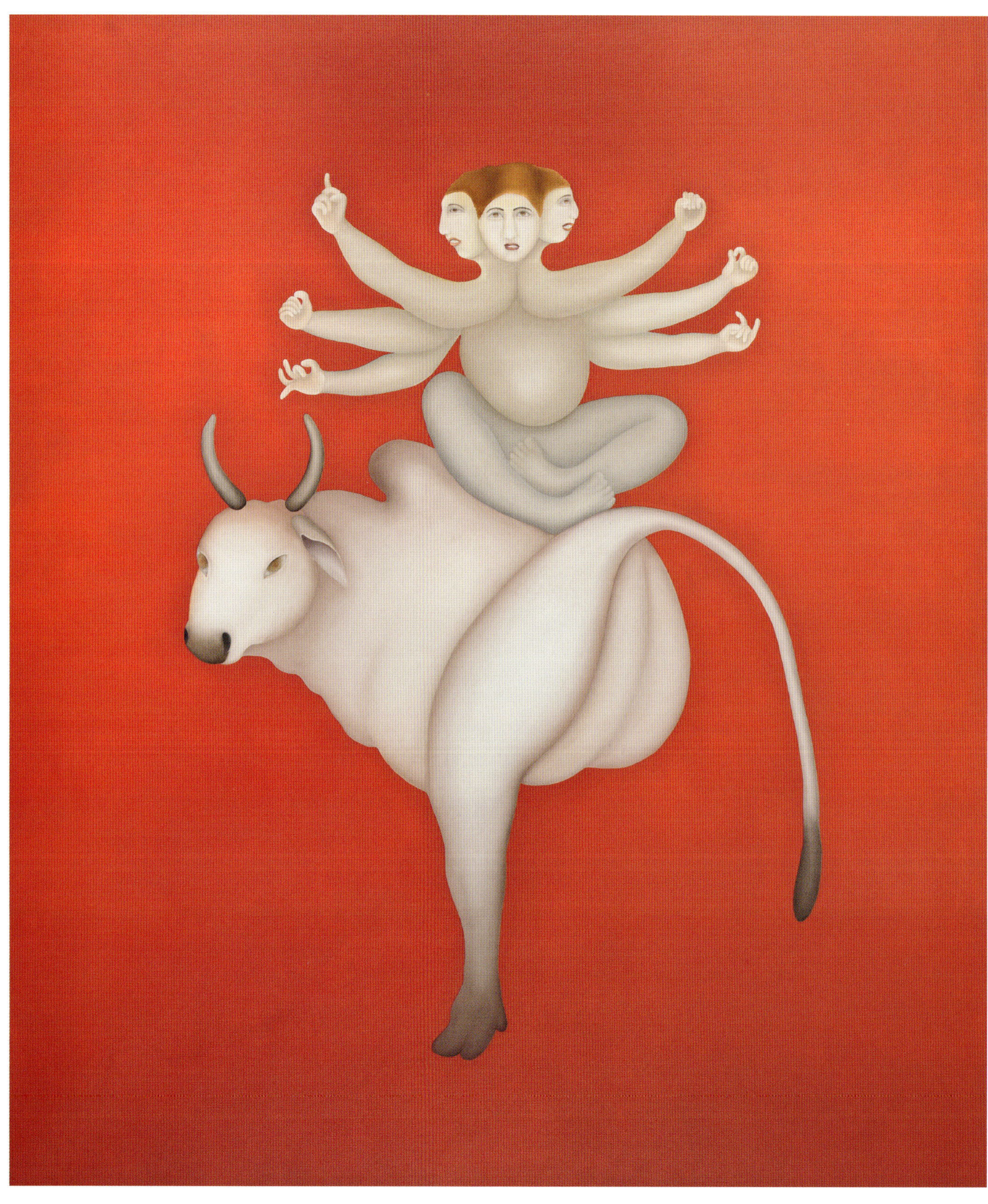

Plate 25.
Dharma and the God, 1984
Oil on canvas
85 ½ × 73 ¼ inches (217.2 × 186.1 cm)

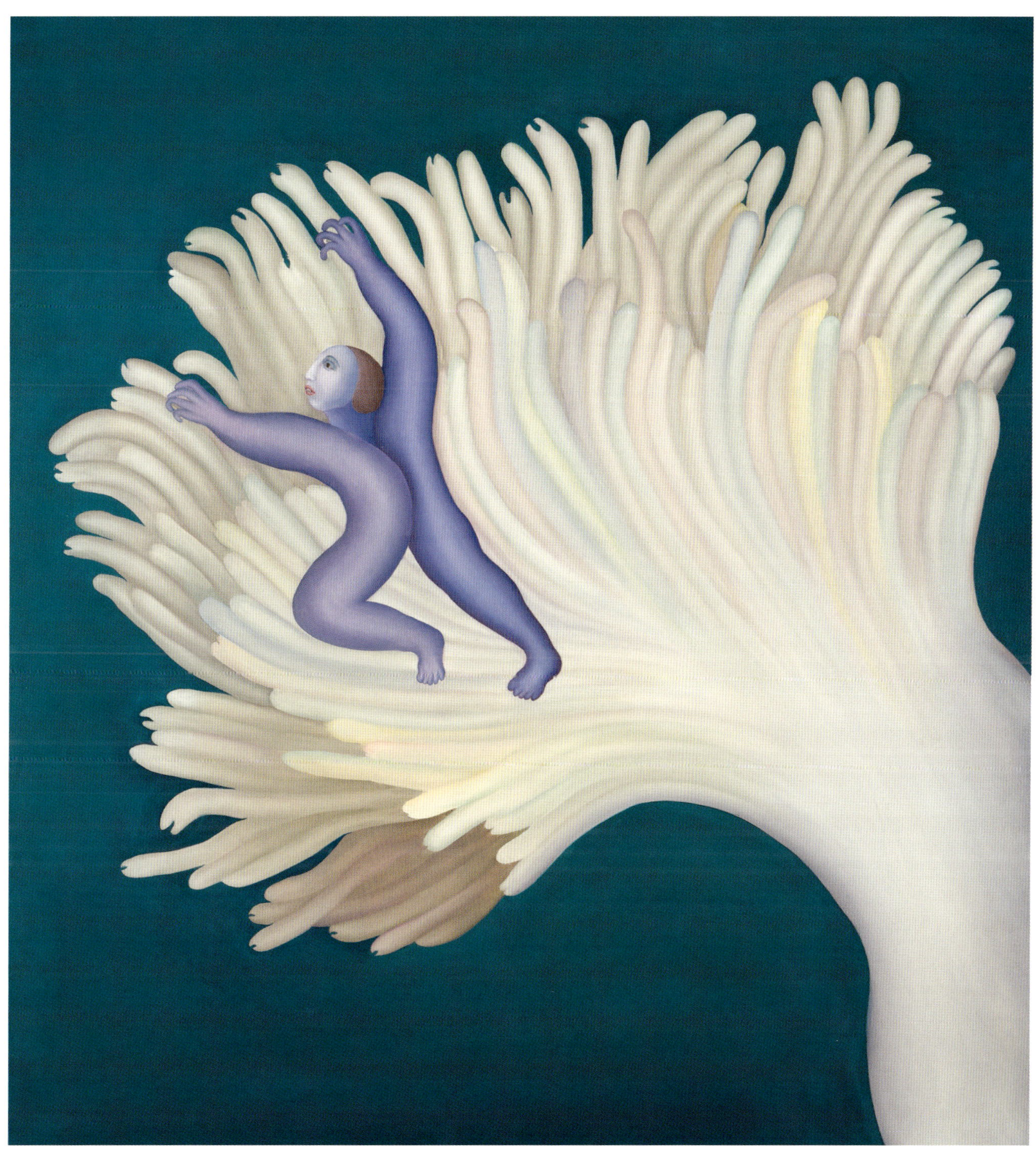

Plate 26.
Untitled, 1987
Oil on canvas
70 × 65 inches (177.8 × 165.1 cm)

BIKASH BHATTACHARJEE

Born in Calcutta, 1940–2006
died in Calcutta
Lived and worked in Calcutta

In the 1980s, Bikash Bhattacharjee brought his sensitivity as a portraitist along with a tinge of the surreal into his explorations of life in Calcutta. His trenchant portrayals include *Inauguration of a Tube Well* (plate 27), *Durga* (plate 28), and *The Lady with the Gas Cylinder* (plate 29).[1] A maverick among his contemporaries, Bhattacharjee built his practice on the academic realism still entrenched in Indian art schools, but resoundingly rejected by most of his peers as an outmoded colonial style.

Bhattacharjee found validation and inspiration for his direction when he discovered the work of the American painter Andrew Wyeth. He recalled: "But after my graduation…I [came] across an Andrew Wyeth album and an issue of the *Span* [magazine]…. *Christina's World* and other subjects, and even his ambience merged with the subjects, are very familiar to me… and the differences of country, period and characters melted away."[2] Bhattacharjee's affinity for Wyeth and his work was multifaceted. His own preoccupation with life in Calcutta paralleled Wyeth's absorption in the people and places well known to him in Maine and Delaware. Like Bhattacharjee, Wyeth was a committed realist, and had achieved prominence in the art world despite eschewing contemporary trends. Bhattacharjee added every book on Wyeth he could find to his growing art library. He particularly admired the detail in Wyeth's figures, his treatment of light and shadow, his manipulation of monochrome tonalities, and his use of windows and wall-like empty spaces as devices to structure the composition and set a mood (figure 1).[3] He experimented in his own work with Wyeth's light, color, and surface.

Bhattacharjee deployed subtle and dramatic alterations of light and shadow and surface textures to inject his canvases with a mysterious, captivating intensity. Although his realism was at odds with prevailing practice in India, his commitment

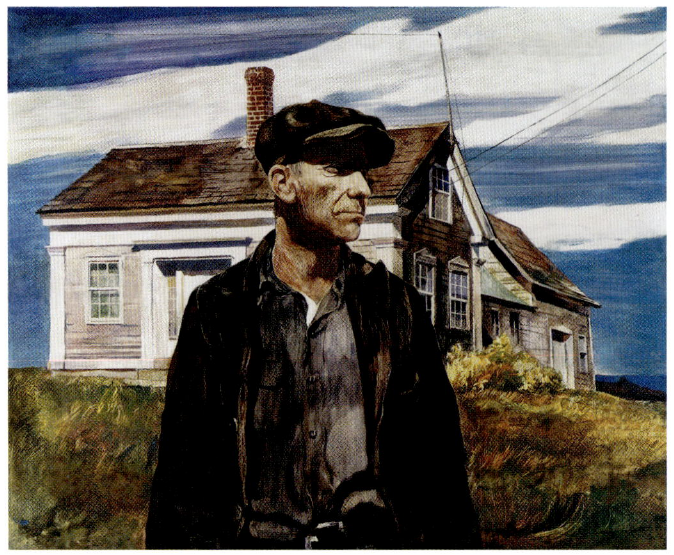

Figure 1.
Andrew Wyeth, *Charlie Ervine*, 1937
Tempera on panel
31 ¾ × 39 ¾ inches (80.6 × 101 cm)
Private Collection

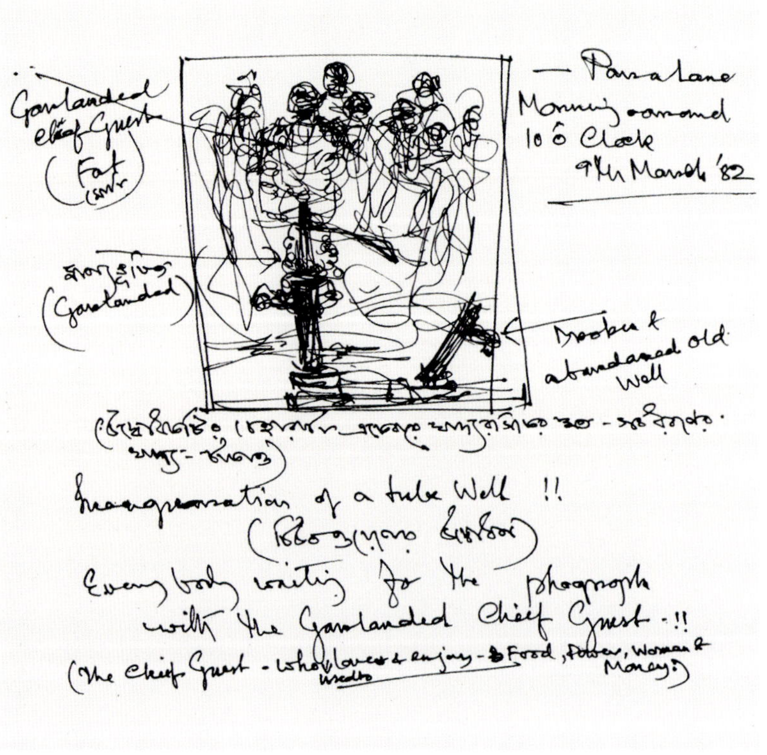

Figure 2.
Bikash Bhattacharjee,
Sketch for *Inauguration of a Tube Well* with inscriptions in English and Bengali, 1983
Pen on paper
Collection of the Bhattacharjee Family

to narrative painting and subjects deeply embedded in the culture of Calcutta was very much in tune with his generation. His canvases are like stills from a film—frozen moments in an ongoing story:

> The scene in front of you is part of a larger one. You know that something has just happened and that there is more to follow. What you see is a single moment in time.... Painting should be like this. It should have a mystery, a story. My passion for narrative and its sudden arrest was formed during the days when I used to watch films at Film Society. The dramatic narrative fascinated me.[4]

In *The Lady with the Gas Cylinder*, a woman in sunglasses with flowing hair and a stylish tunic is pulled along in a rickshaw against the background of a monsoon-filled sky. The gas cylinder she holds—hard to come by at the time—might account for her satisfied expression. A shadow over the face of the gaunt rickshaw-puller renders his feelings unknowable: life in Calcutta is a struggle for the rich and poor, but especially for the poor.

Durga revisits a scene known to the artist since childhood: the courtyard of Maharaja Nabakrishna Deb's palace in Sovabazar.[5] Glass sconces and chandeliers light the evening as a crowd moves toward an image of the powerful goddess Durga installed for Durga Puja, Calcutta's most popular festival. In the foreground, an extraordinary young woman with enormous luminous eyes, her golden skin glowing like the goddess, looks back over her shoulder directly at the viewer. The encounter is observed by another woman just behind, creating a dynamic of intersecting gazes.

Inauguration of a Tube Well is based on a sketch Bhattacharjee made of such an event (figure 2).[6] At the center, a pompous honored guest wears a garland, a hand pump is similarly festooned, and a glass of water rests on the table. Everyone stares straight ahead, squinting into the sun to pose for a photograph, except for the man wearing glasses who looks toward the viewer as if he too is more an observer than a participant. The painting seems as much a commentary on observation and recording—camera, photographer, painter, sketch, posers—as it is about the inaugural ceremony itself.

Bhattacharjee emphasized the reality of these scenes by minimizing his brushstrokes to make the paintings look more like photographs. He injected a sense of movement and narrative progression by placing his chief subjects just off-center and using diagonals to animate the composition. Although firmly rooted in local culture, Bhattacharjee's canvases transcend the society they represent by probing the human condition: the nature of femininity (*Durga*), the vanity and corruptibility of power (*Inauguration of a Tube Well*), and social inequality (*The Lady with the Gas Cylinder*). The dramatic lighting that obscures expressions and establishes an aura of mystery distances the viewer from the action and suggests that despite their familiarity, no acts are ever totally understood. – SSB

1. Also published as *She with a Gas Cylinder* in Marta Jakimowicz-Karle, *Bikash Bhattacharjee* (Bangalore: Kala Yatra, 1991), p. 49.

2. Bikash Bhattacharjee, "Bikash on Bikash," in *Close to Events: Works of Bikash Bhattacharjee*, ed. Manasij Majumder (New Delhi: Niyogi Books, 2007), pp. 182–83.

3. Bhattacharjee family (wife, Parbati, son, Bivas, and daughter, Balaka), conversation with the author, January 13, 2011, Herwitz Archive, Peabody Essex Museum, Salem, Massachusetts.

4. Shubhani Sarkar and Rudrani Sarkar, *Bikash 2000* (Calcutta: Centre of International Modern Art, 2001).

5. Bhattacharjee family, conversation with the author.

6. The sketch is inscribed in Bengali and English: "Everybody waiting for the photograph with the Garlanded Chief Guest: The Chief Guest—who used to love and enjoy food, power, women and money. Para Lane, around 10 a.m. 9th March 82." *Bikash* (Calcutta: Graphic Services, n.d.).

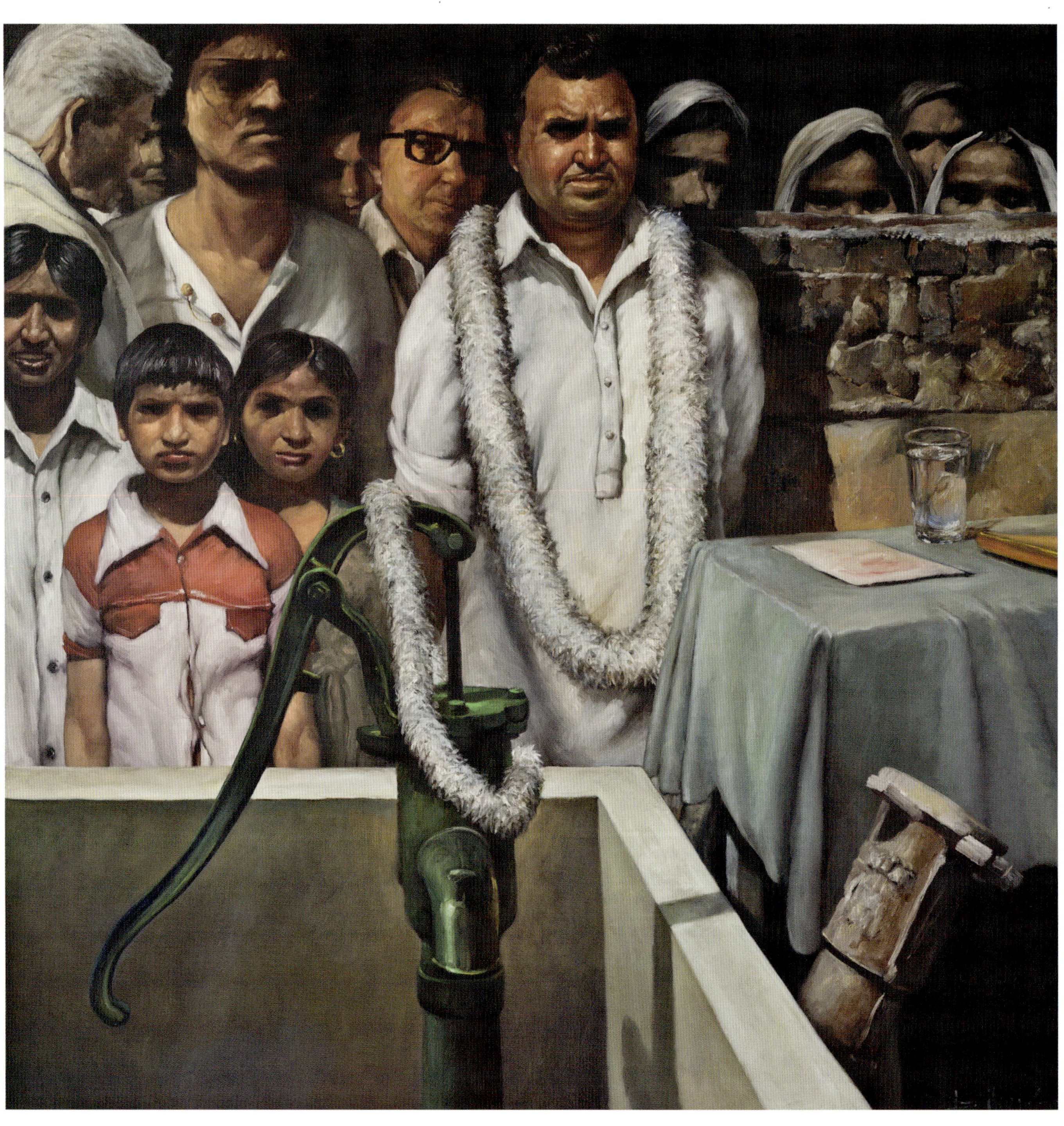

Plate 27.
Inauguration of a Tube Well, 1984
Oil on canvas
47 ¾ × 47 ¾ inches (121.3 × 121.3 cm)

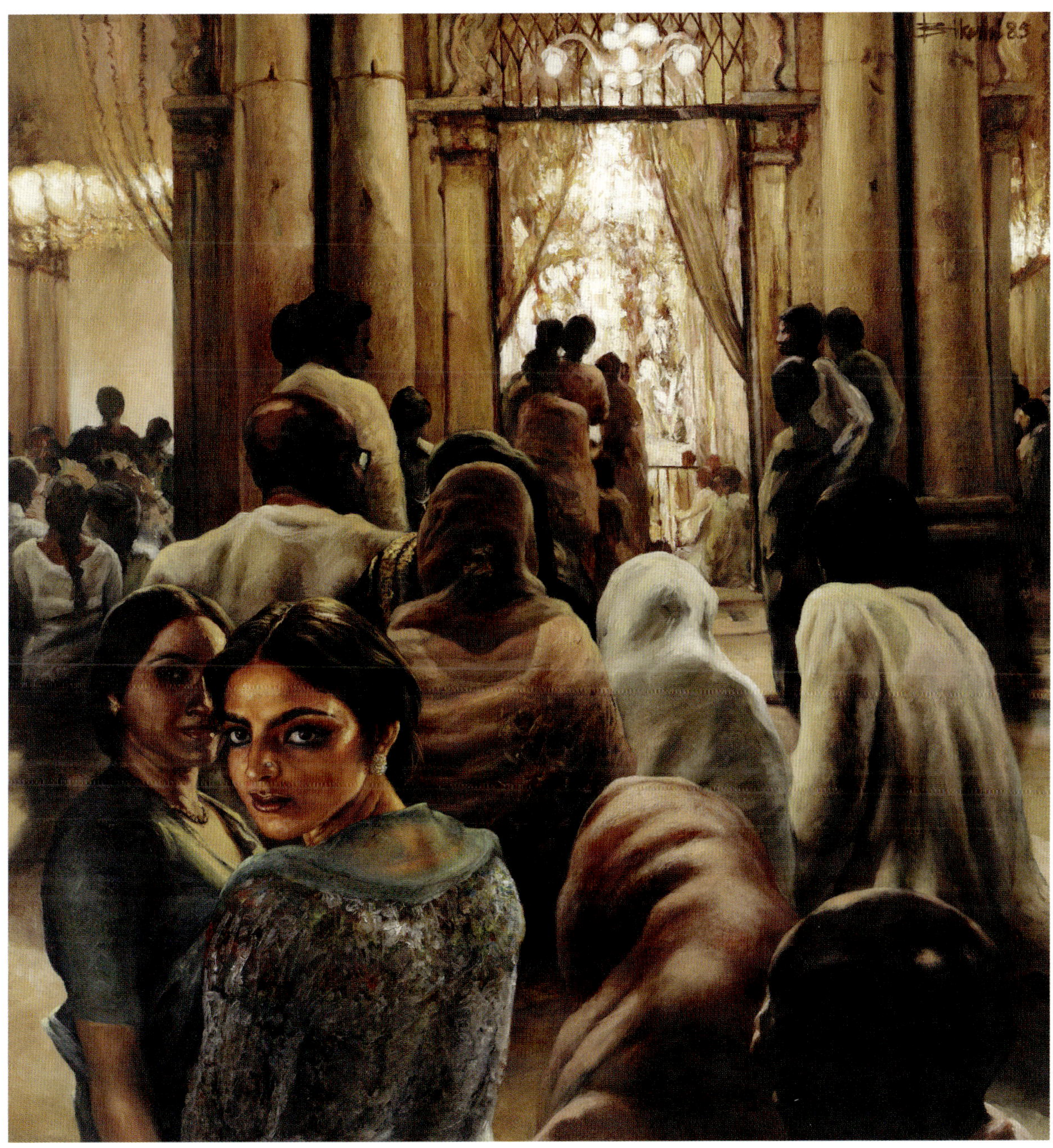

Plate 28.
Durga, 1985
Oil on canvas
41 ½ × 39 ¾ inches (105.4 × 101 cm)

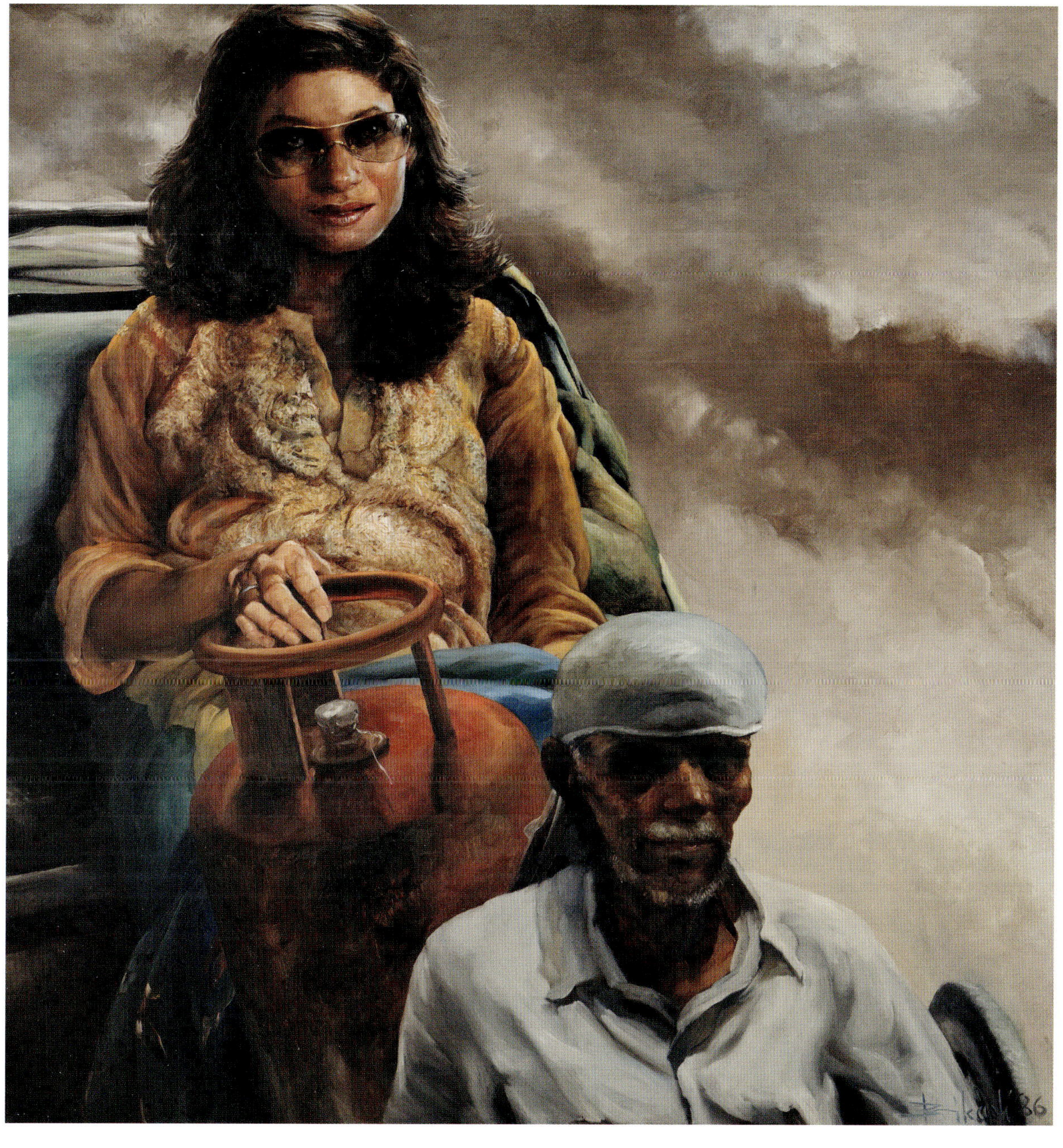

Plate 29.
The Lady with the Gas Cylinder, 1986
Oil on canvas
42 × 40 inches (106.7 × 101.6 cm)

RAMESHWAR BROOTA

Born in Delhi, 1941
Lives and works in Delhi

Rameshwar Broota had the good fortune to be offered a position teaching painting at Triveni Kala Sangam in 1967 shortly after his graduation from the Delhi College of Art (then Delhi Polytechnic); a few years later, he was made head of the department. This home base has provided a stable context for a practice dedicated to meticulously crafted, laboriously executed canvases embodying a singular vision of figural form.

For the first decade after graduation, Broota painted in response to the social inequities, greed, and corruption endemic to life in Delhi, India's political center. Eventually realizing that he did not want the economic and political conundrums of India in the 1970s to govern his art practice, he began to explore new directions. At a time when many of his contemporaries were discovering the local, Broota sought to transcend Indian experience and engage universals of human life: "I thought that this kind of subject is very local, very personal, and art has to go beyond this. It has to have a kind of universality, so that whosoever sees it, it should belong to that person."[1]

In the 1980s and early 1990s, Broota found his subject in the male figure. Simultaneously universal and highly subjective, it has remained at the heart of his practice. *Man (16th)* (plate 30), *Man Through the Ages* (plate 31), and *Through Time and Space (Vanishing Figure)* (plate 32) illustrate the evolution of his treatment. From the beginning, Broota used his own body as model and invented a unique, sculptural technique:

> I just took the canvas, stood before the large mirror without clothes, started just doing scratching, scraping with it, and then from morning till evening, I continuously painted...because that had to be finished when it's wet.... I was dreaming throughout the night, it was such a tortuous night...as if I was scraping my own body with the knife... to reveal this thing....[2]

Man (16th) represents the initial phase of Broota's excavation of the male figure. Captivated by the effects he could produce and mesmerized by the process, he developed a method in which he applied many thin coats of paint beginning with silver and including raw sienna, burnt umber, shades of bluish black as well as pure black, and incorporating linseed oil to preserve the suppleness of the surface for the scraping phase.[3] The absence of color in favor of subtle tints and the austerity of composition generate a stark atmosphere devoid of local references beyond his own body. Broota's deeply craftsmanlike sensibility, however, seems almost an homage to the skilled aesthetic of traditional artisans, weavers, potters, and sculptors, who continue to practice their arts across the country. His very process—painstakingly scraping away paint until a figure emerges—suggests a transcendent aspect, as if the figure already exists in the canvas and has only to be revealed by the artist. Eternal Man is not the artist's creation; the artist is a tool enabling a primordial form to appear. Despite his muscle and bone, the tall, strong figure in his nudity and open posture conveys an aura of vulnerability. Shrouded in shadow, his face is turned away toward a void created from the layers of paint on canvas from which he emerged. This Man is unknowable and unfathomable.

Eventually, as in *Man Through the Ages*, Broota began to place his figures in abstract architectural settings. Here, Man appears as strong and tall as the adjacent vertical elements, suggesting an affinity between human form and man-made geometry. The figure is partially enmeshed within a vague background of sky and clouds, caught between his origin in the natural world and the structures of his own creation. Again vulnerable and exposed, he looks directly at the viewer to engage in a dialogue about the relationship between man and nature. In *Vanishing Figure*, Broota again juxtaposed Man with his creations, using emphatic verticals to empower the imagery. But, this time only the lower torso and thighs are visible, as if Broota was moving away from the effort to fathom and project the nature of Man toward a more purely aesthetic exploration of the sensuality of the human form in juxtapositions with the linear, planar geometries of his creations. In recent work, he has continued to move in this direction, exploiting paint and surface for the sheer sensuousness of texture and form. – SSB

1. Yashodhara Dalmia, *Journeys: Four Generations of Indian Artists in Their Own Words*, 2 vols. (New Delhi: Oxford University Press, 2011), vol. 2, p. 83.

2. Ibid., pp. 89–90.

3. Ibid., pp. 88–89.

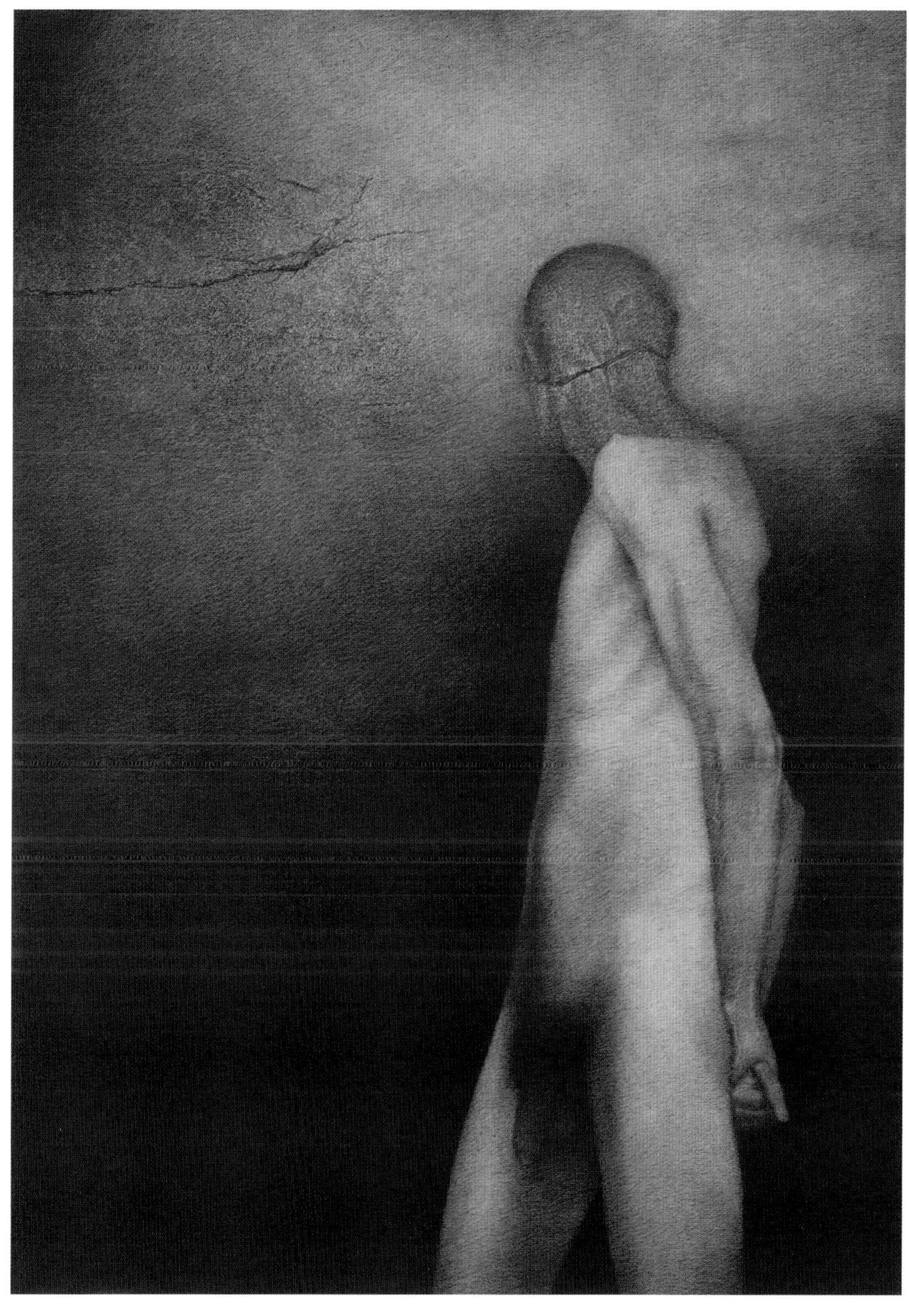

Plate 30.
Man (16th), 1983
Oil on canvas
70 × 50 inches (177.8 × 127 cm)

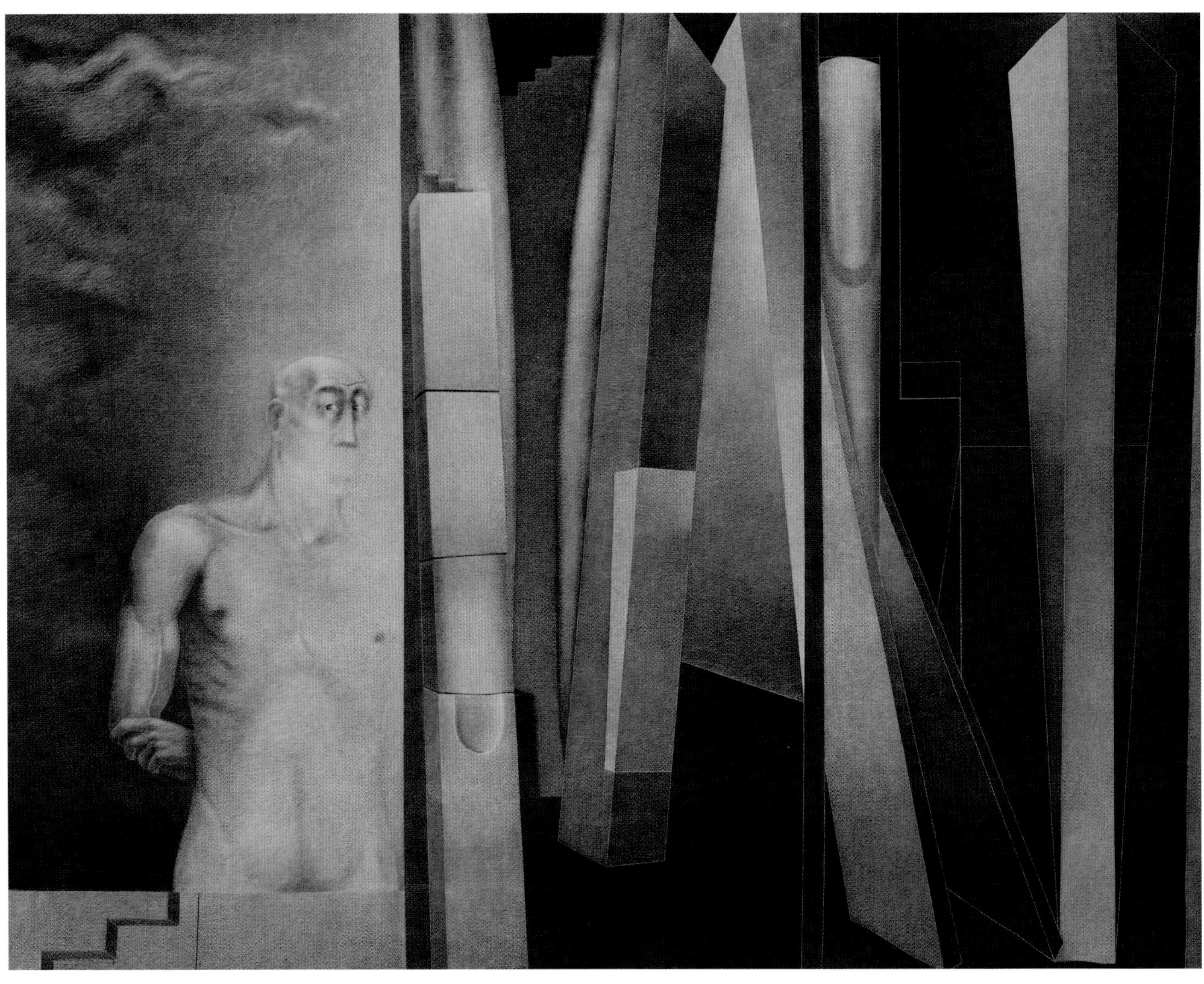

Plate 31.
Man Through the Ages, 1990
Oil on canvas
70 × 89 ¾ inches (177.8 × 228 cm)

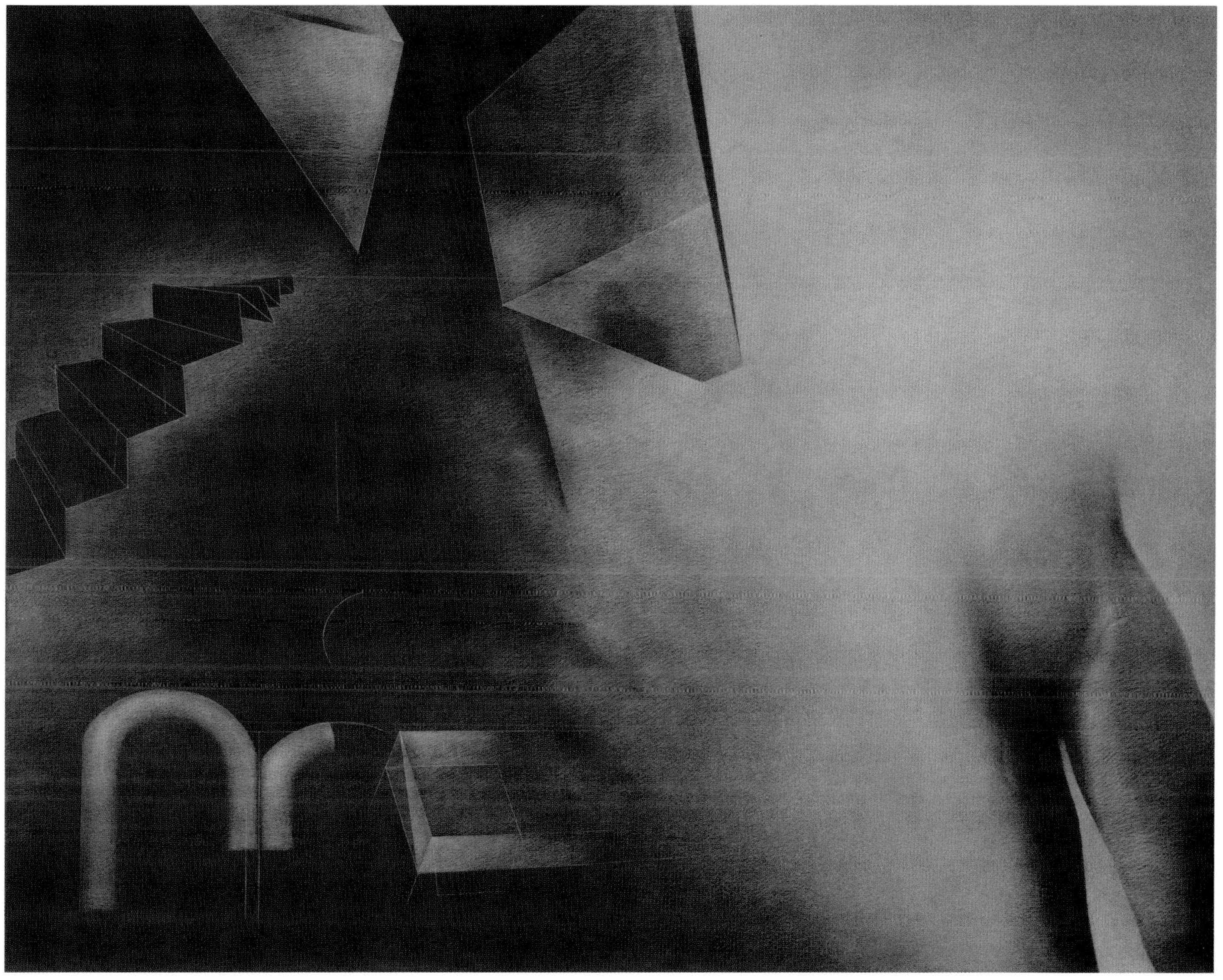

Plate 32.
Through Time and Space (Vanishing Figure), 1991
Oil on canvas
70 × 89 ¾ inches (177.8 × 228 cm)

JOGEN CHOWDHURY

Born in Daharpara, Bengal
(now Bangladesh), 1939
Lives and works in Santiniketan

Looking at Jogen Chowdhury's paintings, it is possible to imagine the artist hunched over his table, building his satires of Bengali middle-class life out of crosshatched lines of ink and subtle applications of pastels. The essence of his work lies at the intersection of these elements, in his skillful and evocative insight into the lives of ordinary and imperfect human beings.

Chowdhury was born in a village in an eastern district of Bengal that in 1947 became part of East Pakistan (now Bangladesh). In the same year, Chowdhury's family moved to Calcutta. Chowdhury's itinerant adult life has in addition included New Delhi, Madras, and Santiniketan. After studying painting at the Calcutta School of Art, he moved to New Delhi, where, like a number of other painters, he became a textile designer. He also spent two years in Paris, studying at the École Nationale Supérieure des Beaux-Arts and in Atelier 17, the print studio set up by British artist Stanley William Hayter in 1927. Sculptor and master printmaker Krishna Reddy studied there with Hayter in the 1950s and became assistant director in 1965, the period when Chowdhury was in Paris. By his own admission, Chowdhury did not develop his mature style until after he returned from Paris in 1967.

He began his landmark series "Reminiscences of a Dream" in 1969 (figure 1).[1] The ink and wash paintings employ crosshatching and other drawing techniques associated with etching, reflecting his work in Paris. They resemble still lifes except that in some cases a pair of hands drifts into the frame to suggest the illusion of a person standing or sitting just in front of the painting, reproducing the artist's point of view. In 1969, Chowdhury wrote: "the artist creates his works from his imagination, from his dreams, from a single image or sound of the past, from the pain of today or from contradictions of his life."[2] These works are, in a sense, self-portraits, but of the artist's internal life, his dreams.

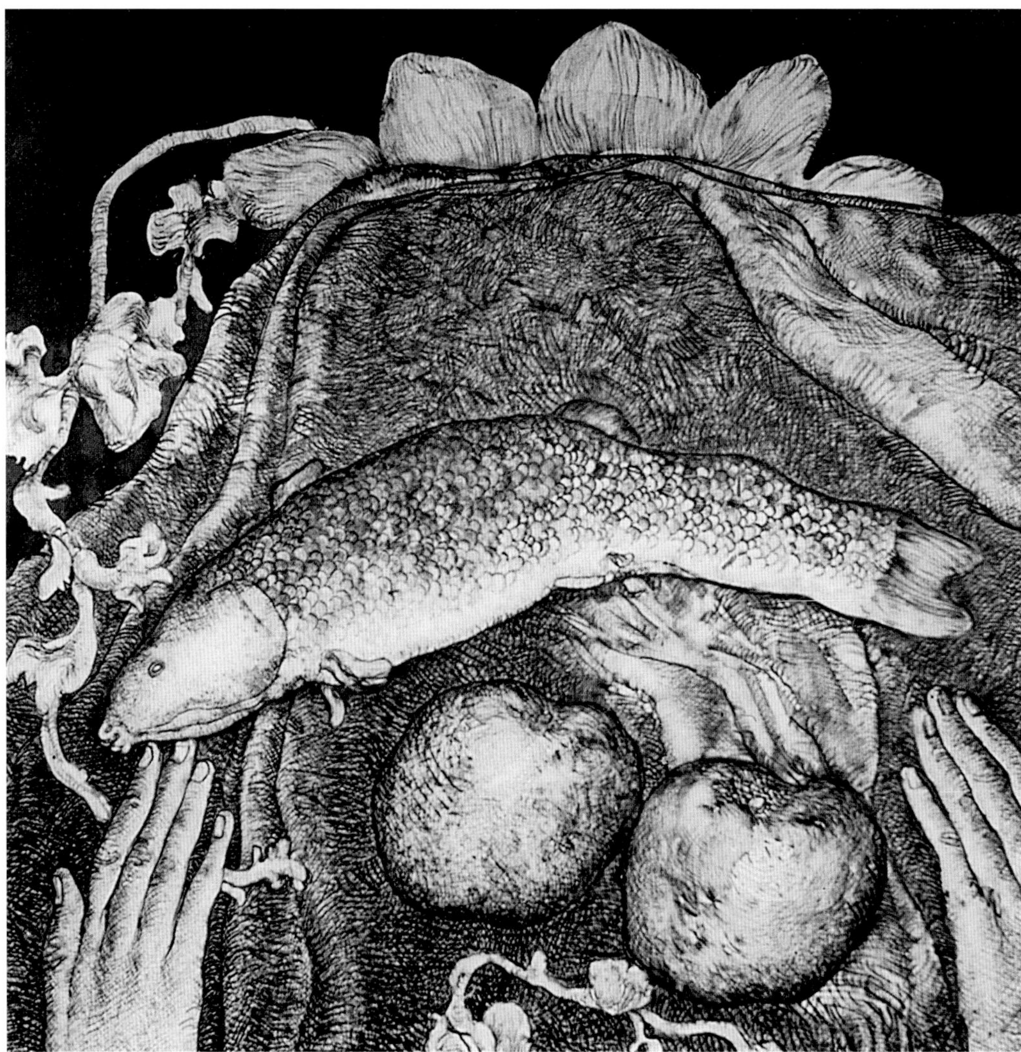

Figure 1.
Jogen Chowdhury,
Reminiscences of a Dream No. 18, 1969
Ink and mixed media on paper
21 × 21 inches (53.3 × 53.3 cm)
National Gallery of Modern Art, New Delhi

During the 1970s and 1980s, Chowdhury began to integrate his own expression with popular visual culture. During this period, he developed an idiosyncratic approach to the figure.[3] Built on his observations of folk art styles, Chowdhury embraced the decorative while exploring the capacity for drawing to invoke the fleshiness of a medium like terra cotta, which was in common use in Calcutta at the time. *Waiting for Her Lover* (plate 33) riffs on the portraits of women in the paintings and prints of Raja Ravi Varma, whose imagery became ubiquitous in the twentieth century. Chowdhury's lover shares the posture and columned setting of Varma's *Hamsa Damayanti*, the heroine of a tale from the Mahabharata in which a swan carries messages between lovers. But, whereas Varma's heroine is young, voluptuous, and beautiful, resplendent in a nine-yard gold-edged sari, Chowdhury's bulbous, cross-eyed figure in a rumpled cotton sari is decidedly unerotic; her impersonation of Varma's icon of desire is humorous, not seductive. Her counterpart appears in

Waiting for His Beloved (plate 35), in which a Gandhi-capped, *khadi*-clad man likewise holds a droopy flower in anticipation. This icon of self-satisfied and hypocritical "respectability" builds on the history of satires of the Bengali *babu* (gentleman), a staple of nineteenth-century popular visual culture. In prints and cartoons, as well as Battala woodcuts and Kalighat paintings, the two most significant popular art forms of Calcutta, the *babu* was presented as a pathetic and usually gloriously fat man, overtaken by desire and delusions of grandeur, and also, commonly, as a dandy. Chowdhury's *babu* politician is round and infantile, like an overgrown six-month-old. This painting was completed shortly after the two-year period of martial law declared as a national emergency by the leader of the Congress Party, Prime Minister Indira Gandhi, in 1975. In this provocative image, politics is seen as a site of corrupt self-indulgence and frustrated impotence.

Chowdhury's satire of Congress leaders continues in his 1982 *Couple* (plate 36), which he says was inspired by a news item concerning a politician in the neighboring state of Orissa, who propositioned an unemployed woman.[4] With limbs coiled like snakes, this couple is still somewhat grotesque, but the folds of their garments unite them and their arms and legs seem tangled together in a classic trope of romantic love. The figural distortions that symbolize corruption are also awkwardly sensual here.

That potent combination carries over into Chowdhury's image of Ganapati. Chowdhury has noted that this elephant-headed deity, also known as Ganesha, is particularly beloved by the business-minded Marwari community in Calcutta.[5] The artist reported that *Ganapati the Warrior* (plate 34) is meant to represent that community, rather than the god himself. Not at all martial, he is an aging and grotesque assemblage of thin limbs, floppy breasts, and rolls of belly fat. He carries arrows and a bow and is accompanied by a humble version of his traditional mount, a rat or mouse. He is also a fitting icon for the late 1970s, a bitter period for many in India, particularly artists, who suffered chilling constraints on freedom of expression during the emergency. – KZ

1. See Geeti Sen, *Image and Imagination: Five Contemporary Artists in India* (Ahmedabad: Mapin Publishing, 1996), pp. 44–71.

2. Jogen Chowdhury, "'Young Printers' Problems in India and Their Responsibility to Be Serious Painters—A Stray Thought!,'' artist's statement written in 1969 and distributed in mimeograph by the artist in 1981, Department of Art History Archives, Maharaja Sayajirao University, Baroda.

3. Chowdhury is generally understood to be a highly individual artist, relatively free from associations with the various movements in Indian painting. See Rita Dutta, *Jogen Chowdhury: His Life and Times* (Calcutta: Centre of International Modern Art, 2006).

4. Jogen Chowdhury, conversation with Susan S. Bean, December 2009, Herwitz Archive, Peabody Essex Museum, Salem, Massachusetts.

5. Ibid.

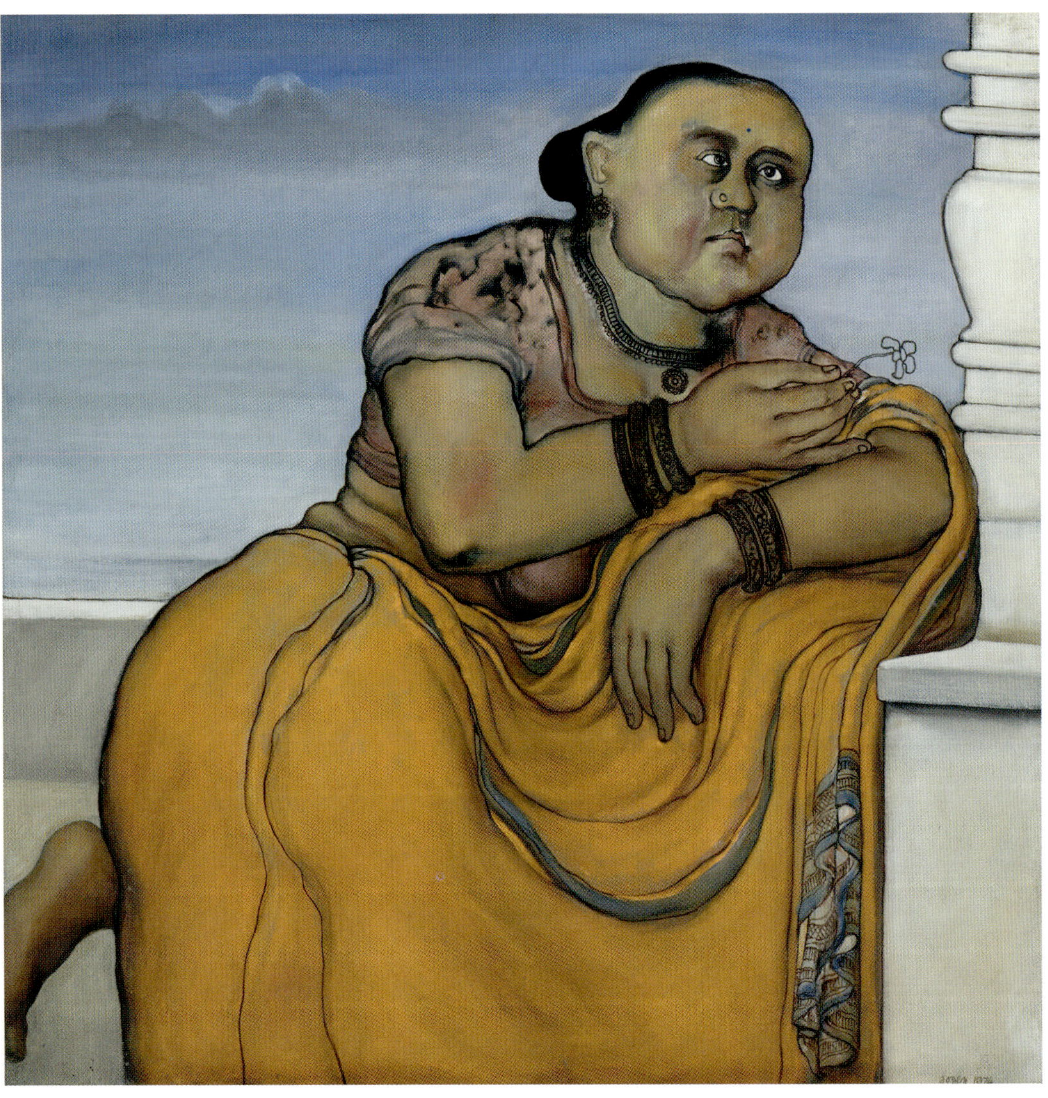

Plate 33.
Waiting for Her Lover, 1974
Oil on canvas
24 × 24 inches (61 × 61 cm)

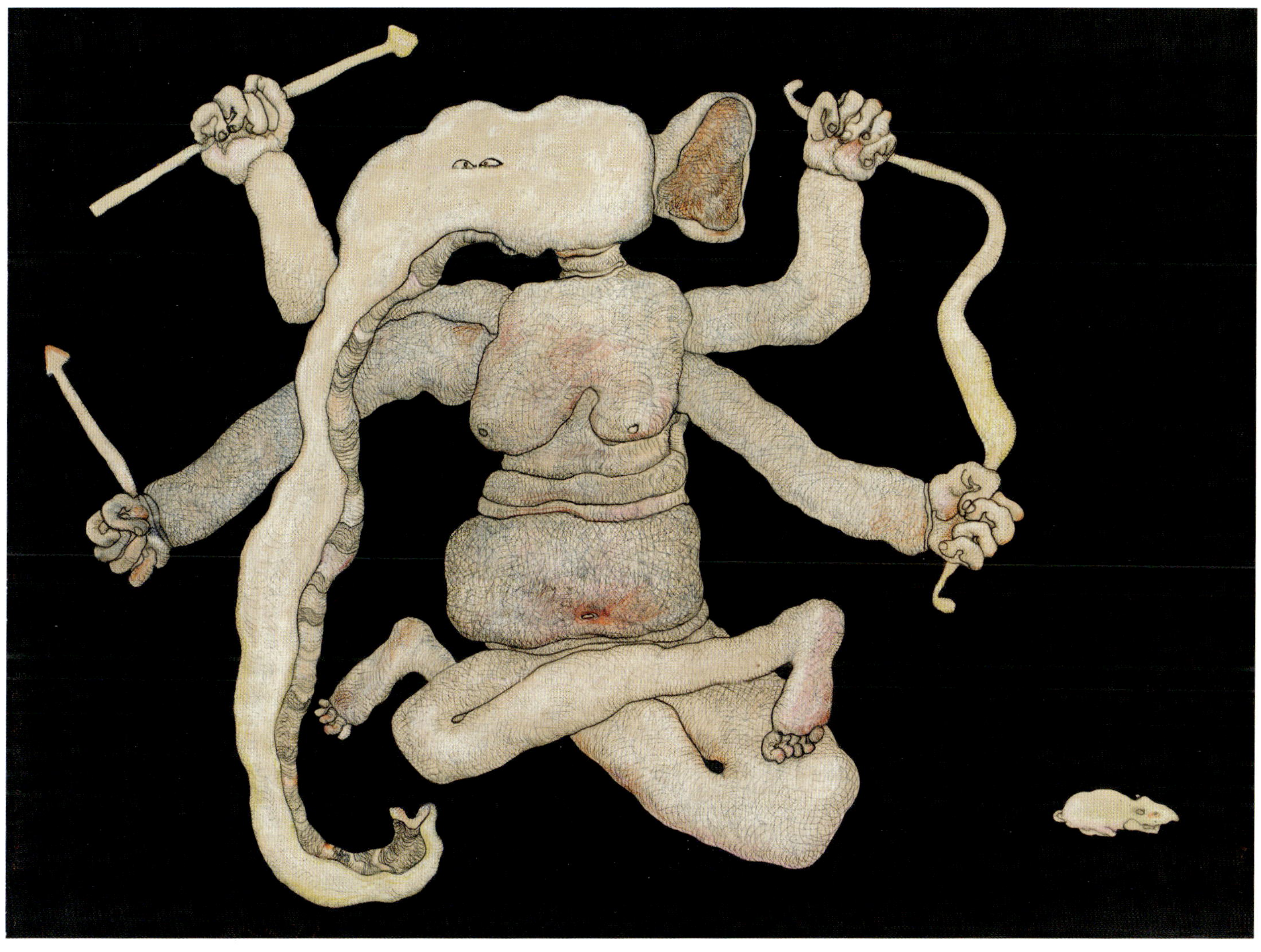

Plate 34.
Ganapati the Warrior, 1977
Pen, ink, pastel, and lacquer on paper
21 ¾ × 29 ¾ inches (55.2 × 75.6 cm)

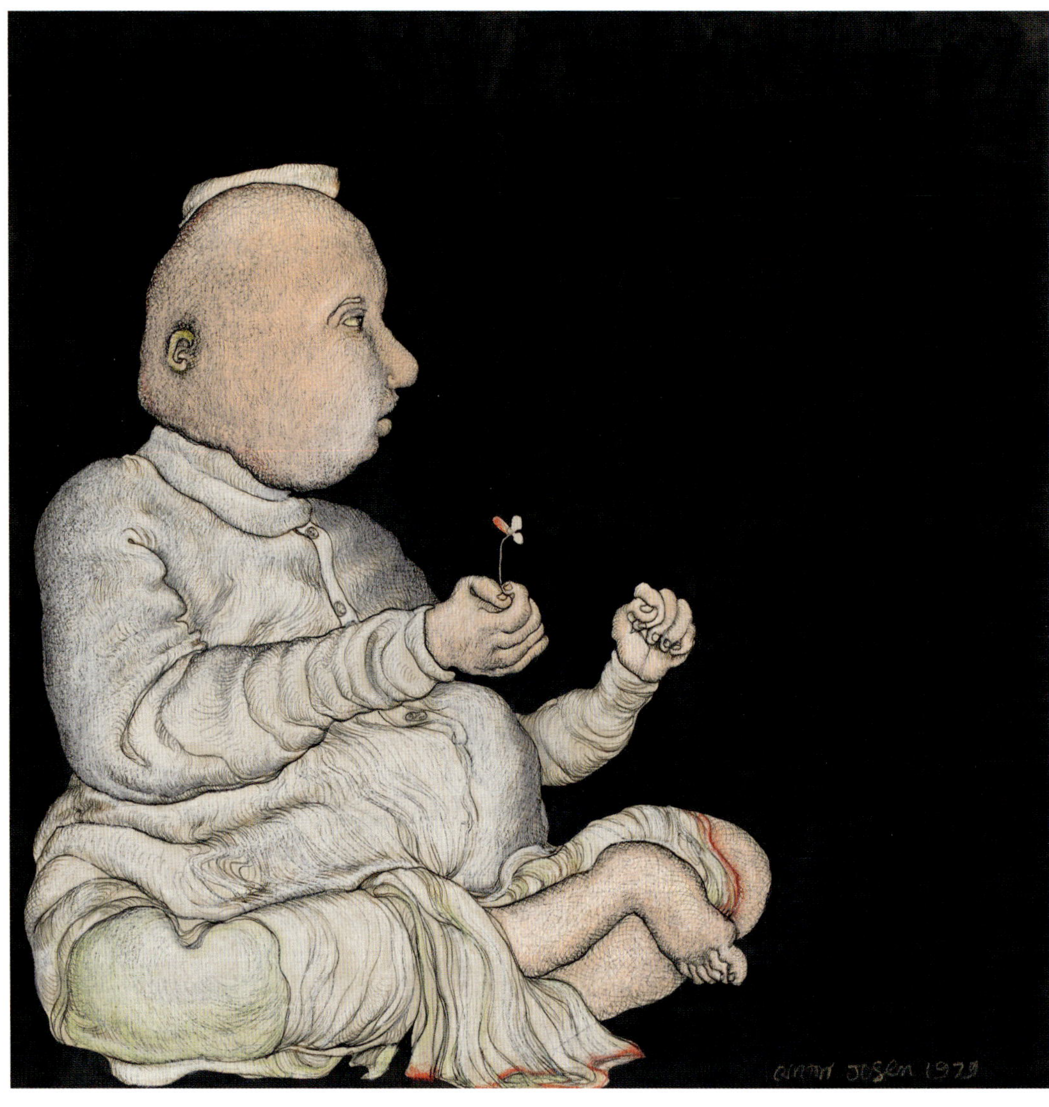

Plate 35.
Waiting for His Beloved, 1979
Pen, ink, pastel, and lacquer on paper
21 ¾ × 21 ¾ inches (55.2 × 55.2 cm)

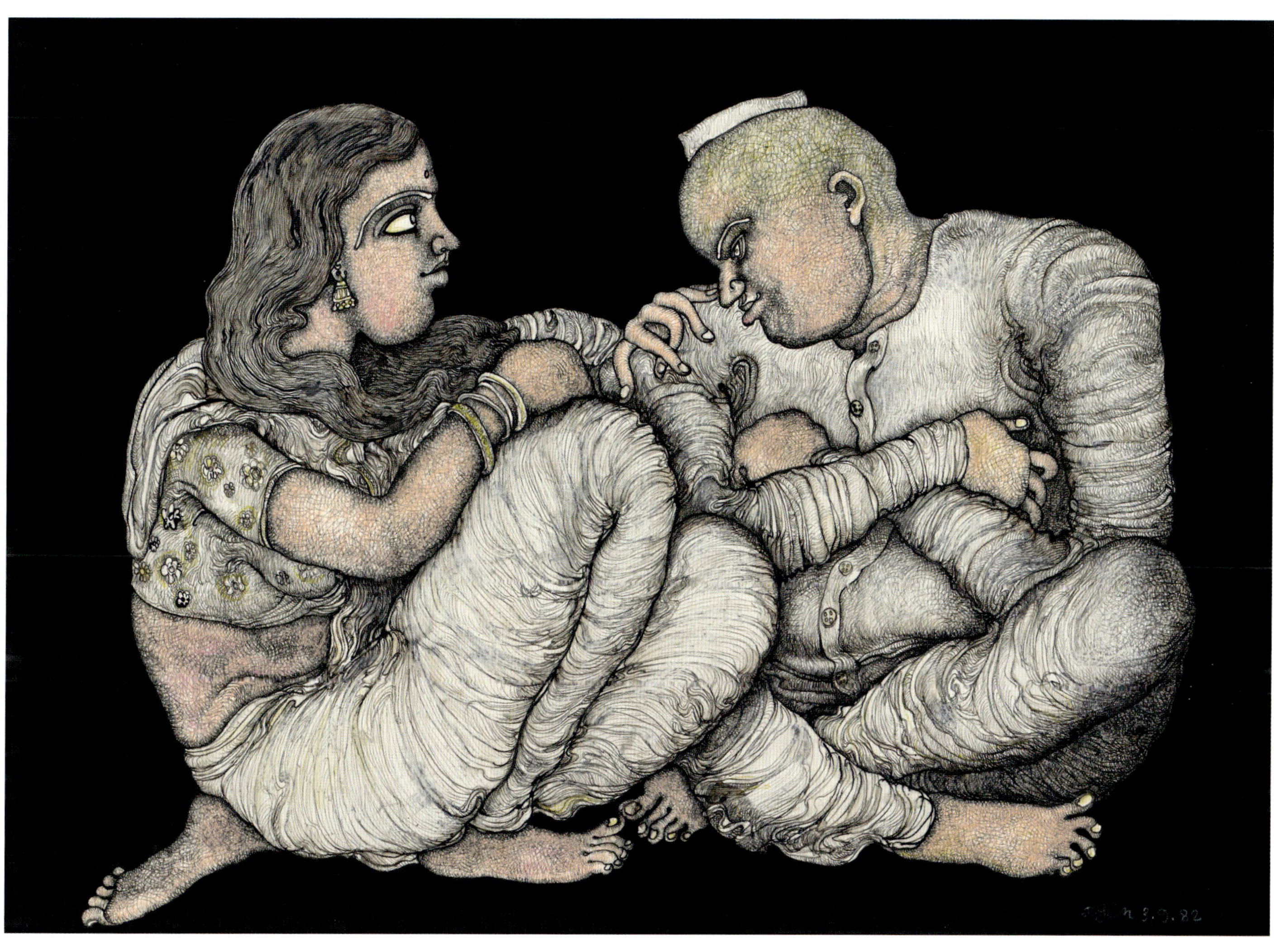

Plate 36.
Couple, 1982
Pen, ink, pastel, and lacquer on paper
24 ½ × 35 inches (62.2 × 88.9 cm)

K. LAXMA GOUD

Born in Nizampur, Andhra Pradesh, 1940
Lives and works in Hyderabad

Kalal Laxma Goud's pencil drawing of a peasant couple (plate 37) embodies the heart of his practice. The couple are poor laborers whose struggle to maintain their family is daily and unending. Nonetheless, through his careful, detailed depiction of the woman's ornaments and the flowers in her hair, Goud asserted their dignity—reflected strongly as well in the closely observed exchange of touch and gaze that flows between the two. Like much of Goud's work, this drawing was laboriously produced with the most basic of tools: an HB pencil—a standard writing instrument—meticulously sharpened with sandpaper. Goud slowly and lovingly builds his figures with tiny marks. He sits at a table, close to the paper, and surrenders himself to the labor and intimacy of the work. For Goud, "drawing is very pure."[1] It requires only the simplest tools. The process is meditative, spiritual, seductive, and elevating; it is both sensual (gratifying to the physical senses) and sensuous (aesthetically pleasing). Goud wants viewers to experience these pleasures, too: "I want to seduce them with my line."[2]

Goud discovered drawing as a child in a poor and remote region of Andhra Pradesh. He describes his family as lower middle-class, belonging to a caste known as toddy-brewers. His father maintained the village's tax revenue accounts and farmed a modest amount of land on which the family grew rice and legumes for their household and to exchange for other necessities. Goud felt a deep attraction to artisanal labor. The local weaver made some of his clothing and Goud spent hours intently watching the village potter at his wheel. He enjoyed making pictures and devising costumes inspired by the village production of the Ramayana. Goud's father and elder brother, a schoolteacher, recognized his talent. His father took special pride in his drawing ability and encouraged Goud to attend art school in the state capital, Hyderabad. His supportive community, with a loving family and interested neighbors who indulged his curiosity, sustained Goud in his dedication to an art practice.

Goud's passion for the line blossomed during his postgraduate studies in the mid-1960s at Maharaja Sayajirao University, Baroda, where he concentrated on printmaking and drawing. In the process of drawing through wax to make etchings, he became aware of a physical attraction to the act of creating the line. During these years, he learned from examining the work of other artists—Picasso's delicate linear realism, the experimental spirit of Paul Klee's drawing.[3] He appreciated the way Ram Kumar (plates 7 and 8 and see figure 1) constructed his abstractions with strokes of the palette knife: "You like the labor he is putting in." Goud's prints and drawings of the time are redolent with raw sensuality. He admired Auguste Rodin's erotic drawings and the treatment of the nude by Bombay artist K.H. Ara. In Goud's early work, raw erotic impulses, feelings he considered so natural in village life but complicated and taboo in middle-class urban life, were central preoccupations. Goud began to build a practice that wove together his obsession with the sensual and his abiding connection to his roots in rural Andhra Pradesh. Increasingly, in his drawings he probed the inner lives of people similar to those with whom he grew up. This focus on the lived realities of his native locale aligned him with an actively growing movement centered in Baroda that privileged and explored everyday existence and subjective experience.

Goud's drawings convey the ordinariness of the people he knew, their ties to the land, their sturdy strength, their passions and affections. In works produced from the 1980s onward, Goud conveyed their gentler and more subtle passions and his deep devotion to them. In a drawing of a standing woman (plate 38), the sepia tone and reddish background infuse the subject with warmth. Goud overfilled the picture space so that the figure seems confined by its boundaries, bowing her head and pushing her hands close to her body. Her posture and expression convey life's trials and disappointments. In a large colored drawing of two couples and a woman with a goat (plate 39), Goud's close-up focus on them draws the viewer to contemplate their presence and relationships. The couples gesture toward one another with a touch of the hand, a tilt of the head. They seem absorbed in one another, as do the woman and the goat, which likewise gaze into each other's eyes. The scene conveys a sense of allegory, suggesting that animal attraction is the fount of life for all creatures.

Fascinated by the technique and the shimmering surface effects in the work of his teacher and mentor, K.G. Subramanyan (plates 20–23), Goud took up painting on glass and acrylic. In the process of applying paint to the back of a transparent surface, he experienced an almost magical response to building figures in reverse, from details to background. The luminosity of the reflective surface attracted him and he was excited by the possibilities of color—especially as one who worked so much without it. Goud's knowledge of the medium's South Indian vernacular roots appealed to him, too, as something close to home. In a reverse painting of a couple in the doorway of their village home (plate 40), the patterns and textures of their clothing and ornaments are lusciously detailed. They stand close to each other and gaze out at the viewer with such intensity that erotic sparks seem to fly. With emphatic directness, they invite us into their world, into Goud's world, a place where people are at ease with their own true feelings. – SSB

1. Unless otherwise noted, all quotations and autobiographical comments are from K. Laxma Goud, conversation with the author, January 16, 2011.

2. K. Laxma Goud, quoted in Geeta Doctor, "A Meeting with Laxma Goud," in *Laxma Goud* (Bombay: Cymroza Art Gallery, 1992), p. 24.

3. Gulammohammed Sheikh, *K. Laxma Goud* (Hyderabad: Andhra Lalit Kala Akademi, 1981).

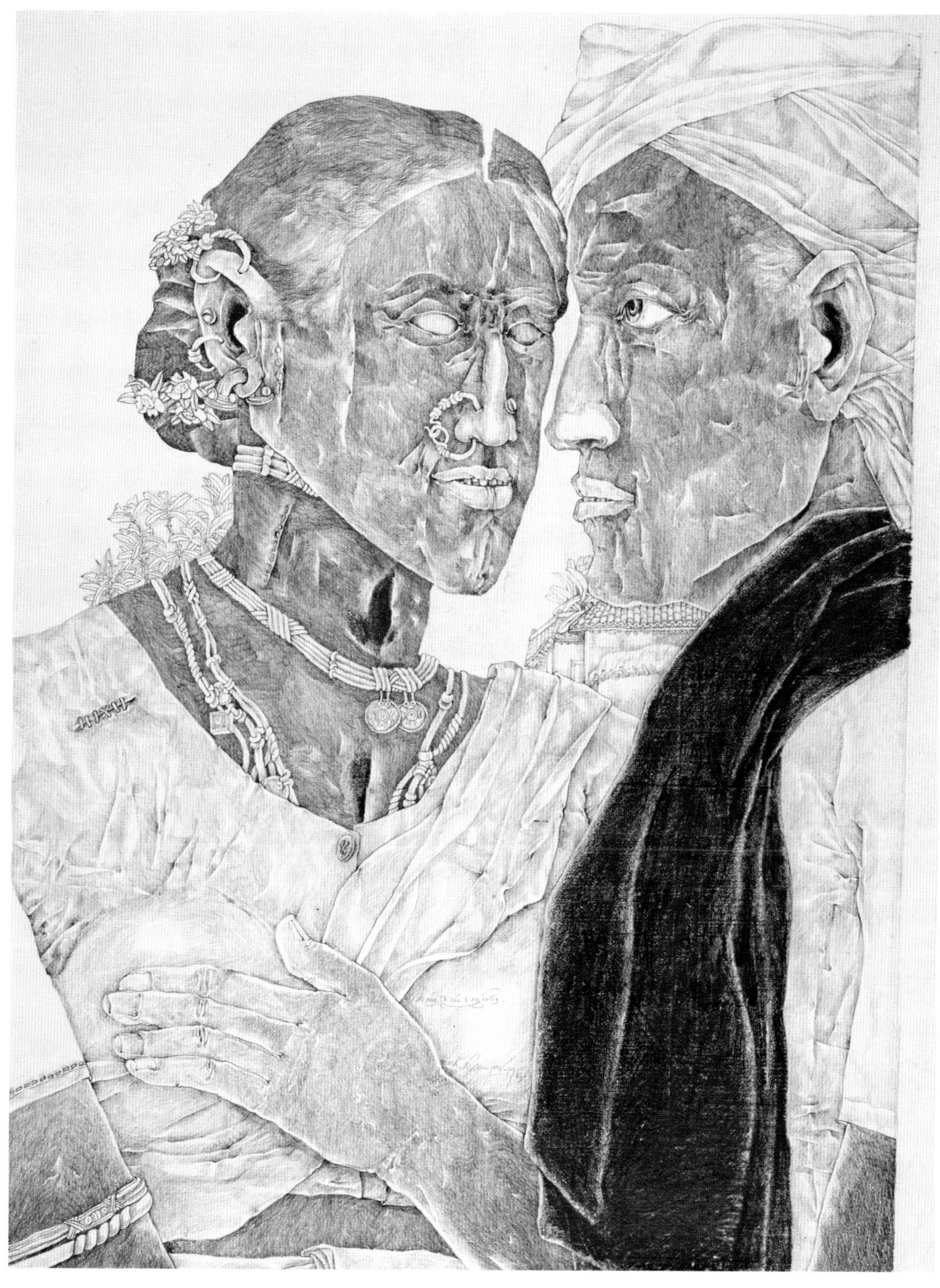

Plate 37.
Untitled, 1983
Pencil and charcoal on paper
20 ¼ × 15 ¼ inches (51.4 × 38.7 cm)

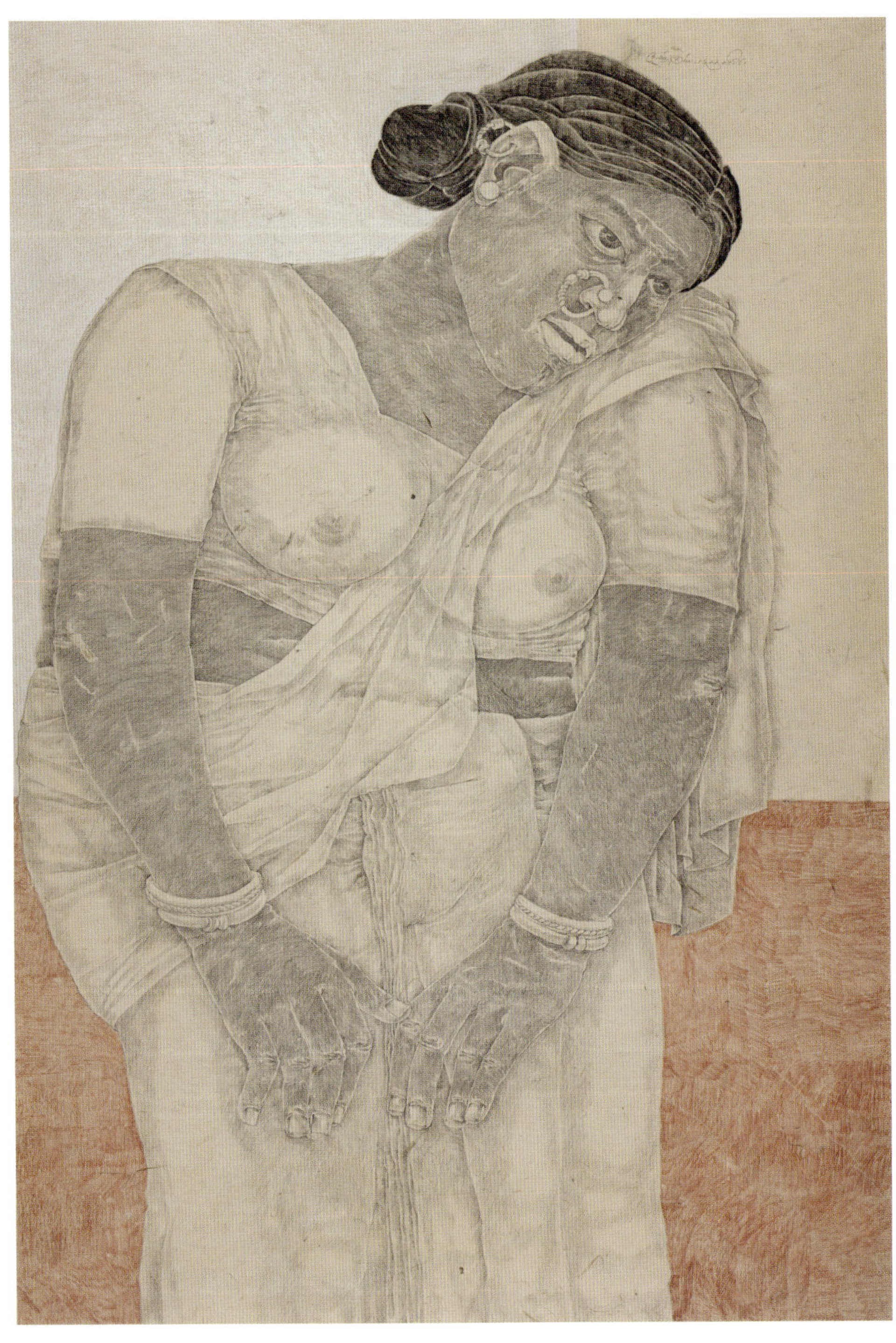

Plate 38.
Untitled, 1984
Pencil and crayon on paper
26 × 18 inches (66 × 45.7 cm)

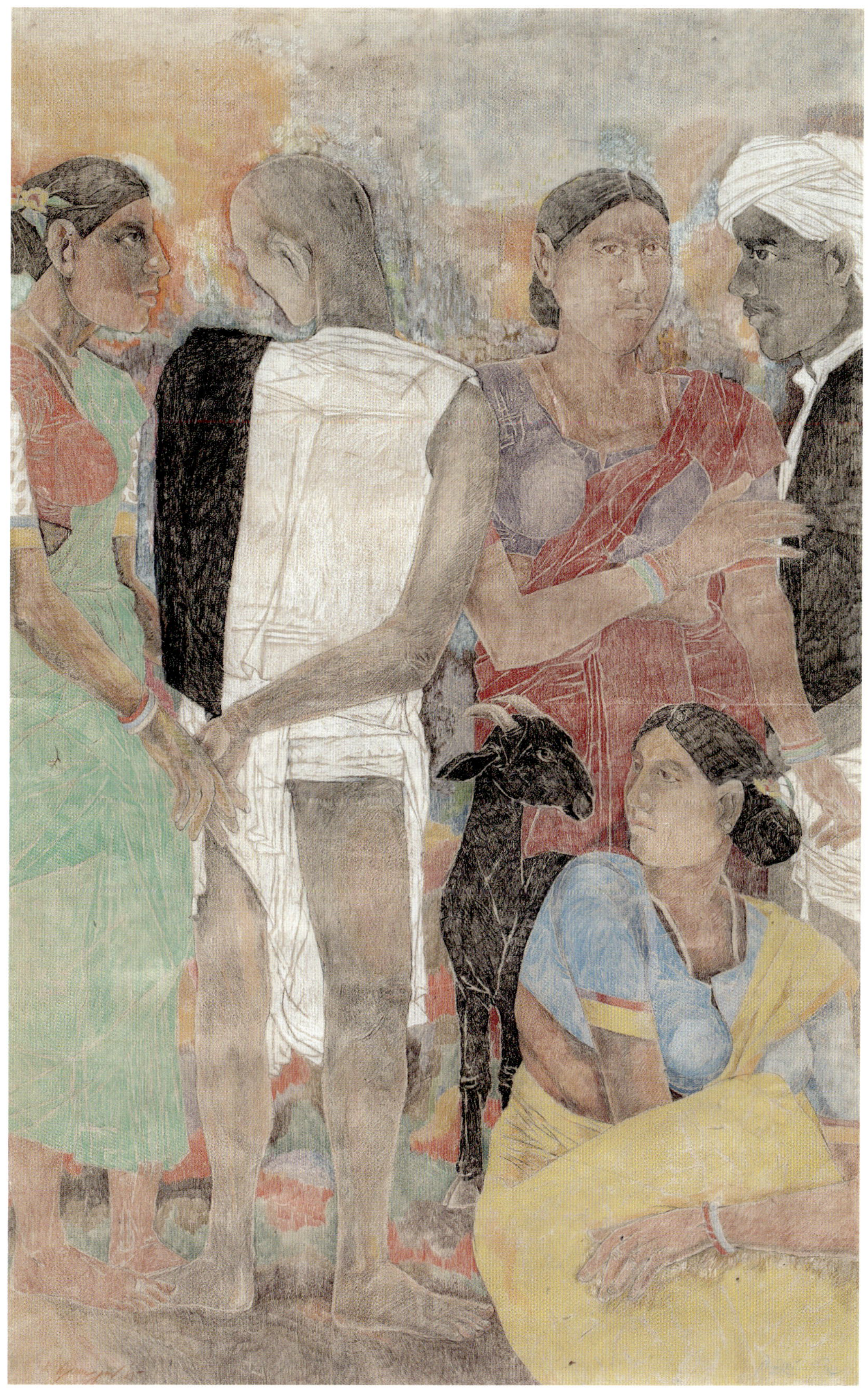

Plate 39.
Untitled, 1987
Oil pastel and pencil on paper
46 × 29 ¾ inches (116.8 × 75.6 cm)

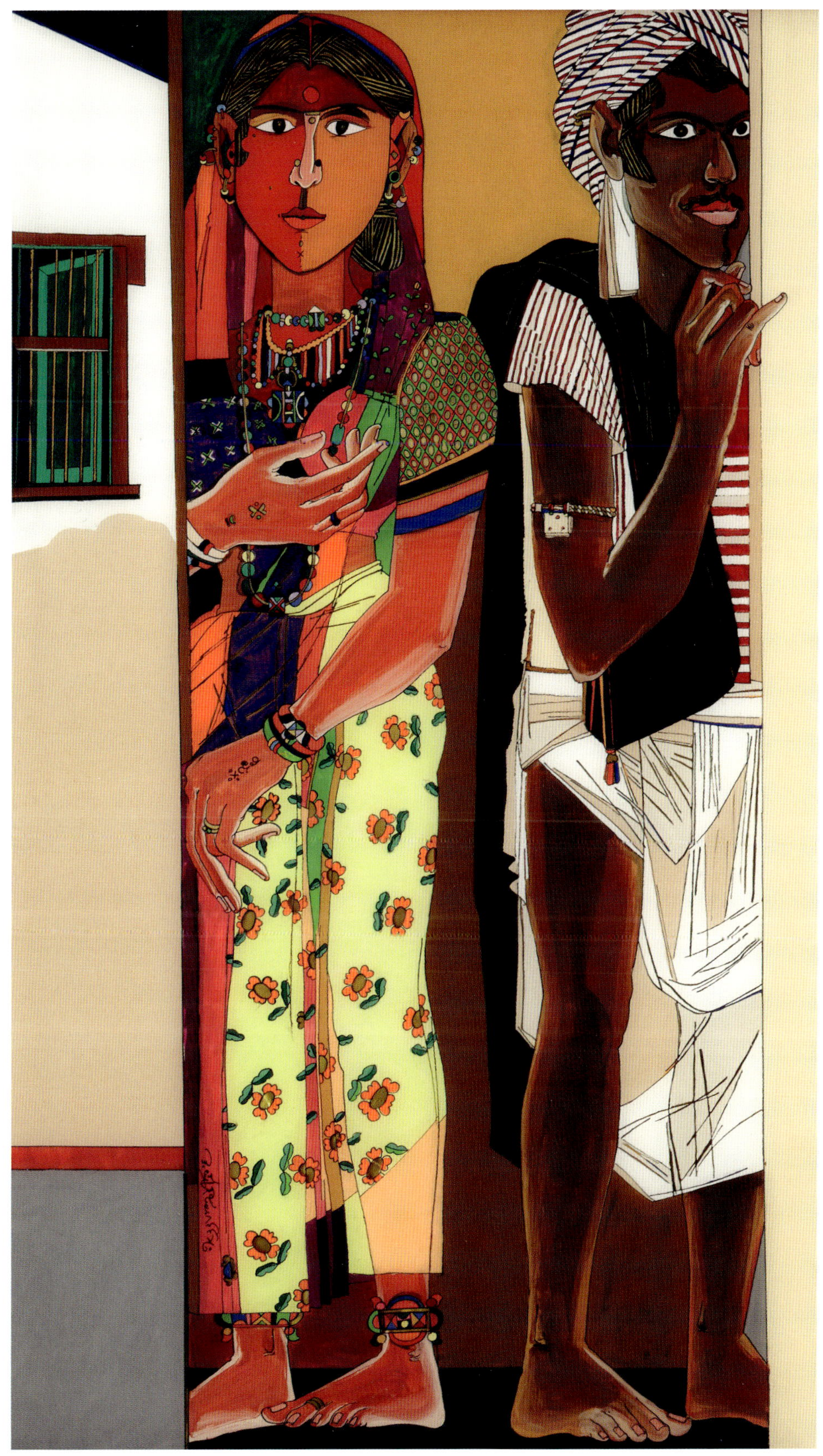

Plate 40.
Untitled, 1991
Reverse painting on acrylic
36 ⅜ × 20 ⅜ inches (92.4 × 51.8 cm)

BHUPEN KHAKHAR

Born in Bombay, 1934–2003 died in Baroda
Lived and worked in Baroda

In 1972, Bhupen Khakhar declared: "All revolutions in painting come about by change in subject matter."[1] This brash and even inaccurate statement speaks well, however, for Khakhar's own work, in which formal change was often driven by the desire to represent something new. He pushed at the boundaries of appropriate subjects for painting, whether by celebrating the questionable taste of the middle class or representing gay men making love. Khakhar widely expanded the area of Indian life visible in painting, but a unique and consistent tone unites his body of work. Often called "serious jokes," Bhupen's paintings balance satirical distance and loving intimacy with his subjects.

Born in Bombay, Khakhar spent much of his adulthood in the artists' haven of Baroda. Dissatisfied with his life as an accountant, he desired to become an artist and writer—he wrote short stories in Gujarati throughout his life. Even before his first solo exhibition in 1965, Khakhar's artistic promise was recognized and his work was included in important group shows, including those traveling to Europe. By the time he held his second solo show in Delhi in 1967, his place among the most influential Indian contemporary artists was assured.

Khakhar was associated with the group of artists focused upon the development of narrative and figurative painting. Throughout the 1970s, he represented the lives of what Geeta Kapur called the "insignificant man."[2] These seemingly straightforward portraits usually placed men alongside simple props—a scarf, a bouquet, or a *jalebi* sweet—but their sensitive rendering suggests that these common men lead rich internal lives.[3] In these paintings, Khakhar first began to explore the realm of desire that later became his central preoccupation.

The landmark 1981 exhibition *Place for People* included what has come to be understood as Khakhar's "coming out" painting: *You Can't Please All* (figure 1). It illustrates Aesop's fable of a man and his son taking a donkey to market, which is plotted in continuous narration. The nude figure watching the story from a balcony is a self-portrait. This painting marks the beginning of the explorations of gay sexuality that characterized Bhupen's work in the 1980s and 1990s.[4] Ranging from ecstatic scenes of sexual play to glimpses of intimacy, many include self-portraits. *My Dear Friend* (1983), for instance, finds Khakhar gazing at his lover, who shares his bed, while the town around them goes about its business. *Man Embracing* (plate 43) presents a similar but heterosexual scene, making this a rare instance in the artist's oeuvre in which a female nude appears. This medium likewise is unusual—reverse painting on glass—a technique he used briefly in the 1980s after being inspired by the use of a similar process by fellow Baroda painter K.G. Subramanyan (plates 20–23).[5] A more typical aspect of *Man Embracing* is the inclusion of a window, a compositional device that allowed Khakhar to include additional narrative elements in his canvases. Behind a lattice appears to be a kitchen, with jars and plates displayed in the manner typical of the Gujarati middle class. The small detail establishes the social context and joins the scene to Khakhar's earlier explorations of "insignificant men."

A windowlike space also appears in *First Day in New York* (plate 41), a self-portrait commemorating his taxi ride into the city. Behind diagonal slats, the city skyline is obscured by rain clouds and occasional trees growing in bright green parks. Khakhar was often struck by the dreary weather of the West, so different from hot, arid Gujarat. When he went to England in 1979, he painted a television weatherman, whom he noted was an extraordinarily important figure in British life. Khakhar found such details quite wonderful and was a wry observer while traveling. *First Day in New York* shows him in that role, blithely staring out the window as his companion clutches the city map and assumes responsibility.

An untitled 1984 watercolor (plate 42) demonstrates the artist's fascination with the human body, which increased throughout his career. In this interior, a nude man stretched out on a bed carries twin fetuses in his belly. Outside the window, a tropical landscape befits the story behind the painting: the miraculous birth of twins to a man in Bangladesh. Such a story would have fascinated Khakhar, whose interest in sexuality led him to explore a number of body issues, from the somatic effects of desire to the ravages of violence and disease, in paintings he did while enduring treatment for prostate cancer.[6] This painting is also an example of Khakhar's extraordinary facility with watercolor, a difficult and unforgiving medium that he used increasingly in the 1990s. The most famous example is *An Old Man from Vasad Who Had Five Penises Suffered from a Runny Nose* (figure 2). Like the pregnant man, he stares out of the painting while frankly displaying his physical predicament. *Old Man* draws humorously on an elaborate but very commonplace notion of the body shared by Hindus, in which yogic practices allow men to contain the vital substance of semen. Ordinary methods for disciplining the body's unruliness are clearly insufficient here, so the hapless man is overcome by mucous.

Khakhar is admired as one of the most innovative and original Indian artists of the twentieth century. Although he shared the deep engagement with visual culture and figurative painting of his fellow artists in Baroda, his kinship with popular aesthetics and sense of dry wit were unique among his peers. – KZ

1. Gieve Patel, "Interview with Bhupen Khakhar," *The Times of India*, June 25, 1967.

2. Geeta Kapur, *Contemporary Indian Artists* (New Delhi: Vikas Publishing House, 1978), pp. 147–77.

3. See Gieve Patel, "Contemporary Indian Painting," *Daedalus* 118, 4 (Fall 1989), pp. 171–205; and the essays in Usha Mirchandani, *Bhupen Khakhar: A Retrospective* (Mumbai: National Gallery of Modern Art and The Fine Art Resource, 2003).

4. See Timothy Hyman, *Bhupen Khakhar* (Bombay: Chemould Publications, 1998); Geeta Kapur, "Lightness of Being: Bhupen Khakhar's Recent Watercolours," *Art Asia Pacific* 14 (September 1997), n.p.; and Rustom Bharucha, "Genet in Manila," *Third Text* 17, 1 (January 2003), pp. 15–28.

5. Kamala Kapoor, "Splash: Images on Glass: Individualistic Harmonies," *The Economic Times*, November 10, 1990.

6. See *Bhupen Khakhar* (Madrid: Museo Nacional Centro de Arte Reina Sofia, 2002).

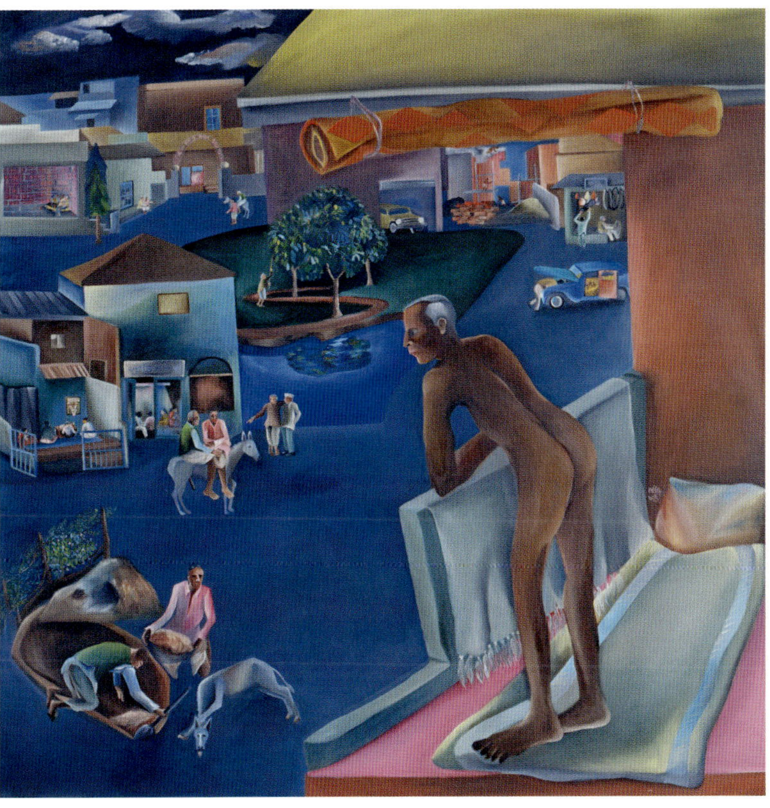

Figure 1.
Bhupen Khakhar,
You Can't Please All, 1981
Oil on canvas
69 × 69 inches (175.3 × 175.3 cm)
Tate Collection, London

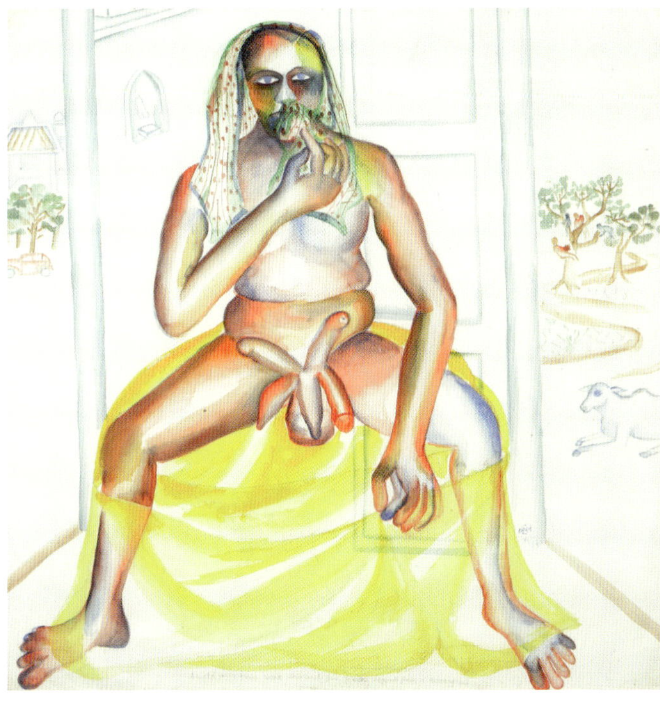

Figure 2.
Bhupen Khakhar,
An Old Man from Vasad Who Had Five Penises Suffered from a Runny Nose, 1995
Watercolor on paper
43 × 43 inches (109.2 × 109.2 cm)
Bhupen Khakhar Estate

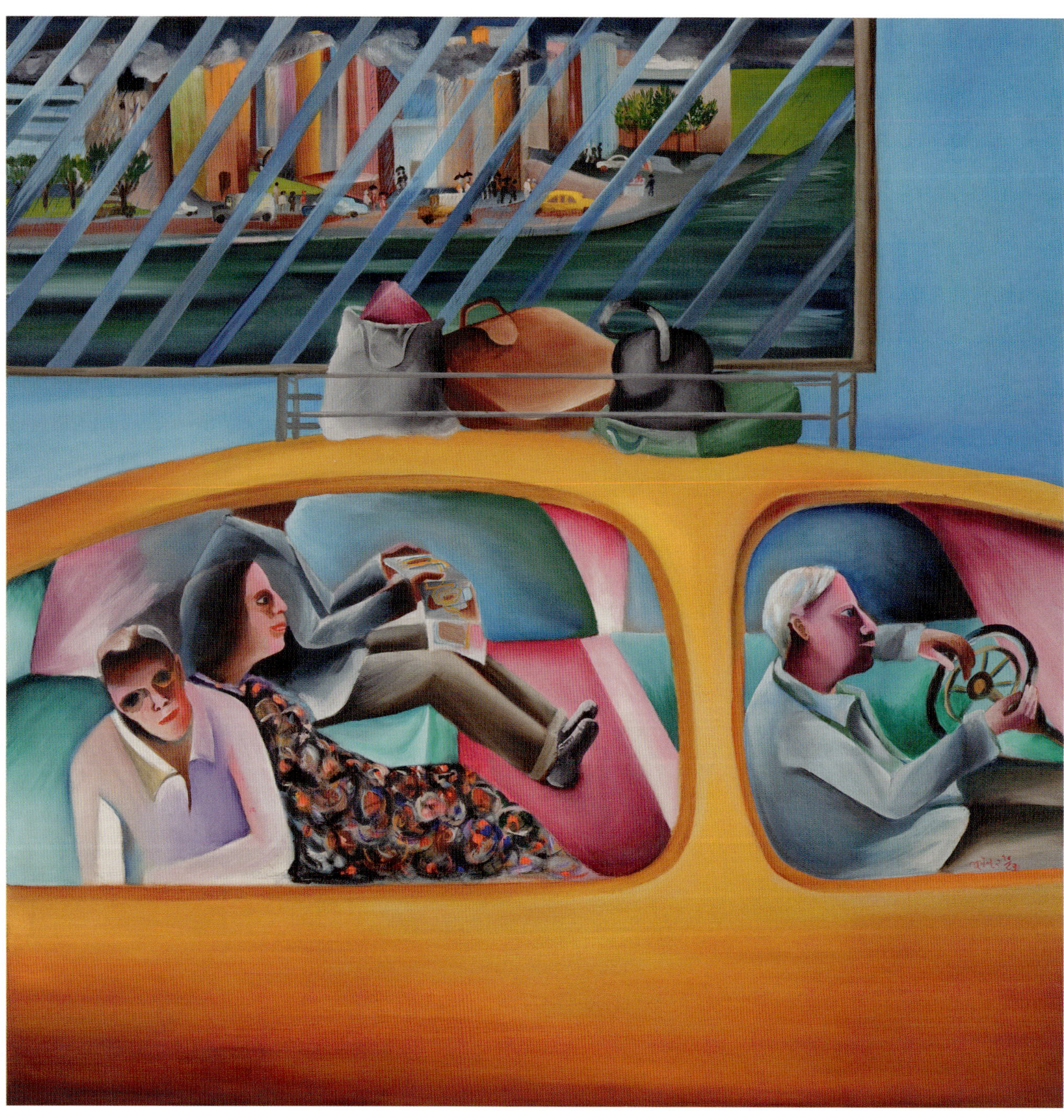

Plate 41.
First Day in New York, 1983
Oil on canvas
44 × 44 inches (111.8 × 111.8 cm)

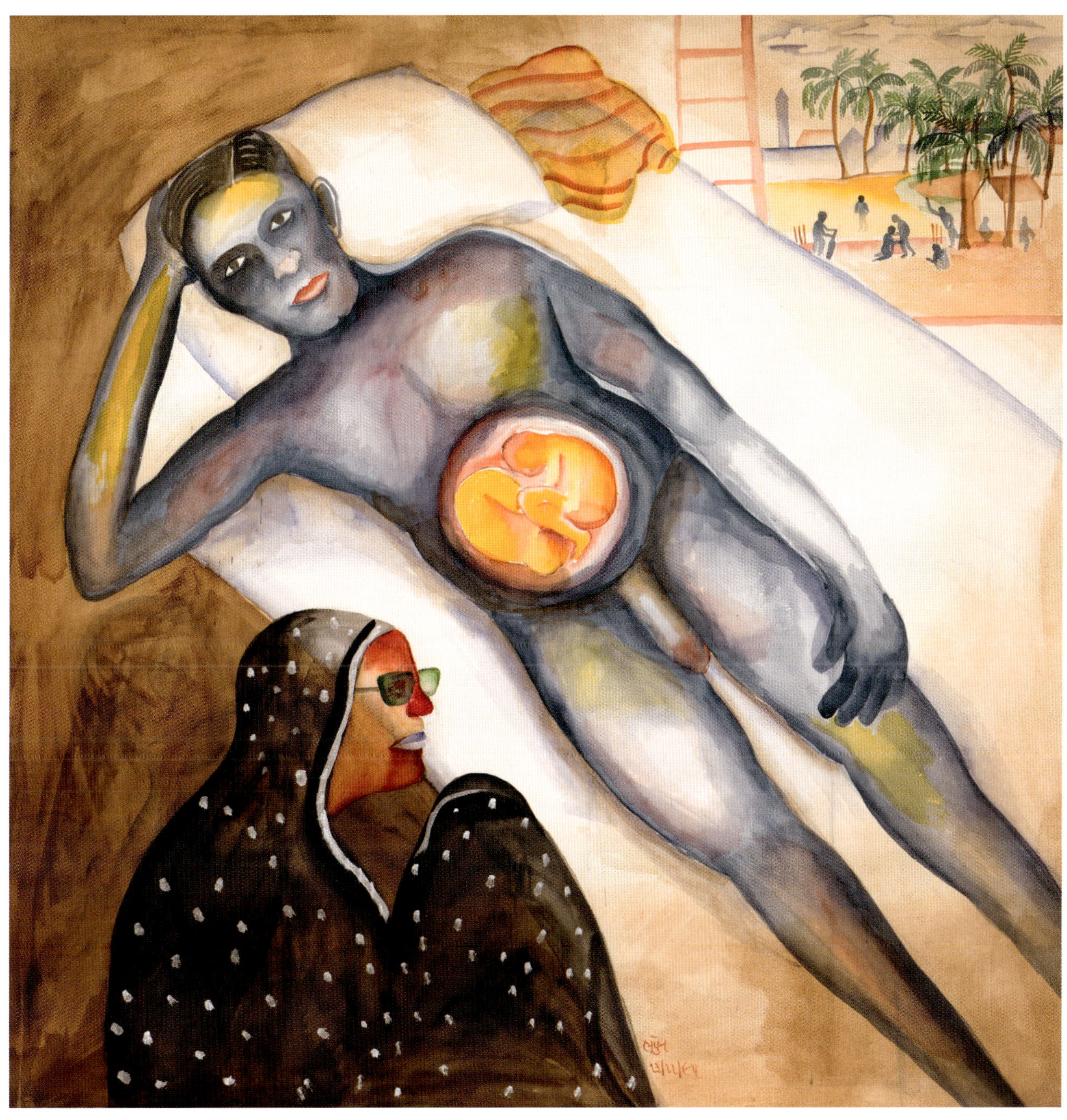

Plate 42.
Untitled, 1984
Watercolor on paper
42 ½ × 42 ½ inches (108 × 108 cm)

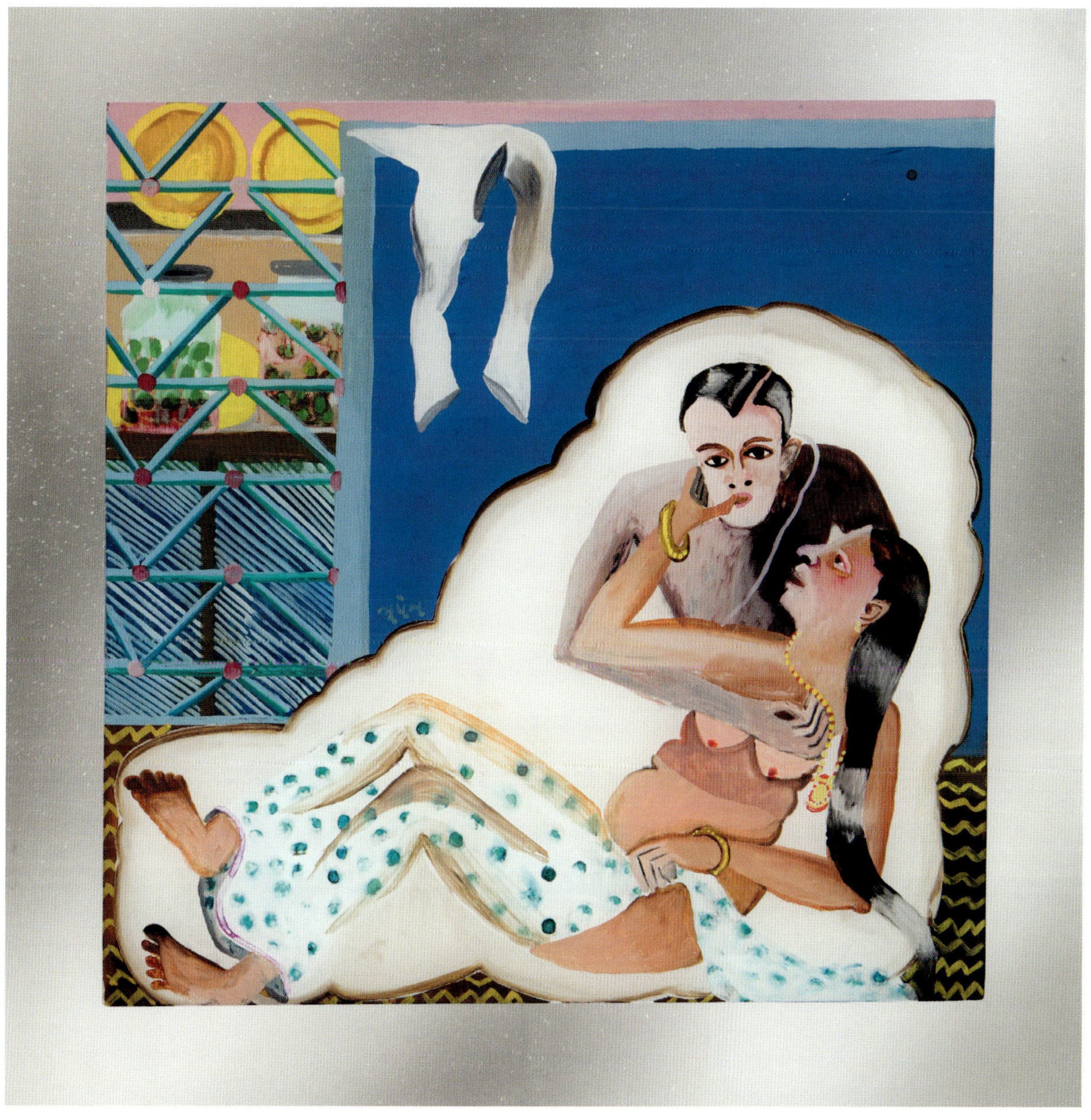

Plate 43.
Man Embracing, 1980s
Reverse painting on glass with mirror surround
18 ⅛ × 18 ¼ inches (46 × 46.4 cm)

NASREEN MOHAMEDI

Born in Karachi (now in Pakistan), 1937–1990 died in Kihim, near Bombay
Lived and worked in Baroda and Bombay

Nasreen Mohamedi's work invites the viewer to consider gesture and geometry, spatial and formal abstraction, the mystical and the concrete. Mohamedi pursued a path distinct from her contemporaries in South Asia, exploring geometric patterns through photographs and delicate drawings in pen and pencil on paper. Her photographs (figure 1) operated as studies: never exhibited during her lifetime, they isolate the lines of a crosswalk, frame the patterns of stone pavement at the sixteenth-century Mughal palace-city Fatehpur Sikri, or highlight the fuzzy perspective of a weaver's loom. Four drawings emblematic of her work in the 1980s feature clusters of lines coalescing to form intersecting planes, set against a fragile background of blank paper (plates 44–47). Earlier drawings of the 1970s pursue patterns that take up the entire sheet and echo her casual diary pages in which textual entries are overcome by—or transform into—linear patterns.

Mohamedi was born in Karachi in British India (now Pakistan) and moved with her family to Bombay at the age of seven. She studied at St. Martin's School of Art in London in 1954–57, then returned to India, living and working in Bombay for several years before settling in Baroda, where she taught in the Fine Arts Department of Maharaja Sayajirao University beginning in 1973. Her work has been shown in a variety of contexts, from Delhi to Paris and Oslo.[1]

Mohamedi had a particular way of seeing the world in terms of gesture and mark-making. Her photographs reveal attention to the marks living things make on the world and resonate with the touch of her hand and the careful movement of the pen or pencil across the paper. Concerned with the ways in which the grid and the pattern emerge in nature, she attempted in her compositions not to order the world through modernist structure, but instead to seek the underlying rhythms of natural phenomena. Mohamedi's attention to the natural world undermines many of the connections viewers make to European and American Minimalism. Therefore, despite the visual resonance, Mohamedi's art diverges significantly from the paintings of Agnes Martin, to whom she is often compared but whose work Mohamedi saw only late in life.[2] Both women engaged the grid and both explored the idea of the flaw or the mark of the hand within the structure of geometric pattern. But, Mohamedi did not incorporate color in her work, nor did she turn to painting, preferring drawing on paper in much smaller scale than her contemporary Martin. Rather than making monumental work akin to Abstract Expressionism, Mohamedi created an experience of the trace of the human on an intimate scale through scant gestures and the minute flutter of the hand.

Like her contemporaries in Europe, America, Japan, Korea, and South Asia, Mohamedi too turned to the spiritual in her work, exploring the concept of the void through Zen philosophy and linking the microcosm of her gesture to the macrocosm of the universe through the lessons of India's Tantric Buddhist and Hindu traditions. She drew as well on questions of optics and perspective, manipulating three-dimensional space on a two-dimensional surface—particularly salient for drawings from the 1980s. Like other painters of her generation, she was inspired by earlier masters such as Paul Klee, whose abstractions link the natural and the otherworldly. Mohamedi's diaries highlight a need for "good design," emphasizing an efficiency of gesture and a sought-after perfection in her artistic process. Her floating spatial line drawings bring together the mechanical and the human, the mundane, everyday gesture and the grand patterns of nature.

Geeta Kapur, in an elegy to her late friend, saw Mohamedi's work as undermining a frontal, challenging gaze in favor of a sideways glance.[3] The intimate scale, delicate, sometimes almost effaced lines, and the thin shake of the human gesture do not face the viewer head-on. Nor do these works envelop the body like those of Abstract Expressionists Barnett Newman, Mark Rothko, or Agnes Martin, all of whom drew on similar spiritual language to articulate their work. Instead, Mohamedi explored the diagonal, the nonfrontal, the miniature. Her work might be more fruitfully situated with the 1970s work of Park Seo-bo and other Korean Monochrome artists of that period who experimented with gesture and line in repetitive, simple paintings. Where Korean Monochrome art looked to Northeast Asian calligraphic tradition and the Joeson dynasty's (1392–1897) privileging of the color white, Mohamedi's intimate compositions evoke the small scale of India's manuscript painting and calligraphy traditions, with their attention to minute detail and the honed, repeated artist's gesture.[4] Mohamedi drew prolifically throughout the last decade of her life, working through the growing instability of her body as she suffered the effects of Parkinson's disease. Her marks, therefore, trace a transcendence, perhaps in part spiritual but also poignantly human and physical. – RMB

1. Venues include the Third Triennial in New Delhi (1975), Paris in 1985, several exhibitions of the Herwitz Collection, a show of contemporary Indian drawing in 2000, at Documenta 12 in 2007, and in a retrospective exhibition that toured to Oslo's Office for Contemporary Art, Basel's Kunsthalle, and England's Milton Keynes Gallery in 2009 and 2010. Soman Gopinath and Grant Watson, *Nasreen Mohamedi: Notes: Reflections on Indian Modernism* (Oslo: Office for Contemporary Art Norway, 2009).

2. Geeta Kapur, *When Was Modernism: Essays on Contemporary Cultural Practice in India* (New Delhi: Tulika Press, 2000), p. 73; Grant Watson, "Passage and Placement: Nasreen Mohamedi," *Afterall* 21 (Summer 2009), n.p.

3. Kapur, p. 68.

4. For more on the gesture and repetition in Indian painting, see Molly Emma Aitken, *The Intelligence of Tradition in Rajput Court Painting* (New Haven and London: Yale University Press, 2010), pp. 57–109.

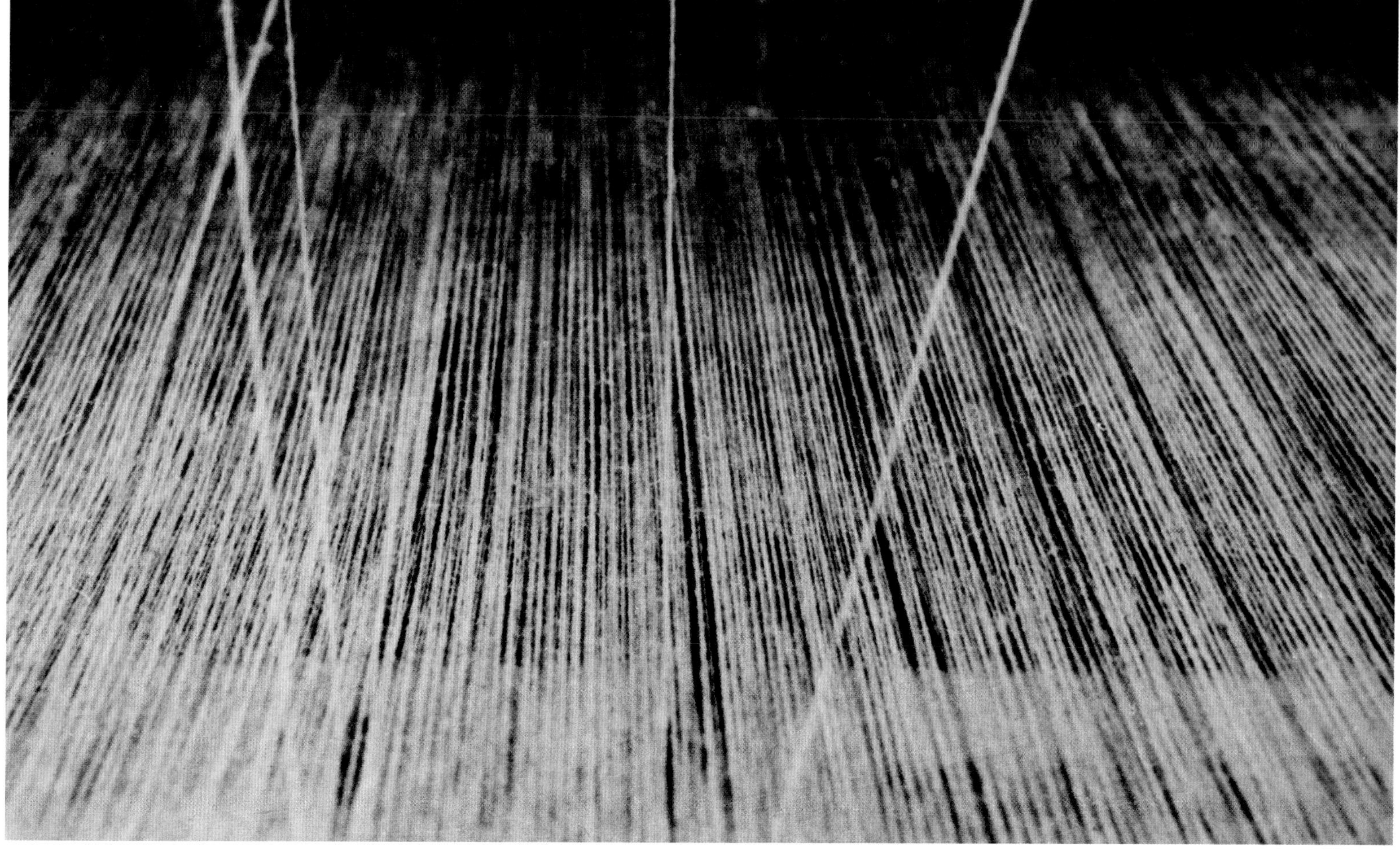

Figure 1.
Nasreen Mohamedi, *Untitled 5*, ca. 1970
Photograph
8 ⅝ × 14 ½ inches (21.9 × 36.8 cm)
Talwar Gallery, New York/New Delhi

Plate 44.
Untitled, ca. 1983
Ink and pencil on paper
22 ⅞ × 28 ⅞ inches (58.1 × 73.3 cm)

Plate 45.
Untitled, ca. 1984
Ink and pencil on paper
20 × 19 ⅞ inches (50.8 × 50.5 cm)

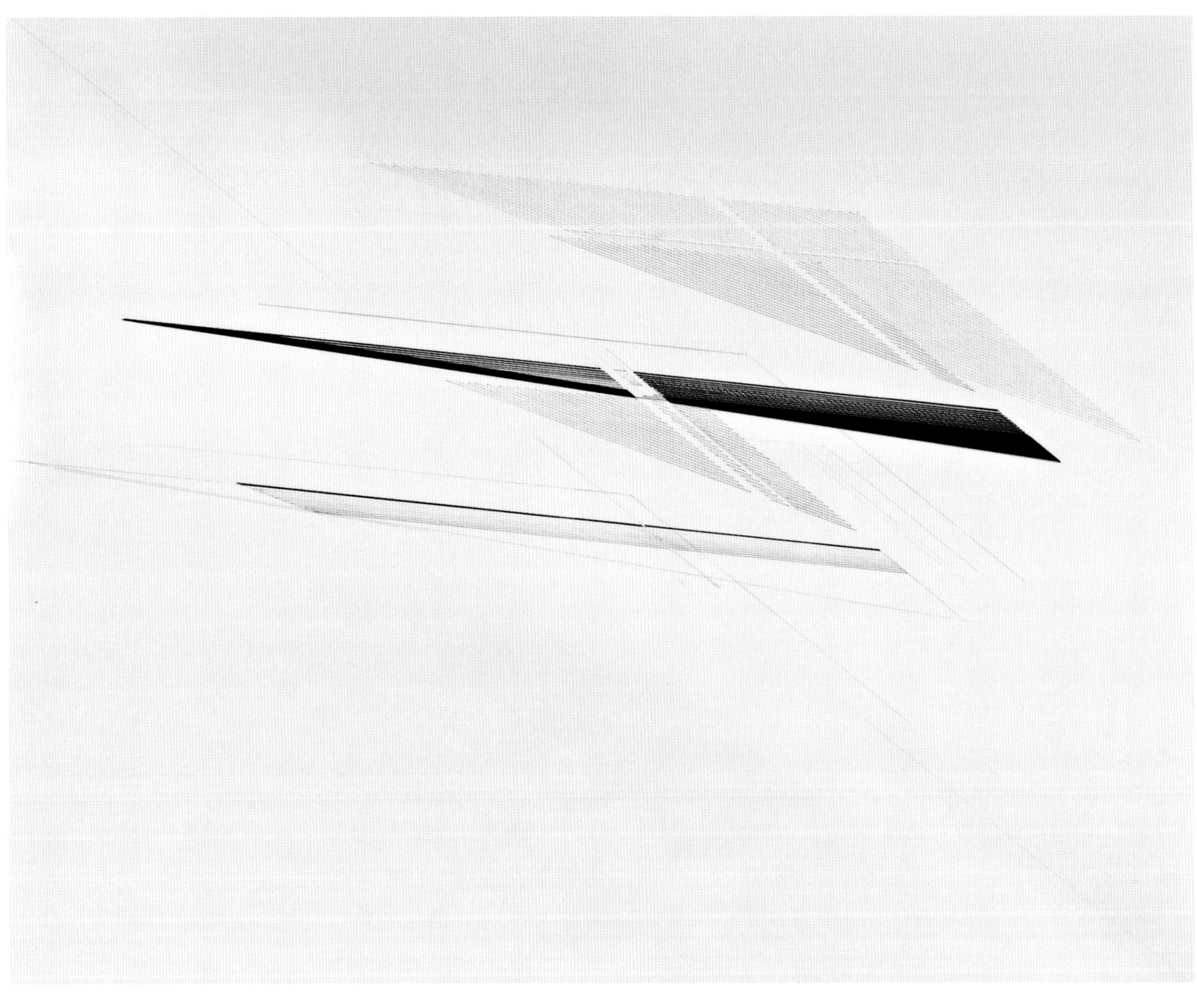

Plate 46.
Untitled, ca. 1985
Ink and pencil on paper
23 × 29 inches (58.4 × 73.7 cm)

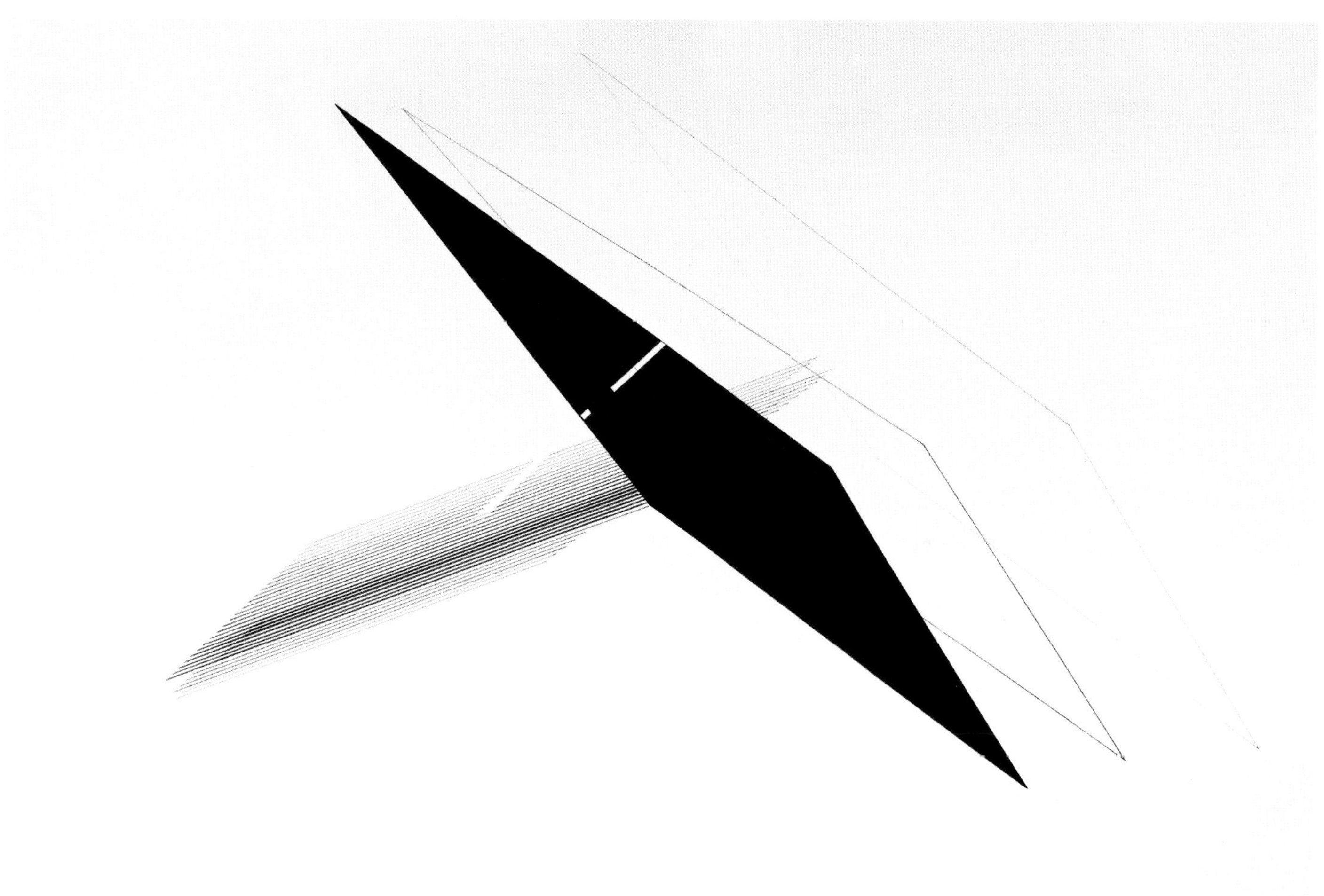

Plate 47.
Untitled, ca. 1985
Ink and pencil on paper on board
20 × 28 inches (50.8 × 71.1 cm)

GIEVE PATEL

Born in Bombay, 1940
Lives and works in Bombay

Gieve Patel was born and raised in Bombay. His aesthetic sensibility is in tune with the experience of living in that mammoth city, which is aware of its own monumentality and intimidating to the individual. In his paintings, as in his poetry and plays, Patel considers people with a clinical detachment and total lack of sentimentality. But, in a city dominated by grand architecture, his paintings foreground the enduring presence of people.

A member of Bombay's Parsi community, Patel grew up in South Bombay and attended St. Xavier's College and Grant Medical College. He also spent time on his family's estate in rural Gujarat. Up until 2005, he worked as a general practitioner in clinics in the city and the countryside. He began to paint after he was given a book about Peter Paul Rubens, but he also wrote, first poetry and then plays. He held his first solo show and published his first book of poetry in the same year, 1966, and has since remained an important presence across the arts in the city.[1] In all three forms, Patel's work is characterized by a keen eye for telling detail, particularly for the physical signs of moral entanglements. Paradigmatic of his moral outlook is his best-known and beloved poem, "On Killing a Tree," which is commonly taught to Indian high school students. It begins by wryly observing that "It takes much time to kill a tree,/Not a simple jab of the knife/Will do it," before describing in detail the resilience of the tree against superficial attacks. Next, the poem calmly recommends that it be pulled out by its roots, for then, "the strength of the tree exposed, [...] Browning, hardening,/ Twisting, withering," the sun and air will finish the task of destruction that man began. By maintaining a careful distance from the suffering it so thoroughly describes, this poem exposes the violence with which human beings dominate the natural world.

Patel's paintings take a similarly dispassionate view of everyday human tragedies, whether they have recognizably political implications or more intimate social reverberations.[2] *Two Men with Handcart* (plate 48), *Early Guest* (plate 49), and *Gateway* (plate 50) show Patel at his very finest, in a period during which he solidified his approach to painting and produced his most iconic images. Preoccupied with color, finding painterly challenges in the pinks and greens that, surprisingly enough, are quite commonly found on buildings in India, Patel tempered his broad planes of color with patterns that at once suggest depth and remain resolutely on the surface, reminding the viewer of the artifice of painting.

Patel participated in the revival of narrative painting associated with the avant-garde movement in Baroda, which sought a "place for people" in Indian art.[3] Like snapshots, his paintings fix a single moment in time while suggesting a sequence of events. But, the paintings emit a sense of repose and feature people when they are inactive, possibly even bored. For example, in *Early Guest*, it is not clear what event the elderly woman is about to attend, but her sense of duty and quiet anticipation are evident in the way she holds her body. This painting is also very sociologically precise: her plain rumpled sari, trailing shawl, and tightly held pocketbook place her at the middle of middle-class respectability. Nevertheless, although she is easy to identify as a type, her impassive stare allows her to remain unknowable as an individual.

Gateway and *Two Men with Handcart* are equally exact in their recording of social position, but they add two further layers of social meaning. First, they record the interactions of individuals who may be friends; second, they plot relationships between human archetypes of urban poverty and the monumental architecture of the city.[4] The man and woman in *Gateway* are obviously attached to one another in a social sense. But, they are also grotesque figures, either in fact or in Patel's representation of the facts. Her face may actually be disfigured or it might be a metaphor; his legs may truly be stick thin or it might be an effect of the paint. There is no mistaking their relationship to the glorious monument that looms behind them, however: the Gateway of India is a symbolic portal to the city, an artifact of British rule that has been thoroughly domesticated as a site of tourism and Bombay street culture. This painting records the manner in which the contrast between that layered urban mythology and the facts of everyday life are enacted daily.

In *Two Men with Handcart*, the men in question are chatting alongside a low building with a tile roof.[5] They stand perhaps in a small lane, the type of urban space occupied almost exclusively by working people. Towering over them are apartment buildings typical of the area in which Patel had his clinic, a jumble of nineteenth- and twentieth-century architectural styles. Unlike the haggard figures in the other two examples, these two men, though clearly poor, are absolutely self-assured. The small detail of one figure momentarily and absentmindedly lifting his foot out of his sandal as he talks transforms what might have been a forceful juxtaposition of luxury with labor into an empathetic study of specific individuals.

As a painter, Patel adopts the role of the observer, never quite bridging the distance between himself and the people he represents. But, like the poet he is, he also carefully preserves the significant gestures, things, and scenes that, especially when frozen in time, evoke multiple layers of meaning. In a significant portion of his body of work, he has applied these strategies to his hometown of Bombay, creating a set of iconic images of the city that insist upon the primacy of the social life it contains. – KZ

1. Gieve Patel, *Poems* (Bombay: Nissim Ezekiel, 1966); also see his *How Do You Withstand, Body* (Bombay: Clearing House, 1976), and *Mirrored, Mirroring* (New Delhi: Oxford University Press, 1991). For commentary, see Bruce King, *Modern Indian Poetry in English* (New Delhi: Oxford University Press, 2001). Patel's plays were collected in *Mister Behram and Other Plays* (Calcutta: Seagull Books, 2008).

2. He accounts for his approach in Gieve Patel, "Contemporary Indian Painting," *Daedalus* 118, 4 (Fall 1989), pp. 171–205.

3. See Ajay Sinha, "Envisioning the Seventies and Eighties," in Gulammohammed Sheikh, ed., *Contemporary Art in Baroda* (New Delhi: Tulika Press, 1997), pp. 145–209.

4. Karin Zitzewitz, "The Moral Economy of the Street: the Bombay Paintings of Gieve Patel and Sudhir Patwardhan," *Third Text* 23, 2 (March 2009), pp. 151–63.

5. See also Rebecca M. Brown, *Art for a Modern India, 1947–1980* (Durham, North Carolina: Duke University Press, 2009).

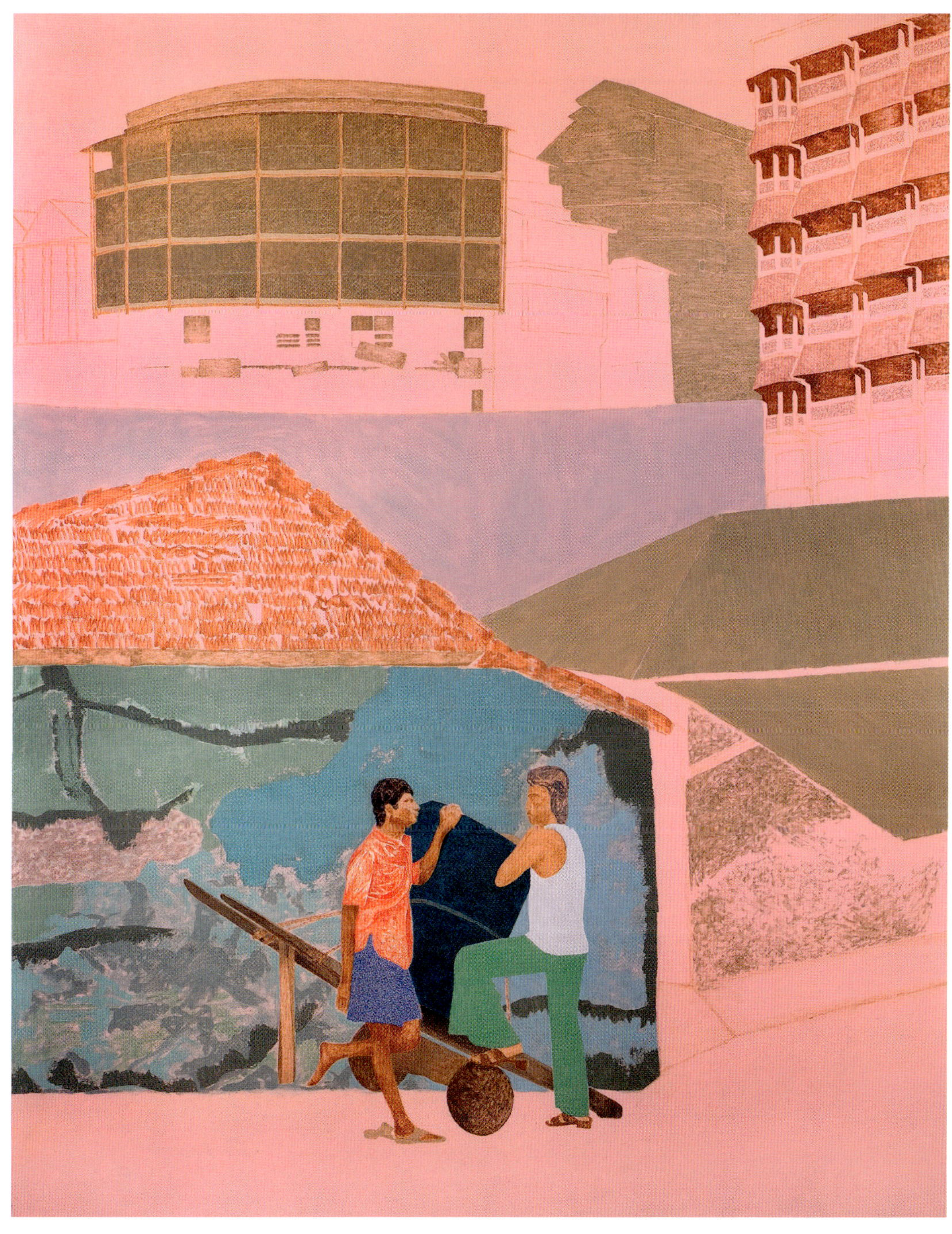

Plate 48.
Two Men with Handcart, 1979
Oil on canvas
69 ½ × 57 inches (176.5 × 144.8 cm)

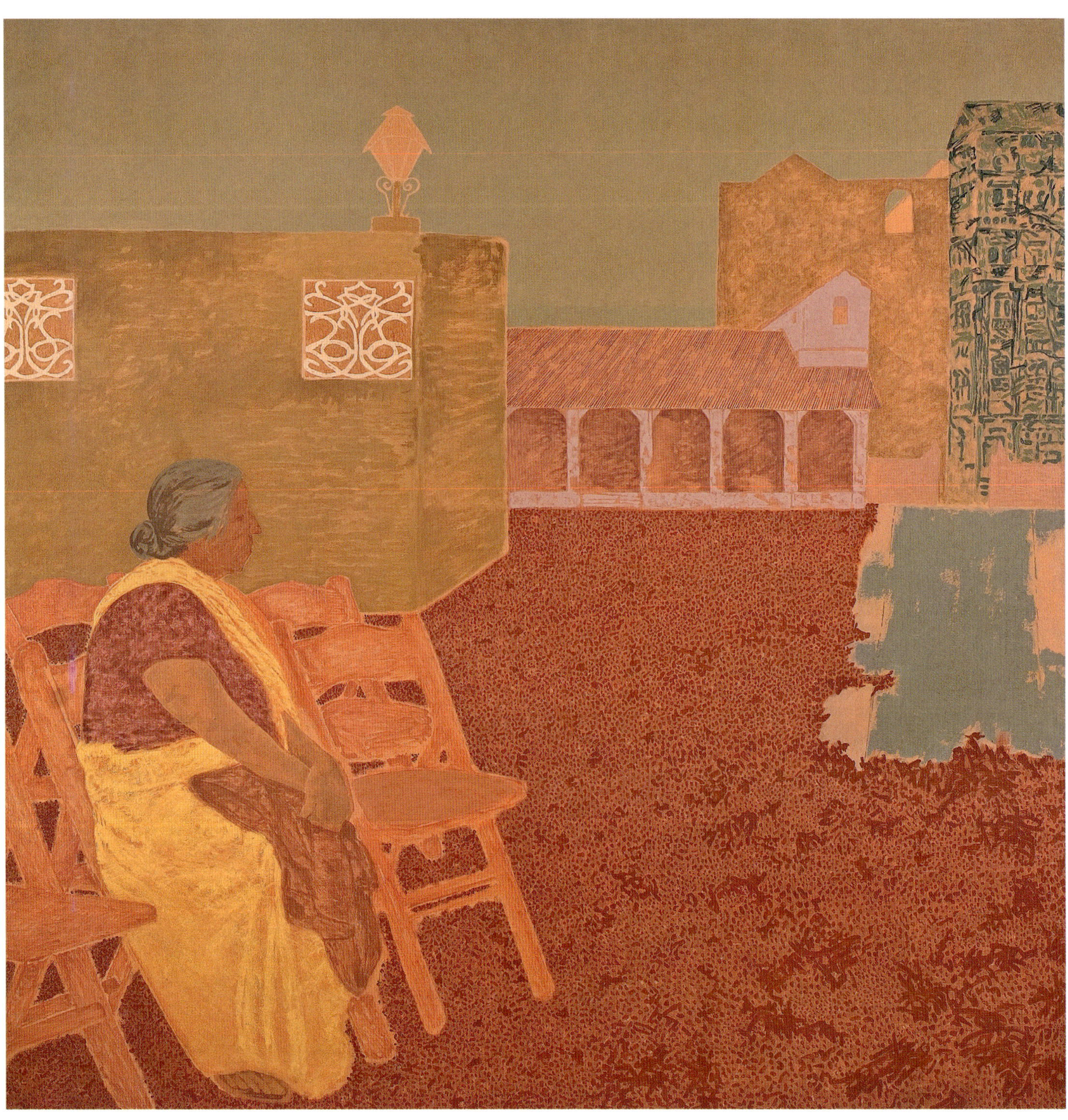

Plate 49.
Early Guest, 1981
Oil on canvas
53 ⅞ × 54 inches (136.8 × 137.2 cm)

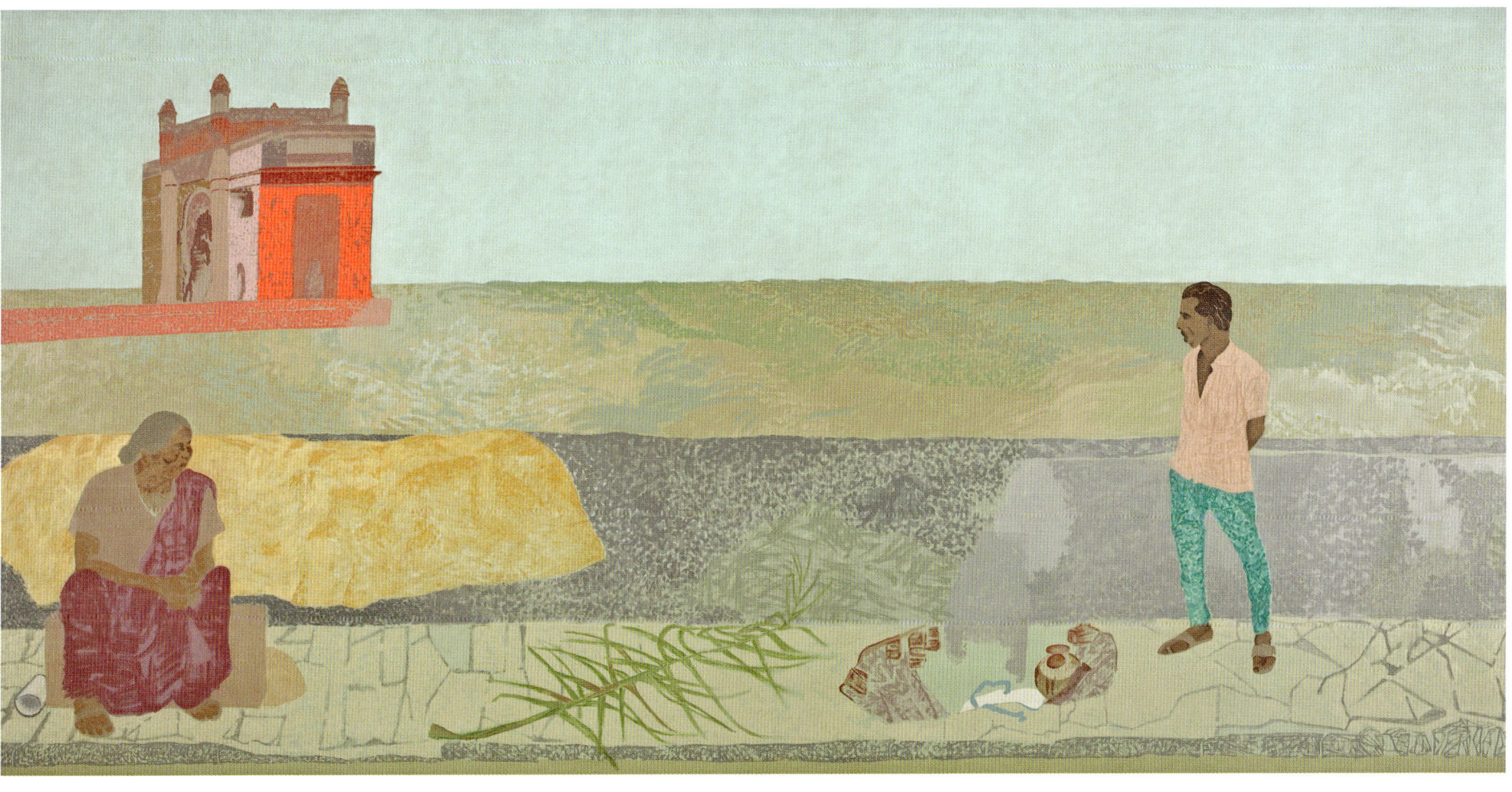

Plate 50.
Gateway, 1981
Oil on canvas
54 × 107 ⅜ inches (137.2 × 272.7 cm)

GANESH PYNE

Born in Calcutta, 1937
Lives and works in Calcutta

Ganesh Pyne's work is often described as melancholic, with watery canvases depicting dark scenes of ghostly, skeletal figures and spindly vegetation. His figures populate the interstices between living and dead, mundane and otherworldly, present and past: "the twilight zone means the meeting point of day and night, of life and death, of love and agony—where everything is seen in a different light."[1]

Pyne was born in Calcutta, ten years before independence. Some of his earliest and most formative memories center on the city's 1946 riots. Evacuated from his home, and with the entire city contorted in conflict, Pyne wandered into the streets where he saw a handcart filled with dead people, including an old woman whose gold necklace gleamed around her neck but whose body had turned gray: "I was shaken by the sight. Since then, I have been obsessed with the dark world."[2] In his paintings, he often plumbs the darker aspects of humanity, using ashen tones, wide, staring eyes, and spectral bodies to explore how we live and breathe in concert with the otherworldly and the ghostly.

Many critics have linked Pyne's melancholic mood to the city where he has lived his entire life. Calcutta was the center of intellectual, artistic, and political activity prior to independence, and Pyne draws from the delicate and careful watercolor and drawing traditions of Abanindranath Tagore and the Bengal School and the experimentations with local painting traditions that took place at Santiniketan, an art school founded by Rabindranath Tagore.[3] At fifteen, Pyne saw an exhibition of Abanindranath Tagore's paintings at the Indian Museum that deeply shaped his eventual artistic language and demonstrated the power of art to engage politically with the formation of the new nation.[4] Pyne attended the Government College of Arts and Crafts in Calcutta between 1955 and 1959, and lived in his family's home in north Calcutta for most of his adult life. His grandmother shaped his visions of Bengali life by narrating folk tales and opening a view into the richness of the vernacular tradition. Pyne circulated among poets, playwrights, musicians and artists, gained exposure to European art through lectures and reproductions, and immersed himself in European and Japanese film.

The 1960s was a vibrant, exciting time in the city's intellectual and artistic circles. Coffee houses served as centers for debate and discussion, continuing earlier artistic and political activism decrying the 1943 famine in Calcutta and supporting workers' movements. In 1963, Pyne joined the Society of Contemporary Artists and developed a new idiom based on the human skeletal form. The death of his beloved grandmother in 1965 coincided with a darkening of subject matter. During the 1960s, Pyne's art had fully emerged and his work was included in prestigious exhibitions and collections such as the National Gallery of Modern Art in New Delhi and the first Delhi Triennial, where he exhibited along with Bikash Bhattacharjee (plates 27–29).

At the opening of the 1970s, Calcutta again witnessed war and death, as Bangladesh won independence from Pakistan in a bloody civil war that ended in 1971. Refugees flooded the city from the conflict just across the border, reviving memories of earlier famines and communal violence. Pyne turned inward to develop a personal iconography based on Bengali folk literature, his memories of violence, and a newfound interest in the teachings of the Hindu saint Chaitanya. He also continued to develop earlier themes in his paintings of the 1980s, weaving them together in his signature style of applying lighter colors that hover and glow over a dark undercoat of paint. The personal and political upheavals he experienced into the 1990s—a decade that saw both the economic opening of India to the world and a marked rise in communal violence and destruction—further shaped his work.

Four paintings from Pyne's mature work in the 1970s and 1980s illustrate intimate moments; two feature a single, tightly framed figure and two feature a place. *The Cobbler* and *The Rag Picker* (plates 51 and 52) present laborers found on Calcutta's streets. They are modeled after nineteenth-century colonial paintings of Indian craftsmen and household servants, but Pyne has chosen workers who recycle old, discarded materials to make a living. Rag pickers comb through trash heaps in cities across India in search of something to sell. Cobblers work with objects that are considered dirty: shoes are removed before entering the temple or the home. Pyne's ghostly atmosphere envelops these figures who operate at the edges of society. This aura of mystery reinforces the figures' liminal status and their often unacknowledged importance to the workings of the Indian city.

The Pond (plate 53) focuses on the countryside, depicting a sari-clad woman collecting twigs and branches in a fragmented, watery landscape. Pyne played with scale to give the scene a magical quality, highlighting the mottled tree root as it seeks the water of the pond and balancing its bulk against a small palm at right. In *The Fair* (plate 54), a performer has pushed back his mask to reveal a masklike face whose eyes eerily echo those of an adjacent wooden horse. Pyne found theater inspiring and here he explored the artificiality of urban and village fairs. In addition to celebrating the playfulness of performance, he used theater to focus on the shifting registers of living and performing, animate and inanimate. His palette is striking in its muted, sonorous, and saturated hues. Such works call out moments of quiet within a city and a world that continue to convulse in events rife with violence and tension. Rather than shying away from that violence, Pyne accepts and analyzes its presence by examining those who work and live in-between: on the pavement, in the theater, or across pond and shore. – RMB

1. Ganesh Pyne, quoted in Geeti Sen, *Image and Imagination: Five Contemporary Artists in India* (Ahmedabad: Mapin Publishing, 1996), p. 126.

2. Mitra Banerjee, "Ganesh Pyne: Artist Interview," *Saffron Art*, http://saffronart.com, 2005.

3. Partha Mitter, *Art and Nationalism in Colonial India, 1850–1922: Occidental Orientations* (Cambridge: Cambridge University Press, 1994); Debashish Banerji, *The Alternate Nation of Abanindranath Tagore* (New Delhi: Sage, 2010).

4. Ella Datta, *Ganesh Pyne: His Life and Times* (Calcutta: Centre of International Modern Art, 1998), p. 26; the biographical information given here relies on Datta and on Sen.

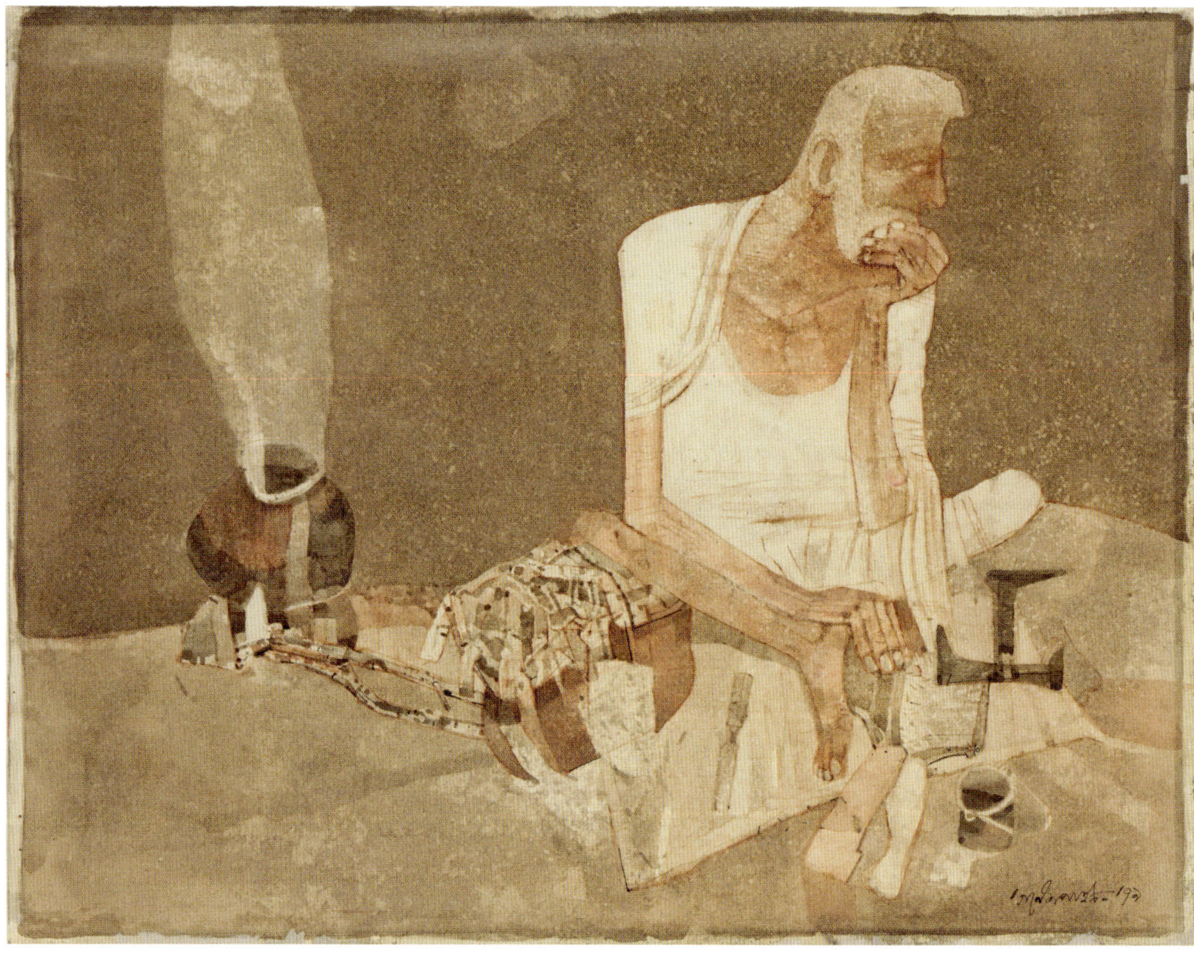

Plate 51.
The Cobbler, 1979
Tempera and ink on paper
10 ⅞ × 14 inches (27.6 × 35.6 cm)

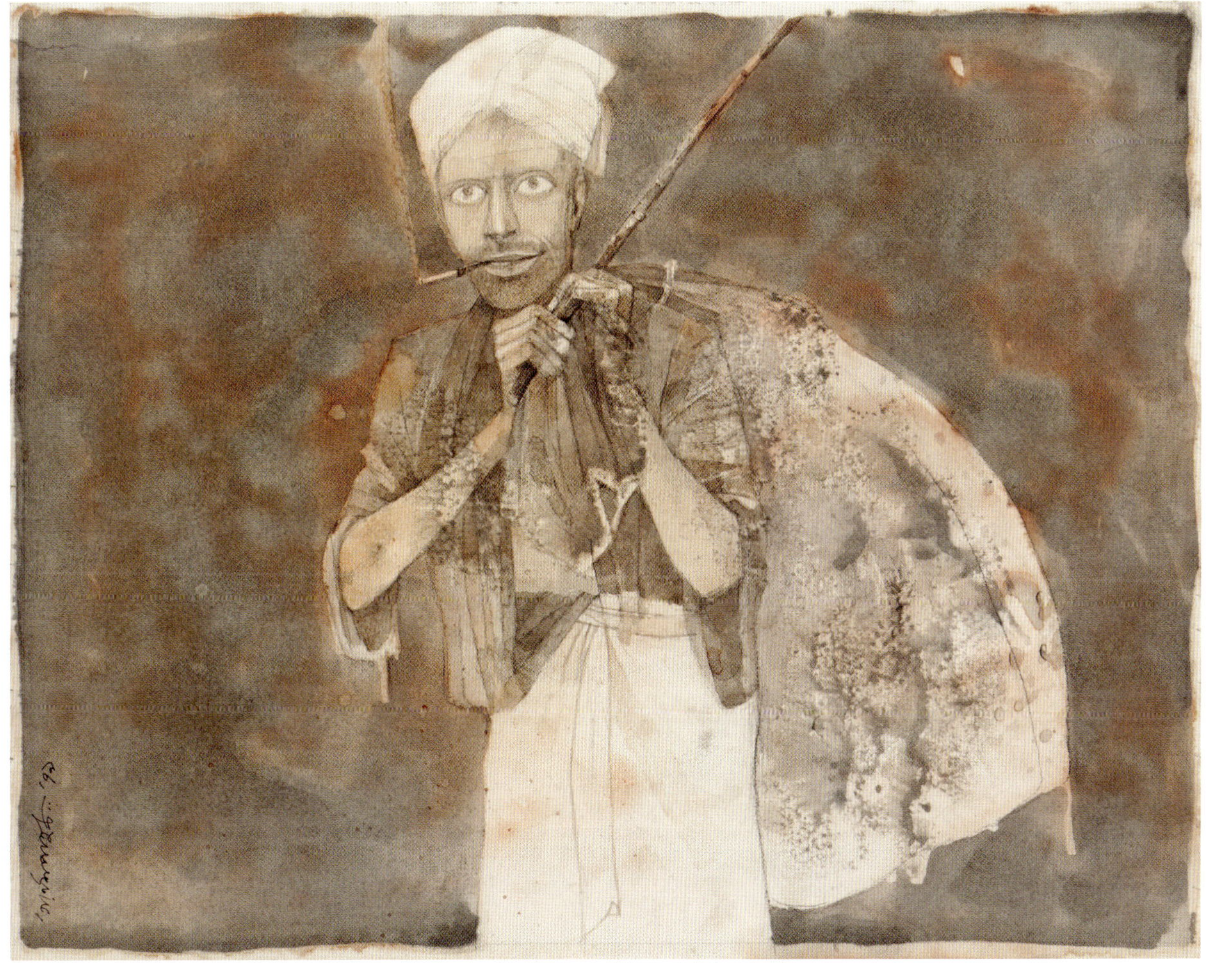

Plate 52.
The Rag Picker, 1979
Watercolor and pencil on paper
10 ¾ × 13 ¾ inches (27.3 × 34.9 cm)

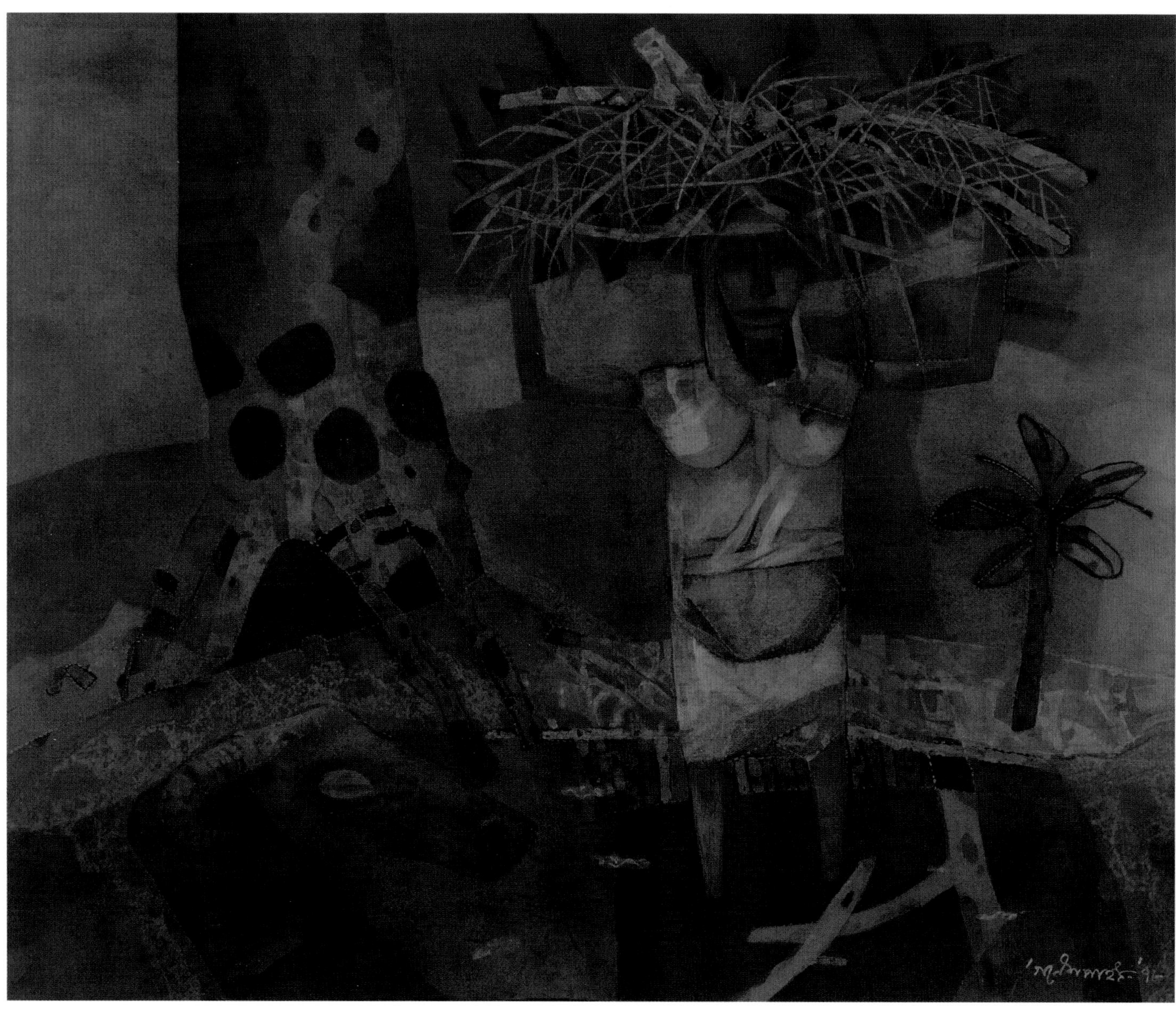

Plate 53.
The Pond, 1983
Tempera on canvas
19 ¼ × 23 ¼ inches (48.9 × 59.7 cm)

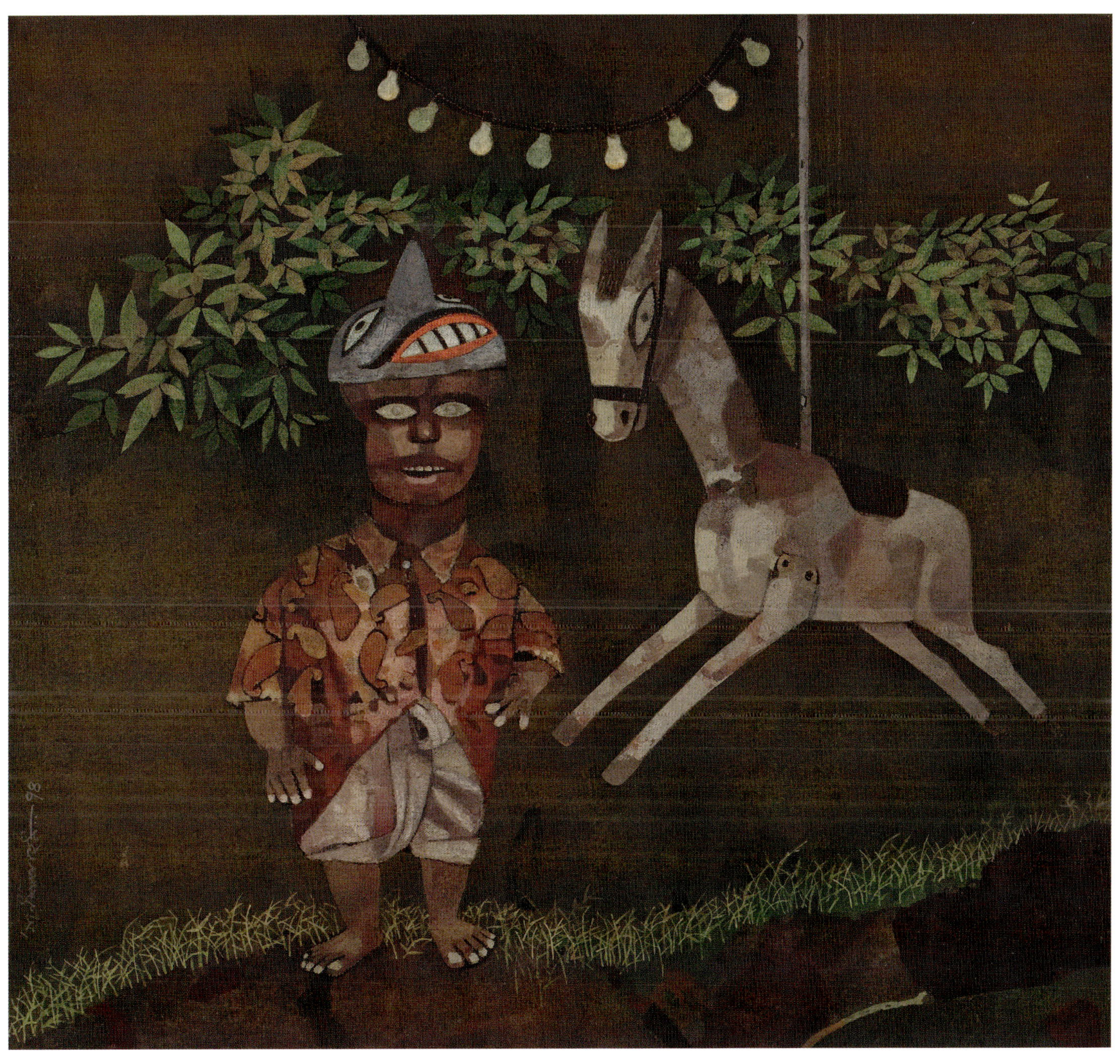

Plate 54.
The Fair, 1986
Tempera on canvas
21 ½ × 23 ½ inches (54.6 × 59.7 cm)

GULAMMOHAMMED SHEIKH

Born in Surendranagar, Gujarat, 1937
Lives and works in Baroda and Delhi

Teacher, scholar, poet, arts activist, and painter, Gulammohammed Sheikh is one of the most influential artists of his generation. By the late 1980s, he was a leading figure in the Indian art world. He was awarded the Padma Shri, one of India's highest civilian honors, and the Maharaja Sayajirao University of Baroda, where he studied and taught, made him head of the department of painting. In Baroda, Sheikh and his wife, the painter Nilima Sheikh, were for many years the vital center of the most active and innovative art community in India.

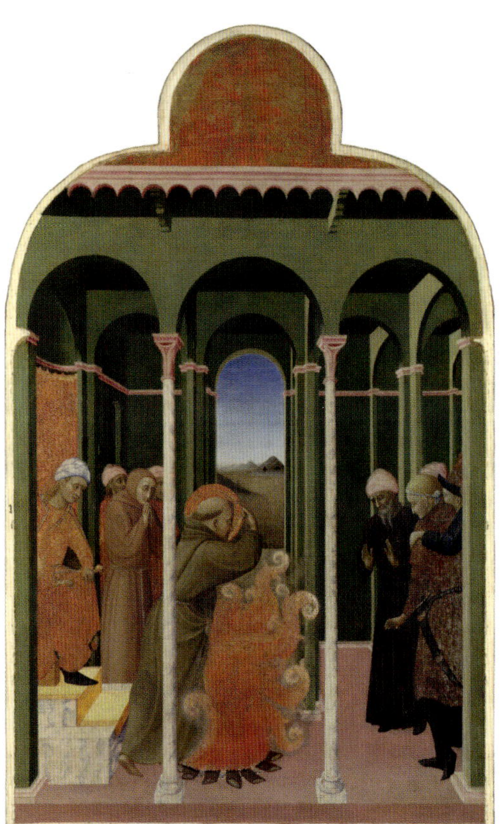

Figure 1.
Sassetta (Stefano di Giovanni),
Saint Francis before the Sultan from San Sepolcro Altar Piece, 1437–44
Egg tempera on poplar
34 × 21 inches (86.4 × 53.3 cm)
The National Gallery, London

In and Out of Story (plate 56), the triptych *Passing Angel, A Life, Summer Diary* (plate 55), and *Characters Questioning the Narrator* (plate 57) are part of Sheikh's central project exploring visual possibilities of complex, multilayered narrative. The canvases are aglow with color and crowded with figures. Sheikh arrived at his approach in the late 1960s during his years in Europe. Based at the Royal College of Art, London, he found the practices he observed in the school and local galleries less interesting than the Indian court paintings of the sixteenth-eighteenth centuries at the nearby Victoria and Albert Museum. On a trip to Italy, he discovered the early Sienese painters Duccio di Buoninsegna, Ambrogio Lorenzetti, and Sassetta (Stephano di Giovanni) (figure 1). Through their works, Sheikh learned the power of color to create mood and atmosphere. The luminous hues in Sienese paintings, "untainted by cast shadows" or "dramatic effects of light and dark," impart "an incredible sensuous seduction to the surface. The eye [is] invited to caress every form...."[1] Similarly, in paintings from the Indian courts of Mewar, Malwa, and Basohli, color seemed "derived from light and air, aromas and sounds, rather than... complexions and surface tints of objects...."[2] For his own paintings, Sheikh chose deeply saturated, luminous jewel tones to create an intense, sensuous, and mystical atmosphere.

Sheikh also made discoveries about pictorial space that became important to his work. He observed how vistas in a Lorenzetti mural opened up as one moved along its length. Mughal court paintings revealed a way to shift the horizontal to vertical and create multiple sightlines so that buildings and hills posed no barrier to viewing distant action. Rajput paintings showed how multiple episodes of a complex narrative could be integrated within a single frame. Sheikh shared his insights in influential published essays and informal discussions with students and colleagues.

In and Out of Story uses a compositional schema from the sixteenth-century illustrated manuscript of the Hamzanama (the adventures of Amir Hamza) (figure 2). Action takes place on the picture plane with no illusion of depth. All figures are given equal importance, so that a viewer searching for a point of entry wanders through the picture and becomes caught up in making the story. The subject is derived from the *Kathasaritsagara (Ocean of Streams of Story)*, a traditional narrative featuring complexly interrelated stories within stories. In the painting's center, five figures, each carrying another, are arrayed almost in a circle. The pairings are based on the well-known tale of King Vikram and the zombie Vetala. The demon rode on the king telling riddles that the king had to solve to free himself. Across the painting are areas that seem like holes containing scenes that appear to be beyond the surface. One wonders if the figures on the picture plane could be the dream-nightmare of the nude woman on the bed at the lower left, or, perhaps, at the bottom right of a passenger inside a bus who bears a striking resemblance to the artist. Sheikh revels in interconnected narrative that "guides you and leads you, but you are unable to get rid of it; it is always there."[3] The viewer must make and remake the narrative, never quite certain about the stories within.

In *Characters Questioning the Narrator*, Sheikh pursued the relationship of tales to storytellers and their audiences. The canvas is sharply bisected into green- and red-hued sections. Two large figures look out at the viewer: the one on the left seems to be gesturing the way into a magical, heavenly landscape; the other, a winged woman-beast, somewhat like the Buraq who transported the Prophet Mohammed, carries a figure resembling Osiris, Egyptian god of the netherworld. On the right side, three rectangles contain, from the top, a two-headed demonic deer, a figure seated on a throne, and a cityscape. Sheikh's enigmatic title sends the viewer on an impossible quest, since the identity of the narrator is unknown. As Sheikh put it: "It is the sum total of a variety of experience, difficult to unravel, impossible to recover the process. Are they narrators or characters? You have an invitation to make your own story."[4]

Sheikh took his relationship with visual narration a step farther by placing himself at the center of *Passing Angel, A Life*, and *Summer Diary*. In *Passing Angel*, a scene below is opened up and viewed from above by a winged figure as well as by viewers, much as in a Mughal painting. At the top are university offices; below are studios in the art college. At the right, in the doorway of Sheikh's home, stands the artist's daughter; his wife, Nilima, sits inside, but can also be seen working in one of the rooms; monkeys cavort on the rooftop. At the left, Sheikh is leaving on his motor scooter. *A Life* is structured like a popular calendar print: the central image, a favorite neem tree with monkeys, is surrounded by scenes set in rectangular spaces, showing two self-portraits of Sheikh at the top, and at the bottom right a magician capable of stopping trains whom Sheikh knew about as a child. *Summer Diary* is divided into horizontal sections like a storyteller's scroll painting. Scenes include occupants of the university flats where Sheikh lived, students rioting, a firing squad quoted from Manet's series "The Execution of the Emperor Maximilian" (1867–69), itself quoted from Goya's *The Third of May 1808* (1814). At the left, Sheikh's upstairs neighbor, the painter Bhupen Khakhar (plates 41–43), with his friend standing nearby, peers through a hole in the floor at Sheikh sleeping. Below are small scenes of summer in Baroda. Nilima is painting at the right. Sheikh explained: "All three paintings are about summer, heat. I love summer."[5]

In all of these paintings, Sheikh pushed the limits of narrative possibility, structuring pictorial space to incorporate and interconnect stories. He has thrown into question the role of the painter and his relation to the narrative created, to the lives of figures on the canvas, to viewers, and to the process and substance of narration.
– SSB

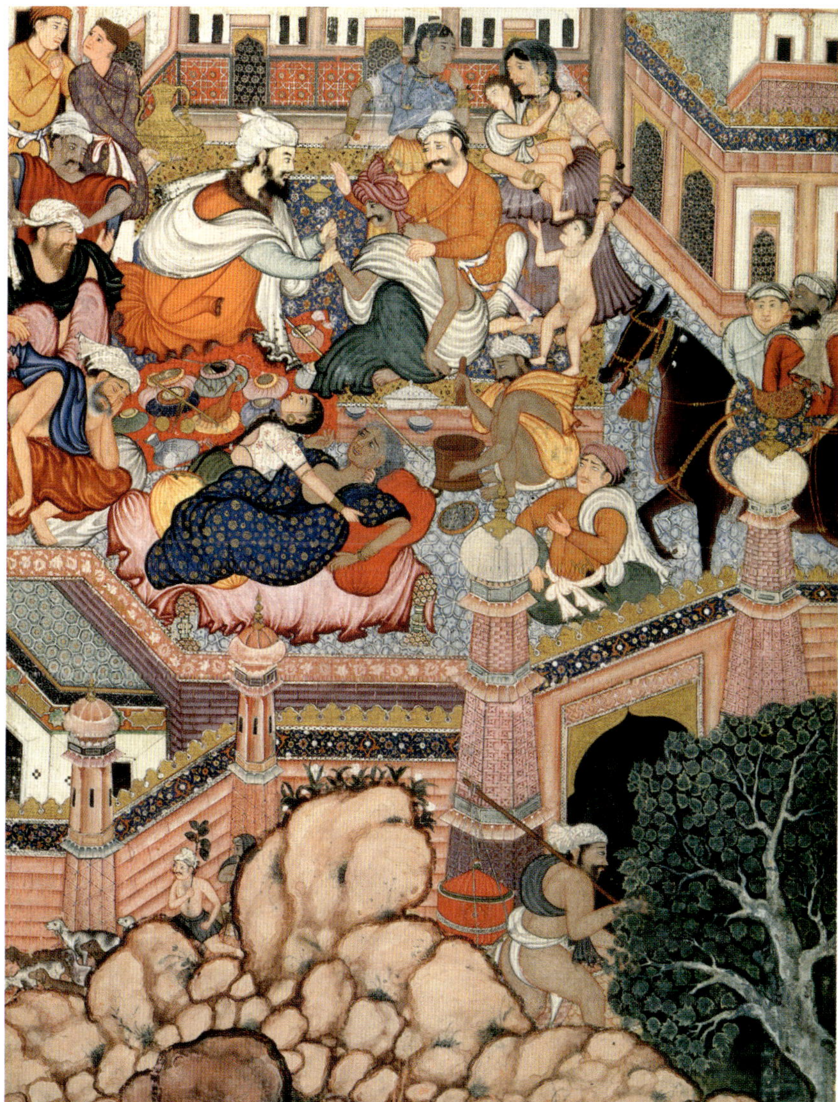

Figure 2.
Attributed to Dasavanta, Shravana, and Mahesa,
Umar, Disguised as Mazmahil the Surgeon, Practices Quackery on the Sorcerers of Antali, 1557–72
Opaque watercolor and gold on cotton cloth
Painting 26 ¾ × 20 ⅝ inches (68 × 52.4 cm)
Caroline H. Polhemus Fund, Brooklyn Museum of Art, New York, 24.49

1. Gulammohammed Sheikh, "Among Several Cultures and Times," in Carla Borden, ed., *Contemporary Indian Tradition* (Washington, DC: Smithsonian Institution, 1989), pp. 111–12.

2. Ibid., p. 112.

3. Gulammohammed Sheikh, conversation with the author, January 20, 2011, Herwitz Archive, Peabody Essex Museum, Salem, Massachusetts.

4. Ibid. See also Geeta Kapur, "The Paintings of Gulammohammed Sheikh," *Marg* 49, 3 (March 1998), p. 55.

5. Sheikh, conversation with the author.

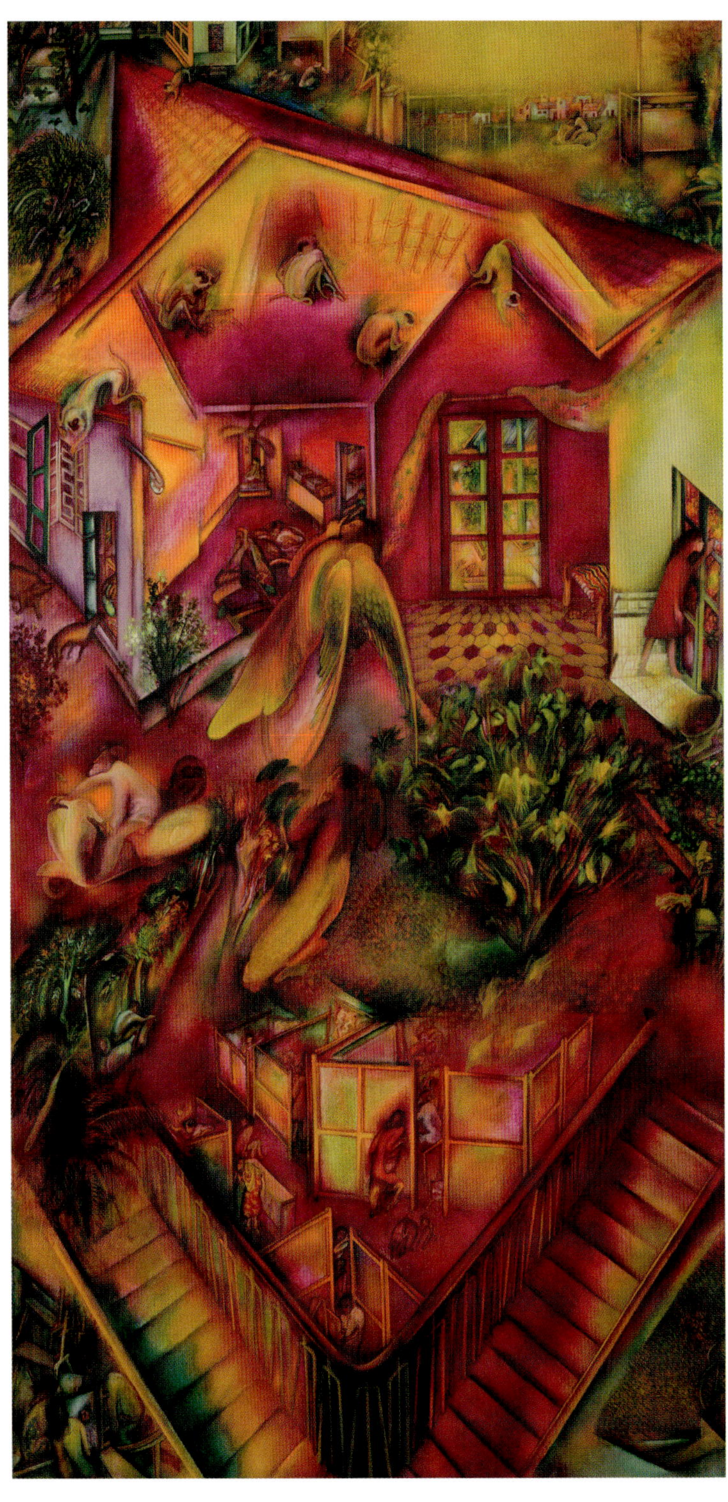

Plate 55.
Passing Angel, A Life, Summer Diary,
1985–87
Oil on canvas
Three panels, each 60 × 30 ¼ inches
(152.4 × 76.8 cm)

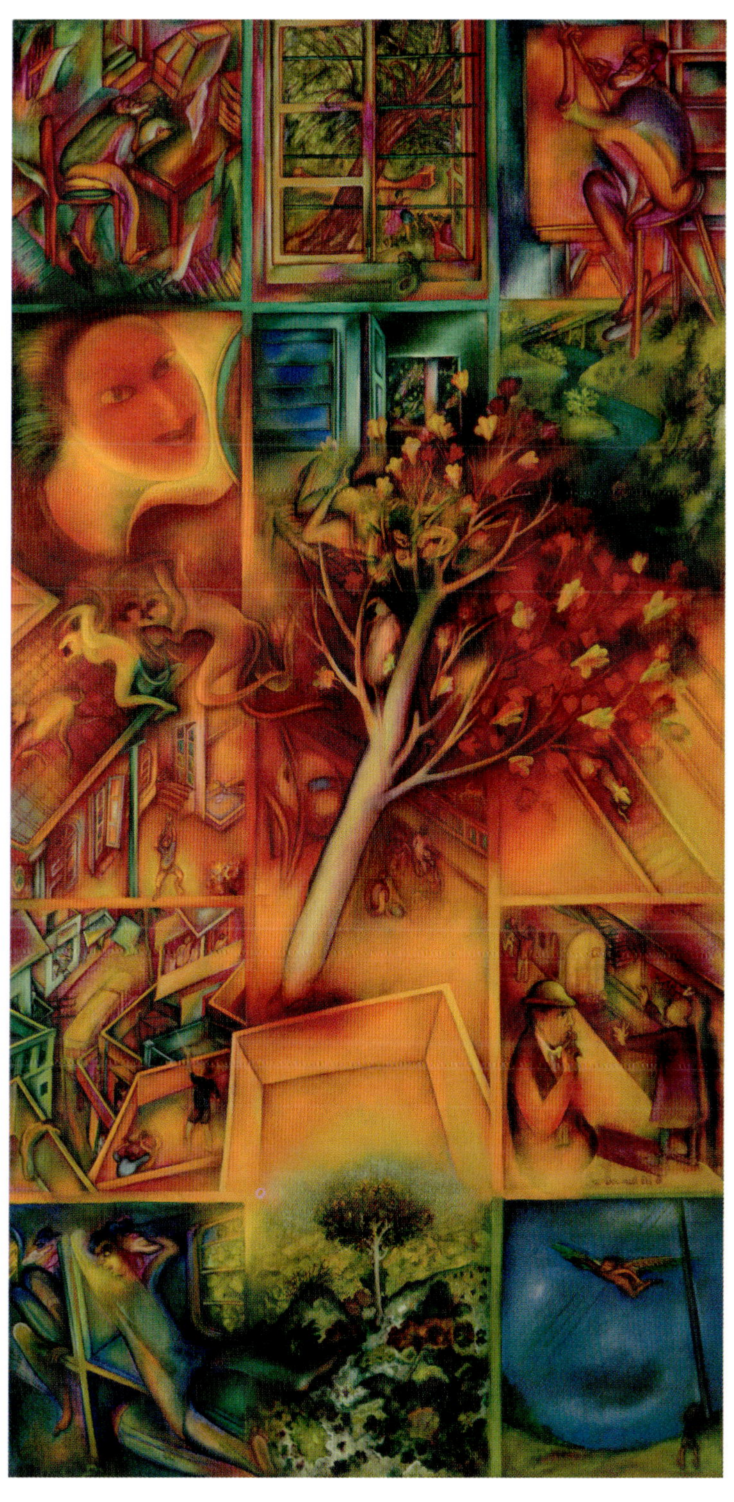

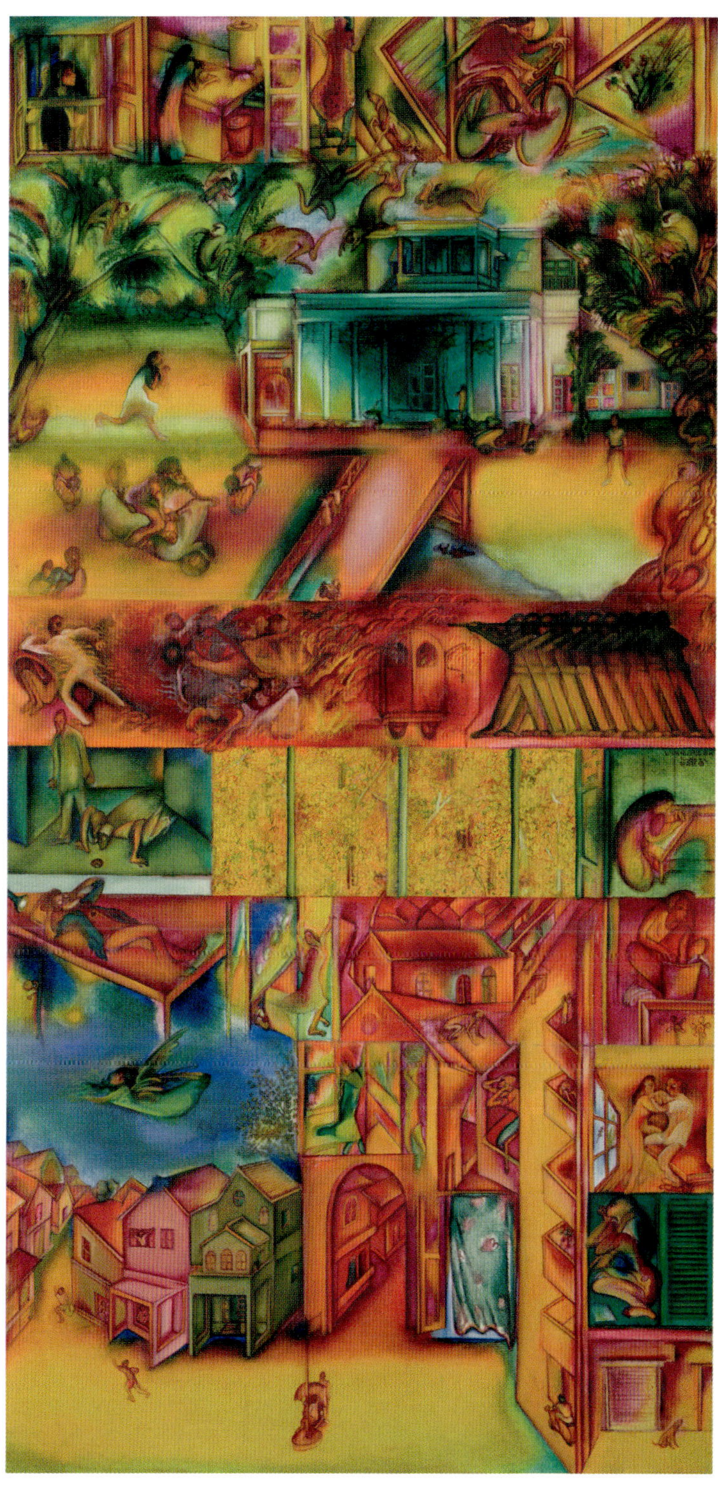

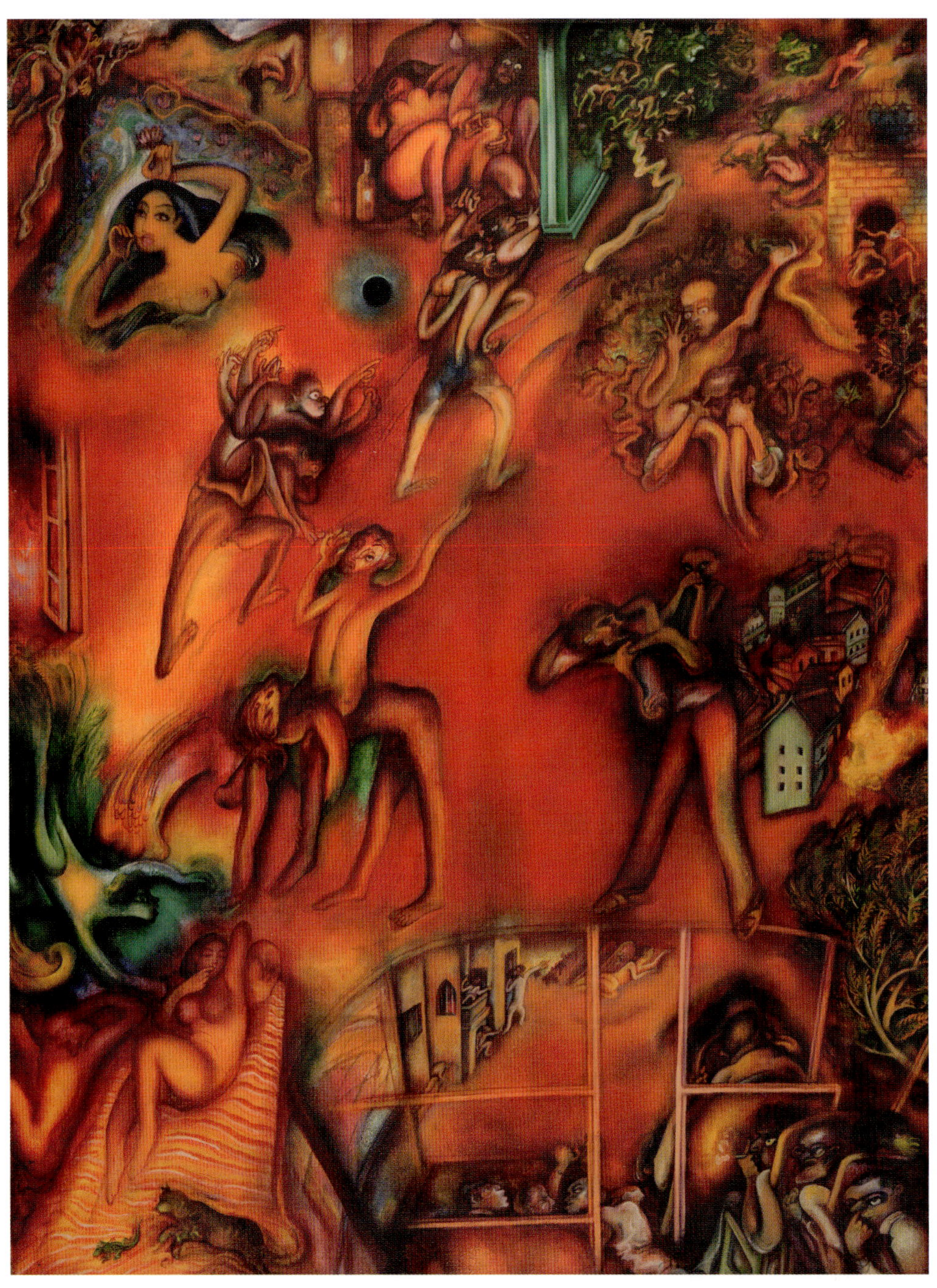

Plate 56.
In and Out of Story, 1984–85
Oil on canvas
32 × 24 inches (81.3 × 61 cm)

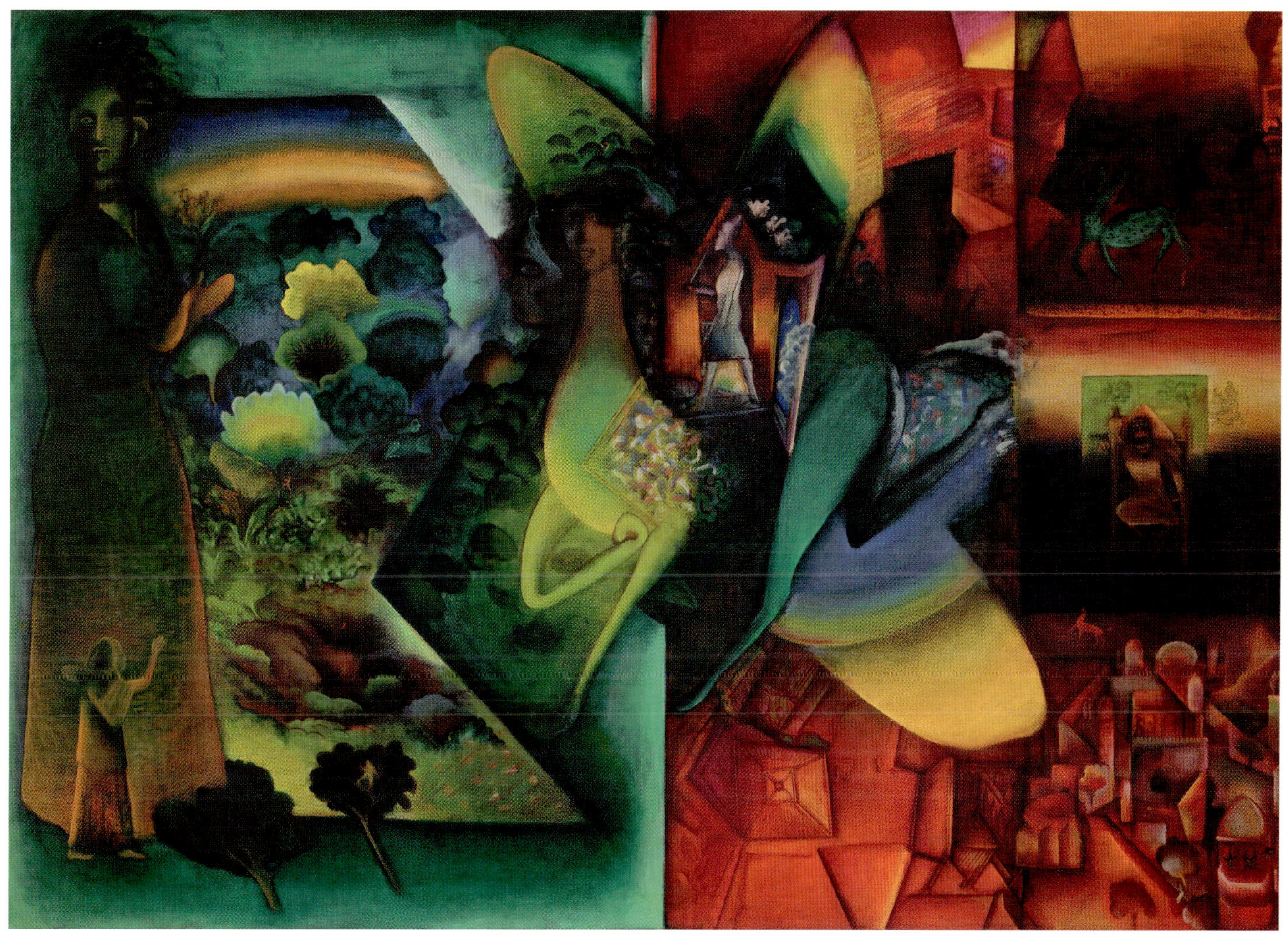

Plate 57.
Characters Questioning the Narrator,
1989–90
Oil on canvas
46 ½ × 66 ½ inches (118.1 × 168.9 cm)

ARPITA SINGH

Born in Baranagar, Bengal
(now in Bangladesh), 1937
Lives and works in Delhi

Arpita Singh is among the few women of her generation in India to gain recognition as a leading artist. Though she does not consider herself a feminist, she acknowledges her woman's perspective as central to her art practice: "I paint these things not because I am a woman. At the same time, it is important that I am a woman."[1] In her works, people jostle with domestic objects—sofas, flowers, framed pictures—sometimes joined with images from the outside world—cars, planes, guns, soldiers. Her whimsical, poignant, and disquieting compositions focus on the deployment and arrangement of these elements and tempt viewers to discover their stories.

In the 1980s, Singh returned to familiar forms after spending nearly eight years working in black-and-white abstraction, deliberately rebuilding her technique. She explained her self-imposed discipline: "at some point, I stopped and realised that I was thinking too much…[it was] not coming very naturally to me. So I stopped painting, and made drawings, just working with basic elements like dots and lines."[2] She removed color from the equation and concentrated on texture. She explored ways to interact with surfaces, to abrade, erase, and build, as a craftsman makes an object. Over these years, as she increased her intimacy with her materials, she achieved a greater ease, an unselfconscious capacity to move from visualization to image—the unmediated connection with her work that she had been seeking. Singh begins her compositions with a familiar form, perhaps a chair or a table like one in her house. She then adds other pictorial elements, spontaneously building the composition. She finds aesthetic satisfaction in the way this impromptu procedure evokes memories and creates unexpected results, leading her in new directions.

Though this inward focus strengthened her practice, she has also gained from her deeply felt affinities with other artists and art forms. For example, Singh engaged her roots in eastern Bengal where women embroidering countless tiny stitches transformed old white garments (saris and dhotis) into exquisitely ornamented quilts or *kantha* (figure 1). Singh's appreciation for these arts deepened later while she was working at a government agency supporting India's rich handmade-textile traditions. In *The Child Bride* (plate 58), the stitchlike white marks that cover the surface relate to these quilts: "The stitches in a *kantha* give body to the limp cloth, give it form. I feel that textures give strength to my painting—an added dimension."[3] *The Child Bride* also evokes the composition of *kantha* in which embroiderers embellish surfaces with familiar objects—combs, mirrors, winnowing fans, circus acrobats, playing cards, and locomotives—placing them wherever they seem to belong.

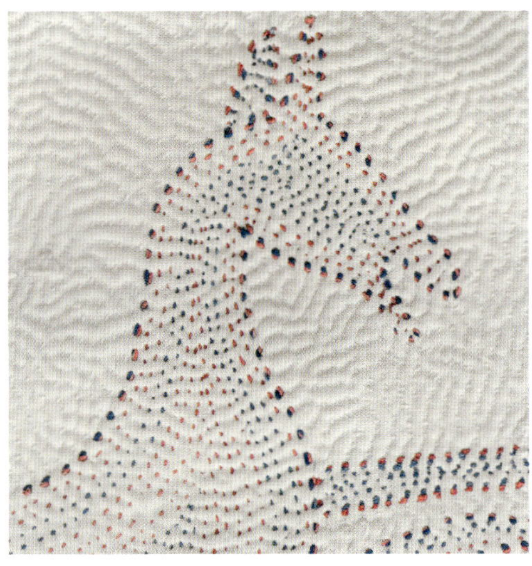

Figure 1.
Kantha (quilt), detail, early 1900s
Cotton

Peabody Essex Museum,
Gift of the Davida Herwitz Fine Arts Trust

The painting has additional, more far-flung affinities. Singh has great admiration for the work of Marc Chagall (figure 2), with whom she feels a connection rooted in their similar folk origins, his in a Jewish stetl in Czarist Russia and hers in rural undivided Bengal, where family and home were of paramount importance. "Maybe we had the same kind of background, similar stock…folk memories" preserved in songs and stories.[4] Beyond the folk background that infuses their work, Singh and Chagall share an approach to composition that propels local imagery beyond reality by transcending spatial logic. Singh observed: "you cannot define space, whether it is earth or whether it is sky… indefinite boundary. That is very interesting to me."[5]

Two oil paintings, *The Draped Woman* (plate 59) and *Munna Apa, Morning, and a Seated Man* (plate 60), are among many works incorporating members of the Kidwai family, neighbors whom Singh found intriguing. In both works, the placement of the figures produces a peculiar tension. In *Munna Apa*, the woman in a painted photograph looks toward a seated man fully absorbed in his morning newspaper. But, as she exists only as a photograph, what could their relationship be? In *The Draped Woman*, the figure luxuriating in her furry pink wrap seems the focus of attention for a woman in a contrasting state of undress. Does she feel envy? Admiration? Their common feminine sensuality is subtly echoed in the viscous pigment. In both paintings, textured surfaces resonate with tension between the figures. And, in both paintings, cars and planes are present in the background, links to the impositions of a wider world.

For *The Worshippers* (plate 61), as for *The Draped Woman*, Singh used a floral border to define the picture space—a device used in textiles. Such borders accentuate and empower what transpires in the main space. Flowers invade the watercolor painting, covering the women's garments and the spaces between them, knitting them into their surroundings: cars, planes, and figures that are active, sleeping, or even dead. The prayerful, solemn worshippers do their utmost to intercede in the face of life's uncertainties, but "Death is always there."[6]
– SSB

1. Geeti Sen, *Image and Imagination: Five Contemporary Artists in India* (Ahmedabad: Mapin Publishing, 1996), p. 98.

2. Neville Tuli, *The Flamed Mosaic: Contemporary Indian Painting* (New York: Harry N. Abrams, 1998), pp. 388–89.

3. Sen, p. 116.

4. Arpita Singh, conversation with the author, January 2011, Herwitz Archive, Peabody Essex Museum, Salem, Massachusetts.

5. Ibid.

6. Ibid.

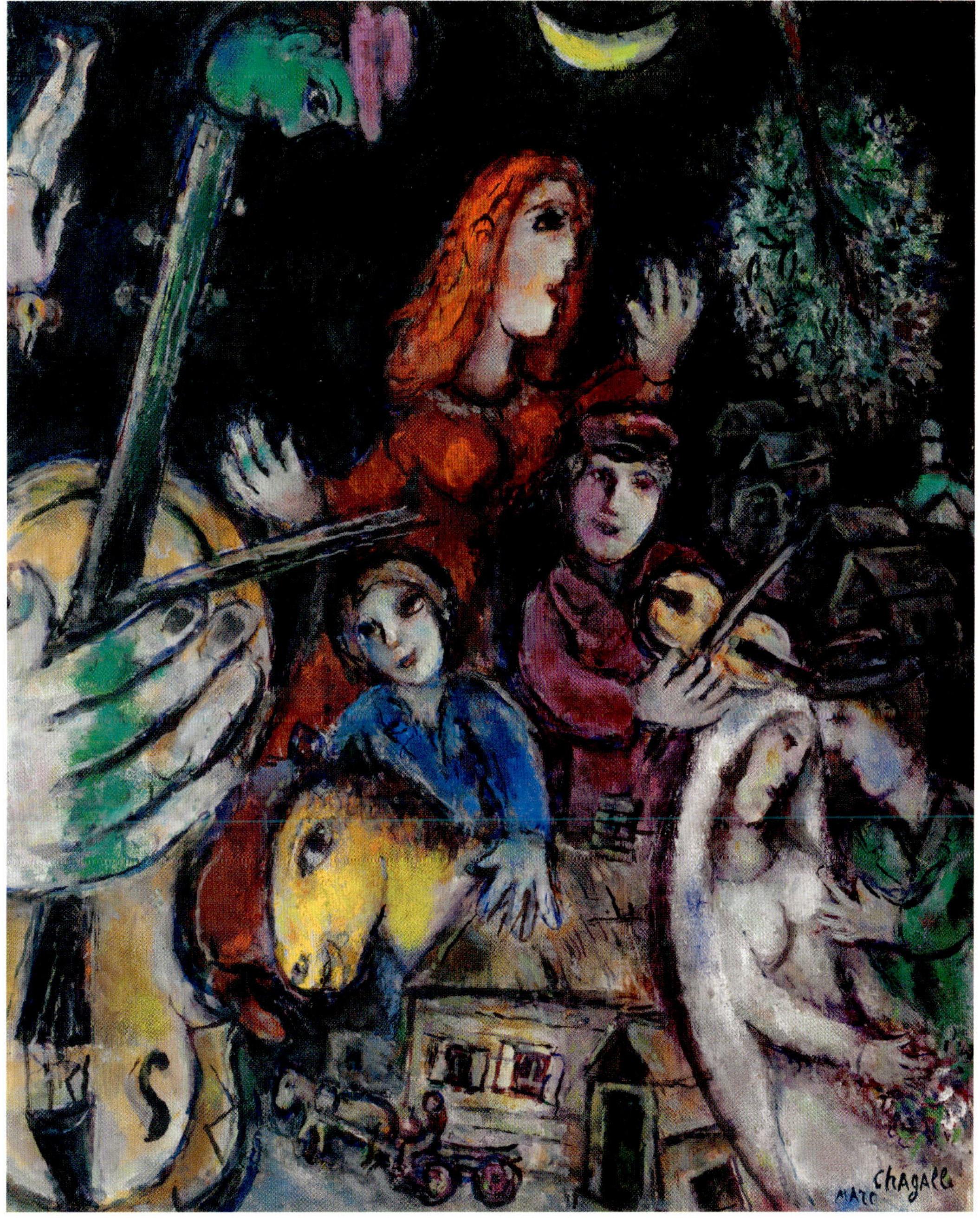

Figure 2.
Marc Chagall, *The Little Concert*, ca. 1968
Oil on canvas
25 ⅝ × 21 ¼ inches (65.1 × 54 cm)
The Baltimore Museum of Art, Anonymous Bequest,
BMA 1994.197

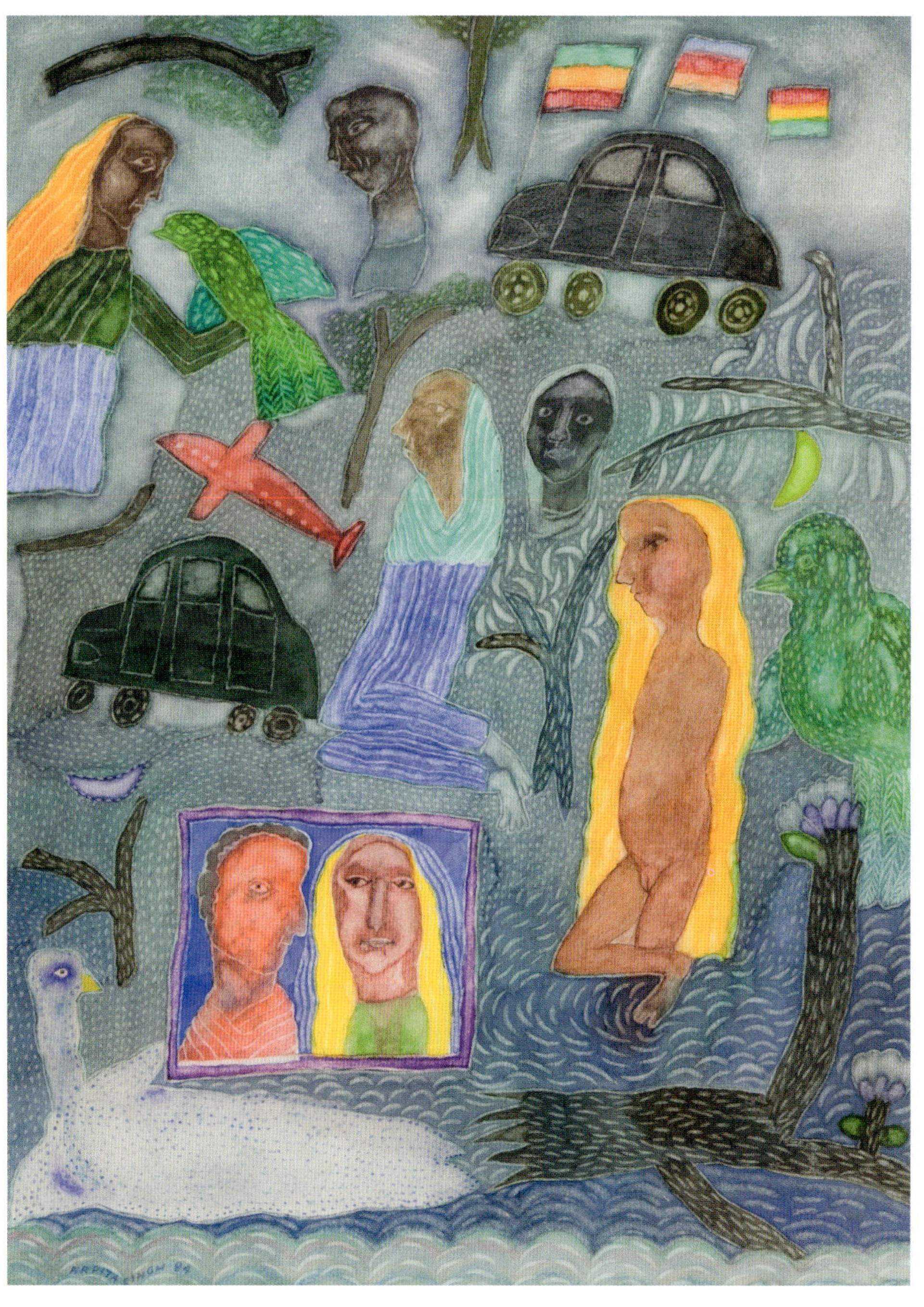

Plate 58.
The Child Bride, 1984
Watercolor on paper
15 ½ × 11 ¾ inches (39.4 × 29.8 cm)

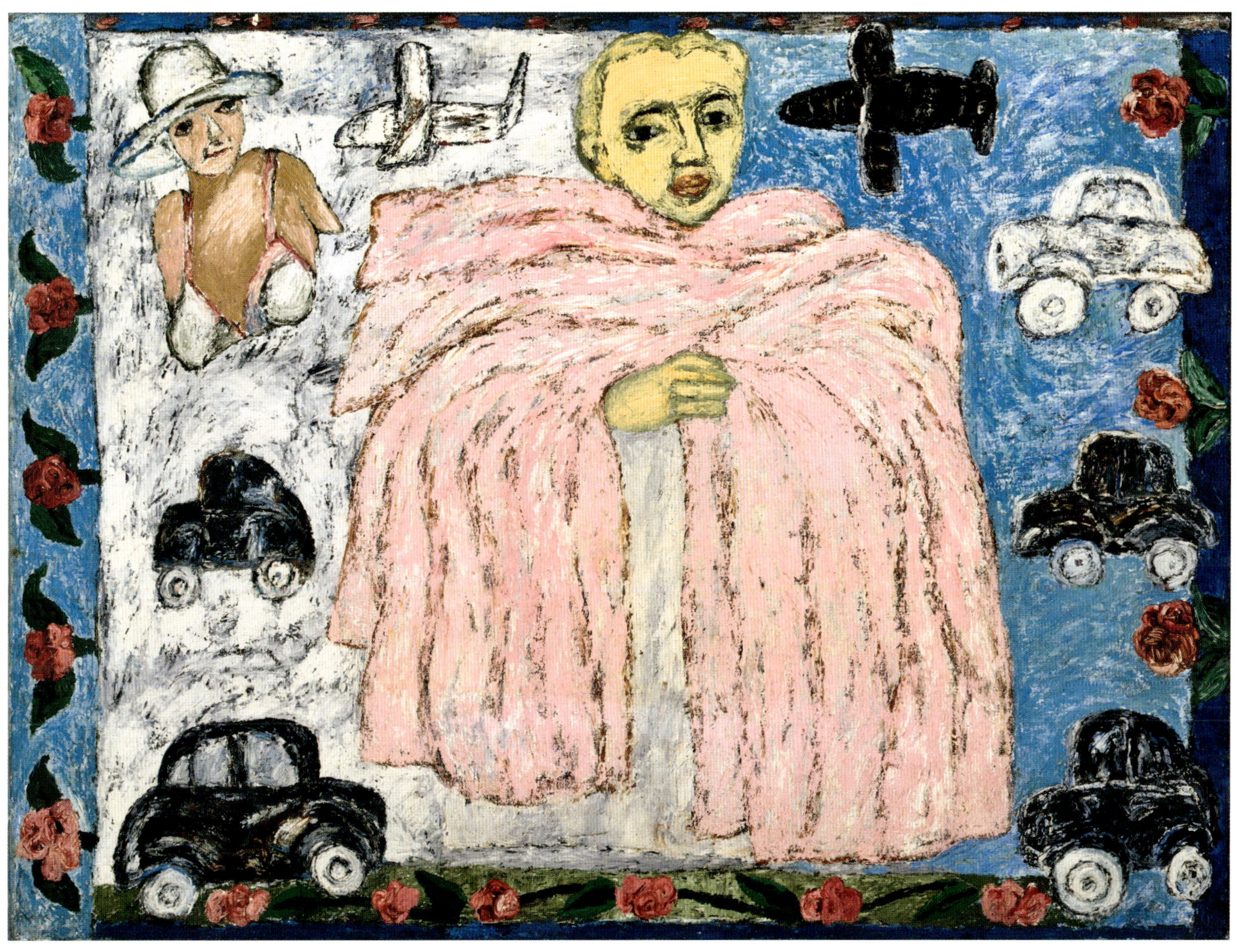

Plate 59.
The Draped Woman, 1989
Oil on canvas
23 ½ × 31 ¼ inches (59.7 × 79.4 cm)

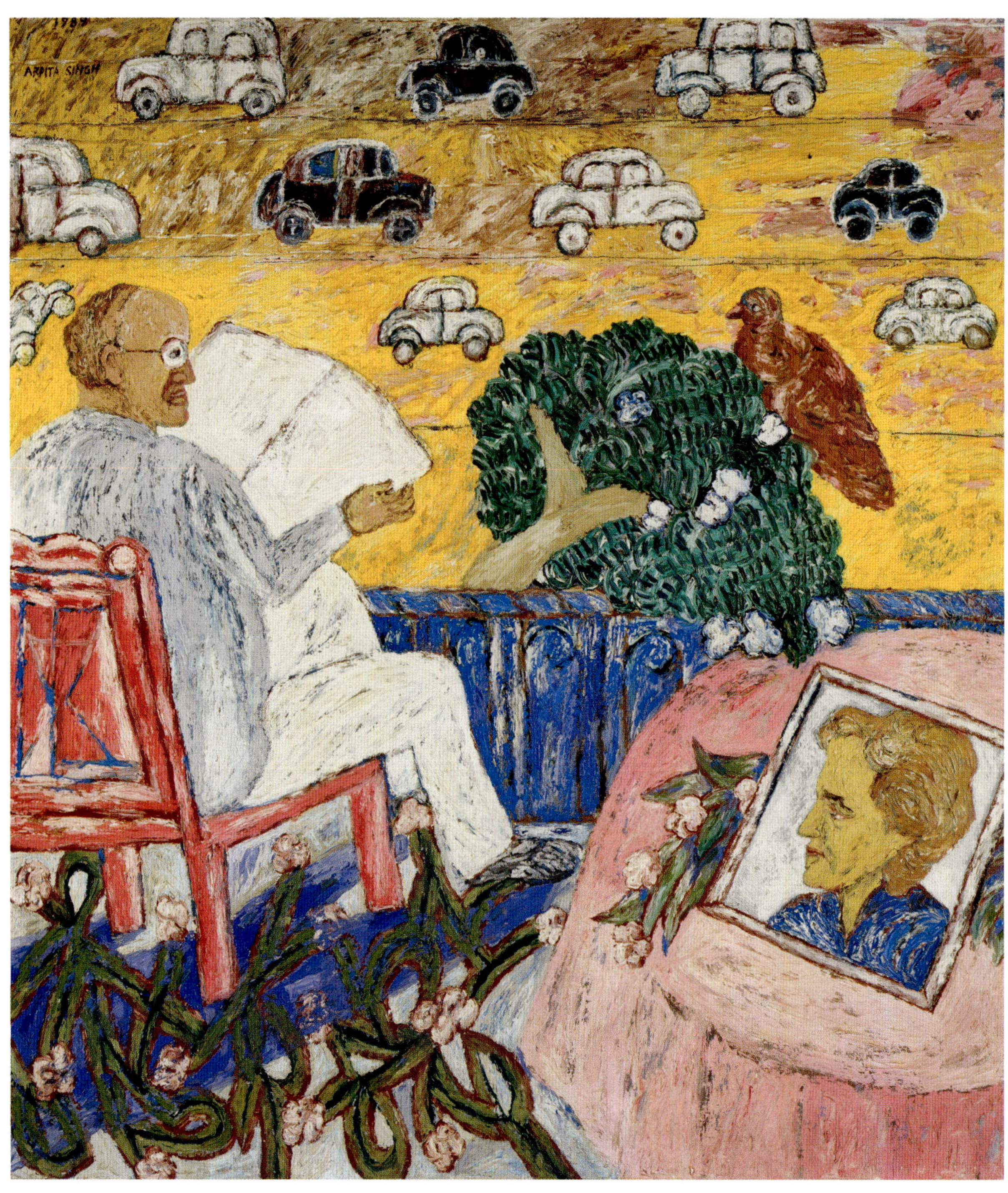

Plate 60.
Munna Apa, Morning, and a Seated Man, 1989
Oil on canvas
33 ¾ × 29 ⅞ inches (85.7 × 75.9 cm)

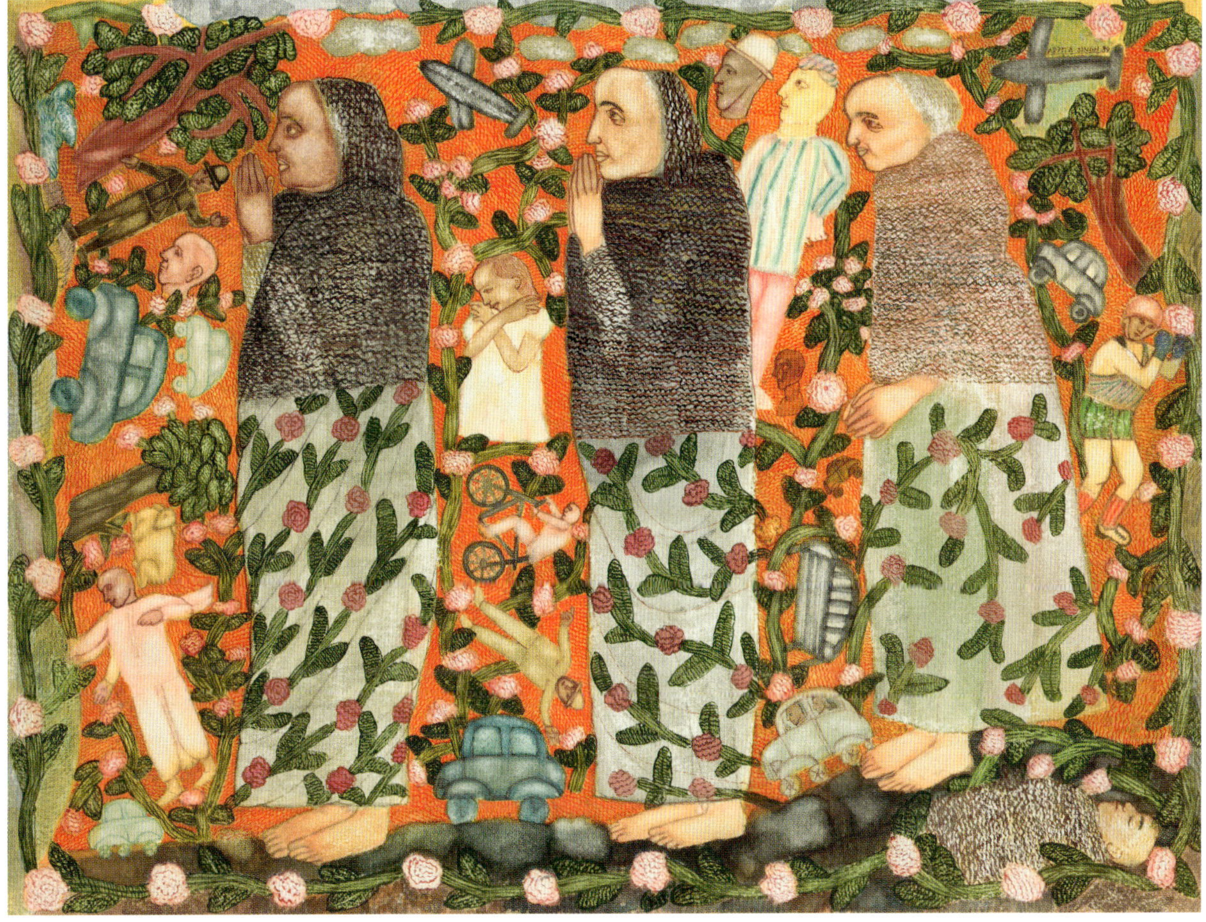

Plate 61.
The Worshippers, 1989
Watercolor on paper
14 × 18 ¾ inches (35.6 × 47.6 cm)

NEW MEDIATORS

The Third Generation

Atul Dodiya

Ranbir Singh Kaleka

Nalini Malani

Sudhir Patwardhan

Rekha Rodwittiya

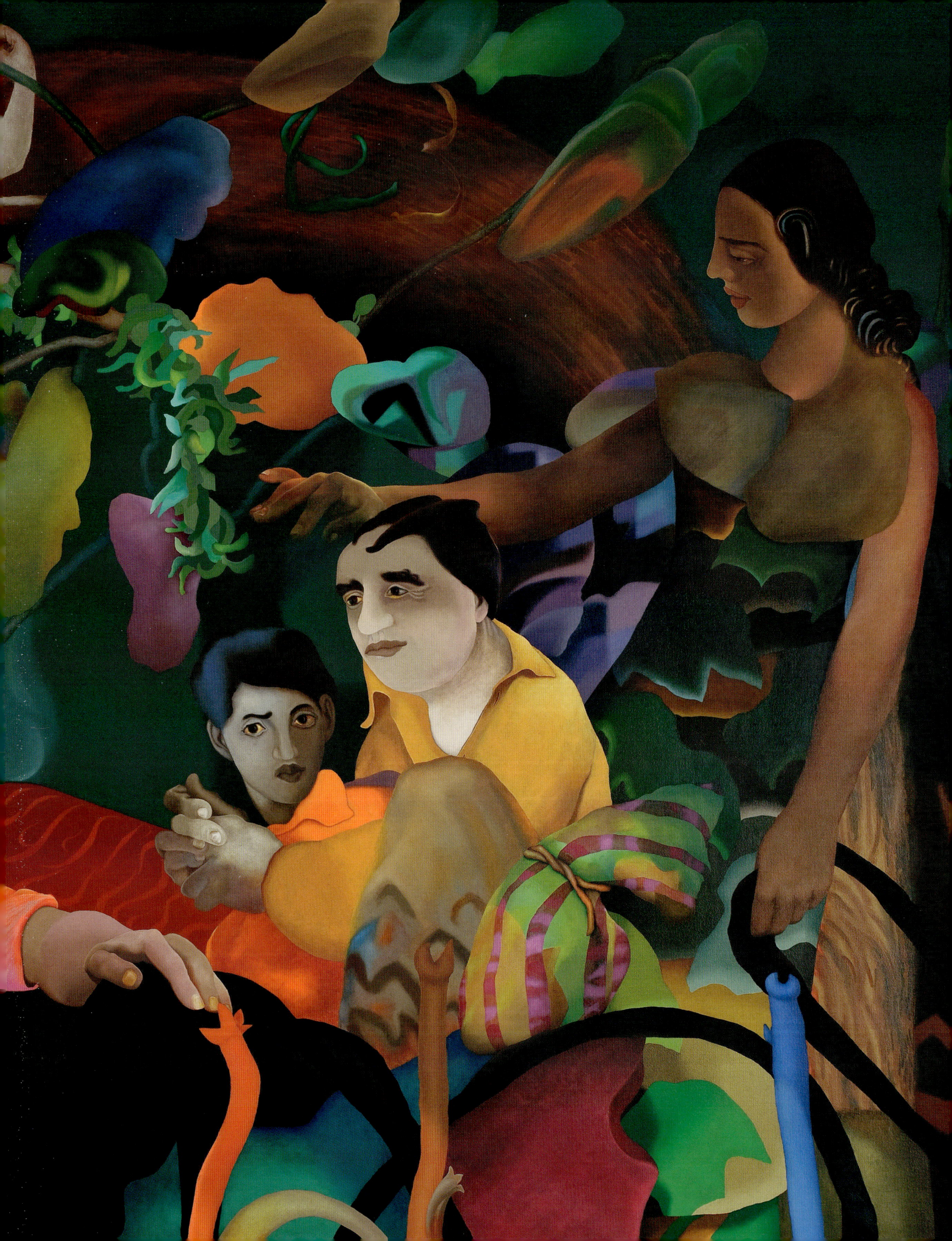

NEW MEDIATORS: THE THIRD GENERATION

Beth Citron

In the wake of India's nineteen-month period of emergency in 1975–77, during which civil liberties and elections were suspended, artists and intellectuals began to occupy a public political position. They stood in opposition to the challenged government and their stance was most often aligned with leftist ideals. Artists developed and articulated their positions through dialogues such as the interdisciplinary workshops at Kasauli that Vivan Sundaram organized in the late 1970s. Leading critic Geeta Kapur was a central participant and interpreter of these intellectual discourses. She was instrumental in crafting a critical and theoretical language for the Indian art world; a primary goal was to contextualize the Marxist platform that underlay her thinking at that time.[1] As an example, one of Sundaram's workshops included a seminar on "Marxism and Aesthetics" that related historical discourses on realism and modernism—originally staged by George Lukacs and Bertolt Brecht, among others, in 1930s Germany—to cultural expression in contemporary India. Seminars such as this directly catalyzed a new movement in the urban Indian art world that took shape in 1981 with the important *Place for People* exhibition held in Bombay and Delhi. This group exhibition included paintings by Jogen Chowdhury (plates 33–36), Bhupen Khakhar (plates 41–43), Nalini Malani (plates 66–68), Sudhir Patwardhan (plates 69–71), Gulammohammed Sheikh (plates 55–57), and Vivan Sundaram. The catalogue included an essay by Kapur.[2] The exhibition asserted artists' priorities on narrative figuration and on the representation of everyday figures in local environments. It emphasized and strengthened the movement toward political activism and marked a critical turn from the priority on self-expression of preceding generations of artists.

Many artists' concerns with political and social processes solidified in the 1980s, as they reacted to disasters such as the Bhopal gas tragedy in December 1984, in which a leak resulted in the death and illness of many thousands of people—considered one of the worst-ever industrial catastrophes. Yet, even as many artists developed their practices around common engagements as activists, and with an almost unilateral political position, those emerging in India in this decade also took up an unprecedented diversity of styles and forms of creative expression. Many of these artists sought to establish ideological stances beyond the limitations of the canvas and the infrastructure of a conventional art world. For example, in 1980 Patwardhan participated in the

Detail of Plate 64.
Ranbir Singh Kaleka, *Family—1*, 1983

Pratishabda 80 festival of many leftist parties held in housing chawls in Bombay by painting a large mural that depicted a mass of working-class people—the audience who would have seen the mural at this festival.[3] For the same festival, he also mounted an exhibition of reproductions of artworks and texts in Marathi that sought to explain the history of modern Indian art to the audience of activists, workers, and farm laborers from all over Maharashtra in their language.[4] Acts such as these also resonated with widespread critiques of modernism, which had often separated the elite, commercial art world from everyday life and mass culture throughout the twentieth century. This division had been maintained both through modern movements and styles (especially abstraction) and through certain types of art criticism, especially formalism, as that discourse tended to isolate artworks from social and political concerns. Internationally, critiques of modernism led to the advent of postmodernism and broader explorations of installation and new media arts that engaged and intervened directly in diverse environments.

Painting remained the dominant and foundational medium of artistic expression in India through the 1980s. This had distinguished modernist art in India from Euro-American or "global" trends for several decades. Through the 1980s, "New Mediators" and other artists continued to work primarily in painting, but the artists who emerged in this decade were the last group for whom painting was the focal medium for innovations in contemporary art. Increasing political fragmentation in India in the 1980s led to several landmark events in the early 1990s that fundamentally changed public life and the nation's cultural imperatives. The most transformational among them all took place in a two-year period: the opening of the Indian economy to capitalism in 1991; the Mandal Commission report of 1992 that sought to eliminate caste from political and social life; and the continuing rise of right-wing Hindu nationalism in Indian cities, seen especially through a series of sectarian riots and bomb explosions following the demolition of the Babri Mosque in Ayodhya by Hindu extremists in December 1992.

As artists responded to the radical upheavals that were taking place in their challenged nation, many "New Mediators" sensed that the presumed autonomy of a canvas was not the right vehicle through which to explore cataclysmic subjects like Ayodhya and resurgent Hindu-Muslim tensions. This led to a sudden shift in the early and mid-1990s to conceptual art, as well as installation, video, and other new media arts. These new forms and the languages that artists developed in them addressed the confusion and difficulty of the contemporary moment, and also built upon the nascent possibilities offered by technology and a growing capitalist economy. A few artists, including Sundaram and Malani, born in 1943 and 1946 on the cusp between generations, pioneered these new directions. Artists such as Sundaram and Rummana Hussain, who had previously identified themselves as painters, consciously and completely turned away from the medium in the early to mid-1990s. They dedicated themselves to large-scale installation projects that, respectively, memorialized Ayodhya and its victims, and considered personal identity in the wake of new sectarian violence across India (figure 1). Other artists, such as Malani, began to incorporate politically minded installations and new media into their practices while still continuing work in painting. For example, in 1992 Malani created *City of Desires* (figure 2), an exhibition

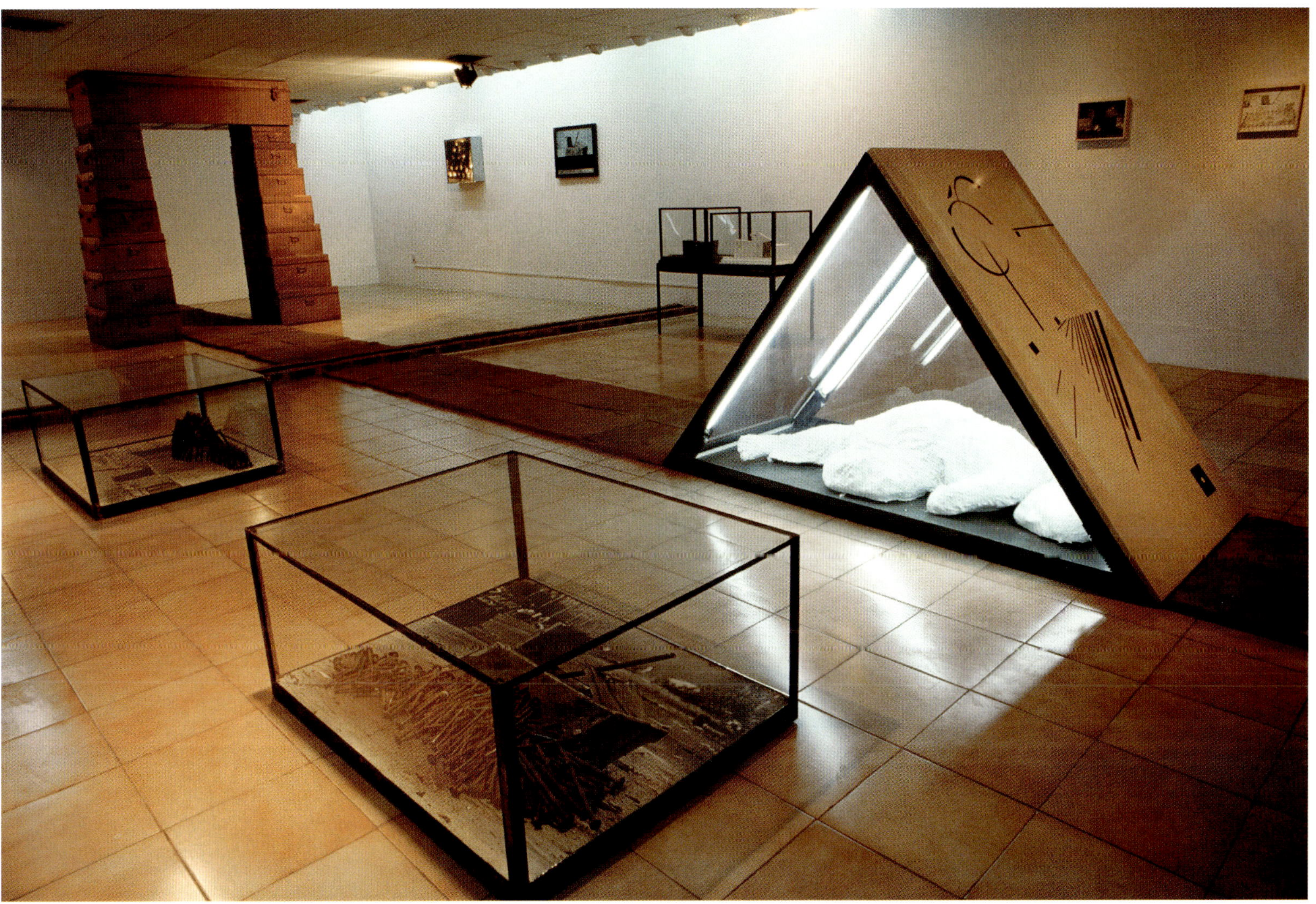

Figure 1.
Vivan Sundaram, *Memorial*, 1993–2000
Mixed-media installation at AIFACS Gallery, New Delhi
Collection of the artist

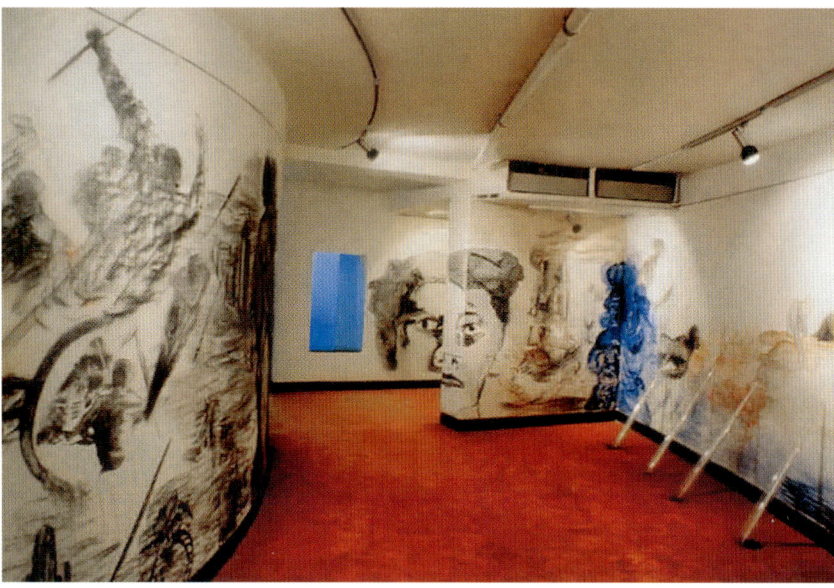

Figure 2.
Nalini Malani, *City of Desires*, 1992
Mixed-media installation and erasure performance at Chemould Prescott Road—Contemporary Art Gallery, Mumbai

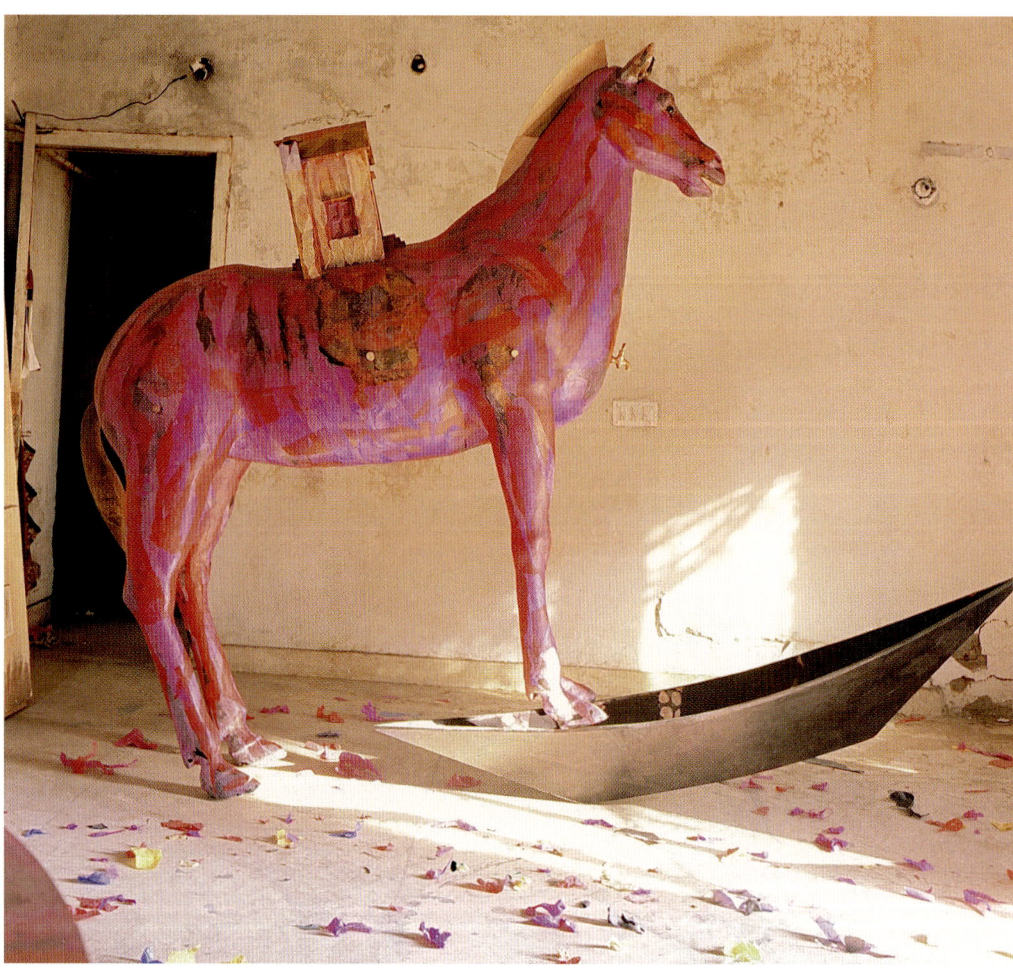

Figure 3.
Sudarshan Shetty, *Paper Moon*, 1995
Mixed-media installation at Pundole Art Gallery and Framji Cawasjee Hall, Mumbai and Ravindra Bhavan, New Delhi
Private Collection, India

of ephemeral drawings and paintings executed on the walls of Bombay's Gallery Chemould. The work was intentionally destroyed after the show as a political act to underscore the fragility of cultural heritage in the face of rising Hindu fundamentalism. Malani's 1994 *Medea* video project and subsequent new media works have integrated imagery of contemporary and partition violence with universal mythologies. In part, Malani's feminist intervention sought to break the male modernist tradition that had dominated India's art world until the 1980s, especially in her home city where the so-called "Bombay Boys" led the art scene.

"New Mediators" such as Atul Dodiya (plates 62 and 63) and Rekha Rodwittiya (plates 72 and 73) have continued to identify themselves as painters, working in oil and acrylic on canvas even as they have actively sought to expand the place for painting in contemporary India. Rodwittiya has done so by offering autobiographical written narratives that attempt to demonstrate how the personal subjects she paints relate directly to her external public interests. In this manner, she has sought to shape the viewer's experience of her painting and the world she inhabits; recently, this has even taken the form of regular posts on a public blog reflecting on her art and daily life in Baroda. For Dodiya, this commitment has included developing strategies to expand the physical limitations and conventions of painting. Beginning in the early 1990s, he has evoked contemporary events and politics in his work through progressive shifts in subject and medium. After exploring the limitations of both the surface of the canvas (as in *2nd October*, plate 62) and the space around the painting (as in *The Bombay Buccaneer*, plate 63), Dodiya moved beyond the canvas and developed his important "shutter series" beginning in 1999. These are paintings executed on actual metal shutters that can be closed and opened, referencing the moment during the Bombay riots in 1993 in which the city was completely "shut" (see Dodiya, figure 1). With this innovative series, Dodiya expanded painting practices in India while maintaining the dialogue with those artists who sought to create alternatives to painting and challenge its dominance. For other "New Mediators," such as Ranbir Singh Kaleka (plates 64 and 65), experimentation in other art forms has been an extension of the artist's painting practice and not expressly political. In the 1990s, Kaleka began to develop video-based projects that dovetailed with the fantastical narratives of his painting; in the past decade, he has even produced works that elaborately integrate video and painting by projecting a moving image onto a painted canvas.

As the art market began to expand through India's newly capitalist economy and interest from non-resident Indian (NRI) communities in the 1990s, there were new opportunities to produce and show new media and installation-based artworks. Younger—fourth-generation—artists began to turn to large-scale projects that did not draw directly on recent politics or the traditions of Indian painting. For his 1994 *Paper Moon* exhibition (figure 3) in Bombay, Sudarshan Shetty created an explosive wonderland featuring enormous, human-scale wooden toys decorated with bright, cheap kite paper. Several years later, Subodh Gupta began to use stainless-steel kitchen utensils to make installation projects that explored everyday Indian life (figure 4). Works like these aligned readily with the aesthetics and consumerism of the global art world, in which India had begun to participate.

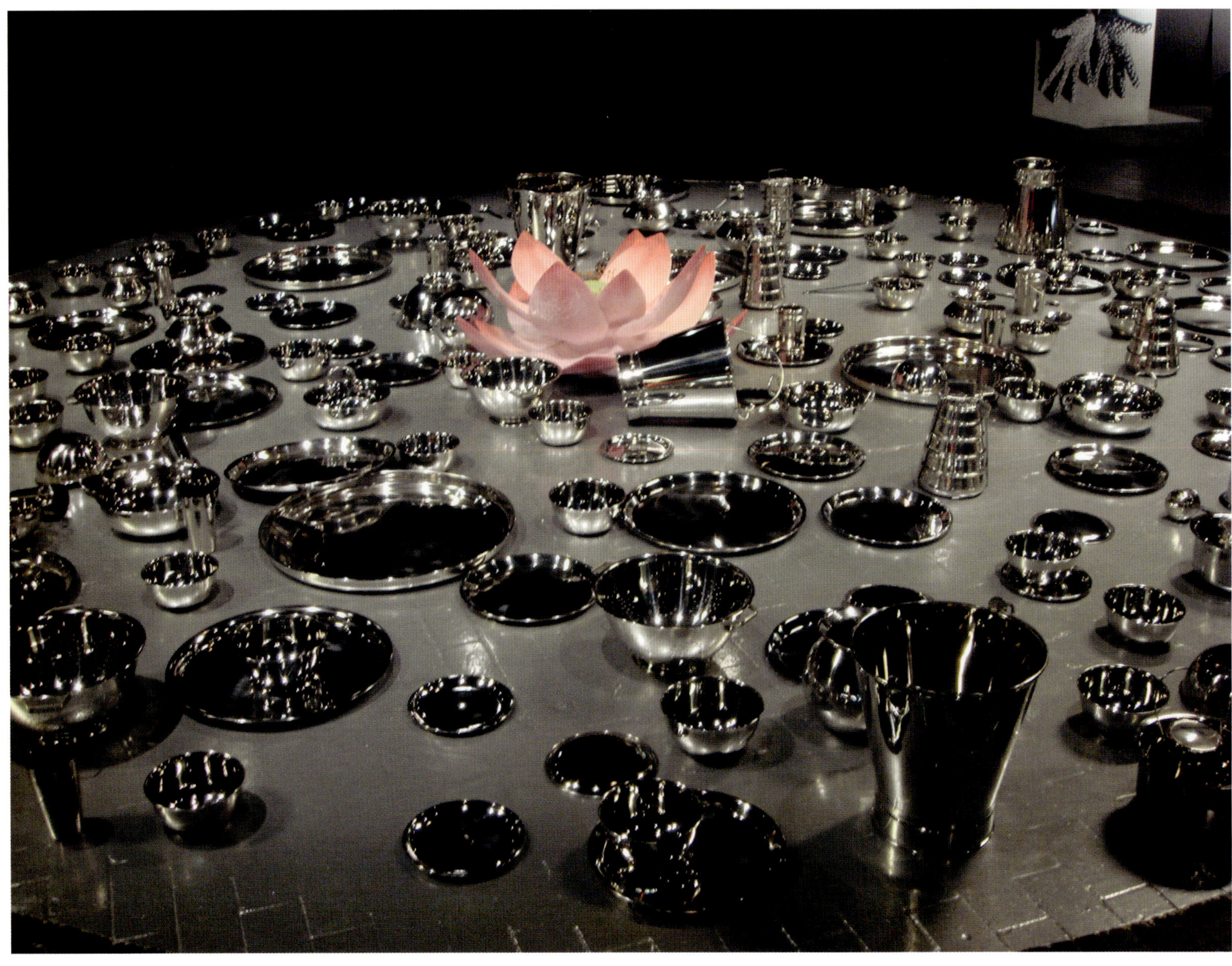

Figure 4.
Subodh Gupta, *The Way Home*, 1998–99
Mixed-media installation at Chemould Prescott Road—Contemporary Art Gallery, Mumbai
Location unknown

By the mid-to-late 1990s, India and the direction of its contemporary art had fundamentally changed. Artists faced new, diverse challenges, as they needed to grasp India's immediate political and social concerns and accordingly reinterpret ever-shifting local, regional, urban, national, and "global" identities. Art produced in the past decade in India has often been conceived, exhibited, and sold alongside contemporary art across the world. This shift accelerated particularly with an unprecedented commercial boom in the art world in India and abroad between 2005 and 2008. Though artists continue to engage culturally specific referents and histories, and their art is still labeled "Indian," contemporary Indian art is increasingly contextualized as part of a global art phenomenon—reflecting an extraordinary shift in the very way in which such art may be defined and historicized in generations to come.

1. Geeta Kapur, "Realism and Modernism: A Polemic For Present-Day Art," *Social Scientist* 8, 89–90 (1979), pp. 91ff.

2. In order to clear up a prevailing assumption that Kapur curated the exhibition, Sudhir Patwardhan, Vivan Sundaram, and Kapur herself have repeatedly and emphatically told this author that Kapur was not the curator of *Place for People*. Instead, they considered her one of them—her contribution was an essay, whereas theirs was painting. Sudhir Sonalkar's report on the exhibition corroborates this, and remarks upon Kapur's importance in the dynamic of the exhibition: "there is a seventh member, a critic, Geeta Kapur, who is as much a part of the venture as the painters in a way probably unprecedented in the country, giving a different shape to the very conception of an exhibition. A different relationship between critic and artist, one in fact in which the critic or at least criticism as a formative force seems to be equally if not most important." In "Six Painters Engaged in Research," *The Illustrated Weekly of India*, n.d., p. 16.

3. Sudhir Patwardan, e-mail correspondence with the author, April 25, 2009.

4. Ibid.

ATUL DODIYA

Born in Bombay, 1959
Lives and works in Bombay

Atul Dodiya belongs to the first generation of artists in India who identified themselves as postmodern and "global" within an international art world. Dodiya was born and raised in Ghatkopar, a traditionally middle-class Gujarati suburb of Bombay, and graduated from Bombay's J.J. School of Art in 1982. Though exposed to popular styles of abstraction in college, Dodiya began his career painting autobiographically and primarily in a Photorealist mode. Accessing a rich vocabulary of stylistic and iconographic allusions from Indian and Euro-American art, along with imagery and ideas rooted in film, popular culture, and literature, he has been known since early in his career for painting clever art-historical citations and compositional witticisms, as well as for an unparalleled ability to improvise and reinvent.

Dodiya's first—and acclaimed—solo exhibition of oil paintings was held in 1988 at Gallery Chemould in Bombay. Subsequent projects included assisting Bhupen Khakhar (plates 41–43) on the production of stage settings for a Gujarati play in 1989. In Paris in 1991–92 on a scholarship at the École des Beaux-Arts, Dodiya encountered works by the European masters and modernists he had earlier admired in books and reproductions. Though he had already moved away from realist painting by this time, he grew interested in recent European art that drew on or manipulated realist styles. Dodiya identified particularly with modernist Francia Picabia for his experimentations in Dada and Surrealism; and with pioneering contemporary artists including Sigmar Polke, for his inventiveness in different mediums, and David Salle, especially for his figurative pastiche.[1] From this time on, strategies associated with Western postmodernist art—such as a free use of art-historical quotation and juxtaposition of disparate sources from high and low culture—became focal in Dodiya's painting practice. As his own development was almost simultaneous with related interrogations by his Western colleagues, Dodiya entered a discourse with international contemporary art as no other Indian artist had done previously.

Following his return to India in late 1992, Dodiya painted *2nd October* (plate 62), making reference to Bombay's landmarks and politics, both of which he has continued to address regularly. This work marks Dodiya's most direct engagement with the tragic situation and increased religious tension in Bombay following the demolition of the Babri Mosque in Ayodhya by Hindu extremists and the violent sectarian riots that beset Bombay in December 1992 and early 1993. The painting depicts a man on an elevated platform garlanding an iconic monument of Gandhi located in South Bombay at Mantralaya, the administrative headquarters of the Maharashtra state government. The painting's title honors Gandhi's birth anniversary. Flanking him on either side are a palm tree with a sunflower, which is a symbol of environmentalist politics, and Bombay's famed revolving restaurant atop the Ambassador Hotel, a symbol of new middle-class aspiration in the 1990s. While the actual monument at Mantralaya is a robust and imposing larger-than-life statue, Dodiya's Gandhi looks weak and ghostly. This transformation is coupled with a faded palette, bleeding colors, and the illusion of peeling patches in accordance with the artist's interest at this time to match the surface appearance of his canvases to their subjects through manipulations of oil paint. *2nd October* is Dodiya's unequivocal response to what many perceived as a tarnishing of Gandhian ethics and ideals in Indian society in the early 1990s. Dodiya has continued to remember Gandhi and inscribe the leader's politics into his work, most prominently as the subject of a seminal exhibition at Gallery Chemould in 1999: *Atul Dodiya: An Artist of Non-Violence.*

Throughout 1994, Dodiya worked on the canvases that would comprise his next solo exhibition, to be held at Gallery Chemould in January 1995. The paintings in this series present a deliberately wide range of subjects, styles, and techniques. Their common conceptual thread is that Dodiya sought through each work to subvert the limits or inherent expectations of what "painting" was at this time in India, including the strategy of painting "peeled" trompe-l'oeil surface patches that he introduced in *2nd October*. The final and crowning work in the series for this exhibition is the breakthrough canvas *The Bombay Buccaneer* (plate 63). This realistic, sober self-portrait is accompanied by "attributes" in the form of small vignettes drawn from art-historical sources. These include the lenses of Dodiya's eyeglasses, which mirror brightly colored images of the British and Indian Pop artists David Hockney and Bhupen Khakhar, at left and right, respectively. The addition of a wooden film clapstick to the upper left corner of the painting represents the first time Dodiya was able to break a painting out of the rectangular form of the canvas and extend it into a real environment, even when the clapstick is "shut." The work can thus be seen as one of the artist's earliest explorations of media and assemblage. Since the mid-1990s, Dodiya has explored and expanded on the interplay between the visual address (and conventions) of the canvas and the space surrounding it, including in his movable "shutter" works beginning in 2000 (figure 1) and in the cabinets comprising his "Broken Branches" series (2002–2003).

In exploring new mediums and pushing the boundaries between painting and other forms of art, Dodiya quite singularly expanded the definition and scope of painting in India in the 1990s. He has continued to identify himself and his work within a painting discourse, and he participated in the important Documenta XII in Kassel, Germany, in 2007 with his large-scale watercolor "Antler Anthology" series (2003–2004). Yet, he also returns frequently to oil on canvas as he questions and reinvents his own painting practice and the place of contemporary art in a transforming India. – BC

1. Peter Nagy, "Atul Dodiya: A Gargantuan Responsibility," in Peter Nagy and Gayatri Sinha, *Atul Dodiya: Broken Branches* (New York: Bose Pacia Modern, 2003), n.p.

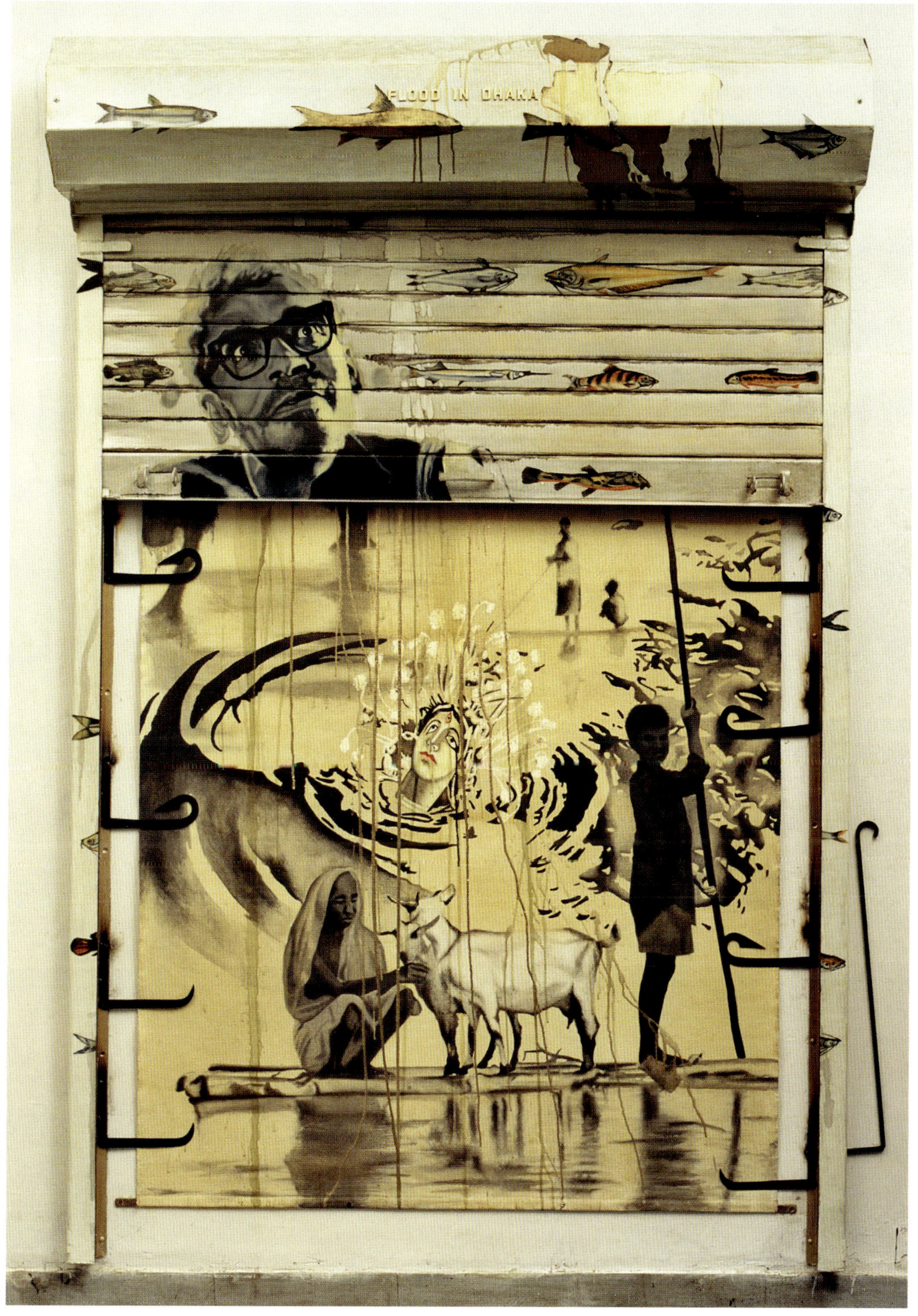

Figure 1.
Atul Dodiya, *The Flood in Dhaka*, 2002
Paint on metal shutter
109 × 72 inches (276.9 × 182.9 cm)
Collection of Arani and Shumita Bose

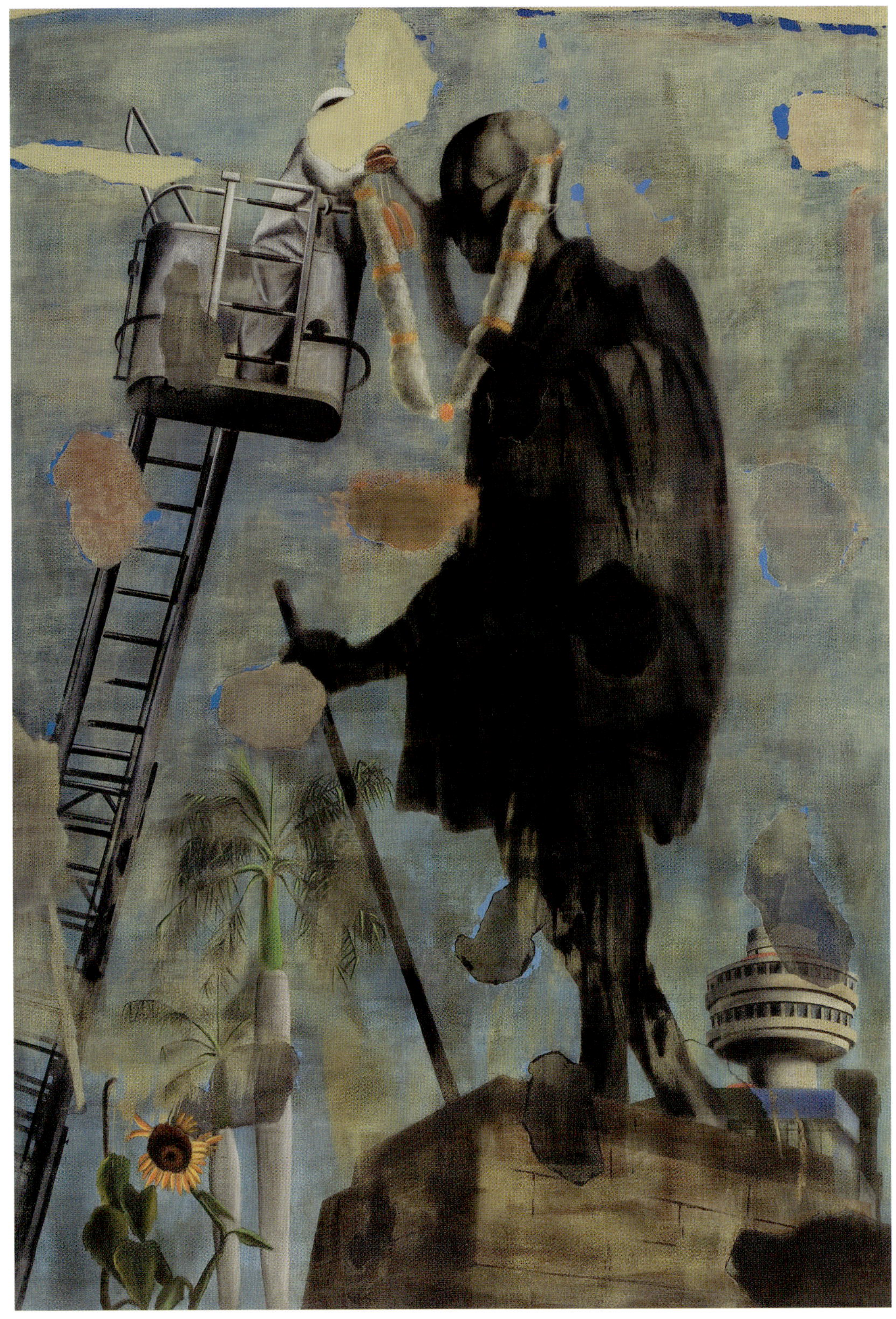

Plate 62.
2nd October, 1993
Oil and acrylic on canvas
69 ⅛ × 48 inches (175.6 × 121.9 cm)

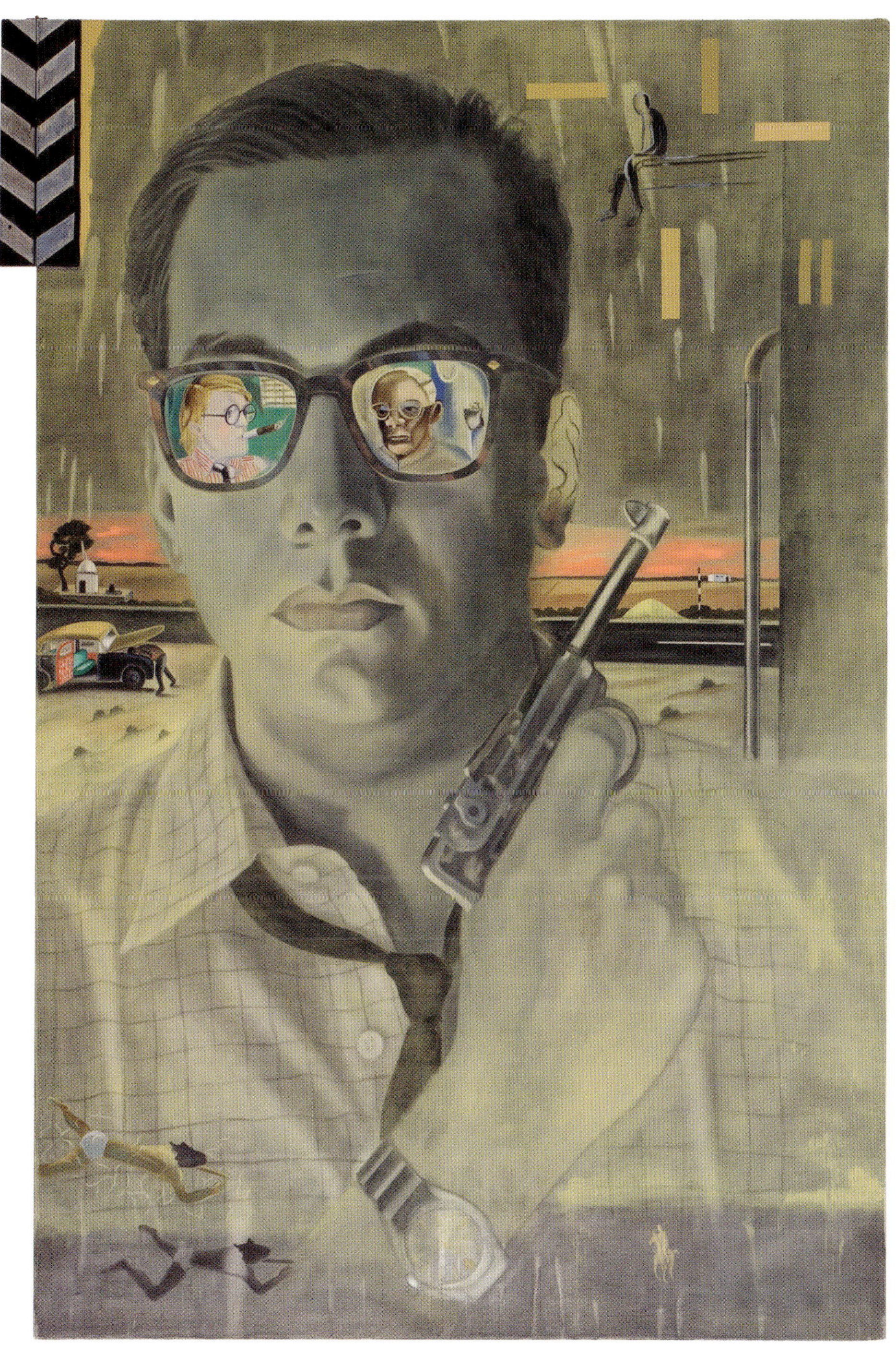

Plate 63.
The Bombay Buccaneer, 1994
Oil and acrylic on canvas with film clapstick
72 × 48 inches (182.9 × 121.9 cm)

RANBIR SINGH KALEKA

Born in Patiala, 1953
Lives and work in New Delhi

Balancing in his art the whimsy of surreal illusionism and the rituals of everyday life, Ranbir Singh Kaleka explores and invents strategies that integrate painting on canvas, time-based video work, and large-scale installations. Kaleka was trained as a painter at Punjab University in Chandigarh and the Royal College of Art in London in the late 1970s; he spent much of the 1980s in London before returning to New Delhi in the 1990s.

In his early career, Kaleka focused on multifigure compositions, drawing on the narrative figuration movement that gained prominence in Indian art in the 1980s, though he was not a direct peer of the artists who pioneered that trend. To a degree greater than that of the artists generally associated with narrative figuration, Kaleka artfully invented his scenes to suggest magical, dreamlike spaces: reality is never presumed and the relationship between internal and external worlds is often blurred. This is true even in a work such as *Family—1* (plate 64), an unusual, theatrical scene for which Kaleka used his relatives, including his father, uncle, and cousins, as models. The boy in the middle of the canvas appears as to be the pivotal figure, though the viewer can see only his face. His relationship to the woman at the left and man at the right who look at him caringly remains undefined other than by the implications of the painting's title. The elegant woman in profile standing over them at the right and the recessed and smaller upward-flying male mythical figure visually frame the scene, though their strange presence leaves the relationship among all of the figures even more uncertain. The figures are placed behind a group of colorful, almost psychedelic, cane-shaped railings, which separate the pictorial protagonists from the viewer and affirm the distance between the narrative of the work and our external reality. Kaleka emphasized the surreal and uncertain quality of this narrative by eliminating any external source of light that would ground and orient the time and space of the setting; this is a strategy learned from miniature painting, which Kaleka has admired and looked to often as a source.

Conjurer's Fire on My Palm (plate 65) draws on many of the playful and dramatic conventions of *Family*, but engages more directly with Surrealist ideas and even the trope of magic. The dynamic main figure, an acrobat or traveling performer who balances his contorted, cloudlike body on one strong, muscular hand, seems to generate fire on his palm of his other hand. Behind the erupting flames is what appears to be a white sheet grasped by the hand of an unseen figure in the background. Its placement turns the fire into almost an abstract composition on or in front of a canvas, and draws a clear parallel between the "magic" devised by this performer and that of the contemporary painter. The conjurer unleashes his magic in a fantastical open space lit by a series of red lights common at country fairs in India. The presence of a sculptural sleeping man at the right suggests that the dramatic scene may perhaps be a figment of his imaginative dreaming. The lack of a clear horizon line and solid ground, and especially the fluid, organic forms of the composition, indicate continual movement, foreshadowing what Kaleka would so successfully create in his video projections just a few years later. Kaleka has maintained the painterliness of his work even in video compositions such as the subtle and masterful *Man with Cockerel* (2004), which traces over a six-minute loop the movement of a bird being caught by, and then escaping from, the man at the center of the projection.

In his hybrid painting-video installations—even more than in those works that can be readily categorized as one medium or the other—Kaleka has explored the relationship between illumination and illusion. This can be seen especially in *The Kettle* (2010) and *Sweet Unease* (figure 1). Both works involve moving images projected on top of oil paintings, though at times in their sequences the boundaries and layers between the two mediums is deliberately and expertly blurred. *The Kettle* suggests a still life centered around a commonplace steel tea kettle painted on a canvas, though the entire scene continually shifts and even includes moments when the kettle is unseen. *Sweet Unease*, Kaleka's most recent and most elaborate large-scale work, presents two canvases with individual male figures whose environments and relationship change over the eleven-minute loop of the video projection.

Kaleka pursued painting as his primary medium until the mid-1990s, and his subsequent forays into video and multimedia have relied conceptually on many aspects of narrative painting and the tradition of figuration. In referring to painterly practices even in his video projections, Kaleka has drawn attention to the conventions by which both mediums usually operate. He has also repeatedly succeeded at blurring the boundaries between painting and new media, and questioned the notion that they necessarily remain distinct mediums in contemporary art. In accord with the "presentness" of video as a medium, Kaleka has considered all of his work to be in progress; he frequently reworks details years after the initial fabrication of an installation. Thus, the movement and process evident in Kaleka's imagery remain an integral part of his practice and keep his work—whether from the 1980s or today, and painting, video, or both—resolutely contemporary. – BC

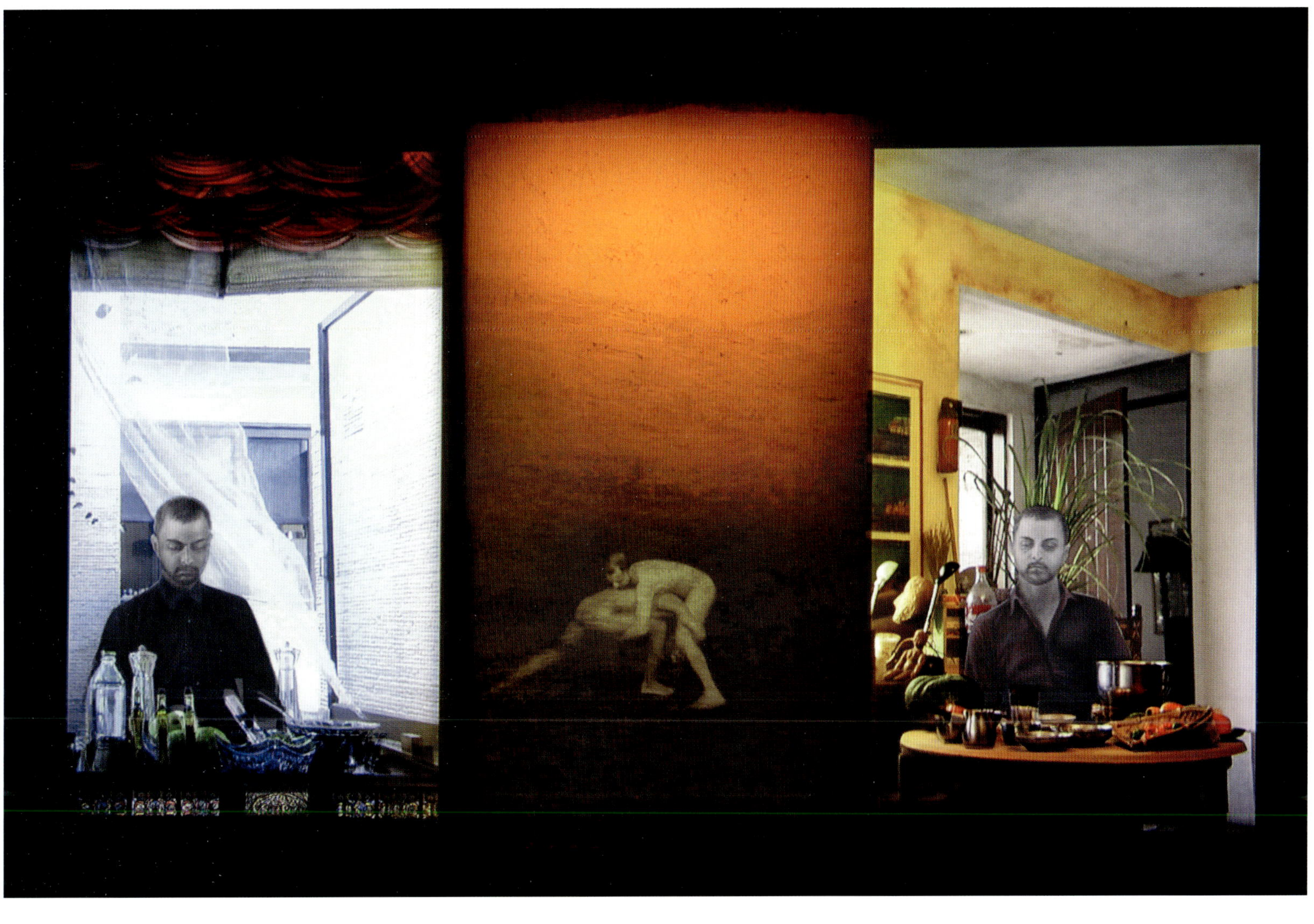

Figure 1.
Ranbir Singh Kaleka, *Sweet Unease*, 2010
Single channel HD video projection on painted canvas mounted on fractured wall
61 ⅞ × 110 ¼ inches (157 × 280 cm)
Volte Gallery, Mumbai

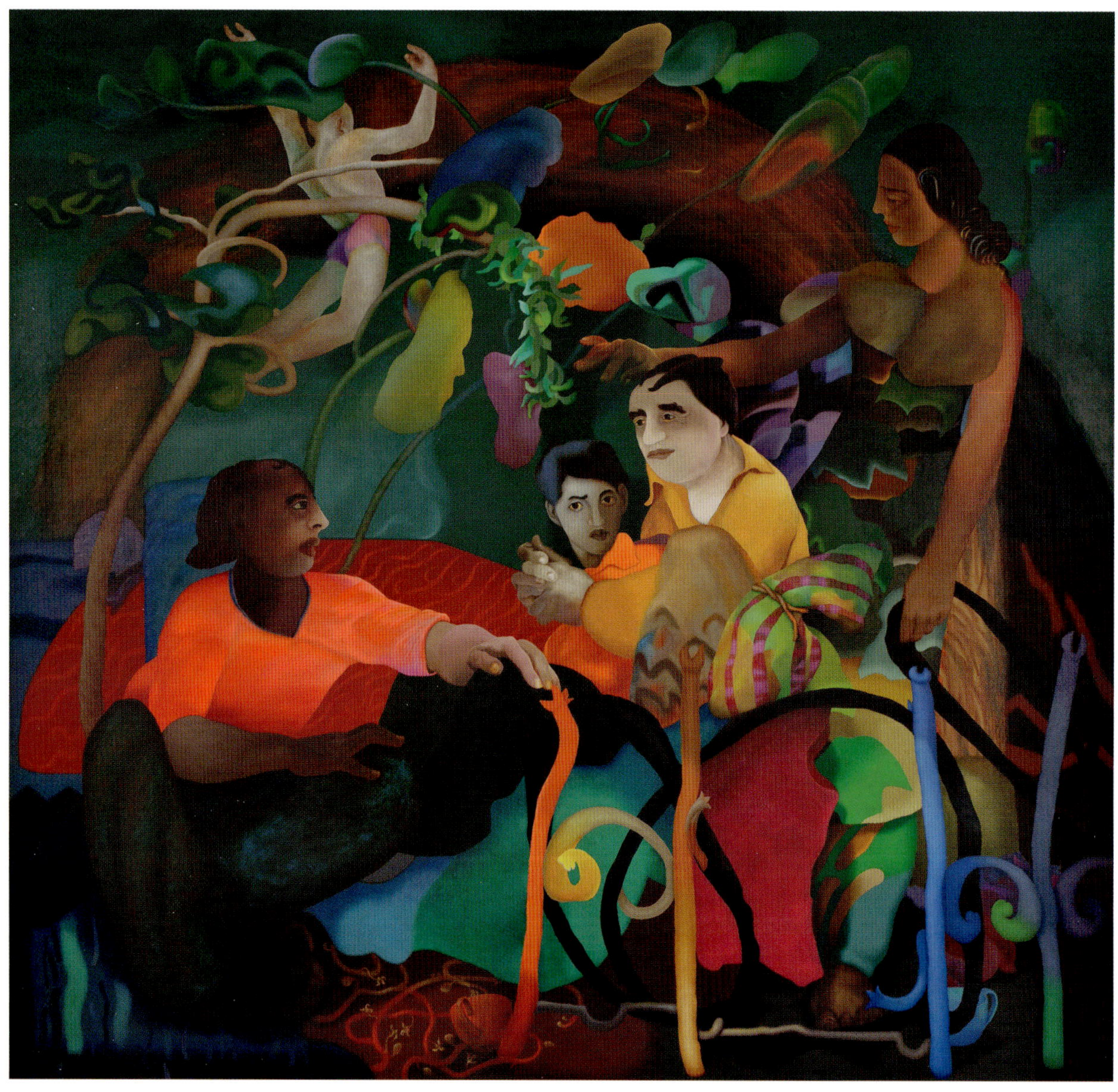

Plate 64.
Family—1, 1983
Oil on canvas
80 ½ × 85 ¼ inches (204.5 × 216.5 cm)

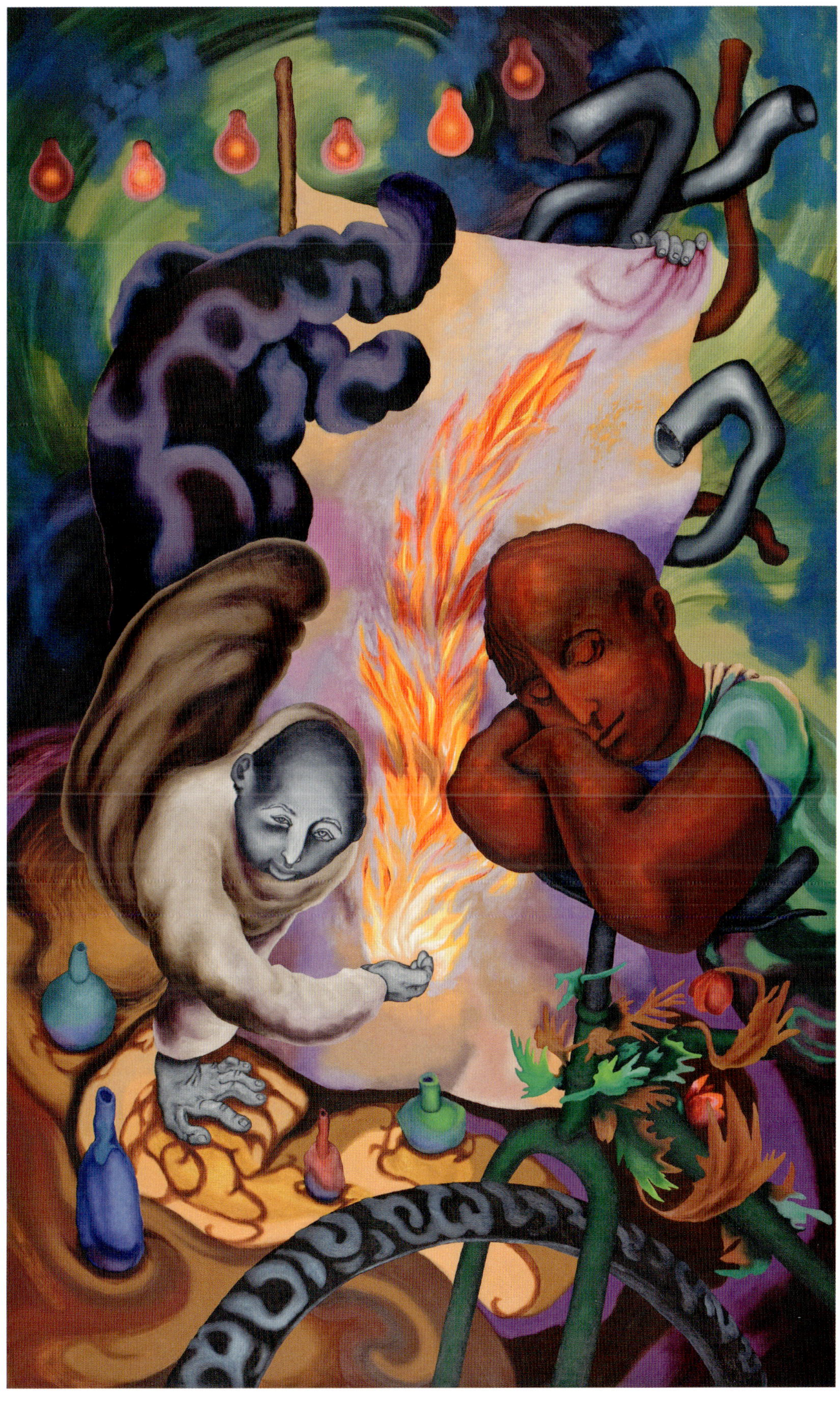

Plate 65.
Conjurer's Fire on My Palm, 1985–86
Oil on canvas
95 ¾ × 59 ¾ inches (243.2 × 151.8 cm)

NALINI MALANI

Born in Karachi (now in Pakistan), 1946
Lives and works in Bombay

In the 1990s, Nalini Malani was in the vanguard of artists who sought to take art in India into new directions. She transformed her painting practice, integrating performance, installation, and video, and became a presence in the global contemporary arena. A survey of the development of her practice since the mid-1970s reveals a striking progression. In early oil paintings, Malani delved deeply into her self and her experience as a middle-class woman among friends and family. Familiar figures people her canvases. Their bodies seem vulnerable, soft and rounded, lacking angularity. Yet, their facial expressions are intense, with heads tilted, jutting chins, and sideways glances. Their touches convey wariness, yearning, sadness, and isolation. No happiness here—only existential angst. Malani commented in 1982: "My concern is with these primary instincts which manifest themselves in external reality and also in the inner chaos of the mind. I work from my personal experience and fantasy, aiming to move from the particular to the general...."[1] Malani's experience as a woman and her deep connection to her own emotional life are still at the center of her art.

Around 1980, Malani discovered the work of Benodebehari Mukherjee in a small book put out by the Lalit Kala Akademi. Mukherjee's painting of a man wearing a shawl and his landscapes moved her. She admired his use of watercolor and his approach to composition. The book prompted new developments in her painting and changed her attitude toward figuration. A few years later, when months of renovations kept her from her studio and she had to put aside oil painting, she turned in earnest to watercolor, which could be managed at home. *City of Pain/City of Escape* (plate 66) represents the new direction in her work in which figures take form from the pigment itself, more suggestive than structured. They remain transparent, and forms are layered, retaining inklings of what lies beneath. To achieve this effect, Malani applied gesso to create a nonabsorbent surface on which daubs of watercolor could be manipulated and contours moved or removed. Malani used this technique to interpret the character of her city, Bombay: "Beneath its everyday skin lies a vast alternate world; sometimes secret; sometimes blatant. Piercing the layers, you encounter odd mosaics and montages, a whole archaeology of the city and its inhabitants and immigrants."[2] Presiding over the composition are Gangadevi, goddess of the waters, and Ganesh, patron deity of the city and of commerce that is the city's lifeblood. They are flanked on either side by tightly massed skyscrapers conveying the press of life in the world's second largest city. Below them, the streets seethe with the turmoil of sectarian aggression and greed for land and power.[3]

Also in 1989, Malani integrated transparency and layering into an oil painting reflecting on her predecessors Frida Kahlo and Amrita Sher-Gil. *Old Arguments on Indigenism* (plate 67) was painted after a trip to the United States where she once again saw the work of Kahlo and a documentary film on the artist.[4] Malani was intrigued by Kahlo's parallels with India's pioneering modernist Sher-Gil. Both were women from elite families of mixed ancestry, with local and European Jewish antecedents. Like Malani, they sourced their art practices in their own life experiences. Though both painters drew on indigenous sources in their work, Malani found Kahlo's identification with the people of Mexico deeper and more convincing than the fashionable, bourgeois Sher-Gil's connection to village India. In Malani's painting, Kahlo and Sher-Gil's icons—a woman with a damaged, exposed, and bleeding spine; a temple sculpture; and a village girl—rest in their laps like dolls or babies, recalling that both women were childless. Malani placed herself at the left, looking back over her shoulder and surrounded by her own troubling symbols: severed limbs and a woman with leg-braces (see Bhabha and Bean, figure 3). Perhaps her apprehensive look and the turn of her body away from the viewer reflect Malani's fear of the heavy toll of being an artist and of carrying forward an aesthetic legacy, especially for a woman from the third world.

Malani's "Mutant" series, originally inspired by the story of Medea (in both Euripides' and Heiner Mueller's versions), probes exploitation and victimization as universal experiences of women and the stuff of mythic tales. In the 1990s, as she extended outward from her own experience to that of all women, Malani used the experience of women to interpret the human propensity for violence and domination. Malani's "Mutants" are damaged women, witnesses and victims. Most works in the series are on milk-carton paper, which, for Malani, additionally referred to the shipments of powdered milk to India from the radiation-contaminated region of Chernobyl. In *After Pina Bausch—Mutant B* (plate 68), Malani turned from this ephemeral medium to the durability of canvas, in keeping with the enormity of the sectarian violence unleashed by the 1992 destruction of the Babri Mosque in Ayodhya and the subsequent murderous riots in Bombay. She also drew on Pina Bausch's performance of "Carnations" in Bombay and her dance's eloquence in evoking the destructive effects of distorted relationships and the victimization of others in gross and subtle ways.[5]

The desire to interpret global exploitation of people and the environment impelled Malani to seek new media and expand beyond the canvas. In 2001, she created her first shadow play combining painting, installation, and video. She turned to the technique of reverse painting on transparent surfaces, which she had learned from Bhupen Khakhar (plates 41–43) during their 1989 collaboration with Vivan Sundaram on a mural for a private home in Bombay. Malani had found a new nonabsorbent surface to further the technique she had developed with watercolor. She bent the Mylar sheets into cylinders and motorized them to revolve so that light projected through them casts moving shadows of the painted images. Works like *Remembering Mad Meg* (figure 1) draw on her own experience and fantasies and reach outward from the experience of women to probe victimhood and violence, whether from persecution, imperialism, or the exploitation of the planet. – SSB

1. *India: Myth & Reality—Aspects of Modern Indian Art* (Oxford: Museum of Modern Art, 1982), p. 43.

2. *Nalini Malani: Under the Skin* (Bombay: Gallery 7, 1989).

3. Nalini Malani, conversations with the author, December 2007 and December 2009, Herwitz Archive, Peabody Essex Museum, Salem, Massachusetts.

4. Malani, conversation with the author, December 2009.

5. Nalini Malani, e-mail to the author, September 2008.

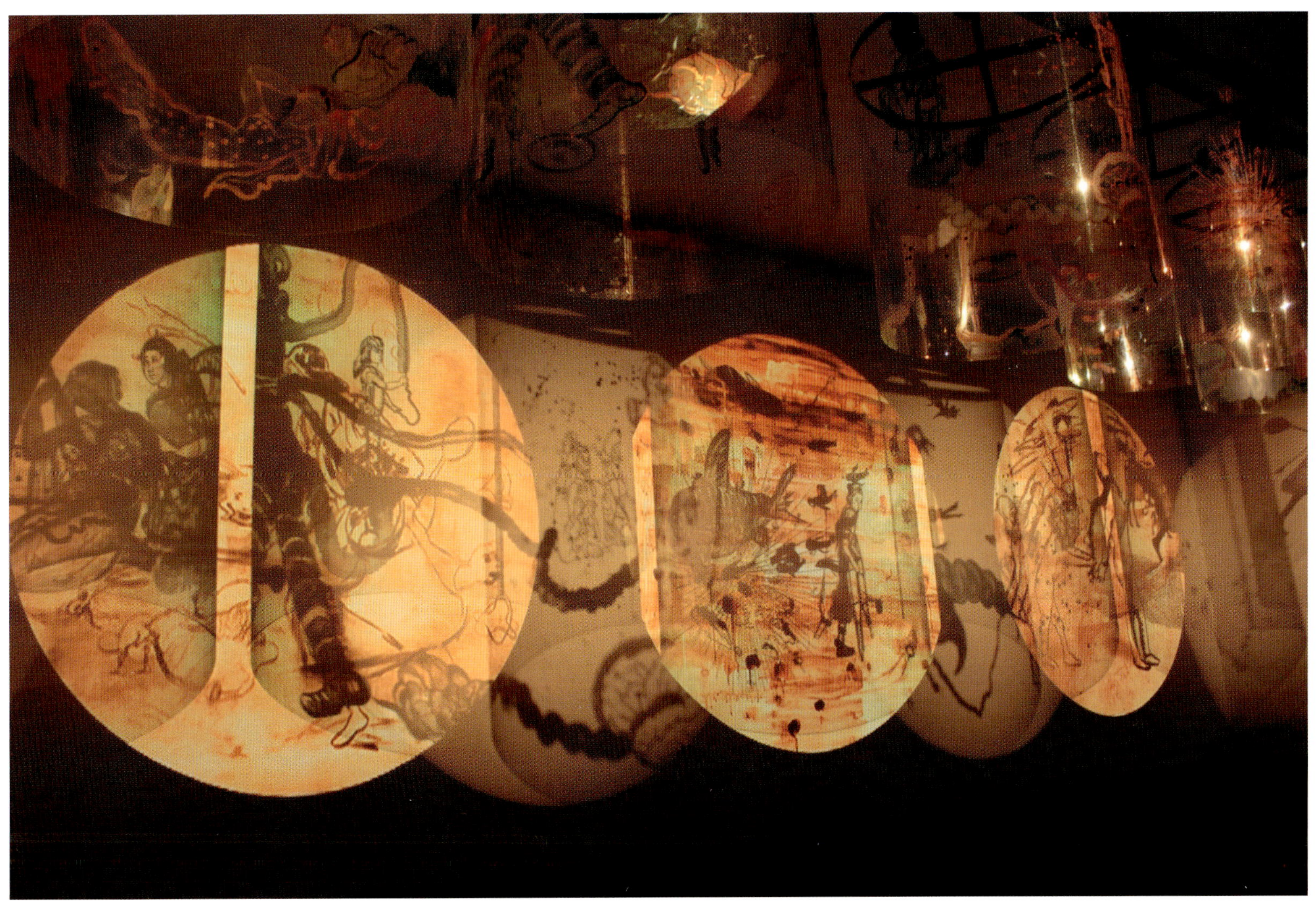

Figure 1.
Nalini Malani,
Remembering Mad Meg, 2007–11
Video shadow play, three single channel animations, lights, and eight rotating reverse painted Lexan cylinders, sound, three minutes
Centre Pompidou, Paris

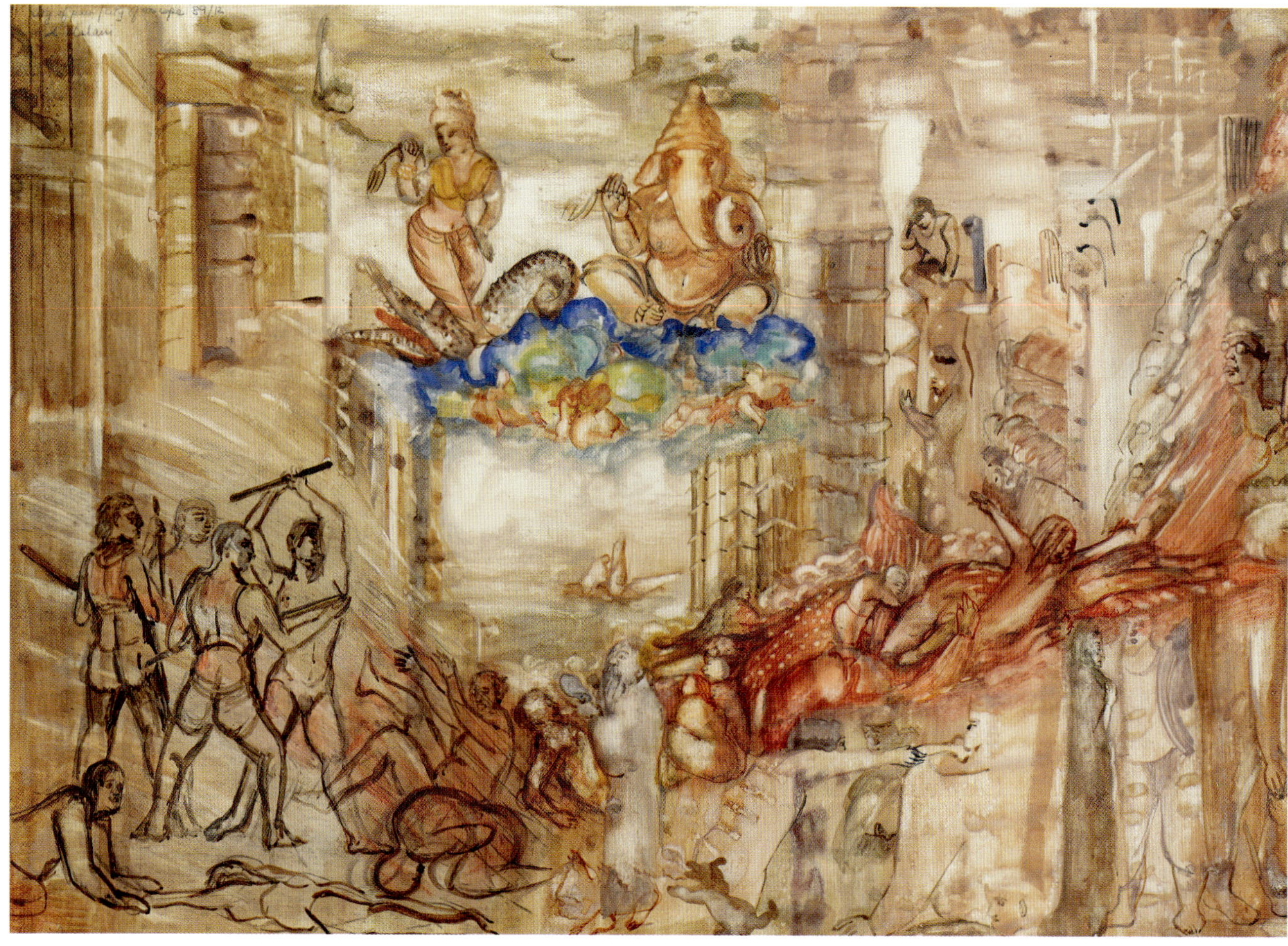

Plate 66.
City of Pain/City of Escape, 1989
Watercolor and pencil on paper
21 ½ × 29 ½ inches (54.6 × 74.9 cm)

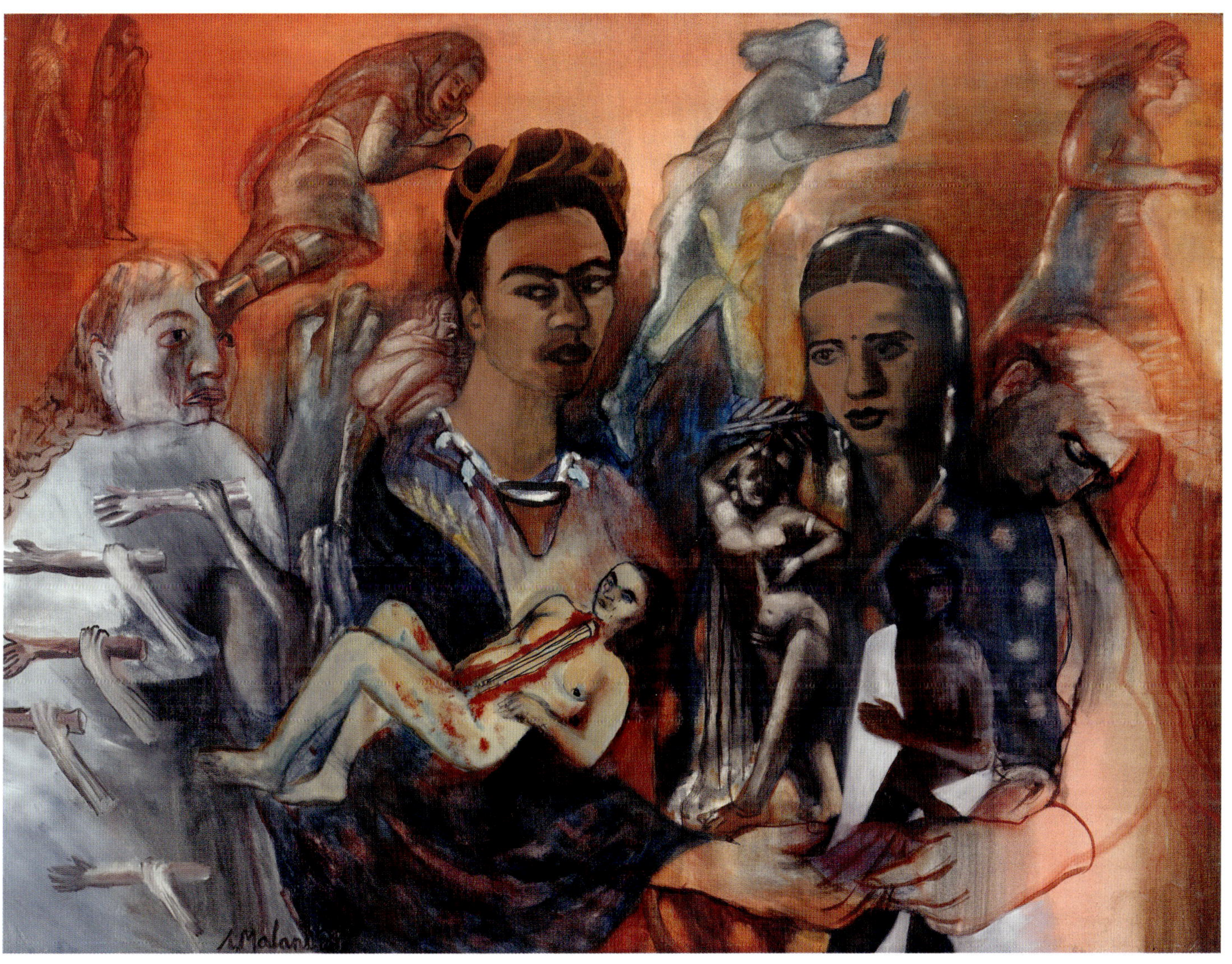

Plate 67.
Old Arguments on Indigenism, 1989
Oil and acrylic on canvas
36 × 48 inches (91.4 × 121.9 cm)

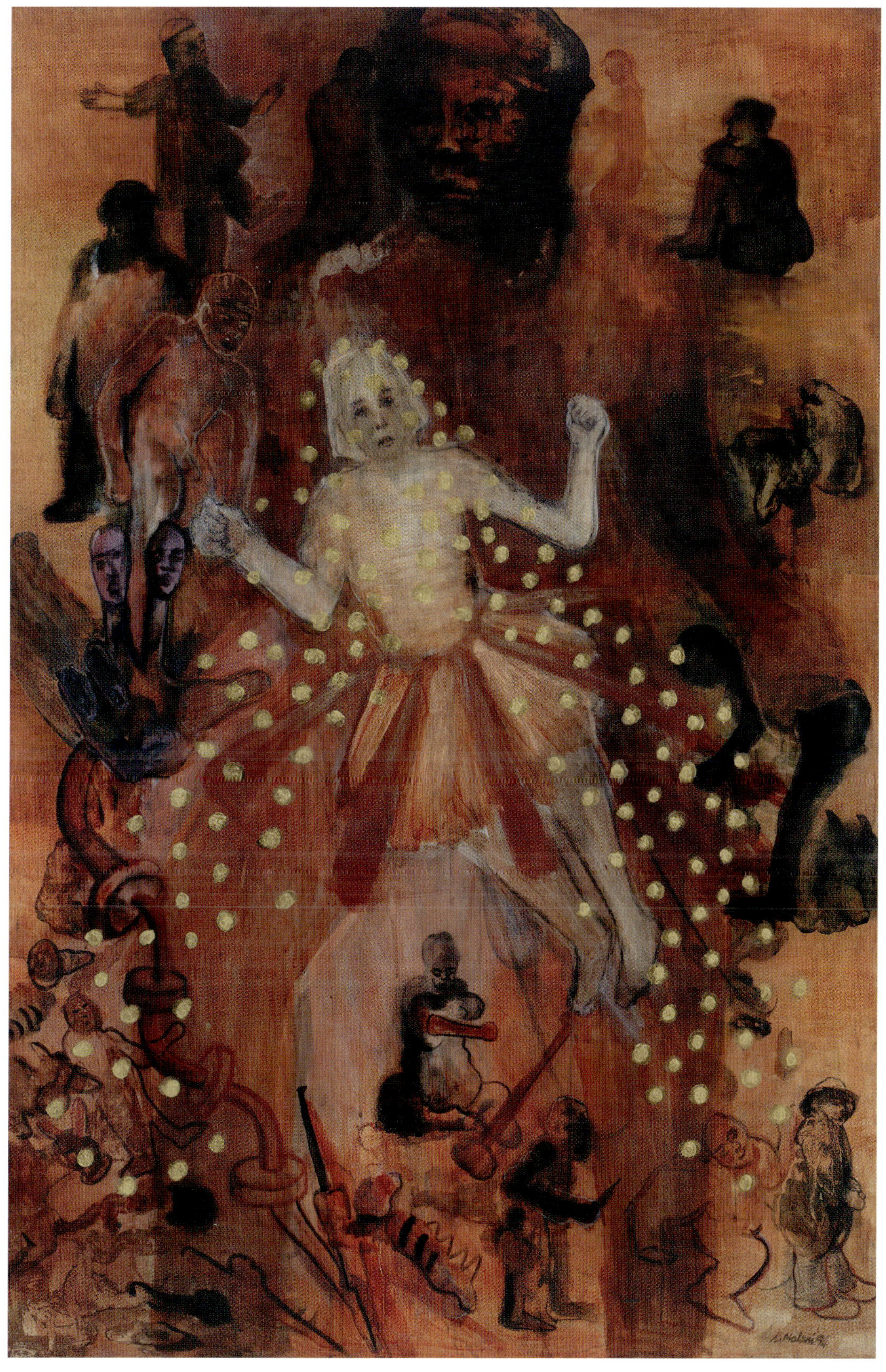

Plate 68.
After Pina Bausch—Mutant B, 1994
Oil on canvas
60 × 40 inches (154.4 × 101.6 cm)

SUDHIR PATWARDHAN

Born in Pune, 1949
Lives and works in Bombay

A self-taught artist (and also a practicing radiologist until his 2007 retirement), Sudhir Patwardhan began to paint professionally in the mid-1970s, following a move to Bombay after medical school. The cosmopolitan city offered new opportunities to Patwardhan, originally from Pune in Maharashtra. He participated in an emerging leftist subculture responding to threats of war with Pakistan, oil embargoes, and nonalliance (in which India chose not to align with any power bloc) at the height of the Cold War, all of which contributed to India's period of emergency from 1975 to 1977. As part of this process, Patwardhan found social, linguistic, and intellectual community with greater Bombay's Maharashtrians: his affinity with the Konkani-Marathi working classes distinguished his painting practice and career from that of fellow artists in urban India's cosmopolitan art world.

Patwardhan's art has reflected his politics—an engagement with Marxist and "New Left" thought and his sense that he ought to be a "painter of people."[1] Indeed, his desire to extend the long tradition of figuration in Indian art into the living politics and society around his painting is reflected in both his activism and his language (prioritizing "people" over the more common artistic term "figure"). In his paintings, he has explored general social issues like class relations and urbanization through multiple viewpoints, while depicting specific local urban and suburban places and relationships from his personal experiences. In part resisting earlier generations of artists who were intellectually engaged by a universalist, but self-contained, existentialism (and who often looked stylistically to expressionism associated with the West), Patwardhan was among a group of artists in India in the late 1970s and early 1980s who pioneered the locally rooted "narrative figuration" movement. Narrative figuration asserted itself as a new, interventionist direction in Indian painting through the landmark 1981 exhibition *Place for People* in Bombay and Delhi. Patwardhan was one of the six participating painters and his submissions marked the peak of his leftist activism and his experimentations with strategies to represent the lower and working urban classes. In those works from 1979 to 1981, Patwardhan began to incorporate an adaptable style of realism to render figures and narrative scenes, intending that the work remain legible to his "ideal audience, which included the people...represented,"[2] engaging the diverse communities that were most often outside of the conventional art world.

In the early 1980s, Patwardhan's relationship to his working-class subjects began to shift somewhat. He had moved from Bombay to the satellite city of Thane (today a large suburb of Bombay). As the final dissolution of Bombay's once leading textile mill industry displaced and devastated many city workers in the late 1970s and 1980s, Patwardhan took stock once again of his local surroundings and the changing dynamics of his environment. The panoramic *Town* (plate 70) demonstrates his foray into experimenting with a varying interplay of intimacy and objectivity. Depicting Thane as an expanding urban site, *Town* is principally divided along a central vertical axis of dark water; at the left is a near-empty expanse, while to the right is a dense, mostly residential, urban area. The middle ground is limited by a dry, undeveloped mass of hills behind it and a building project in the foreground that bisects the central vertical partition. While the construction physically overshadows the space of the foreground, day-to-day activities continue: a lone male worker, balanced on a wooden beam, serves as the protagonist of the building project and the figural focus of the painting. Engaging a complex visual device that alludes to Mughal painting, *Town* employs multiple, simultaneous perspectives in an attempt to compress the distant and universal and the personal and intimate into the same plane and landscape. Through this strategy, Patwardhan has presented the transformation underway not as a single object or even a single moment, but in and as a process.

Ceremony (plate 69), painted in the same year, 1984, demonstrates Patwardhan's empathetic portrayal of the community and life within Bombay's shantytowns—up close and at ground level. The central figures erect a canopy for a ritual meal to mark the death of a neighbor or family member.[3] A crow flying overhead and orange garlands hanging in the door of the makeshift shanty in the background are additional visual signs of the recent loss. By contrast with his earlier works and even *Town*, here Patwardhan depicted the central figures with a more painterly, expressive treatment and chiaroscuro. The rendering of the figures and also their closeness to the picture plane generate a sense of intimacy without voyeurism.

Patwardhan has continued to paint "peopled landscapes" that document and respond to changes in Bombay and Thane, but in works such as *Sketch* (plate 71), he has also investigated interiority and relationships at close range. Turning inward, provoked perhaps by the riots and sectarian violence that besieged Bombay in the early 1990s,[4] Patwardhan in much of his work from this time reflected on middle-class domestic life and even private questions of the self. In *Sketch*, a woman reaches toward a set of bookshelves in an unspecified room; a second female figure, visually connected even as the relationship between the two figures remains unclear, faces away toward a back wall. Rather than show the surrounding landscape through the background windows, Patwardhan attached his sketch of the interior scene. This solution doubled the focus on the internal action and evinced consciously postmodern strategies of quotation, repetition, and translation that were at this time being integrated into contemporary Indian art. The work, and Patwardhan's subsequent dual engagements with figuration and landscape, is evidence of his commitment to the articulation of "people" and the environment, and his constant questioning of the artist's role and intervention in the surrounding urban environment. – BC

1. Sudhir Patwardhan, "Near and Far," in *Sudhir Patwardhan* (Paris: Association Française d'Action Artistique in association with Centre Georges Pompidou, Musée National d'Art Moderne, 1986), n.p.

2. Sudhir Patwardhan, e-mails to the author, April 24 and 25, 2009.

3. Susan S. Bean, *Gateway Bombay* (Salem, Massachusetts: Peabody Essex Museum, 2007), p. 17.

4. As suggested by Ranjit Hoskote, *Sudhir Patwardhan: The Complicit Observer* (Mumbai: Sakshi Gallery, 2005), p. 30.

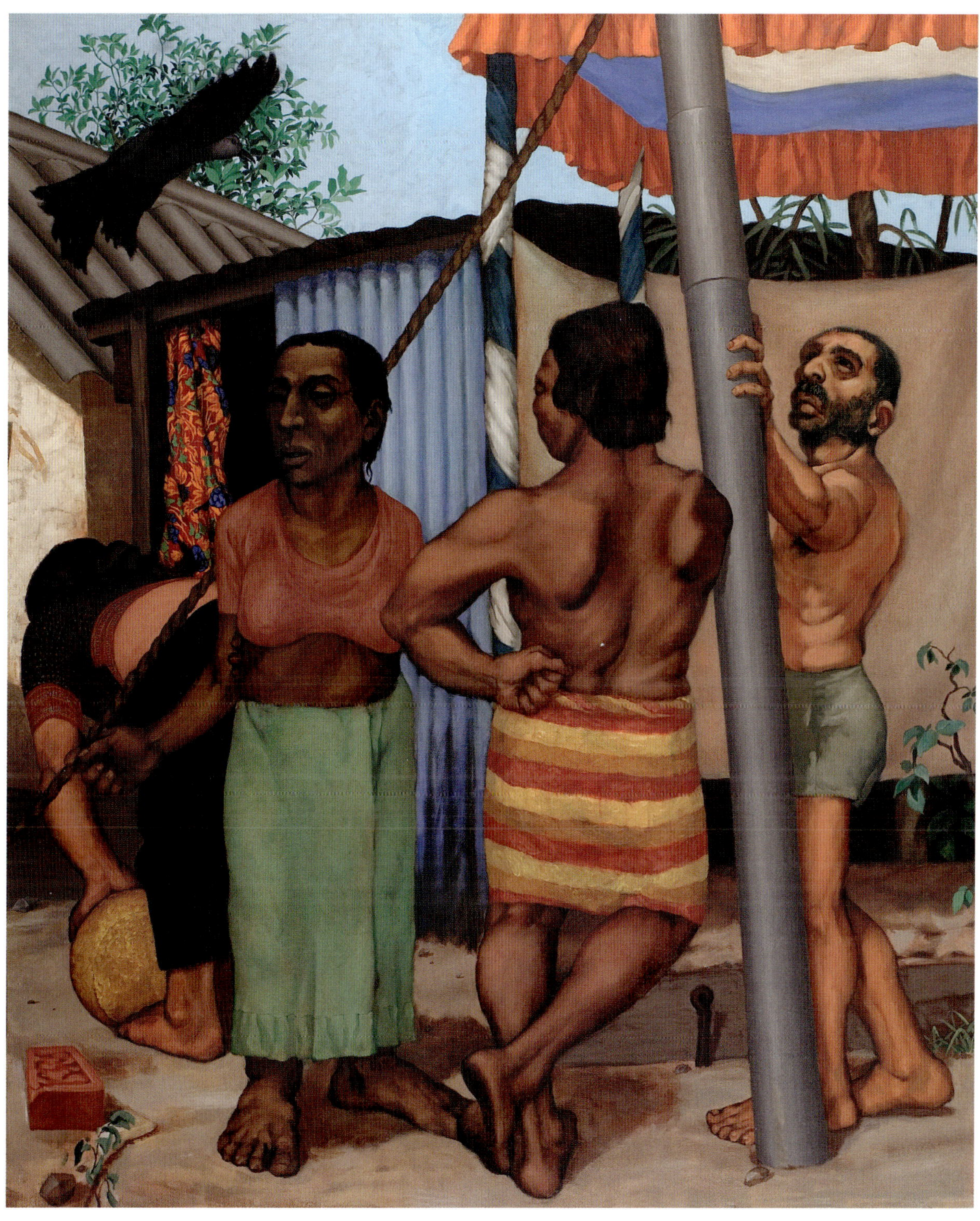

Plate 69.
Ceremony, 1984
Oil on canvas
50 × 42 ⅛ inches (127 × 107 cm)

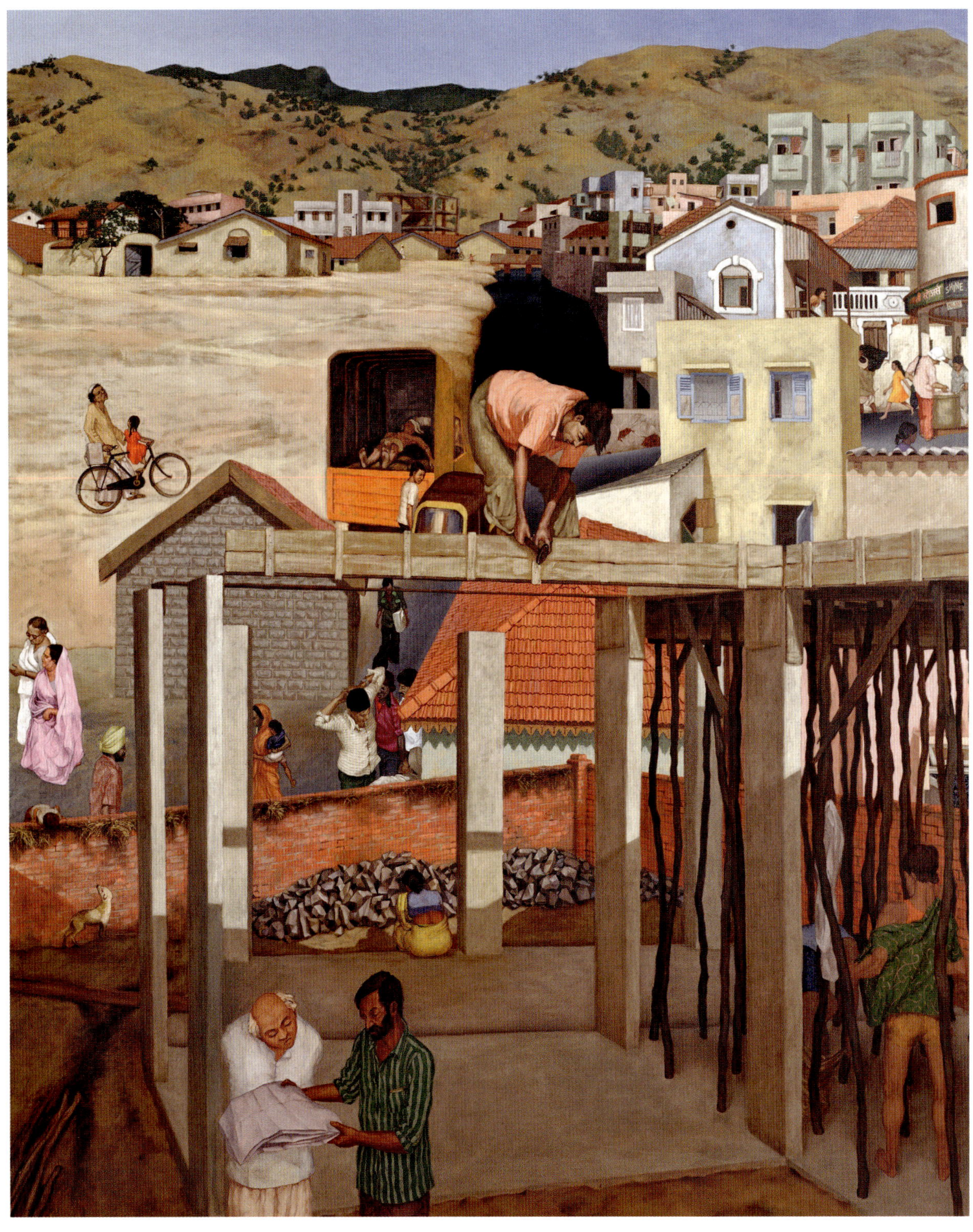

Plate 70.
Town, 1984
Oil on canvas
73 × 61 inches (185.4 × 157.5 cm)

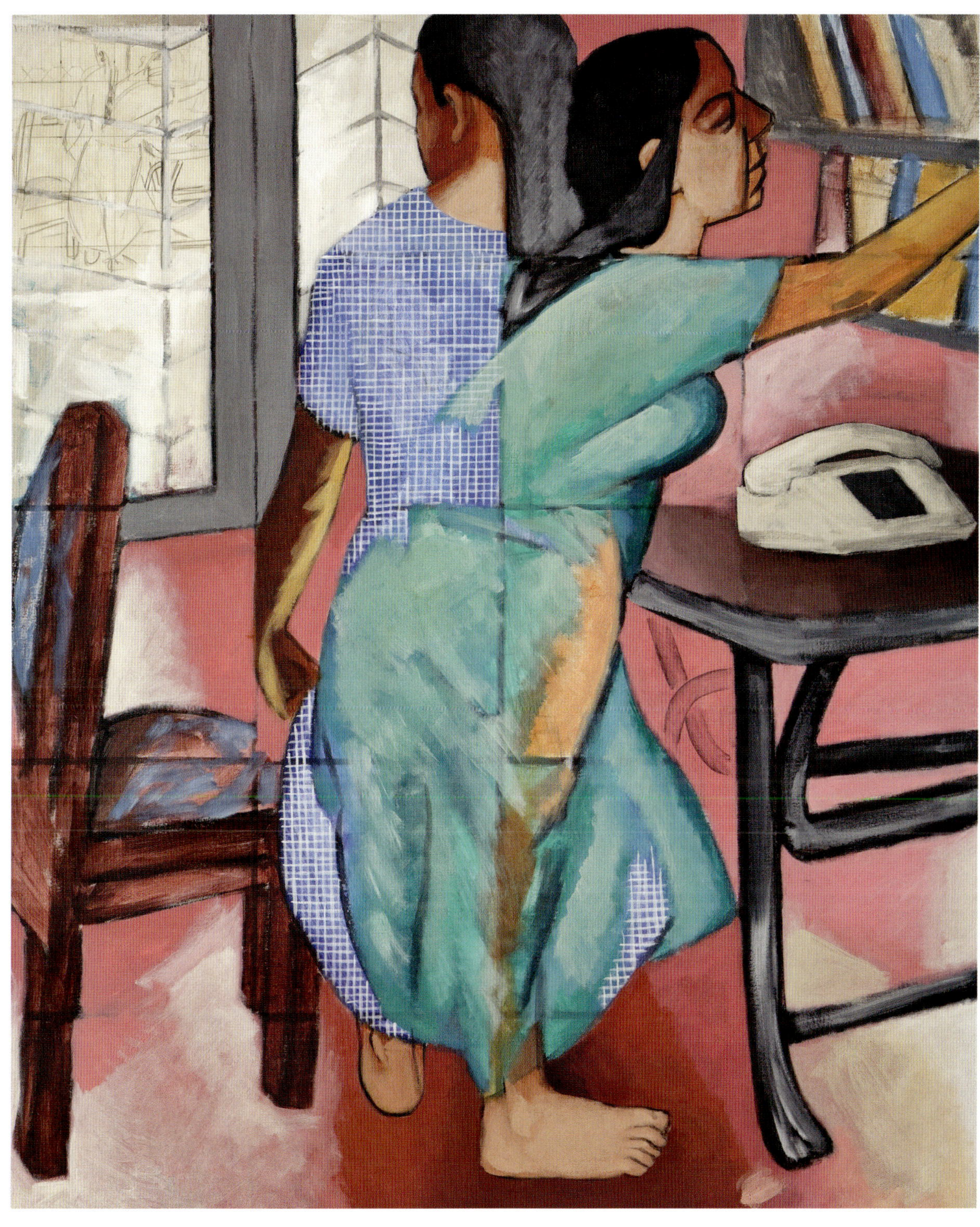

Plate 71.
Sketch, 1994
Oil on canvas with pencil on paper drawing
48 × 40 inches (121.9 × 101.6 cm)

REKHA RODWITTIYA

Born in Bangalore, 1958
Lives and works in Baroda

Rekha Rodwittiya emerged as a pioneering feminist Marxist artist in Baroda in the mid-1980s. Rodwittiya studied painting at Maharaja Sayajirao University in Baroda, then at the Royal College of Art in London. Following her extended stay in London, Rodwittiya returned to settle in Baroda, where she aligned herself intellectually and politically with the Indian Radical Painters and Sculptors' Association, which supported extreme leftist politics and ideas. Key members, including Alex Mathew and K.P. Krishnakumar who hailed from the southern state of Kerala, spread their influence and traveled to Baroda in the late 1980s, invigorating its very different artistic climate. By this time, Baroda had become an important "think tank" for the Indian art world; Maharaja Sayajirao University had surpassed Bombay's J.J. School as the nation's leading academic art center. The influence of the Kerala Radicals (as they were known to many) did not arise because their politics diverged from that of artists who associated themselves with socialist and communist activism (including Vivan Sundaram and Sudhir Patwardhan [plates 69–71]), but rather because the group was perceived by some as the leaders of a new generation of more politically aware artists.[1] The outspoken and overt politics of the Kerala Radicals appealed to Rodwittiya as a vehicle to reject what she perceived as a traditional, patriarchal structure in Baroda, and to change and reexamine both language and representation in contemporary art.[2] Consciously integrating her artistic practice and politics into the broader rhythms and narrative of her life, she has presented autobiographical texts alongside her painting to frame their perspectives.[3] This solution has enabled Rodwittiya to maintain and articulate her feminine point of view within an artistic and political culture that discouraged it.

At that time, Rodwittiya was—by choice—a single mother. She was committed to discourses of gender politics that enabled her to present herself openly and to intervene in society through her feminism. This is quite aggressively and cannily shown in *How Naked Shall I Stand For You* (plate 72), which depicts a woman positioned frontally, but looking away and disaffected as she rips open her skin to reveal a burning red interior. Though the central figure is seated calmly, the dramatic tearing of her flesh speaks to the violence afflicting women globally. The woman is among a kaleidoscopic chorus of faces and figures in the background; several cats, with visages eerily similar to hers, surround and peer at her. (Rodwittiya has regularly associated women and cats in her work.) Though this woman is exposed even more deeply than simple nakedness, Rodwittiya has kept her anonymous and universal so as to address conditions for women in general. The painting also reflects Rodwittiya's process of working out the conflict between a focus on her personal life and the need to engage with external issues, a problem she has continued to address.

In the diptych *The Excavation of Weathered Dreams* (plate 73), Rodwittiya commented on the idealism and aspiration of her generation in the late 1980s. She has noted the excitement of the artistic journey for an emerging artist, and the collective passion felt among young artists working in dialogue with each other at this time.[4] The figures who make their way through the painting's unmapped, fantastical forests, with no end or objective in plain sight, are torchbearers of tomorrow and remind the viewer of the importance of the journey (in her case, artistic) itself. In comparison to the primal woman in *How Naked Shall I Stand For You*, the travelers in *The Excavation of Weathered Dreams* appear androgynous and undefined in terms of race or ethnicity. Interestingly, however, crosses mark the graveyard behind the three wanderers in the first panel, alluding to an aspect of Rodwittiya's own identity as a Christian in India. The figures carry tools—a shovel, walking stick, and axe—that suggest the very utilitarian nature of their progression. Yet, with a fabulist title and the representation of time-honored symbols of youth and optimism, such as a perfect crescent moon and a colorful, flowing river winding through a forest, the work offers a double-edged message of eternal promise and no reward in sight.

In her writings, Rodwittiya has commented on several personal and career turns in her practice, and has noted that from around 1990 onward, her work became more oriented toward the public. From that time, she tried more assertively to reconcile her interest in the private self, family, and her inner life with the collective public and politics to which she was committed. Unlike many artists of her generation who turned to new media in the 1990s and subsequently, Rodwittiya has remained resolutely committed to painting as her principal medium, engaging the canvas as a space for confrontation with the viewer. Through her writing and the articulation of her life journey and evolving politics (including recently through an online blog that she regularly posts), Rodwittiya and her work are able to participate in the discourse and interventions of younger generations in ways that are perhaps different from those feminist painters who seemed to be her direct peers, like Nilima Sheikh and Nalini Malani. Indeed, Rodwittiya's art has been read as an "aesthetic rollercoaster," with a sheer volume of work that gives her a "vanguardist edge,"[5] and it continues to be part of Baroda's artistic currents. – BC

1. Ashish Rajadyaksha, "The Last Decade," in Gulammohammed Sheikh, ed., *Contemporary Art in Baroda* (Delhi: Tulika Press, 1997), p. 260.

2. Rekha Rodwittiya, e-mail to Susan S. Bean, September 20, 2009.

3. Rajadyaksha, p. 260.

4. Rodwittiya, e-mail to Susan S. Bean.

5. Rajadyaksha, pp. 260–61.

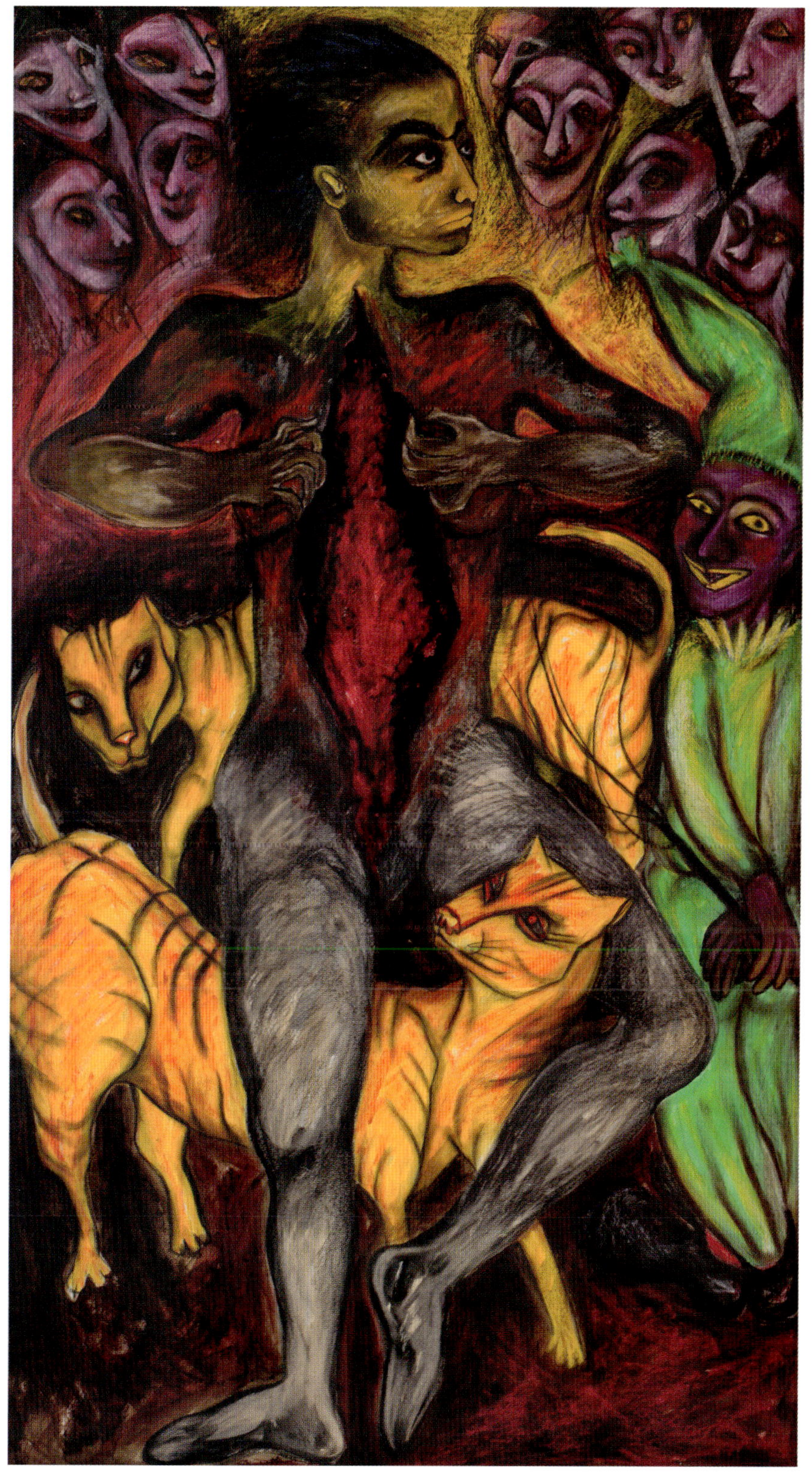

Plate 72.
How Naked Shall I Stand For You, 1986
Watercolor, gouache, graphite pencil,
and pastel on paper
72 ½ × 41 ¼ inches (184.2 × 104.8 cm)

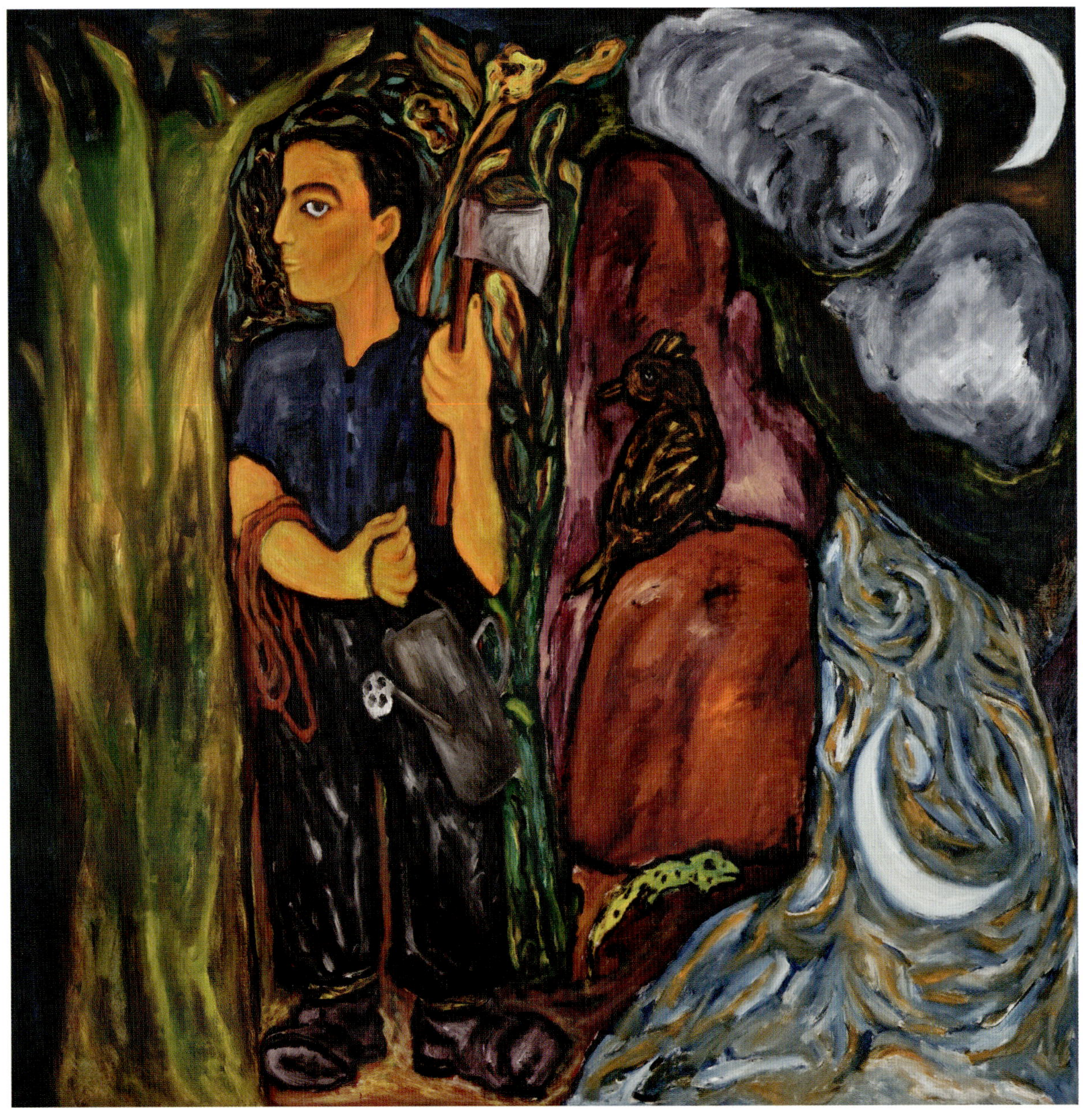

Plate 73.
The Excavation of Weathered Dreams, 1988
Oil on canvas
Two panels, each 54 ½ × 54 ½ inches
(138.4 × 138.4 cm)

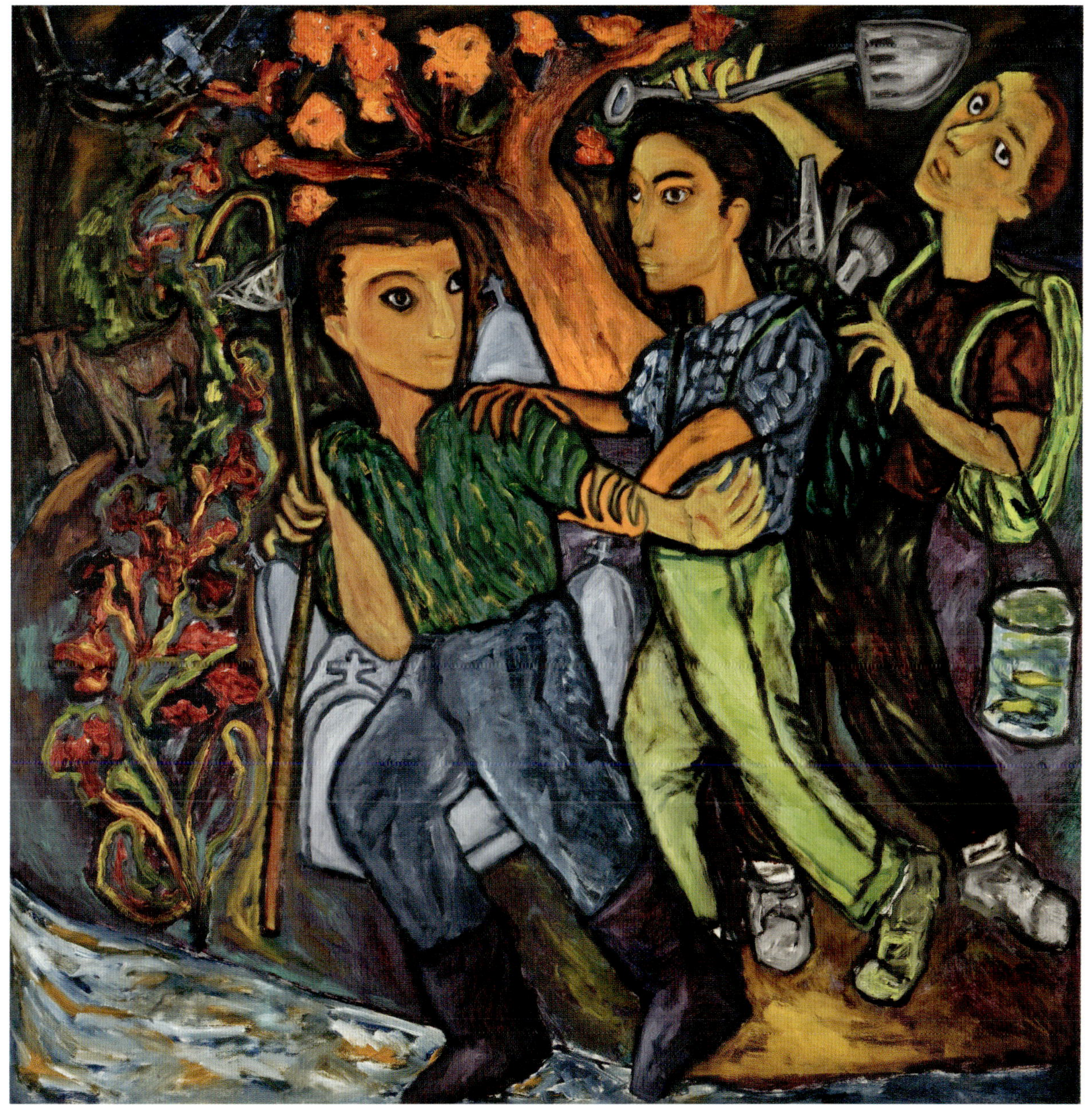

BIBLIOGRAPHY

Aitken, Molly Emma. *The Intelligence of Tradition in Rajput Court Painting*. New Haven and London: Yale University Press, 2010.

Alkazi, Ebrahim. *M.F. Husain: The Modern Artist and Tradition*. New Delhi: Art Heritage, 1978.

Banerjee, Mitra. "Ganesh Pyne: Artist Interview." *Saffron Art*, http://saffronart.com, 2005.

Banerji, Debashish. *The Alternate Nation of Abanindranath Tagore*. New Delhi: Sage, 2010.

Bartholomew, Richard. "Paintings of Ramkumar." *Hindustan Times*, October 1955, p. 6.

Bartholomew, Richard, and Shiv S. Kapur. *Maqbool Fida Husain*. New York: Harry N. Abrams, ca. 1971.

Bawa, Manjit. *Manjit Bawa in His Own Words*. As told to Ina Puri. New Delhi: Roli Books, 2000.

——. *Manjit Bawa*. As told to Ina Puri. Mumbai: Sakshi Gallery, 2002.

Bean, Susan S. *Timeless Visions: Contemporary Art of India from the Chester and Davida Herwitz Collection*. Salem, Massachusetts: Peabody Essex Museum, 1999.

——. "East Meets East in Husain's Horses." In *Lightning: From Private Collection of Marguerite and Kent Charugundla*. New York: Tamarind Gallery, 2007, pp. 11–16.

——. *Gateway Bombay*. Salem, Massachusetts: Peabody Essex Museum, 2007.

Bharucha, Rustom. "Genet in Manila." *Third Text* 17, 1 (January 2003), pp. 15–28.

Bhattacharjee, Bikash. "Bikash on Bikash." In *Close to Events: Works of Bikash Bhattacharjee*. Ed. Manasij Majumder. New Delhi: Niyogi Books, 2007, pp. 182–83.

Bhupen Khakhar. Madrid: Museo Nacional Centro de Arte Reina Sofia, 2002.

Bikash. Calcutta: Graphic Services, n.d.

Borden, Carla M., ed. *Contemporary Indian Tradition: Voices on Culture, Nature, and the Challenge of Change*. Washington, DC: Smithsonian Institution Press, 1989.

Brown, Rebecca M. "P.T. Reddy, Neo-Tantrism, and Modern Indian Art." *Art Journal* 64, 4 (Winter 2005), pp. 26–49.

——. *Art for a Modern India, 1947–1980*. Durham, North Carolina: Duke University Press, 2009.

——. *Gandhi's Spinning Wheel and the Making of India*. London: Routledge, 2010.

Butalia, Urvashi. *The Other Side of Silence: Voices from the Partition of India*. Durham, North Carolina: Duke University Press, 2000.

Chakrabarti, Jayanta, R. Siva Kumar, and Arun Kumar Nag. *The Santiniketan Murals*. Calcutta: Seagull Books in association with Visva-Bharati, 1995.

Chatterjee, Mortimer, and Tara Lal. *The TIFR Art Collection*. Mumbai: Tata Institute of Fundamental Research, 2010.

Chattopadhyay, Kamaladevi. *The Glory of Indian Handicrafts*. New Delhi: Clarion Books, 1985.

Chowdhury, Jogen. "Young Printers' Problems in India and Their Responsibility to Be Serious Painters—A Stray Thought!," Artist's statement written in 1969 and distributed in mimeograph by the artist in 1981. Department of Art History Archives, Maharaja Sayajirao University, Baroda.

Contemporary Indian Art: The Gesture, and Motif and *Stories, Situations*. London: Royal Academy, 1982.

Contemporary Indian Art from the Chester and Davida Herwitz Family Collection. New York: Grey Art Gallery and Study Center, New York University, 1985.

Dalmia, Yashodhara. *The Making of Modern Indian Art: The Progressives*. New Delhi: Oxford University Press, 2001.

——. *Amrita Sher-Gil: A Life*. New Delhi: Penguin Viking, 2006.

——. *Journeys: Four Generations of Indian Artists in Their Own Words*. 2 vols. New Delhi: Oxford University Press, 2011.

Datta, Ella. *Ganesh Pyne: His Life and Times*. Calcutta: Centre of International Modern Art, 1998.

Datta, Sona. *Urban Patua: The Art of Jamini Roy*. Mumbai: Marg Publications, 2010.

Davey's Handbag Collection. Worcester Historical Museum, Worcester, Massachusetts.

De, Biren. "Pictorial Space—A Journey Within." In *Concepts of Space, Ancient and Modern*. Ed. Kapila Vatsyayan. New Delhi: Indira Gandhi National Centre for the Arts, 1991, p. 572.

Devraj, Rajesh. "Making Showcards." In Dewan, Deepali, ed. *Bollywood Cinema Showcards: Indian Film Art from the 1950s to the 1980s*. Toronto: Royal Ontario Museum Press, 2011.

Dewan, Deepali, ed. *Bollywood Cinema Showcards: Indian Film Art from the 1950s to the 1980s*. Toronto: Royal Ontario Museum Press, 2011.

Doctor, Geeta. "A Meeting with Laxma Goud." In *Laxma Goud*. Bombay: Cymroza Art Gallery, 1992, pp. 23–24.

Dodiya, Atul. "Untitled." Trans. from Gujarati by Gieve Patel. In *Akbar Padamsee: Work in Language*. Eds. Bhanumati Padamsee and Annapurna Garimella. Mumbai: Marg Publications in association with Pundole Art Gallery, 2010, pp. 281–85.

Dutta, Rita. *Jogen Chowdhury: His Life and Times*. Calcutta: Centre of International Modern Art, 2006.

Fields, Rick. *How the Swans Came to the Lake: A Narrative History of Buddhism in America*. Boulder, Colorado: Shambala, 1992.

Gamboni, Dario. "Composing the Body Politic: Composite Images and Political Representation, 1651–2004." In *Making Things Public: Atmospheres of Democracy*. Eds. Bruno Latour and Peter Weibel. Karlsruhe: ZKM Center for Art and Media, and Cambridge, Massachusetts: MIT Press, 2005, pp. 162–95.

Gandhy, Kekoo. "The Beginnings of the Art Movement." In "City of Dreams: A Symposium on the Many Facets of Bombay." *Seminar* 528 (August 2003).

Gill, Gagan, ed. *Ram Kumar: A Journey Within*. New Delhi: Vadehra Art Gallery, 1996.

Gopinath, Soman, and Grant Watson. *Nasreen Mohamedi: Notes: Reflections on Indian Modernism*. Oslo: Office for Contemporary Art Norway, 2009.

Guardiola, Juan. "Modern India: An Introduction." In *India Moderna*. Valencia: Institut Valencià d'Art Modern, 2008, pp. 347–50.

Guha, Ramachandra. "Travelling with Tagore." In *Theorizing the Present: Essays for Partha Chatterjee*. Eds. Anjan Ghosh, Tapati Guha-Thakurta, and Jakani Nair. New Delhi: Oxford University Press, 2011, pp. 152–87.

Guha-Thakurta, Tapati. *The Making of a New 'Indian' Art: Artists, Aesthetics and Nationalism in Bengal, c. 1850–1920*. Cambridge: Cambridge University Press, 1992.

——. *Monuments, Objects, Histories: Institutions of Art in Colonial and Postcolonial India*. New York: Columbia University Press, 2004.

Gupta, Atreyee. "The Promise of the Modern: Silpi Chakra and the Politics of Art in New Delhi." In *Twentieth Century Indian Art*. Eds. Partha Mitter and Parul Dave Mukherji. New Delhi: Art Alive Gallery, in press.

Harris, Clare. *In the Image of Tibet: Tibetan Painting after 1959*. London: Reaktion Books, 1999.

Heehs, Peter. *Indian Religions: A Historical Reader of Spiritual Expression and Experience*. New York: New York University Press, 2002.

Herwitz Archive. Peabody Essex Museum, Salem, Massachusetts.

Herwitz, Daniel. *Husain*. Bombay: Tata Steel, 1988.

——. *Husain*. Chattanooga, Tennessee: Hunter Museum of Art, 1988.

Hoskote, Ranjit. *Sudhir Patwardhan: The Complicit Observer*. Mumbai: Sakshi Gallery, 2005.

——. "Images of Transcendence: Towards a New Reading of Tyeb Mehta's Art." In *Tyeb Mehta: Ideas, Images, Exchanges*. New Delhi: Vadehra Art Gallery, 2005, pp. 1–48.

Hyman, Timothy. *Bhupen Khakhar*. Bombay: Chemould Publications, 1998.

India Moderna. Valencia: Institut Valencià d'Art Modern, 2008.

India: Myth & Reality—Aspects of Modern Indian Art. Oxford: Museum of Modern Art, 1982.

Indian Art Today—Four Artists from the Chester and Davida Herwitz Family Collection. Washington, DC: The Phillips Collection, 1986.

Jakimowicz-Karle, Marta. *Bikash Bhattacharjee*. Bangalore: Kala Yatra, 1991.

Jain, Kajri. *Gods in the Bazaar: the Economies of Indian Calendar Art*. Durham, North Carolina: Duke University Press, 2007.

——. "The Showcard: Traveling Still." In Dewan, Deepali, ed., *Bollywood Cinema Showcards: Indian Film Art from the 1950s to the 1980s*. Toronto: Royal Ontario Museum Press, 2011, pp. 44–48.

Jayakar, Pupul. *The Earthen Drum: An Introduction to the Ritual Arts of Rural India*. New Delhi: National Museum, p. 180.

Kapoor, Kamala. "Splash: Images on Glass: Individualistic Harmonies." *The Economic Times*, November 10, 1990.

Kapur, Geeta. *Contemporary Indian Artists*. New Delhi: Vikas Publishing House, 1978.

——. "Six Painters Engaged in Research." *The Illustrated Weekly of India*, n.d., p. 16.

——. "Realism and Modernism: A Polemic for Present-Day Art." *Social Scientist* 8, 89–90 (1979), pp. 91–100.

——. "Partisan Views about the Human Figure." In *Place for People*. Bombay: Jehangir Art Gallery, and New Delhi: Rabindra Bhavan, 1981, n.p.

——. *K.G. Subramanyan*. New Delhi: Lalit Kala Akademi, 1987.

——. "Lightness of Being: Bhupen Khakhar's Recent Watercolours." *ART Asia Pacific* 14 (September 1997), n.p.

——. "The Paintings of Gulammohammed Sheikh." *Marg* 49, 3 (March 1998), pp. 52–61.

——. *When Was Modernism: Essays on Contemporary Cultural Practice in India*. New Delhi: Tulika Press, 2000.

——. "subTerrain: artists dig the contemporary." In Chandrasekhar, Indira, and Peter C. Seel, eds. *body.city: siting contemporary culture in India*. Berlin: Haus der Kulteren der Welt, 2003, pp. 47–83.

——. "Modernist Myths and the Exile of Maqbool Fida Husain." In *Barefoot Across the Nation: Maqbool Fida Husain and the Idea of India*. Ed. Sumathi Ramaswamy. New York: Routledge, 2011, pp. 21–53.

Keehn, Thomas, ed. *India Ink: Letters from India by Martha McKee Keehn, 1953–61*. New Delhi: Vadehra Art Gallery, 2000.

King, Bruce. *Modern Indian Poetry in English*. New Delhi: Oxford University Press, 2001.

Kripal, Jeffrey. *Kali's Child: The Mystical and Erotic Life of Ramakrishna Paramahansa*. Chicago: The University of Chicago Press, 1998.

Kumar, R. Siva. *K.G. Subramanyan: A Retrospective*. New Delhi: National Gallery of Modern Art, 2003.

Kumar, Ram. *Yuropa ke skaica [Sketch of Europe]*. Noida, India: Remadhava, 2007; originally published 1957.

Mathur, Saloni. "Charles and Ray Eames in India." *Art Journal* 70, 1 (Spring 2011), pp. 34–53.

Mehrotra, Arvind Krishna. "Koffee Korner." In Padamsee, Bhanumati, and Annapurna Garimella, eds. *Akbar Padamsee: Work in Language*. Mumbai: Marg Publications in association with Pundole Art Gallery, 2010, pp. 274–79.

Mirchandani, Usha. *Bhupen Khakhar: A Retrospective*. Mumbai: National Gallery of Modern Art and The Fine Art Resource, 2003.

Mitter, Partha. *Art and Nationalism in Colonial India, 1850–1922: Occidental Orientations*. Cambridge: Cambridge University Press, 1994.

——. *The Triumph of Modernism: India's Artists and the Avant-Garde, 1922–1947*. London: Reaktion Books, 2007.

Mookerjee, Ajit. *Tantra Art*. New Delhi, New York, and Paris: Ravi Kumar Gallery, 1966.

Muller-Ortega, Paul E. *The Triadic Heart of Śiva: Kaula Tantricism of Abhinavagupta in the Non-Dual Shaivism of Kashmir*. Albany: State University of New York Press, 1989.

Nagy, Peter. "Atul Dodiya: A Gargantuan Responsibility." In Nagy, Peter, and Gayatri Sinha. *Atul Dodiya: Broken Branches*. New York: Bose Pacia Modern, 2003, n.p.

Nalini Malani: Under the Skin. Bombay: Gallery 7, 1989.

Nath, Aman. "Manjit Bawa." *Swagat*, April 1985, pp. 21–24.

Padamsee, Bhanumati, and Annapurna Garimella, eds. *Akbar Padamsee: Work in Language*. Mumbai: Marg Publications in association with Pundole Art Gallery, 2010.

Pandey, Gyanendra. *Remembering Partition: Violence, Nationalism and History in India*. Cambridge: Cambridge University Press, 2001.

Patel, Gieve. *Poems*. Bombay: Nissim Ezekial, 1966.

——. "Interview with Bhupen Khakhar." *The Times of India*, June 25, 1967.

——. *How Do You Withstand, Body*. Bombay: Clearing House, 1976.

——. "To Pick Up a Brush." In *Contemporary Indian Art from the Chester and Davida Herwitz Family Collection* New York: Grey Art Gallery and Study Center, New York University, 1985, pp. 8–16.

——. "Contemporary Indian Painting." *Daedalus* 118, 4 (Fall 1989), pp. 171–205.

——. *Mirrored, Mirroring*. New Delhi: Oxford University Press, 1991.

——. *Mister Behram and Other Plays*. Calcutta: Seagull Books, 2008.

Patwardhan, Sudhir. "Near and Far." In *Sudhir Patwardhan*. Paris: Association Française d'Action Artistique in association with Centre Georges Pompidou, Musée National d'Art Moderne, 1986, n.p.

Peerbhoy, Ayaz S. *Paintings of Husain*. Bombay: Thacker, 1955.

Pinney, Christopher. "Some Indian 'Views of India': The Ethics of Representation." In *Traces of India: Photography, Architecture, and the Politics of Representation, 1850–1900*. Ed. Maria Antonella Pelizzari. Montreal: Canadian Centre for Architecture, and New Haven, Connecticut: Yale Center for British Art, 2003, pp. 262–75.

——. *Photos of the Gods: The Printed Image and Political Struggle in India*. London: Reaktion Books, 2004.

Place for People. Bombay: Jehangir Art Gallery, and New Delhi: Rabindra Bhavan, 1981.

Prakash, Gyan. *Mumbai Fables*. Princeton, New Jersey: Princeton University Press, 2010.

Quintanilla, Sonya Rhie, ed. *Rhythms of India: The Art of Nandalal Bose*. San Diego: San Diego Museum of Art, 2008.

Rajadyaksha, Ashish. "The Last Decade." In Sheikh, Gulammohammed, ed. *Contemporary Art in Baroda*. New Delhi: Tulika Press, 1997, pp. 211–65.

Rawson, Philip. *Tantra*. London: Arts Council of Great Britain, 1972.

——. *The Art of Tantra*. Greenwich, Connecticut: New York Graphic Society, 1973.

Raza, Sayed Haider, and Ashok Vajpeyi. *Passion: Life and Art of Raza*. New Delhi: Rajkamal Books, 2005.

Roszak, Theodore. *The Making of a Counter Culture: Reflections on the Technocratic Society and its Youthful Opposition*. Garden City, New York: Doubleday, 1969.

Rushdie, Salman. *Midnight's Children*. London: Cape, 1981.

Santosh, G.R. *Santosh, A Decade of Realization*. New Delhi: Chanakya Gallery, 1978.

Sarkar, Shubhani, and Rudrani Sarkar. *Bikash 2000*. Calcutta: Centre of International Modern Art, 2001.

Sarkar, Sumit. "'Kaliyuga,' 'Chakri,' and 'Bhakti': Ramakrishna and His Times." *Economic and Political Weekly* 27, 29 (July 18, 1992), pp. 1543–59, 1561–66.

Savant, Shukla. "Artist Collectives in the Age of Anxiety, 1940–50." In *Art and Visual Culture in India, 1857–2007*. Ed. Gayatri Sinha. Mumbai: Marg Publications, 2009, pp. 136–49.

Sen, Aveek. "Vanishing Point." In *Richard Bartholomew: A Critic's Eye*. Mumbai: Chatterjee & Lal, New Delhi: PhotoInk, and New York: Sepia International, 2009, pp. 84–95.

Sen, Geeti. *Raza*. New Delhi: Lalit Kala Akademi, 1990.

——. *Image and Imagination: Five Contemporary Artists in India*. Ahmedabad: Mapin Publishing, 1996.

Sen-Gupta, Achinto. "Neo-Tantric 20th-Century Indian Painting." *Arts of Asia* 31, 3 (May/June 2001), pp. 104–15.

Seth, Nikki Ty-Tomkins, interview with Tyeb Mehta. "The Human Figure Is What I Primarily React To." *Sunday Observer* (Bombay), February 1984, pp. 14–15.

Shedde, Meenakshi. "Art in the River of Life." In *Akbar Padamsee: Work in Language*. Eds. Bhanumati Padamsee and Annapurna Garimella. Mumbai: Marg Publications in association with Pundole Art Gallery, 2010, pp. 309–21.

Sheikh, Gulammohammed. *K. Laxma Goud*. Hyderabad: Andhra Lalit Kala Akademi, 1981.

——. "Among Several Cultures and Times." In Borden, Carla M., ed. *Contemporary Indian Tradition: Voices on Culture, Nature, and the Challenge of Change*. Washington, DC: Smithsonian Institution Press, 1989, pp. 107–20.

Sheikh, Gulammohammed, ed. *Contemporary Art in Baroda*. New Delhi: Tulika Press, 1997.

Sheikh, Nilima. "A Post-Independence Initiative in Art." In Sheikh, Gulammohammed, ed. *Contemporary Art in Baroda*. New Delhi: Tulika Press, 1997, pp. 53–143.

Sinha, Ajay. "Envisioning the Seventies and Eighties." In Sheikh, Gulammohammed, ed. *Contemporary Art in Baroda*. New Delhi: Tulika Press, 1997, pp. 145–209.

Six Indian Painters. London: Tate Gallery, 1982.

Sonalkar, Sudhir. "Six Painters Engaged in Research." *The Illustrated Weekly of India*, n.d., p. 16.

Subramanyan, K.G. *Moving Focus*. Calcutta: Seagull Books, 1978.

——. *The Living Tradition: Perspectives on Modern Indian art*. Calcutta: Seagull Books, 1987.

——. *The Creative Circuit*. Calcutta: Seagull Books, 1992.

——. *The Magic of Making: Essays on Art and Culture*. Calcutta: Seagull Books, 2007.

Sudhir Patwardhan. Paris: Association Française d'Action Artistique in association with Centre Georges Pompidou, Musée National d'Art Moderne, 1986.

Swaminathan, J. *Manjit Bawa*. New Delhi: Dhoomimal Gallery, 1979.

Tarlo, Emma. *Clothing Matters: Dress and Identity in India*. Chicago: The University of Chicago Press, 1996.

Tharoor, Shashi, and Bean, Susan S. *Epic India: M.F. Husain's Mahabharata Project*. Salem, Massachusetts: Peabody Essex Museum, 2006.

Thompson, Frank. "The Splintered Glass: Painting and Religion in Modern India." *Studies in Religion/Sciences Religieuses* 10, 2 (June 1981), pp. 175–86.

Tonelli, Edith, ed. *Neo-Tantra: Contemporary Indian Painting Inspired by Tradition*. Los Angeles: Frederick S. Wight Art Gallery, University of California, Los Angeles, 1985.

Tuli, Neville. *The Flamed Mosaic: Contemporary Indian Painting*. New York: Harry N. Abrams, 1998.

Tyeb Mehta: Ideas, Images, Exchanges. New Delhi: Vadehra Art Gallery, 2005.

Viswanathan, Prema. "The Human Figure Is a Distraction." *Free Press Journal* 19 (October 1986).

Watson, Grant. "Passage and Placement: Nasreen Mohamedi." *Afterall* 21 (Summer 2009), n.p.

White, David Gordon. "Tantra in Practice: Mapping a Tradition." In White, David Gordon, ed. *Tantra in Practice*. Princeton, New Jersey: Princeton University Press, 2000, pp. 3–40.

Zitzewitz, Karin. *The Perfect Frame: Presenting Indian Art*. Mumbai: Gallery Chemould, 2003.

——. "The Secular Icon: Secularist Practice and Indian Visual Culture." *Visual Anthropology Review* 24, 1 (2008), pp. 12–28.

——. "The Moral Economy of the Street: the Bombay Paintings of Gieve Patel and Sudhir Patwardhan." *Third Text* 23, 2 (March 2009), pp. 151–63.

PHOTOGRAPHY CREDITS

Image courtesy of Art Resource: Raza, figure 2, Khakhar, figure 1. © 2012 Artist Rights Society (ARS), New York/ADAGP, Paris, Image courtesy the Baltimore Museum of Art, Photograph by Mitro Hood: Singh, figure 2. © 2012 Artist Rights Society (ARS), New York/DACS, London, Image courtesy of Umesh Gaur, Photograph by Nayeem Modan: Brown, figure 3. © Estate of Richard Bartholomew/Photoink, Image courtesy of Pablo Bartholomew: Zitzewitz, figure 5. Image courtesy of Bivas Bhattacharjee: Bhattacharjee, figure 2. Image courtesy of Bose Pacia Gallery: Dodiya, figure 1. Image courtesy of Brooklyn Museum of Art, Brooklyn, New York: Sheikh, figure 2. Image courtesy of Chemould Prescott Road—Contemporary Art Gallery, Mumbai: Zitzewitz, figure 1, Citron, figures 2, 4. Image courtesy of Jogen Chowdhury: Chowdhury, figure 1. Image by Digital Imaging, Salem, Massachusetts: Bean, "American Collectors," figures 2, 4. Image courtesy of Atul Dodiya: Sinha, figures 2, 3, 4. Image courtesy of Farnsworth Museum: Bhattacharjee, figure 1. Image courtesy of Gallery SKE, Bangalore: Citron, figure 3. Image courtesy of the Michael Gallis Collection: Husain, figure 1. © Shawn G. Henry: Bean, "American Collectors," figure 1. Image courtesy of Ranbir Singh Kaleka: Kaleka, figure 1. Image courtesy of R. Siva Kumar: Subramanyan, figure 1. Image courtesy of R. Siva Kumar, Photograph by Jyoti Bhatt: Zitzewitz, figure 7, Bean, "Midnight's Children," figure 1. Image courtesy of Nalini Malani, Photograph by Payal Kapadia: Malani, figure 1. Digital Image © The Museum of Modern Art/ Liscensed by SCALA/Art Resource, NY: Mehta, figure 2. Image courtesy of The National Gallery, London/Art Resource, New York NG4761: Sheikh, figure 1. Image courtesy of the National Gallery of Art, Washington, DC: Raza, figure 1. © 2012 The Barnett Newman Foundation, New York/ Artists Rights Society (ARS), New York, Image courtesy of Art Resource, 527.1971: Mehta, figure 1. Image © 2006 Peabody Essex Museum, Photograph by Mark Sexton/ Jeffrey Dykes: plates 50, 70. Image © 2007 Peabody Essex Museum, Photograph by Joe Budd: plates 62, 63; Photograph by Barbara Kennedy: plates 48, 49, 69; Photograph by Mark Sexton: plates 42, 59, 60. Image © 2010 Peabody Essex Museum, Photograph by Kathy Tarantola: plate 46. Image © 2011 Peabody Essex Museum, Photograph by Kathy Tarantola: Zitzewitz, figure 2, De, figure 1. Image courtesy of Christopher Pinney: Sinha, figure 5. Image courtesy of Praful and Shilpa Shah: Khakhar, figure 2. Image courtesy of Geeti Sen: Zitzewitz, figure 3. Image courtesy of Sotheby's: Husain, figure 2. Image courtesy of Vivan Sundaram: Bhabha, figure 1. Image courtesy of Vivan Sundaram and the Asian Art Archives, Hong Kong: Zitzewitz, figure 8, Citron, figure 1. © J. Swaminathan Foundation, Image courtesy of J. Swaminathan Foundation, New Delhi: Zitzewitz, figure 6. Image courtesy of Talwar Gallery: Mohamedi, figure 1. Image courtesy of Vadehra Art Gallery, New Delhi: Kumar, figure 1. © Homai Vyarawalla Archive in the Alkazi Collection of Photography, Image courtesy of Alkazi Foundation for the Arts, New Delhi: Brown, figure 2.

AUTHOR BIOGRAPHIES

Susan S. Bean, Former Curator of South Asian and Korean Art at the Peabody Essex Museum, has produced a number of exhibitions and publications that address art from the colonial period to the present and include the Chester and Davida Herwitz Collection of modern and contemporary Indian art. She also writes on Indian textiles and clay sculpture.

Homi K. Bhabha is the Anne F. Rothenberg Professor of the Humanities in the Department of English, director of the Mahindra Humanities Center, and senior advisor on the Humanities to the president and provost at Harvard University. His numerous publications address postcolonial theory, cultural change and power, and cosmopolitanism, among other themes.

Rebecca M. Brown, teaching professor in the History of Art at Johns Hopkins University, focuses her research and curatorial projects on colonial and post-independence South Asian visual culture.

Beth Citron, assistant curator at the Rubin Museum of Art and adjunct assistant professor of Art History at New York University, is engaged in exploring modern South Asian art and photography.

Ajay Sinha, a professor of Art History at Mount Holyoke College, specializes in Indian art and film and is currently researching the visual culture of India in the eighteenth and nineteenth centuries with particular attention to the position of oil painting.

Karin Zitzewitz, assistant professor of Art History and Visual Culture at Michigan State University, has done extensive fieldwork in three centers of the Indian art world: Mumbai, Vadodara (Gujarat), and New Delhi, with special emphasis on the effects of Hindu nationalism on the profoundly secularist practice of modernist art.

INDEX

Page numbers in *italics* refer to illustrations.